D1596058

DISCARDED

Samuel Johnson has become known to posterity in two capacities: through his own works as the great literary essayist of the eighteenth century, and, through Boswell's *Life*, as a man – notoriously a medical patient with a string of physical and psychological ailments. John Wiltshire brings the two together in this original study of Johnson the writer as 'Doctor' and patient. The subject of modern medical historians' case studies, Johnson also cultivated the acquaintance of doctors in his own day, and was himself a 'dabbler in physic'. Dr Wiltshire illuminates Jonhson's life and work by setting them in their medical context and also examines the importance of medical themes in Johnson's own writings. He discusses the many parts of Johnson's work, touching on doctors, medicine, hospitals and medical experimentation, and analyses the central theme, running throughout, of human suffering – in body and mind – and its alleviation.

SAMUEL JOHNSON IN THE
MEDICAL WORLD

Plaster cast of a bust of Samuel Johnson, incorporating his death-mask (1784). William Cumberland and James Hoskins. National Portrait Gallery, London.

SAMUEL JOHNSON IN THE MEDICAL WORLD

THE DOCTOR AND THE PATIENT

JOHN WILTSHIRE

English Department, La Trobe University, Melbourne

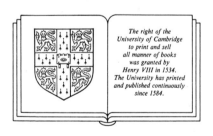

The right of the
University of Cambridge
to print and sell
all manner of books
was granted by
Henry VIII in 1534.
The University has printed
and published continuously
since 1584.

CAMBRIDGE UNIVERSITY PRESS

CAMBRIDGE

NEW YORK   PORT CHESTER

MELBOURNE   SYDNEY

IN MEMORY OF
LEONTINE DINGA
AND
NORAH WILTSHIRE

Published by the Press Syndicate of the University of Cambridge
The Pitt Building, Trumpington Street, Cambridge CB2 1RP
40 West 20th Street, New York, NY 10011–4211, USA
10 Stamford Road, Oakleigh, Melbourne 3166, Australia

First published 1991

Printed in Great Britain at the University Press, Cambridge

British Library cataloguing in publication data
Wiltshire, John
Samuel Johnson in the medical world: the Doctor and the
patient.
1. English Literature. Johnson, Samuel, 1709–1784
1 Title
828.609

Library of Congress cataloguing in publication data
applied for

ISBN 0 521 38326 9 hardback

CE

CONTENTS

PREFACE

MEDICINE HAS been written as the story of doctors, their practices and achievements. Recently, there has been a shift to the patient. Writers from widely different fields – neurology (Oliver Sacks, *Awakenings*, 1973, revised edition 1982), literary criticism (Elaine Scarry, *The Body in Pain*, 1985), medical history (Roy Porter, *Patients and Practitioners*, 1985; *Mind Forg'd Manacles*, 1987) and anthropology, (Arthur Kleinman, *Social Origins of Distress and Disease*, 1986; *The Illness Narratives*, 1988) – have converged to focus upon the history and experience of the individual sufferer. This book seeks to build upon and augment their work by examining the words and experience of a major writer and spectacular patient.

I wish to acknowledge the help of the following scholars and medical historians in preparation of this book: Miss E. Allen, Curator of the Hunterian Museum; Professor Harold Attwood; Dr C. H. Brock; the late Professor Kenneth Dewhurst; Dr J. D. Fleeman; Dr Graham Nicholls of the Birthplace Museum. I am especially indebted to Dr Dennis Gibbs of the London Hospital.

The editors of the Australian journals *The Critical Review* and *Meridian* published earlier versions of parts of chapters 6 and 7 respectively, and I thank them. The Research Grants Committee of the School of Humanities, La Trobe University, gave me a travel grant which allowed me to research part of chapter 3.

My colleagues and friends in the English Department, La Trobe University, have helped me in dozens of ways, with suggestions and comments, criticisms and translations, and not least in enduring the papers in which I tried out parts of this book. I am very grateful to them. To Susan Louise Burns, Judi Benney and Dorothy Johnstone I am especially indebted for typing the various drafts: and to Richard McGregor for his help with the proofs and index.

David Ellis and Howard Mills gave me encouragement when I needed it most.

A NOTE ON REFERENCES

REFERENCES TO Boswell's *Life of Johnson* are normally to the edition edited by G. B. Hill, revised by L. F. Powell, *Boswell's Life of Johnson* (6 vols., second edition, Oxford, 1964, reprinted 1975) which will be cited in the notes as *Life*. Occasional reference will also be made to the edition published in 1938 by the Limited Editions Club and edited by Edward G. Fletcher, *The Life of Samuel Johnson by James Boswell, with Marginal Comments by Mrs Piozzi*, and to Hill's original edition (6 vols., Oxford, 1889).

G. B. Hill's *Johnsonian Miscellanies* (2 vols., Oxford, 1897) (which includes Mrs Thrale's *Anecdotes*) is cited as *Miscellanies*.

Sir John Hawkins, *The Life of Samuel Johnson L.L.D.* (second edition 1787) is cited as Hawkins.

Johnson's letters are usually cited by number only in the edition edited by R. W. Chapman, *The Letters of Samuel Johnson with Mrs Thrale's Genuine Letters to him* (3 vols., Oxford, 1952). References to essays by Johnson are also normally by number only: the text is taken from the Yale edition of the *Works of Samuel Johnson*, vol. 2, *Idler and Adventurer*, edited by W. J. Bate, J. M. Bullitt and L. F. Powell, (1963) vol. 3, vol. 4 and vol. 5, *The Rambler*, edited by W. J. Bate and Albrecht B. Strauss (1969).

Johnson's *Diaries, Prayers and Annals*, edited by E. L. McAdam Jr, with Donald and Mary Hyde, vol. 1 in the Yale edition (1958), is cited as *Diaries*.

Thraliana: The Diary of Mrs Hester Lynch Thrale (later Mrs Piozzi) 1776–1809, edited by Katharine C. Balderston (2nd edn, 2 vols., Oxford, 1951), is cited as *Thraliana*.

INTRODUCTION

THIS BOOK considers Samuel Johnson as a patient, as an amateur doctor, and as a writer about medicine. Everyone calls him 'Doctor Johnson' and the title no doubt acknowledges his scholarship, his learning and authority. But it also suggests how persistently he is thought of as a sage, and – perhaps less consciously – as a healer. To look at Johnson as a sufferer, and as physician, both of the body and the mind, becomes inseparable, then, from thinking about the sources and nature of that cultural authority.

In the first of these roles Johnson has gained some fame or notoriety among doctors. A continuous stream of articles on his melancholy and depression, his gout, his abnormal movements, his 'alcohol problem' (to give only some more recent examples), has appeared in the pages of medical and medical-historical journals. That Johnson was a 'dabbler in physick' and that he cultivated the acquaintance of doctors is almost as well-known, though neither the extent of his medical friendships, nor the nature of his medical knowledge is much recognised. You would not guess from Boswell, or from modern biographies, that at least four of his closest friends were doctors, and that three of these friendships lasted over decades. But it is in the third role, as a writer about medical matters, that Johnson is so often overlooked. As I will show, he wrote a good many pieces which touch on or discuss doctoring, medicine, hospitals and medical experimentation. Much more important, though, is the fact that medical themes – in the broadest sense, themes of suffering and its remedy or alleviation – form the core of his thought and writing. Johnson, we know, is a moralist: but the particular force of his moral writing lies in its attention to both physical and psychological suffering. I want to draw some connections between Samuel Johnson, the amateur doctor and enthusiast for medicine, and the Doctor Johnson who figures so largely in the cultural imagination.

Johnson's medical friends came from all walks of life, and part of my purpose is, by looking at them, to reconstruct some of the complexity of relations that characterised the medical world in which Johnson moved. Certainly, it can be shown, Johnson was surrounded by doctors all his life. He was born into a household in which Dr Samuel Swinfen, who became his godfather, was the lodger. His father sold medical preparations in his bookseller's shop and published two medical treatises by his friend, the eminent local physician Sir John Floyer, who – or so it was said – intervened early in Johnson's long and eventful medical history. Two of Johnson's companions at school later became doctors; one of them belonged to a local medical family and practised all his life in the Midlands, the other went up to London and became one of the age's most notable medical figures. The three kept up their friendship and Johnson was visiting Edmund Hector, the Birmingham surgeon, a few weeks before his death in 1784. At the other end of his life Johnson's famous household at Bolt Court, that collection of human memorabilia, included Mrs Desmoulins, the daughter of Samuel Swinfen, and the blind Anna Williams, whose father, a medical practitioner in Wales, had come to London hoping to win the reward offered by the government for an improved method of finding the longitude at sea. Francis Barber, Johnson's negro servant, had been left to his charge by Colonel Bathurst, father of Johnson's dearest friend, a physician who had struggled to make a living in London for a decade, Dr Richard Bathurst. And there was Robert Levet, whose obscure existence as one of the many uncredited doctors who must have tended the poor of London is brought into history by its proximity to Johnson's own life, and who invites us to ponder the distinction, so vigorously promoted by the profession in the eighteenth century, between the accredited doctor or surgeon and the 'quack'. During the intervening years, Johnson had spent two years living with Hector whilst he was a practising surgeon in Birmingham, and on coming to London served what was in effect an apprenticeship to Dr Robert James, his other school-companion, as they worked together planning and putting together James's major, massive, compilation of medical information, the *Medicinal Dictionary* of 1743–5. His friendship with Richard Bathurst led in turn to an introduction to the learned Thomas Lawrence, soon to become Johnson's own doctor, eight times elected President of the College of Physicians (1767–74), and a life-long friend.

It is not surprising then, that Johnson was very well informed on medical matters. He could write out a prescription for himself in apothecary's characters, and pass, as in the Hebrides, for a physician. He is repeatedly presented by Boswell as seeking the company and conversation of doctors, and though wary of protocol, of seeming to trespass upon professional territory, was well known to his friends as a 'dabbler in physick' – the phrase is used by both Boswell and Hawkins. One might expect that this would leave its mark, in some form or other, on his work.

Look at his life in another way. In 1712, as everyone knows, Samuel Johnson was taken by his mother to London when less than three years old to participate in an ancient magical rite. Queen Anne, who at the behest of her Tory ministers had revived a practice over 600 years old, touched with her wonder-working hands the disfiguring marks of scrofula on the child's neck. It was almost the last occasion on which this ritual was performed in England.[1] As a memento of the ceremony, the Queen presented its participants with a token, or 'touch-piece' (sometimes called an 'angel'), and this Johnson wore round his neck for the rest of his life. After his death, seventy-two years later, his diseased and mutilated body was opened by James Wilson in the presence of three physicians and two surgeons. Specimens were taken, a formal autopsy report was written, and a description of the condition of his lung, its cells 'most of them the size of a common garden pea, and some few so large as to be able to contain a small gooseberry' appears in chapter 4 on 'Diseased Appearances of the Lungs' in a classic and pioneering textbook, Matthew Baillie's *Morbid Anatomy* (1793).[2] Johnson, wearing his magical emblem to the end of his days, had now become the subject of what Michel Foucault has called 'anatomo-clinical' medicine, a medical stripping itself of superstition and guesswork, transforming itself into positivistic science.

The eighteenth century is rarely considered a dramatic period of medical history in England. It is a time of stagnation, whose fitful bursts of innovation tend to come from those on the fringes of the profession, the ship-surgeons and army doctors. Yet there were important new clinical initiatives during the second half of the century, and important changes in the nature and status of the medical profession, though it is difficult to see them as part of a consistent movement or total reorientation. A remarkable number of these events impinged upon Johnson's life, or came within the range of his activities or commentary. If we focus on the figure of Samuel Johnson, the unco-ordinated, discontinuous events of eighteenth-century medicine will seem momentarily at least to converge. He lived a life within medicine, intimate with some of the age's chief practitioners, learned in both the classical and contemporary branches of the art, receiving upon and within his body its various ingenuities and interventions. To contemplate his life and work in its medical connection is to draw together, sometimes upon a thread of irony, some of the disparate themes and topics that the general medical historian may find resistant to unity, to integration: James' fever powders and Mrs Stephens' medicines for the stone, for instance, with the discovery of digitalis, the introduction of the controlled drug trial with the coming of professional obstetrics and the 'man midwife', the origins of psychiatry, the controversy over sensibility and irritability, the founding of the great London and provincial hospitals.

Whatever changes took place in medicine in Johnson's lifetime, though, it would be a mistake to see them as a steady or concerted progress between the poles of, for instance, folklore and magic and rationalistic science. Magic did not leave the field of medicine with the demise of *les rois thaumaturges*, even if it remained, and remains, only in the diffused form of what Oliver Sacks calls the doctor's 'magic of attention and interest'.[3] And if, throughout the century, we take note of a persistent, perhaps growing, interest in mensuration, tabulation and the critical analysis of experimental results in medicine, it is useful to be reminded by Lester King that technological progress does not in itself guarantee the presence of a critical attitude towards diagnosis or prescription, and that an 'empiric' cast of mind may continue to coexist alongside greatly increased expertise and resources.[4]

Johnson himself embodies a powerful illustration of what King means by the exercise of critical judgement in the field of medicine. His sceptical, La Rochefoucauldian attention to the moral life ('Will *any* body's mind bear this eternal microscope that you place upon your own so?' cried Mrs Thrale), and his unwillingness to take any geographical, historical or biographical report on trust ('Distrust is a necessary qualification of a student in history', he remarked in an early review), is replicated in his attitudes towards medicine. Johnson was no passive consumer of health care. Harassed as he was by a variety of ills throughout his life, he was a vigorous proposer and initiator of treatments, sometimes bullying his physicians – the most eminent men of their generation – into giving their consent to a course of action of which their judgement disapproved. He had many disagreements with his doctors over the nature and course of specific disorders, and often he was right. This and the scrupulous recording of his own condition following treatment or the testing of a new drug, is not merely the obsessiveness of the hypochondriac. 'Thus much I have written medically', he notes on one occasion in his diary, 'to show that he who can fast long must have lived plentifully'.[5] He was capable of regarding himself, as early medical amateurs, like Stephen Hales, or even physician experimenters like Floyer, so often did, with detachment as a clinical specimen, an experimental subject. An anti-romantic would, of course, have no time for panaceas or his generation's equivalent of the 'wonder drug'. The eighteenth-century cult of cold bathing, for instance (nothing to do with swimming, which – it's pleasant to report – he enjoyed), he regarded with persistent scepticism. 'I hate immersion', he once muttered. Such slight evidences of his general attitude are reinforced by the recurrent tone of the not insignificant quantity of what I shall call his medical journalism. He wrote numerous notes, reviews and biographies in which his medical interests and scepticism about medical claims frequently come to the surface. A tiny example: in the midst of a review-article on the history of Aleppo, for instance, Johnson remarks that the recommendation of the author (a doctor) 'to breath through a spunge wet with an infusion of rue in vinegar' as a preservative against the 'Aleppo disease' would work just as well if the vinegar alone were used, adding 'the vertues of rue to resist infection being, I fear, imaginary'.[6]

Of moderns, the two most esteemed and influential figures in eighteenth-century medicine were Thomas Sydenham and the Dutchman, Herman Boerhaave. Not long after Johnson's arrival in London in 1737 and recruitment to the staff of the *Gentleman's Magazine*, he produced biographical estimates of these two doctors distinguished already by medical acumen and extreme scepticism as to the provenance of historical 'facts'. In 1743, he joined Robert James on the project of the *Medicinal Dictionary*, for which he wrote the Dedication (to Richard Mead), and co-authored a set of proposals which would, if carried out, have resulted in the *Dictionary*'s cutting a swathe through the jungle of early eighteenth-century medical folklore and the various received knowledges of classical and medieval medicine. Johnson proposed to penetrate the undergrowth, sort out the proliferating remedies, rescue and name the valuable, therapeutically effective plants. But the huge project was never effectively carried out, and all that can be attributed to Johnson in the *Dictionary* are a few estimates of the work of classical physicians, mostly compiled from secondary sources. Over ten years later though, his own *Dictionary* completed, Johnson is found in an editorial capacity on a new journal, the *Literary Magazine*, which like other journals of the time gave much space to 'discoveries' in natural and physical science. In the case of the *Literary Magazine* there seems to be a clear bias towards medical and physiological reviewing and reporting, and several medical associates of Johnson made contributions. Johnson was the chief, sometimes the only, reviewer of books in that 'bounteous year', as he called it, of 1756–7, and his selection included many in which the editor's interest in medicine and stern scrutiny of experimental logic is exercised. The enterprise of the *Literary Magazine* suggests that Johnson was, as he implies in the *Life of Akenside* over twenty years later, an 'acute observer' of 'the transactions of the medical world'.

This book situates Johnson within that 'world', tracing his relationships with physicians and examining his own medical theory and practice. Whilst I hope that this focus on Johnson will illuminate the medical context in which he lived and wrote, I stress that my primary intention is to illuminate his work itself by investigating its medical background and connections. And I use the word 'world' rather than, say, milieu, because of its broader meaning. I include within it the totality of questions and practices that concern both those involved in the alleviation of human suffering and those suffering themselves. In a sense I have used Johnson as the focus – the occasion – for the raising of medical issues. Illness has from ancient times been conceived as punishment, as a derivative of sin (with venereal disease providing the obvious paradigm), and even when this nexus is broken or disavowed by the conscious mind, it is always creeping back in less conscious forms – in the insistent public demand, for instance, to connect illness with some misdemeanour (cancer and emphysema with smoking), or more diffusedly with character, as in the production of 'asthmatic' or 'cancer-prone' personality types. Or it may take another form when a sudden 'attack' of disease is connected – to all intents and purposes arbitrarily – with some personal guilt, and thereby given a form of explanation. Some of these connections between behaviour and illness no doubt are valid enough, but round the core or seed of scientific truth accumulate old superstitions and fears.

A related issue is an apparently quite distinct one: how far are diseases historically specific? Until the last twenty years or so, 'Whig' medical historians have taken for granted that the same illnesses have tormented humankind throughout its history, and therefore that the history of medicine could be conceived and written as a consecutive and integrated body of thinking directed towards the elucidation of an unchanging, passive subject. But – apart from the obvious instances like the disappearance of the plague and the sudden outbreak of viral encephalitis after the First World War – it seems that different illnesses might belong to different periods. 'Hypochondriasis' is described in detail by early eighteenth-century writers, but there is no recognised modern equivalent: 'hysteria' is an equally widespread disease entity at the end of the nineteenth. The 'hyperactive child' or 'pre-menstrual tension' are late twentieth-century constructions or recognitions (choose your word). If this is plausible, it suggests that the idea of a medical entity is drawn from a pool of thought or cultural circumstances from which metaphysical or religious meanings might equally well be drawn, and that the definition of a medical condition is not an isolated act within the history of medical thought alone. It may be argued against this view that this precisely defines such constructions as misdiagnoses – specious and false diseases – since true medical entities are transhistorical and transcultural. Nevertheless, it seems an illuminating way of discussing illness to see how it occurs within a given cultural framework, and how it was performed.

These are some of the issues which lie behind the discussions in the following chapters. Such questions are present, sometimes explicitly and often implicitly in most of Johnson's most important and substantial texts. Stemming perhaps from his own personal condition, Johnson devotes much attention, in the *Rambler* series of essays, for example, to the problem of pain and tolerance of pain. 'Pain', of course, in this context means pain in its broadest possible meaning, like that which Johnson implied when he famously told Mrs Williams that 'he who makes himself a beast' (through drinking) 'gets rid of the pain of being a man'. The pain and suffering these essays discuss is mostly moral or psychological, though Johnson's metaphors insistently attribute to psychological sufferings the harrowing qualities of physical ones, and the essays that treat them borrow more than a hint in their design and approach from the medical textbook. *Rasselas*, too, reaches its extended climax in the depiction of the dangerous courses of two distinct, but equally common, forms of mental disease, Nekayah's mourning for the loss of her maid and friend Pekuah, in which she drifts towards a morbid cultivation of sorrow and withdrawal from life, and the solitary obsession of the astronomer – types of mental illness which may, or may not, correspond to the more modern categories of neurosis and psychosis. Johnson's review of the work of amateur philosophising, Soame Jenyns's *A Free Inquiry into the Nature and Origin of Evil*, confirms the hints in other works that the arbitrary, unpredictable cruelty of the onset of physical diseases had taken strong hold on Johnson's imagination. His biographies of doctors make a particular point of stressing, when appropriate, their Christian piety. Medicine must, Johnson declared in his life of Boerhaave, 'undoubtedly claim the second Place among those [professions] which are of the greatest Benefit to Mankind'. The doctor does not merely treat or prescribe: he is the embodiment of charity and benevolence. So the topic of medicine becomes intertwined too, with that very large strand in Johnson's thinking, his 'tenderness' towards the weaknesses of human nature and hatred of all forms of cruelty.

It was common in the eighteenth century to attribute the peculiar cast of Johnson's mind to his physical infirmities. Sir John Hawkins, for instance, thought that his poor appreciation of music, art and architecture, due to his bad eyesight and hearing, explained Johnson's opinion that life contained more to endure than to enjoy. His 'asperity of manners', Frances Reynolds suggested, was due to his 'inherent melancholy infirmities, both mental and corporeal'.[7] It is difficult to know how one would go about answering what Sir Humphry Rolleston in 1924 called 'the interesting question of how far Johnson's infirmities influenced his view of matters and men and the style and temper of his work',[8] yet it seems right to begin an account of Johnson's medical interests by reviewing his own medical history, particularly as an interesting and fundamental issue emerges as soon as one does so. Specialists in many different fields of medicine and psychiatry have studied aspects of Johnson's case history. Without their work the first chapter of this book could not possibly have been written. But despite their investigations many aspects of Johnson's history remain mysterious or puzzling. When one assembles together some of the diverse and conflicting explanations that have been offered about Johnson's condition one's own 'distrust' tends to be aroused. There is little reason, I shall suggest, to regard the latest analysis of Johnson's condition as more persuasive than the first. I have, indeed, been led by the nature of the material in the first chapter to adjudicate, to offer or imply an opinion on medical maters. (I hope I shall not for that reason be considered a quack; what is involved is not judgement about patients but about texts.) Many questions about Johnson's medical condition – as well as, heaven knows, many questions about medicine – remain open ones. Part of the purpose of this first chapter, apart from assembling as much information about Johnson's medical history as will not utterly prostrate the reader, is to induce some scepticism, relevant to the topics of the succeeding chapters, towards the premature foreclosure of medical discussion.

I introduce Johnson as a non-professional, whose medical thinking has been neglected, and I try to show that it is cogent and persuasive, more so than that of many of the medical writers who were his contemporaries. When we look, for instance, at his considered opinions on phlebotomy we find matters raised that are still controversial. His account of the astronomer's insanity, which certainly had some influence on the development of psychiatry, is of more than historical interest. Johnson's life-history intersected with the work of several men – William Withering, William Heberden, James Lind and the Hunters among them – who have honourable places in the history of medical research. I do not of course claim that Johnson made any contributions of as tangible a value as theirs. He is a patient, an observer, a commentator, on the peripheries of the medical world. The more general question which Johnson's life in medicine raises is how far one can give an adequate history of medicine by considering only the contributions of the profession itself; and the closely related topic of how far the profession can be considered as the sole repository of medical wisdom. These are controversial issues of course: they are touched upon most explicitly in the book's penultimate chapter, on Dr Robert Levet.

The backbone of the book is biographical. It begins with an account of some of the main crises in Johnson's medical history. Chapter 2 discusses his medical education and knowledge; chapter 3 sets him in the context of the medical arrangements of his day, and examines the work (most early) in which he comments on medical writings. After this I suggest that his medical interests find various dispersed and indirect forms of expression. Chapter 4 examines some of the *Rambler* essays as transmuted medical texts. Chapter 5 discusses the astronomer chapters in *Rasselas* as contributions to the theory of insanity. Chapter 6 concentrates on the last English poem Johnson wrote. The last chapter reviews Johnson's friendships with his doctors, and looks briefly at the wealth of medical and psychological advice Johnson offers in his correspondence. Finally, I come to terms with the role he played as doctor (and Doctor) in the life and imagination of James Boswell, whose medical problems were sometimes complementary to his own.

If a book can be said to have a backbone perhaps it can be said to have a nerve centre too. The centre of this is the belief that Johnson is pre-eminent among those writers who have spoken of the experience of pain. His sensibility – a word he rarely uses except in connection with suffering – was acutely responsive to the diverse forms of pain and cruelty in the world. I would argue too that in the face of suffering Johnson wrote with, if not unusual force, for he is almost always forceful, but with unusual agility, pungency and passion. In the review of *A Free Inquiry*, for instance, as well as in parts of his work there has been no space to discuss in this book, in the pamphlet on the Falklands Islands, in *Rambler* 112, on the cruelty of parents, in those passages of the *Lives* of Pope and Swift which concern their physical degeneration, whenever his imagination is led to contemplate pain, whether it be the pain of disease, or the wounds inflicted in social life, he writes with a depth of engagement that makes such passages quintessentially Johnsonian. Tracing this current of imagination from its origins in his response to the world through some of the textual sites through which it flows may lead us at last to pass through the heart.

I

JOHNSON'S MEDICAL HISTORY: FACTS AND MYSTERIES

I

AFTER JOHNSON'S death in 1784, the surviving members of his last club met to discuss what kind of monument to erect to him in St Paul's Cathedral. Some of Johnson's friends were apparently disturbed at the proposal to erect a full-length statue, 'to transmit to posterity', as Malone wrote to Sir Joseph Banks, 'a true and perfect exhibition of the entire man', because, in the fashion of the time, it was to show Johnson attired only in a Roman toga.[1] Sir Joshua Reynolds, who had disapproved of Pigalle's famous statue of Voltaire showing the philosopher 'not only nude but with the withered shanks and scrawny torso of a septuagenarian' was able to reassure them.[2] 'Johnson's limbs', he declared, 'so far from being unsightly', were 'uncommonly well-formed & in the most exact & true proportion'.[3]

Seeing Johnson swim in the sea at Brighton in 1766 the 'dipper' ('Dr Naked', Johnson and Mr Thrale called him) declared, 'Why, Sir, you must have been a stout hearted gentleman forty years ago.'[4] 'His stature was remarkably high, and his limbs exceedingly large', according to Mrs Thrale.[5] When he was first introduced to his future wife, Elizabeth Porter, in 1734, at the age of twenty-five, he was then, according to her daughter, 'lean and lank, so that his immense structure of bones was hideously striking to the eye', but in later years he got more to eat, put on weight and in 1773 Boswell described him as 'large, robust, I may say approaching to the gigantick, and grown unweildy from corpulency'.[6] Descriptions of Johnson's physique by his contemporaries often serve as a metaphor, one suspects, to convey their mingled amazement, respect and disturbance at his extraordinary mental prowess: 'he is as great a *souled* man as a bodied man', wrote Fanny Burney. Anecdotes of his physical feats abound. They tend to suggest a phenomenal, even miraculous strength and agility. Thus Johnson does not only throw someone who has usurped his chair on the stage into the pit, he throws the seat under him too. He runs races with folk much younger than himself and always wins, most amusingly with the diminutive Mr Payne, whom he picks up before they have run half the intended distance, perches on the arm of a tree and then 'running as if he had met with a hard match' returns with great exultation to help his friend down.[7] He climbs gates and walls and swarms up trees, rows down the Thames, rolls down hills at the age of fifty-five and swims in the sea at Brighthelmstone in October at sixty-seven. These feats are so recurrent as to suggest the need to release or discharge great amounts of pent-up energy. They seem also perhaps to have become necessary to Johnson's self-image. On his death bed he was still saying to Charles Burney, 'Tell Fanny I think I could throw the Ball to her yet.'[8]

Though Foote, the actor, might call him 'the Caliban of literature' and such enemies as Horace Walpole a 'monster', Johnson's friends liked to compare his physical appearance to heroes like Hercules or Milo. Johnson preferred to compare himself to Falstaff. The conceit reflected his awareness that his companions were of a different social class and age than he but also his bulk and his energy. He plays Falstaff opposite the aristocratic Topham Beauclerk (descendant of Charles II and Nell Gwynn), and his friend Bennet Langton on their rambles into the countryside: 'What is it you dogs! I'll have a frisk with you.' He plays Falstaff, the Falstaff who fears rejection – 'Go thy ways old Jack' – with Mrs Thrale, Falstaff with Boswell in the Highlands.[9] And when he got his pension, Beauclerk told him he hoped Johnson would 'purge and live cleanly like a gentleman'.[10] This identification can be glimpsed too in his famous remark that a tavern chair is the throne of human felicity.

There is another side to the picture. Johnson was robust, energetic, and adventurous, but also very overweight, subject to chronic lung and breathing problems, tormented by insomnia. These capers and exploits, including the Tour, make a striking contrast to the distress and pain that he was in these very same years continually confiding to his diary. His prayers are constantly for help with his 'troubles and maladies', his 'diseases of mind and body'. During the middle and later years of his life, those years for which we have such abundant records, Johnson suffered from some congenital difficulties – poor eyes and poor hearing among them – insomnia, 'asthma', or bronchial difficulties, melancholy, as well as obsessive behaviour, strange recurrent 'tics', gesticulations, and movements, as well as more humdrum difficulties like flatulence and, in his later years, intermittent visits from the gout.

'So morbid was his temperament', wrote Boswell, 'that he never knew the natural joy of a free and vigorous use of his limbs; when he walked, it was like the struggling gait of one in fetters.'[11] The history of Johnson's diseases is inevitably intertwined with the differing accounts he and other people – his friends and contemporaries as well as later commentators – have given of them. So to write Johnson's medical history is also to thread one's way through a labyrinth, or a battlefield, not only of competing theories, but of competing perceptions, and competing 'facts'. 'The original of diseases is commonly obscure', Johnson notes in the *Life* of Swift. Yet the study of Johnson's medical history, in the eighteenth century and since, has been haunted by the desire to trace his heterogeneous symptoms back to a single source, an original condition or event which may explain them all. In the eighteenth century this explanation is usually some form of the 'morbid constitution' or 'temperament'; in the twentieth it is often related to some trauma of childhood or of sexual development. Tracing Johnson's illnesses to their 'original' reflects a desire, too, to unite them: to see his often bewilderingly diverse symptoms as branches of one underlying pathology. If we leave aside the psychoanalytic accounts, there are two main contenders for this great originating event, Johnson's childhood scrofula and the nervous crisis or illness (whatever it was) of his twentieth year.

The paradox of immense stamina and residual strength contending with appalling afflictions that is the refrain of his friends and biographers is captured in the first, apparently factual, words of Johnson's own account of his life in the document known as his *Annals*:

Sept. 7, 1709, I was born at Lichfield. My mother had a very difficult and dangerous labour, and was assisted by George Hector, a man-midwife of great reputation. I was born almost dead, and could not cry for some time. When he had me in his arms, he said, 'Here is a brave boy.'[12]

Johnson's mother was forty years old, an elderly primipara, in the obstetrician's phrase. It has naturally been suggested that Johnson's later psychological and movement disorders were due to birth trauma and cerebral anoxia, or deficiency in the supply of oxygen to the brain, as a consequence of the difficult birth, though there is little enough evidence for this.[13] The child was put out to a wet-nurse, a common practice among the middle or genteel classes: the wife of John Marklew, a brick maker who worked for Johnson's father Michael Johnson, had had a son in February 1708, and it was to her milk, over eighteen months later, that Samuel Johnson succeeded.[14] Mrs Marklew's milk has also been blamed for the most well-known if not the most serious of Johnson's afflictions:

> Dr Swinfen told me, that the scrofulous sores which afflicted me proceeded from the bad humours of the nurse, whose son had the same distemper, and was likewise short-sighted, but both in a less degree. My mother thought my diseases derived from her family.[15]

Johnson himself defined 'Scrofula' in his *Dictionary* as 'A depravation of the humours of the body, which breaks out in sores, commonly called the king's evil', and cites Richard Wiseman, Charles I's physician: 'if matter in the milk dispose to coagulation, it produces a scrofula'. Scrofula is tuberculosis of the lymphatic glands, and is characterised by their chronic enlargement and degeneration, particularly in the neck.

Mrs Johnson was not alone in her theory that the disease was inherited. Even as late as 1859 'the secondary or bubonic nature of this disease was not then recognised. It was supposed to take its rise in a "vice of the system" and accordingly elaborate medicinal or magical means were wholly relied upon in the treatment of it ... It was a common warning of careful parents that this girl or that was to be shunned as a wife because she carried on her neck this signal of a constitutional vice.'[16] Johnson's biographers have traditionally agreed with Dr Swinfen and ascribed his scrofula to his nurse's infected milk. But it has been very convincingly argued by two doctors, Lawrence McHenry and Ronald MacKeith, that this view cannot be correct since scrofulous infections are not passed on to children through mother's milk, and that if Johnson had had tuberculosis at this very early age, it would almost certainly have led to his death. McHenry and MacKeith in fact suggest that Johnson developed tuberculosis lymphadenitis when he was two years old, as a result, probably, of infected *cow's* milk.[17]

This theory involves some amendments to Johnson's own account. The dramatic sentence in the *Annals*, 'In ten weeks I was taken home, a poor, diseased infant, almost blind', McHenry and MacKeith explain as 'probably a non-specific ophthalmia neonatorium or conjunctivitis and blepharitis', not the same 'blindness' that Johnson later suffered from.[18] What has not been explained is why the child was taken from Mrs Marklew after two and a half months, since the usual period of weaning was from six to eight months. Johnson certainly did have troubles with his eyes later for he was taken by his mother to stay with a relative at Trysull near Wolverhampton, so that a young physician from Worcester, Dr Thomas Attwood, could come over to examine them. But he implies that the cutting of an incision or 'issue' in his left arm was made very early:

Here [at the Marklews] it was discovered that my eyes were bad; and an issue was cut in my left arm; of which I took no great notice, as I think my mother has told me, having my little hand in a custard.[19]

He goes on immediately, as if recognising the unreliability of this reconstruction: 'It is observable, that, having been told of this operation, I always imagined that I remembered it, but I laid the scene in the wrong house. Such confusions of memory I suspect to be common.' Johnson does not, of course, state that the issue was made at the wet-nurse's house (unlikely in any case), and it is probable, McHenry and MacKeith suggest, that he also confuses the time of this operation. A child of a few weeks, they suggest, would hardly have been diverted by a custard, though a child of two might.

It seems strange to us that an incision in the arm should be regarded as an appropriate treatment for 'bad eyes', but it is perfectly consonant with the premises of early eighteenth-century medicine. Both the eye trouble and the scrofulous swellings – if they appeared together – would have been related to the same 'bad humour' which could be drawn from one part of the body to another and might be discharged at any convenient site. The issue ('a vent made in a muscle', Johnson called it) was made on the left, possibly since it was Johnson's left eye which was most affected. In a note Johnson adds that he cannot remember how long this issue was continued (it would have been kept open by a round object such as a bead) and says 'I believe it was suffered to dry when I was about six years old'.

The other mode of treatment led to one of the most famous incidents in Johnsonian biography, though it belongs to the history of politics and magic as much as to Johnson's medical history. The meeting of the elderly Queen Anne (she was to die two years afterwards) and the thirty-month-old Samuel Johnson, in a ceremony vouchsafing the 'royal touch' to poor sufferers from scrufulous sores and swellings, has always struck people's imaginations. Johnson was taken to London, on the advice, so Edmund Hector, his schoolfellow, told Boswell, of the famous, local, and strongly royalist physician, Sir John Floyer. James II had actually touched in Lichfield Cathedral in August 1687, when Michael Johnson was already established as a bookseller in the city.[20] The practice was renewed by Queen Anne in order to reinforce her hereditary right to the throne for the power of healing supposed to reside in the royal hands was a useful weapon in the cause of divine right – especially since the Pretender across the channel was busily performing miracles to establish his own claim. Royalists took it very seriously: Wiseman, the Stuart king's surgeon, mentions 'the great concourse of strumous persons to Whitehall', where the ceremony was held, and declares:

I my self have been frequent Eye-witness of many hundreds of Cures performed by his Majesties Touch alone, without any assistance of Chirurgery; and those, many of them, such as had tyred out the endeavours of able Chirurgeons before they came thither . . .[21]

He adds, as Royalists always did, that the blood of the martyred Charles I had the same power. After three folio pages spent expatiating on these miracles, though, Wiseman goes on to speak of the Evil as 'one of the most obstinate Diseases that I know'.

So it proved in the case of Samuel Johnson. The ceremony is interesting because of the light it casts briefly on the extraordinary conditions of the medical world in which Johnson grew up – a world in which faith in miraculous cures was intertwined with empirical experimenting, Galenic 'vital spirits' with 'medical statics' and antiquarian learning with Newtonian mechanics. It was perfectly possible, though, when medical theory changed, to construct, as Tobias Smollett did at the mid-century, a mechanical explanation for the apparent cure: 'a poor diseased wretch, of low station and weak intellects', he suggested, 'prepossessed with the superstitious notion of a delegated power from Heaven, and struck with the *Apparatus*, as well as with the sublime rank of the operator, acting in the double capacity of apostle and king, could not fail to be extremely affected through the whole system of the nerves, and suffer such agitation in the blood and spirits, as might work great changes in the constitution'.[22] The touch of the monarch's hand here becomes a kind of shock therapy. A twentieth-century doctor, on the other hand, agreed that this experience was indeed a shock, but a pathogenic one, fancying a correlation between the young Johnson's vivid memory of the state occasion – 'somehow a sort of solemn recollection of a lady in diamonds and a long black hood' – and its effect on his nervous system. 'All Johnson's frightful jerkings and grimaces, roarings and puffings', he wrote, 'may possibly be traced back to that one moment of nervous tension when he felt himself a little boy the observed of all observers waiting to be touched'.[23] The failure of the Queen's intervention led to another operation, rather more serious: the scrofulous glands were surgically incised for drainage and the scars remained visible on the underpart of Johnson's face – particularly on the left side – for the rest of his life. They are clearly visible in his death-mask.[24] The disease ran its normal clinical course and Hector told Boswell that Johnson 'was very well when he came to school, and had only the scars'.[25]

Some eighteenth-century doctors associated scrofula with nervous disease, as did George Cheyne:

> I never saw any Person labour under severe obstinate, and strong *Nervous* Complaints, but I always found at last, the *Stomach, Guts, Liver*, Spleen, Mesentary or some of the great and necessary Organs or Glands of the Lower Belly were obstructed, knotted, schirrous, or spoil'd, and perhaps all these together; and it may be very justly affirmed, that no habitual and grievous, or great *nervous* Disorders, ever happen'd to any one who laboured not under some real *glandular* Distemper, either *scrophulous* or *scorbutical*, original or acquired. So that in general, great Nervous Disorders may justly and properly be termed *Glandular* . . .[26]

Scrofula too has often been thought of as providing an origin for Johnson's later medical problems. 'His nerves were affected by that disorder, for which, at two years of age, he was presented to the royal touch', wrote Arthur Murphy. It is probably to beliefs like Cheyne's that Sir John Hawkins alludes when he writes of Johnson's 'morbid affection', melancholy, that 'it is but a surmise that it might be a latent concomitant of that disease which, in his infancy, had induced his mother to seek relief from the royal touch'.[27]

One very likely result of the scrofula was that it left Johnson with impaired eyesight. The correlation between scrofula and bad eyes was noted by contemporaries and is confirmed by modern ophthalmic opinion.[28] 'Disease had deprived him of the use of one eye', wrote Johnson's first biographer, Hawkins, and his two other most important biographers are equally firm. However much they might disagree on other points, Boswell and Mrs Piozzi agree on this one. 'The scrophulous evil ... left such marks as greatly disfigured a countenance naturally harsh and rugged', writes Mrs Piozzi. 'It was owing to that horrible disorder, too, that one eye was perfectly useless to him.' The king's evil, says Boswell, 'disfigured a countenance naturally well formed, and hurt his visual nerves so much, that he did not see at all with one of his eyes'.[29] Both say that the defect was not observable and that Johnson's eyes looked alike. It is an interesting fact that Boswell never realised, whilst Johnson was alive, that there was anything amiss with his eyes.

A 'perfectly useless' eye is not quite the same as a blind one. It is possible that Johnson's visual difficulties have been popularly exaggerated. 'In tuberculous inflammation of the eye', write McHenry and MacKeith,

small collections of lymphoid tissue (called phlyctenules) accumulate on the conjectivae (tunica adnata) and cornea producing phlyctenular kerato-conjunctivitis. The phlyctenules may ulcerate and cause the brilliant surface of the cornea to become scarred, giving it a dull ground-glass appearance. As the years pass, the dulled corneal surface may clear to some extent with enlargement of the visual field. The corneal scarring or opacity can be patchy or quite small (called a nebula) and scarcely apparent to an observer. The nebula may still cause severe visual disturbance on account of the resulting diffusion and irregular refraction of the light rays. Limited vision can be obtained through the unscarred portion, if the individual holds objects closer to the eye for a clearer definition. In Johnson's case corneal scarring probably destroyed enough central vision to make him essentially blind in the left eye. However enough peripheral vision remained to keep the eye in good alignment, since a divergent strabismus with outward drifting of the eye did not develop.[30]

A strabismus is a squint. Johnson's 'eyes', wrote Mrs Piozzi, 'though of a light grey colour, were so wild, so piercing and at times so fierce, that fear was I believe the first emotion in the hearts of all his beholders'.[31]

References to Johnson's 'blindness' are part of the mythology surrounding this disabled giant. On 10 April 1775, for instance, the Rev. Thomas Campbell dined with General Oglethorpe, Johnson and Boswell. 'The Poem of the Graces became the topic; Boswell asked if he had never been under the hands of the dancing master. "Aye, and a dancing mistress too", says the Doctor, "but I own to you I never took a lesson but one or two, my blind eyes showed me I could never make a proficiency." '[32] 'Dr Johnson has asked me', said Philip Metcalfe to Fanny Burney in 1782, 'to go with him to Chichester, to see the Cathedral, and I told him I would certainly go if he pleased; but why, I cannot imagine, for how shall a blind man see a cathedral?' 'I believe', said Fanny Burney in reply, 'his blindness is as much the effect of absence as of infirmity for he sees wonderfully at times.'[33] She was right enough: Johnson was taken to Chichester Cathedral and noted in his diary 'Chichester Cathedral beautiful, the quire elegant – pews in body.'[34] Sir Joshua Reynolds remarked that 'pictures he could not well see', yet in his visit to Paris in 1775 Johnson was able to note that at the Palais Royal 'I thought the pictures of Raphael fine.'[35] 'I have heard him say, and I have often perceived, that he could not distinguish any man's face half a yard distant from him, and not even his most intimate acquaintance', wrote Frances Reynolds, herself a painter.[36] He may not have been able to recognise the faces of his acquaintances, and 'once declared, that he "never saw the human face divine"',[37] but he died possessed of 146 portraits, of which sixty-one were framed and glazed.[38]

Johnson himself spoke frequently of his eye troubles, and one sometimes feels that with this as with some of his other disabilities, he was not beyond what Mr Darcy was to call the 'indirect boast'. 'Are you a botanist, Dr Johnson?' he was asked on his tour to Devonshire in 1762. 'No sir ... should I wish to become a botanist, I must first turn myself into a reptile.'[39] Yet Johnson did not wear spectacles. George Steevens, who worked with him on the revisions to his edition of Shakespeare and in this instance is presumably reliable, wrote:

Though he never made use of glasses to assist his sight, he said he could recollect no production of art to which man has superior obligation. He mentioned the name of the original inventor of spectacles with reverence, and expressed his wonder that not an individual, out of the multitudes who had profited by them, had, through gratitude, written the life of so great a benefactor to society.[40]

'Having by some ridiculous resolution or mad vow, determined never to wear spectacles, he could make little use of books in his later years', Johnson remarks sternly in his *Life* of Swift. If he did not use them himself it must have been either because his problem was not simple myopia, and therefore irremediable by the optics of the day, or because he did not need them.[41] Most of the evidence suggests that

Johnson, though short-sighted in the right eye, and having limited peripheral vision in the left, was by no means 'blind'. In one sense this is obvious. No one could have done the amount of reading Johnson did for the *Dictionary*, as well as supervise the collection, collation, and – presumably – the proof-reading of the quotations without an eyesight which in practice was highly efficient. He 'commonly read with amazing rapidity, glancing his eye [sic] from the top to the bottom of the page in an instant', wrote Miss Reynolds.[42] When on his trip to Paris with the Thrales in 1775 Johnson visited the Bibliothèque du Roi he inspected the incunabula and was able to deduce from the appearances of the letters in several volumes whether they were printed from wooden or metal types.[43] 'Seeing' is of course not entirely a matter of visual acuity. 'So much does mind govern, and even supply the deficiency of organs, that his perceptions were commonly quick and accurate', says Boswell, and he describes how Johnson could make out the shape of a hill, at a distance, better than he could. Johnson worked, as with the catalogue for the Harleian library, with obscure and difficult texts: he once called himself an 'exact inspector of . . . old books.'[44] 'The imprudent use of a small print', he thought, left an inflammation in his 'useful eye' in 1773, but he never once, among his many complaints, complains of headache.

Scrofula may have damaged his ears as well as his eyes, 'doing irreparable damage to the auricular organs, which never could perform their functions since I knew him', wrote Mrs Piozzi, who first met Johnson in 1764 when he was fifty-five.[45] 'Infection of the middle ear may result from tuberculous extension via the Eustachian tube from the nasopharynx.'[46] Johnson's deafness or hearing difficulties may well originate from this period of his childhood. Johnson certainly was rather deaf in the last twenty years of his life, often unable to hear the sermon when he went to church and notoriously disabled by his deafness from any enjoyment of music.[47] At John Taylor's, in 1777, Taylor and two other players entertained the company with 'tunes on the fiddle'. 'Johnson desired to have "Let Ambition fire thy mind" played over again, and appeared to give a patient attention to it, though he owned to me', says Boswell, who was present, 'that he was very insensible to the power of musick.'[48] Johnson usually spoke 'very contemptuously' of music, declaring 'no man of talent, or whose mind was capable of better things, ever would or could devote his time and attention to so idle and frivolous a pursuit'. One of Sir Joshua Reynolds' nieces who was present on this occasion whispered to her neighbour 'I wonder what Dr Johnson thinks of King David'.[49] 'I never would consult him about anything where Music is concerned, as he is wholly deaf & insensible to it', wrote Charles Burney rather petulantly in the midst of compiling his *History of Music* in 1780.[50] This opinion did not stop Burney from asking Johnson for the Dedication – his last – to his *Commemoration* of Handel in 1784 in which he declared:

> The delight which Music affords seems to be one of the first attainments of rational nature; wherever there is humanity, there is modulated sound. The mind set free from the resistless tyranny of painful want employs its first leisure upon some savage melody. Thus in those lands of unprovided wretchedness which Your Majesty's encouragement of naval investigation has brought lately to the knowledge of the polished world, though all things else were wanted, every nation had its Music; an art of which the rudiments accompany the commencements, and the refinements adorn the completion of civility, in which the inhabitants of the earth seek their first refuge from evil, and, perhaps, may find at last the most elegant of their pleasures.
>
> But that this pleasure may be truly elegant, science and nature must assist each other: a quick sensibility of Melody and Harmony is not always originally bestowed, and those who are born with this susceptibility of modulated sounds are often ignorant of its principles and must therefore be in a great degree delighted by chance . . .[51]

'I once bought me a flagelet', Johnson once said, 'but I never made out a tune.'[52] It is touching to find him, not six months before his death, turning to Burney and asking him 'to teach him the Scale of Musick: – "Dr Burney, teach me at least the alphabet of your language"'.[53]

Perhaps the scrofula was the true origin of many more of Johnson's later problems, but it has to compete with a formidable rival for explanatory power. The crisis of 1729 is put at the centre of his medical history by Johnson himself. 'My health has been from my twentieth year such as has seldom afforded me a single day of ease', he told Edmund Hector, probably some time in the seventies.[54] In 1786 Boswell wrote to the Birmingham surgeon who had been a school-fellow of Johnson and the friend of his youth, asking for more information:

> In one of the letters to you with which you favoured me, Dr Johnson says that he had not enjoyed a day's health since his *twentieth* year. *That* may refer to the first vacation he spent at home after being entered in Pembroke College. Was it *then* that he was first seised with a strong fit of 'morbid

melancholy'? or was it later? I *know* it was *about* that period. He never got entirely rid of it. What particulars can you tell of it? and where was you then?

He was honoured with this reply:

1st Q

If that Letter does not carry its own date, I cannot ascertain it. The time He complains of his morbid melancholy must be dated from his first fixing in London and his acquaintance with Mr Thrale.[55]

Marshall Waingrow, the editor of Boswell's papers, suggests that perhaps Hector did not recognise the term 'morbid melancholy' (which seems to be a Johnsonian invention) 'as descriptive of Samuel Johnson's affliction as *he* knew it'.[56] Johnson's statement could be construed as referring to complaints which are preponderantly physical. Lack of 'ease' and 'oppression' – Johnson goes on to say in this letter, 'My disorders are . . . still sufficiently oppressive' – seem to refer more readily to the breathing difficulties which afflicted him throughout at least the last twenty years of his adult life than to melancholy or – to use a modern term – depression. There is another possible explanation. Perhaps Hector had decided not to tell.[57]

Lacking Hector's information, Boswell gives this account of the crisis:

The 'morbid melancholy', which was lurking in his constitution, and to which we may ascribe those particularities, and that aversion to regular life, which, at a very early period, marked his character, gathered such strength in his twentieth year, as to afflict him in a dreadful manner. While he was at Lichfield, in the college vacation of the year 1729, he felt himself overwhelmed with an horrible hypochondria, with perpetual irritation, fretfulness and impatience; and with a dejection, gloom, and despair, which made existence misery. From this dismal malady he never afterwards was perfectly relieved . . .[58]

It has been generally assumed that this crisis was a consequence of Johnson's having to leave Oxford after four terms in December 1729, but as A. L. Reade pointed out, 'Whether it was the onset of these symptoms that caused him to come home, or his coming home under the compulsion of circumstances that caused the onset of the symptoms, we do not know'. Furthermore, 'After his return from Oxford in December 1729 there is not known one single fact of his career until the autumn of 1731.'[59]

Boswell's account of Johnson's malady implies that he – perhaps rather confusedly – conceives of it as originating physiologically, in Johnson's 'constitution'. In N. D. Jewson's summary a 'remarkable feature of 18th century theories of pathology was the absence of a sharp distinction between afflictions of the mind and of the body. Emotional temperament and physical disposition were believed to be closely related, and considerable attention was paid to the patient's subjective impressions of his disease and cure.'[60] Jewson instances hypochondriasis as illustrating the close association thought to exist between psychological disorders and somatic events. 'Hypochondria' has no exact equivalent in modern medicine but in the eighteenth century, and earlier, it was a generally recognised disease entity, a real and serious condition which originated in the upper abdomen and was due to slow, sluggishly moving or too 'heavy' or 'viscid' blood. Like many other eighteenth-century medical aetiologies, this combined a Galenic belief that the disorder was due to a defect in one of the body's 'humours' (a word which by this time was tending to mean simply fluids) and a post-Newtonian conviction that the nature of this defect must be a physical property of that fluid's movement or composition. In Boswell's account can be discerned too the influence of the monistic or unitary premises of eighteenth-century medicine.

The contemporary accounts of Johnson's medical condition almost always adhere to the notion, as Boswell later called it, of 'something morbid in his constitution', a single explanatory concept which links the body and the mind. This constitution – something inherited, fatal and therefore readily excusable – becomes an important aspect of Boswell's defence of Johnson from the charge of rudeness. 'You . . . have shown clearly that his fits of fretfulness and bursts of rudeness proceeded from no innate acrimony of disposition, but from that nervous irritability to which from his constitution he was so unhappily subject',[61] wrote one of his correspondents. Johnson's 'constitution', like every individual's, was mysteriously unique to him. Again, as Jewson suggests, each patient in the eighteenth century was conceived of as 'suffering from his own peculiar combination of factors which accounted for his physiological disequilibrium. Although there was only one pathological condition there were innumerable pathological careers.'[62] When Arthur Murphy writes that 'From the close of his last work, the malady, that persecuted him through life, came upon him with alarming severity, and his constitution declined apace' he leaves the malady unnamed, since it is presumably specific only to Johnson.[63]

It is possible that Johnson suffered from some physical, even infectious, disease in the winter of 1729 or later, but whatever the precise nature of this crisis its effects on Johnson's subsequent life were devastating. During Johnson's interview with King George III in the library at the Queen's house in February 1767 the king observed 'that he supposed he must have read a great deal; Johnson answered, that he thought more than he read; that he had read a great deal in the early part of his life, but having fallen into ill-health, he had not been able to read much, compared with others ...'[64] 'His great period of study', Johnson told Langton, according to Malone, 'was from the age of *twelve* to that of *eighteen*.'[65] After this illness then, it seems, Johnson was no longer able, or thought himself no longer able, to read systematically and intensely. One other result of this crisis has been widely recognised: 'I myself was for some years totally regardless of religion. It had dropped out of my mind.' 'When was that, Sir?' Seward asked Johnson. 'Why, Sir, I think from ten till two and twenty. Sickness brought it back, and I hope I have never lost it since.'[66]

The third result of this illness was the development of the strangest of his characteristics. I shall call them, reluctantly, his 'tics and gesticulations' – the strange, awkward, repeated movements and sounds he made, which always attracted notice and were commented on by many observers.[67] I use the phrase reluctantly (some term has to be used) since to name these phenomena is to risk immediately curtailing the field of explanation, and Johnson's 'tics' cannot be discussed without distinguishing at the same time the ways in which they were perceived, conceived and made sense of.

Johnson's condition, even more in this than in other instances, varies with the observers' altering gaze. In the eighteenth century his strange gestures were usually held to be the result of a 'paralytic' or 'convulsive' malady, one more manifestation of some underlying morbidity of his unique constitution or 'humours'. Alternatively – and incompatibly – Boswell on one occasion presents them as typifying the symptoms of a recognised organic disease. At the same period, these behaviours could be separated from Johnson's other illnesses and isolated as moral misdemeanours – the result of habitually indulged liberties. In the nineteenth century the same gestures have all the bizarre appeal of eccentricity. In the early twentieth century they become the symptomatic manifestation of deep-seated psychological problems, having their origin in Johnson's childhood and youth,

Later still, in the seventies and eighties, they form a neurological syndrome. It is difficult to make one's way through this welter of conflicting readings and explanations, but as a beginning we could note that there is always a choice between a moral or a medical stress in any given account.

The earliest description of Johnson's physical peculiarities is in a letter from one Henry Greswold of Solihull Grammar School explaining why Johnson was unsuccessful in his application for the post of schoolmaster:

he has yᵉ Caracter of being a very haughty, ill natured Gent., E yᵗ he has such a way of distorting his Face (Wᶜʰ though he can't help) yᵉ Gent, think it may affect some Young Ladds ...[68]

'Distorting his face' suggests a twitch or spasm. A similar rejection from another school was reportedly due to 'an apprehension that the paralytick affection, under which our great Philologist laboured through life, might become the object of imitation or of ridicule among the pupils', but this testimony is obviously given long after the event.[69] Another piece of evidence is William Shaw's *Memoirs of Dr Johnson*:

To his dying day, he never thought, recollected, or studied, whether in his closet, or in the street, alone, or in company, without putting his huge unwieldy body, in the same rolling, aukward posture, in which he was in use, while conning his grammar, or construing his lesson, to sit on the form at school.[70]

The phrase 'to his dying day' makes it clear that this evidence too is based on later observation. Shaw is reading back into Johnson's childhood what he has himself noticed about the adult: his informant about Johnson's childhood was Dr Swinfen's daughter so it would have been third-hand testimony anyway. One may doubt, too, whether 'rolling' (a term other observers such as Fanny Burney also used) whilst one reads concentratedly is correctly described as a movement disorder. After the 1729–31 crisis the term most frequently used by contemporary observers was 'convulsive'.

Most if not all of Johnson's strange movements do seem to have originated at this period. That may well be the meaning of the statement to Hector already quoted: 'My health has been since my twentieth year such as has seldom afforded me a single day of *ease*' (my italics). What does Johnson mean by this notion of a long-standing lack of 'ease'? Does he mean something like 'I've been troubled by one illness after another ever since'? Or does it refer more specifically to inability to relax, to be emotionally or mentally at peace, to the 'perpetual irritation, fretfulness and impatience' of Boswell's description of the 'hypochondria' of that time? It might also point, even more specifically, to the movement disorders, the tics and gesticulations described for example by Fanny Burney in 1779. 'He has almost perpetual convulsive movements, either of his hands, lips, feet or knees, and sometimes of all together', she wrote.[71]

It has already been impossible to keep separate the description of this aspect of Johnson's behaviour from diagnostic assumptions. Fanny Burney's is the briefest of descriptions of those 'tics' of which Boswell at the end of the *Life* gives the most full and observant account:

while talking or even musing as he sat in his chair, he commonly held his head to one side towards his right shoulder, and shook it in a tremulous manner, moving his body backwards and forwards, and rubbing his left knee in the same direction, with the palm of his hand. In the intervals of articulating he made various sounds with his mouth, sometimes as if ruminating, or what is called chewing the cud, sometimes giving a half whistle, sometimes making his tongue play backwards from the roof of his mouth, as if clucking like a hen, and sometimes protruding it against his upper gums in front, as if pronouncing quickly under his breath, *too, too, too*: all this accompanied sometimes with a thoughtful look, but more frequently with a smile. Generally when he had concluded a period, in the course of a dispute, by which time he was a good deal exhausted by violence and vociferation, he used to blow out his breath like a Whale . . .[72]

Boswell's account, wonderfully attentive as it is (has anyone at this date described human gestures with such detailed fidelity?), could be supplemented still further by other observers' reports. It is already a complex enough medley – but of what? If we seek to understand these movements we have first to give them names. Are these 'tics', gestures, mannerisms, bad habits, compulsive behaviour? To call them symptoms is to accede at once to the medical claim to explanatory power. To call them 'tics' would be to allow them to be only involuntary, enforced and purposeless: to call them mannerisms or bad habits would foreground the moral dimension of behaviour and therefore pre-empt a neurological explanation. Behind, inter-twined with or interpenetrating oddities of gesture might seem some symptoms which readily prompt a physiological account. As Boswell notices, the gasping for breath seems like the habitual response of the chronic bronchitis sufferer to his breathing difficulties. The shaking of the head and hand movements seem involuntary, but can they be quite so in the context Boswell gives them 'while talking or even musing' as if they were perceived not as discrete, meaningless phenomena, but the necessary accompaniment of other (valuable) behaviour? The lip-movements and mutterings seemed to another observer, Frances Reynolds, to be forms of prayer, though whether this can be construed as still involuntary or not is an open question. 'He seemed to struggle almost incessantly with some mental evil, and often, by the expression of his countenance and the motion of his lips, appeared to be offering up some ejaculation to Heaven to remove it.'[73]

Generally speaking, the less familiar observers were with Johnson the more they were inclined to think his movements involuntary or crazed, as William Hogarth did, for instance at the home of Richardson (1739, according to Boswell). 'While he was talking, he perceived a person standing at a window in the room, shaking his head, and rolling himself about in a strange ridiculous manner. He concluded that he was an ideot, whom his relations had put under the care of Mr Richardson, as a very good man.'[74] 'His head and sometimes also his body', Boswell wrote in his first introductory sketch of Johnson in the *Tour*, 'shook with a kind of motion like the effect of a palsy: he appeared to be frequently disturbed by cramps, or convulsive contractions, of the nature of that distemper called St. Vitus's dance.' 'He was to the last a *convulsionary* . . . His gestures, which were a degree of St Vitus's dance, in the street, attracted the notice of many',[75] wrote Thomas Tyers. 'He has the aspect of an Idiot . . . He is forever dancing the devil's jig', wrote Thomas Campbell in his diary.[76] Boswell initiates the medical account of Johnson's behaviour by quoting from Sydenham's classic description of chorea minor:

This disorder is a kind of convulsion. It manifests itself by halting or unsteadiness of one of the legs, which the patient draws after him like an ideot. If the hand of the same side be applied to the breast, or any other part of the body, he cannot keep it a moment in the same posture, but it will be drawn into a different one by a convulsion, notwithstanding all his efforts to the contrary.[77]

There are many reasons why this diagnosis does not fit the facts. Nowhere else is it suggested that Johnson suffered the kind of violent convulsive movements of the whole arm depicted here.[78] Miss Hawkins speaks of his walking with his left hand in an odd position, 'so as to bring the hand under his chin', but it is of a 'fixed' position.[79] Frances Reynolds and Fanny Burney only describe movements of the *hands* of an unusual kind – 'a singular method of twirling his fingers and twisting his hands' (Burney), 'as for his gestures with his hands ... sometimes he would hold them up with some of his fingers bent, as if he had been seized with the cramp, and sometimes at his Breast in motion like those of a jockey on full speed' (Reynolds).[80] Joshua Reynolds' portrait of 1769 appears to show Johnson's hands in the position his sister describes: they are held in front of him, the thumbs straight, the fingers separate and bent, each hand tensed in a gesture that Reynolds makes both eloquent and tragic. The whole implication of the picture is that these movements of the hands, however strange, are expressive, not involuntary. These three observers agree too in describing Johnson's bodily movements. He moved backwards and forwards, 'see-sawed' especially during conversations, and his body 'rolled' when he was concentrating on his reading. Shaw, as we have seen, spoke of his 'rolling, aukward posture'. Miss Reynolds describes an occasion when his reading of Grotius in Twickenham Meadows caused him to see-saw 'at such a violent rate as to excite the curiosity of some people at a distance to come and see what was the matter with him'.[81]

Whether one should give a medical account of behaviour depends obviously enough on the observer's sense of the limits of the normal or acceptable. Rolling or see-sawing movements whilst one's concentration is absorbed should hardly be called pathological. An early study of the subject, Meige and Feindel's *Tics and their Treatment* (translated in 1907) makes this useful distinction:

Concentration of the attention may diminish the intensity or even inhibit the occurrence of a tic; inversely, a simple bad habit is manifested preferably during this very concentration. In the heat of physical or intellectual labour, we have all our favourite and characteristic tricks: we curl our moustache, we twist our beard, we scratch our forehead, we rub our chin, we nod our head, we fidget with our fingers in reading, speaking, reciting – in any mental or physical exercise requiring our attention we reveal innumerable little oddities of movement; but let our thoughts be directed for an instant to these gestures of distraction, and they disappear forthwith, to reappear afresh when we are absorbed in our work again. Charcot used to twist his hair round his index finger so intricately that to disentangle the finger one day a lock of hair had actually to be cut off. It was a trick of his, not a tic.[82]

Boswell, as we have seen, said that Johnson's movements were present both while he talked and mused. But on this crucial matter Sir Joshua Reynolds disagreed. When Johnson was left out of a conversation, he noted, 'he fell into a reverie accompanied with strange antic gestures; but this he never did when his mind was engaged by the conversation. [These were] therefore improperly called by [Boswell], as well as by others, convulsions; whereas, a word addressed to him, his attention was recovered.'[83] Yet Reynolds' observation may not be inconsistent with the diagnosis of some organic disorder. The nature of the movements as well as their occasions have to be considered.

Meige and Feindel, as disciples of Charcot, perceived ticqueurs as degenerate, sufferers from 'mental infantilism', and extolled the power of the will. Though tics differed from 'tricks' or 'stereotyped acts' in that they were abnormal and functionless movements, and their suppression caused pain, they could and should be controlled. 'The intensity and tenacity of any tic are determined by the degree of volitional imperfection to which its subject has sunk. He who can will can effect a cure; be it simple tic, or be it a case of Gilles de la Tourette's disease . . .'[84] Gilles de la Tourette syndrome was named by Charcot after his pupil who first (1885) published an account of nine patients having 'une affection nerveuse caractérisée par de l'incoordination motrice accompagnée d'écholalie et de coprolalie'.[85] TS (as it is now known) is at present generating much interest and research. It has also been proposed as a means of collecting together and explaining Johnson's varied symptoms, the latest and in some ways the most persuasive assertion of medical explanatory power over Johnson's behaviour.

First suggested, in passing, as a possibility, in 1967 by McHenry, a comprehensive study of the disorder in 1978 (A. K. Shapiro *et al.*, *Gilles de la Tourette Syndrome*) declares that 'Samuel Johnson . . . is the most notable example of a successful adaptation to life despite the liability of Tourette syndrome', though the authors repeatedly stress the difficulty of making a diagnosis of the syndrome even on contemporary patients. A Canadian physician, T. J. Murray, published an article in 1979 in the *British Medical Journal* arguing that Johnson's abnormal movements constitute the clinical picture of Tourette syndrome, and this conclusion has been widely publicised.[86] TS begins in childhood, often with single tics – rapid, repeated, involuntary movements – of the eye and face; in time the movements tend to spread downwards, so that odd jerkings of the shoulders and

the trunk occur simultaneously as well as other varieties of movement. These involuntary gestures are always associated with disorders
of speech: most often the patient will feel compelled to utter
obscenities ('coprolalia') or will make grunting, snorting, barking or
screaming noises in the midst of ordinary speech. In some instances the
patient will be compelled to mutter sequences of sounds, or end their
speech with an expiratory hiss. The symptoms may tend to 'wax and
wane', patients being relatively free of them for considerable periods.
They can also control the tics to some degree at least: tic-ing children,
when brought to the doctor's surgery, for instance, often behave quite
normally, to the consternation of their parents. 'Absorption in a
non-anxious task' will also relieve the tics. It is when the patient is
relaxed, as when watching television, that the movements become
most marked. Shapiro argues that TS is not a psychological disease
and on the evidence of controlled psychological testing of patients, he
finds that it is not necessarily associated either with obsessive-compul-
sive character traits, or with the inhibition of aggressive impulses (two
favourite earlier hypotheses). The success of the drug halperidol, a
dopamine inhibitor, in controlling the symptoms of TS patients,
probably means that the disorder has an organic origin, possibly in the
basal ganglia. The assertion in the study itself, however, that 'patients
can almost always volitionally decrease their symptoms for variable
lengths of time'[87] possibly means that psychological, or 'psycho-
social' factors do have some role to play in the condition or its
management.

This is certainly the impression one takes from case histories of
similar afflictions. The famous 'confessions of a ticqueur' which opens
Meige and Feindel tells us that 'He is a great fisher, and when he "has a
bite", or is expecting one, he will remain motionless indefinitely; his
tics do not hinder him from preparing his bait with the minutest
care.'[88] A recent introspective report by a highly intelligent TS
patient, Joseph Bliss, interestingly insists on the volitional element not
only in the control but in the genesis of the movements. Bliss's
symptoms, as described, show parallel, if not identical, features to
Johnson's. They included 'neck jerking and twisting: ear movements;
stomach to belt twisting, torso movements; nose twitching; brow
lifting ... leg and arm jerking ... sounds made between tongue and
teeth.'[89] In his account Bliss insists that 'Each movement is the result of
a voluntary capitulation to a demanding and relentless urge accompanied by an extraordinarily subtle sensation that provokes and fuels

the urge', a conviction formed over many years of introspective attention to his symptoms:

When attention is trained to be aware of the very first signs, one perceives a sensitive point, a trembling it seems, on the threshold; it slips out almost undetected and evolves quickly into action. Normally, consciousness records only the obvious overt actions. Only when the senses are sharpened by long years of effort is it possibly to detect these faintest of signals skittering over the field of awareness ...

As soon as the senses become aware of any site (through actual or phantom, tactile or kinesthetic impressions), a very rapidly escalating desire to satisfy the sensation with movements intended to free oneself from the insistent feeling ensues. The first evidence of an emerging signal is originally perceived as an unsatisfied or unfulfilled sensation that immediately translates into a craving for relief. Relief for the impulse seemingly can be achieved only by movement against or through the surface of the site. This sensitized surface becomes the target of completely satisfing the urge; each movement to a target gives some relief but does not extinguish the feeling. Each one cries out for more forceful repetition.

The TS movement is not the whole message. The TS movement is not rhythmic, spasmodic, or involuntary. The movement only *seems* involuntary because of the instant capitulation to the unrecognized sensory stimulus. It can be detected and interrupted when in progress and at any stage.

The TS movements are intentional bodily movements. The intention is to relieve a sensation, as surely as the movement to scratch an itch is to relieve the itch. If the itch was so subtle and fast that it escaped detection, would that make the act any less voluntary?[90]

Johnson too, would insist, despite the implication of phrases like 'paralytic affection' or 'morbid infection', that he had connived with or fostered his symptoms. When Christopher Smart's niece asked him 'Pray, Dr Johnson, why do you make such strange gestures?', he replied 'From bad habit. Do you, my dear, take care to guard against bad habits.'[91] Sir Joshua Reynolds agreed: 'My opinion is, that it proceded from a habit which he had indulged himself in, of accompanying his thoughts with certain untoward actions.'[92] Reynolds' sister was also convinced that Johnson's 'extraordinary gestures' were not involuntary, 'Many people have supposed that they were the natural effects of a nervous disorder, but had that been the case he could not have sat still when he chose, which he did, and so still indeed when sitting for his picture, as often to have been complimented with being a pattern for sitters.' 'I dare say the King saw none of these odd gesticulations, nor did he MUCH use them at Church', commented Mrs Thrale.[93]

'Bad habit', as a general explanation, entails the notion that the habitual gesture or movement might be suppressed or abolished by the bringing to bear of a certain contrary energy, in the form of the 'will' or the 'reason'. But if one thinks of Johnson's own abnormal behaviours, as described by Boswell, for instance, it is scarcely conceivable that such a constellation of symptoms could be defeated except by the exertion of such energy, or force of will – maintained continuously – as virtually to change the nature of the person, or at least tax their resources in a way that leaves little energy left for other functions (for example, thought). If we view them in this, admittedly pragmatic, light, Johnson's movements come to have almost a benign quality. Johnson's condemnation (and Reynolds', who in this respect is a disciple) is founded upon a hard and fast distinction between voluntary and involuntary acts; and the term 'habit' seems to resolve, but actually obscures, all the problems that are generated once one adopts those two poles. In any case, naming it 'habit' and invoking reason as its antagonist places emphasis exclusively on the individual and ignores the social circumstances in which it occurs. Frances Reynolds describes another of Johnson's peculiarities:

But the manoeuvre that used the most particularly to engage the attention of the company was his stretching out his arm with a full cup of tea in his hand, in every direction, often to the great annoyance of the person who sat next him, indeed to the imminent danger of their cloaths, perhaps of a Lady's Court dress; sometimes he would twist himself round with his face close to the back of his chair, and finish his cup of tea, breathing very hard, as if making a laborious effort to accomplish it.[94]

Can the genteel standards Miss Reynolds voices here so primly be entirely unconnected with the gestures she describes? These stretching movements – which Johnson sometimes also performed with his legs – seem comprehensible not as the symptoms of (neurological) disease, but as means of dealing with various tensions – though I am well aware that the term 'tensions' in its turn begs innumerable questions. One thing is clear, though. Had these been the 'sudden, lightning-like and jerky' TS movements, the cup of tea would certainly have been spilled.

There are other difficulties in the way of accepting a diagnosis of Gilles de la Tourette syndrome. Whilst one cannot be certain, with

W. J. Bate, that Johnson's 'embarrassing tics and other compulsive mannerisms' developed in the 1729–31 crisis, there is little convincing evidence that peculiarities in Johnson's behaviour were noticed in his youth.[95] If Johnson's own statement that his 'unease' began in his twentieth year is accepted as including, though not necessarily comprehending, these symptoms, then this would make the onset of the disorder extraordinarily, perhaps uniquely, late. The fact that Johnson did not suffer from coprolalia need not preclude a diagnosis of TS since only 55 per cent of patients do in fact show this symptom. On the other hand, there is good evidence that Johnson's mouth movements and mutterings were forms of prayer, and they certainly did not interrupt normal speech. Mrs Thrale said that Johnson's eye trembled, but there is little evidence for other facial movement. Many of his gestures – see-sawing, rolling his head etc. – seem less automatic and bizarre than exaggerations of traits which may be seen in many less gifted and perfectly ordinary mortals.

Besides acts which were perceived as involuntary or 'convulsive', Johnson performed ones which seemed quite the opposite – deliberate, ritualized and quite complex – (though some commentators run them together):

> He had another particularity, of which none of his friends ever ventured to ask an explanation. It appeared to me some superstitious habit, which he had contracted early, and from which he had never called upon his reason to disentangle him. This was his anxious care to go out or in at a door or passage, by a certain number of steps from a certain point, or at least so as that either his right or left foot (I am not certain which,) should constantly make the first actual movement when he came close to the door or passage. Thus I conjecture: for I have, upon innumerable occasions, observed him suddenly stop, and then seem to count his steps with a deep earnestness: and when he had neglected or gone wrong in this sort of magical movement, I have seen him go back, again put himself in a proper posture to begin the ceremony, and, having gone through it, break from his abstraction, walk briskly on, and join his companion.[96]

Boswell's account is corroborated by Miss Reynolds' more excited report of his

> extraordinary gestures or anticks with his hands and feet, particularly when passing over the threshold of a Door, or rather before he would venture to pass through *any* doorway. On entering Sir Joshua's house with poor Mrs Williams, a blind lady who lived with him, he would quit her hand, or else whirl her about on the steps as he whirled and twisted about to perform his

gesticulations; and as soon as he had finish'd, he would give a sudden spring, and make such an extensive stride over the threshold, as if he was trying for a wager how far he could stride, Mrs Williams standing groping about outside the door, unless the servant or the mistress of the House more commonly took hold of her hand to conduct her in, leaving Dr Johnson to perform at the Parlour Door much the same exercise over again.

But the strange positions in which he would place his feet (generally I think before he began his straddles, as if necessarily preparatory) are scarcely credible. Sometimes he would make the back part of his heels to touch, sometimes the extremity of his toes, as if endeavouring to form a triangle, or some geometrical figure ...[97]

Bate has suggested that these rituals demonstrate a 'compulsion neurosis' – 'a powerful unconscious need to release nervous tension through order, pattern, or rhythm and keep it from overwhelming the psyche – a need to "divide up" the welter of subjective feeling and reduce to manageable units, which we also see in his constant resort to arithmetic and counting'.[98] These rituals do seem peculiarly difficult to explain as straightforward results or extensions of neurological disease, though parallel cases of 'arithomania' occur in discussion of various forms of tic. (One patient was compelled to take five steps in a circle before beginning to walk: Shapiro identifies a 'sub-group' 'plagued by the pressure of internal fantasies and compulsive ritualistic behaviour'.[99]) Such acts may, conceivably, be invented by the sufferer and have a diversionary or therapeutic relation to an original disease or disturbance. Alternatively, they may be thought to take their roots in the same 'unease'. Certainly, if, with Russell Brain and other physicians who have studied the evidence one rejects neurological disease as an explanation for Johnson's behaviour, a problem remains. 'His movement and psychological disturbances were not on the basis of brain anoxia or cerebral palsy, but were manifestations of his underlying psychological make-up', concludes McHenry.[100] This gap in the explanation of Johnson's behaviour has been readily filled by psychoanalytic accounts. It is certain, though, that when Johnson wrote of his as a life 'radically wretched', he was not exaggerating; and his extraordinary disabilities were augmented further in his middle years.

II

The study of Johnson's 'tics and gesticulations' makes an interesting commentary on the post-Foucauldian proposition that medical conditions are not naturally occurring entities but are socially produced; or rather (since no one denies the reality of sickness) that ways of perceiving disease, in particular the way in which symptoms are observed and grouped together to form a disease entity, is socially determined and reciprocally reinforces social expectations. Sufferings, it is suggested, 'have no necessary, transhistorical, universal shape'.[101] A brief look at three more of the recurrent problems that beset Johnson's middle and later years may lend some support to these propositions. The three conditions are named 'gout', 'asthma' and 'melancholy'.

These terms represent very different concepts, perhaps very different orders of knowledge. 'Gout' is the easiest of the three to discuss because it was perceived as a localised invasion or disruption of bodily processes, and because there is a clear overlap between modern conceptions of gout, also localised, and the understandings of Johnson's day. Asthma is a far more nebulous, fluid and problematic notion or construct. It is a good candidate for what Johnson meant when he spoke of the disorders that inhibited his ease – though melancholy is another strong contender. The two may have been experientially linked, since Johnson's very frequent inability to breathe freely, especially lying down at night, will have led to the generation of anxiety, tension and general malaise. It is notable, too, that 'convulsions', 'spasms' (the antitheses of 'ease') are the words which Johnson uses most frequently when recording the problems that kept him from sleeping. Johnson's 'melancholy', which he sometimes spoke of as if it were a specific disease entity, is difficult for us to think of as totally separate from symptoms which may be readily assigned disease categories.

Johnson's gout has recently been investigated by Pat Rogers.[102] As Rogers shows, the onset of what Johnson and his doctors called 'gout' was, according to modern ideas, uncharacteristically late. He suffered recorded attacks in 1775, 1776, 1779 and 1781; the first when he was almost sixty-five. In June 1776, for instance, he wrote to Henry Thrale that 'the lameness ... has improved to a very serious and troublesome fit of the gout. I creep about and hang by both hands ... I enjoy all the dignity of lameness. I receive ladies and dismiss them sitting. *Painful pre-eminence.*' Though Johnson speaks of 'arthritick' pains (6 October 1783) and in his *Dictionary* conflated gout with arthritis, it seems clear that the disorder was confined to his feet and lower legs: he told William Bowles after the attack in 1783 that 'the Gout has treated me with more severity than any former time, it however never climbed higher than my ankles'. Johnson shared the vagueness of diagnostic terminology with his contemporaries, so it is possible, Rogers concludes, that a form of degenerative arthritis would be a more likely modern diagnosis.

It was a common belief that gout, as an acute, intense disorder, would drive out other ailments. Dr Mudge of Plymouth told Johnson, for instance, that the gout would secure him 'from every-thing paralitick'. The unitary premises of eighteenth-century medi-cine led Johnson to a similar belief that his stroke the previous summer had improved his general health. 'My disorders are in other respects less than usual', he told Mrs Thrale, 'my disease whatever it was seems collected into this one dreadful effect. My Breath is free, the constrictions of the chest are suspended, and my nights pass without oppression.'[103] In the case of gout though Johnson's views were heretical. 'I have had a little catch of the gout', he told John Taylor in October 1779, 'but as I have had no great opinion of the benefits which it is supposed to convey, I made haste to be easy, and drove it away after two days.' Taylor, like Mrs Thrale and his doctor, Thomas Lawrence, disapproved, for in December Johnson was replying:

> My Gout never came again. You blame me, but I think very well of myself. Dr Laurence does not seem much to like the trick, but he does not deny that it was very dexterously performed. That the Gout is a remedy I never perceived, for when I had it most in my foot I had the spasms in my breast. At best the Gout is only a dog that drives the wolf away and eats the Sheep himself, for if the Gout has time for growth, it will certainly destroy, and destroy by long and lingering torture. If it comes again I purpose to show it no better hospitality.[104]

Lawrence believed that gout would have a beneficial effect on Johnson's breathing difficulties, and this was why he resisted John-son's own pleas for the procedure he believed would relieve him – phlebotomy. What the 'trick' was we can only guess. Mrs Thrale thought meddling with his gout had led ultimately to Johnson's death. Many years afterwards she wrote of an incident that must have occurred at Sunninghill Park, Berkshire in July 1781: 'I am persuaded that Dr Johnson died of repelled Gout – You may remember the trick he played at Sunninghill, putting his feet in cold water. He never was well after.'[105] She seems to have been right about his general health – for from this time, after two years of comparatively good health, Johnson's condition took a turn for the worse. Yet it seems at first sight difficult to reconcile this opinion with Johnson's letter of 29 August 1775 where he jokes about treating his gout by sea-bathing. 'Into the sea, I suppose, you will send it, and into the sea I design it shall go ... ' As Rogers notes, Mrs Thrale's diagnosis is 'crude and indeed in modern terms unintelligible'.[106]

One can reconstruct the therapeutic rationale which restores meaning to her comment. It rests on the notion that gout or 'the gouty matter' as it was sometimes called, is a specific quantity which would be located somewhere in the veins or nerves of the foot. Cold water shrinks, so the minute vessels in which the gout resides would compress, 'constringe', and expel their contents. It would be forced to move to some other, almost certainly more dangerous, site of the body.[107] For gout was well known to be incurable. Mrs Thrale deplores Johnson's interference in what she perceives as a naturally prophylactic event, a blessing in disguise. This belief in the properties of gout can hardly be separable – as the social constructivists of medicine would insist – from the truth of Rogers' concluding observation that 'there was a certain dignity in the disease, as it was then conceived'.[108] He assembles an impressive array of other eighteenth-century sufferers from this badge of status, among them dukes, earls, admirals, bishops and heiresses.

Gout's visits were intermittent: so-called 'asthmatick' complaints dogged Johnson for many years of his life, and are very frequently mentioned alongside a variety of other symptoms. 'I have been accustomed to bleed frequently for an asthmatick complaint' Johnson told William Heberden at the time of his stroke in June 1783, isolating this, as he always did, from an accompanying symptom, 'a painful, or more properly an oppressive constriction of my chest'. It is partly the fact that what has been called Johnson's asthma is almost always accompanied by other complaints that makes discussion of it a tricky business. So does the fact that there is little consensus even today on the nature and treatment of the condition: immunological approaches still vie with psychosomatic explanations. The experience of the asthma sufferer – to use the term loosely – is often a terrifying one. Inability to breathe, and the location of pain or constriction in the lungs or the bronchial tree produce a sense of 'radical' unwellness which can rise to life-threatening intensity. Johnson's most eloquent description of his symptoms is in a Latin letter to Thomas Lawrence of 13 March 1782 in which he compares the sensations from which he suffers to the accumulated weights piled on the chest of a prisoner who stubbornly refuses to plead. It is difficult, then as now, to be certain of what the term asthma actually meant to an individual patient, but it is interesting, at least, that Anthony Storr's more recent first-hand account uses exactly the same comparison:

> Severe attacks of asthma are alarming; and even if the thought of death itself is not necessarily threatening, inability to get enough air in and out of one's lungs is in itself a horrible, frightening experience, which provokes considerable anxiety. So much is this the case, that, in various parts of the world, mechanical interference with respiration is a well-known method of torture. In many prisons, those who are being interrogated have their heads plunged under water, which is often full of excreta, until they are nearly drowning. Another well-tried technique is to lie the victim down and pile slabs of stone on to his chest until it becomes more and more difficult for him to breathe at all. I can imagine exactly what such a prisoner feels ...[109]

Historically the term asthma has been used of patients suffering from many different symptoms. Areteus of Cappadocia gave, in the second century, what was for long the accepted description of the disease, which begins: 'If from running, gymnastic exercise or any other work, the breathing becomes difficult it is called asthma.' During the long period in which Galen's authority held sway, asthma was thought of as a symptom of disordered humours, not as a diagnostic entity.[110] When this conception developed, as in the works of the iatrochemist J.-B. van Helmont (1577–1644), and Sir John Floyer – with both of whose works Johnson was acquainted – it was the stomach which was considered the originating site of the disease. Floyer considered that a collection of ill-fermented or 'mucilaginous' humours in the abdomen, passing to the lungs, brought about the disease. The remedies were, as they continued to be, despite fundamentally different aetiologies for the disease, until well into the nineteenth century, emetics, vomits and bleeding. 'My respiration was once so difficult', Johnson wrote as he reviewed the past year at Easter 1778, 'that an asthma was suspected.' Until then at least, Johnson's chest problems, however severe, had not seemed to require this specific diagnosis. His recorded history begins in December 1755, when he was forty-six, with 'a cough so violent that I once fainted under its convulsions. I was afraid of my lungs.' In later years, the winters regularly brought problems: a 'vexacious catarrh' for at least ten weeks in the winter of 1773–4, 'great labour of respiration' in January 1777. In November of the same year 'obstructed respiration' is again complained of; in March 1779 'tight and short breath', in January 1780' vexacious and incessant cough', a violent cough in the delayed spring of '82 ... there is no need to go on.[111]

These episodes seem to have been separate again from what Johnson records as an endemic problem, 'spasms', sometimes located in the stomach, sometimes in the breast or throat. During an attack of rheumatism in April 1770 he noted in his diary that one night

between the pain and the spasms in my stomach I was insupportably distressed. On the next night, I think, I laid a blister to my back, and took opium; my night was tolerable, and from that time the spasms in my stomach which disturbed me for many years, and for the two past harassed almost to distraction, have nearly ceased. I suppose the breast is relaxed by the opium.

In 1777 he wrote that 'the flatulence which torments me has sometimes so obstructed my breath that the act of respiration became not only voluntary but laborous in a decumbent posture'. Reviewing his health over the past ten years he told Robert Chambers in 1783 that he had endured 'spasms in the breast' for more than twenty years. His diary for 18 June 1780 speaks similarly of 'those convulsions in my breast which had distressed me for more than twenty years'.

It seems that here were at least four inter-related and mutually reinforcing groups of symptoms. Violent but comparatively brief episodes of coughing: 'spasms' in the chest, which were quieted by opium, difficulty of respiration, sometimes acute, and 'a sensation like flatulence or intumescence which I cannot describe' as Johnson put it in his letter to Chambers. The 'catarrh' and violent coughs sound obviously enough like viral infections, but given the complexity of the picture it seems rash for anyone to submit a retrospective diagnosis, though the results of the autopsy on Johnson's body have encouraged many to do so.[112] There is general agreement among the twentieth-century doctors who have studied Johnson's case that some, at least, of his symptoms lead without difficulty to a diagnosis of bronchitis, or a chronic bronchial infection, which afflicted him during the last two decades of his life and, as with all sufferers, occasionally became acute. Chronic bronchitis is inflammation of the bronchi, the air passages in the lungs, and is associated, as is well known, with damp climates and atmospheric pollution. The disease follows an inexorably progressive course, and is accompanied by emphysema, a lung condition in which the small air sacs or alveoli of the lung surface are destroyed or hardened, making difficult the normal gaseous exchange between air and blood. Such patients are, like Johnson, breathless on exertion and find the act of respiration, as he did, laborious. The report of Johnson's autopsy is in fact headed 'Asthma' and notes that 'On opening the cavity of the chest the lungs did not collapse as they usually do when air is admitted, but remained distended, as if they had lost the power of contraction; the air cells on the surface of the lungs were also very much enlarged'.[113] This is a typical picture of emphysema produced by chronic bronchitis.[114] A gallstone 'the size of a pigeon's egg' which was removed from the gall bladder possibly explains the flatulence. The colicky stomach pain obviously would make for anxiety which would not improve his breathing, and pulmonary congestion was undoubtedly another contributing factor.

Johnson's 'melancholy' has been much written upon, but this again is difficult to separate (nor should it be separated) entirely from his other disorders. The difficulty is compounded by the habit that Johnson shared with other eighteenth-century figures of speaking about his 'morbid melancholy' as if it were, indeed, a physical illness, a survival no doubt of the older humoral pathology. How does one interpret the series of diary entries over early August 1767, for instance, in which Johnson speaks of being 'disturbed and unsettled', of being 'extremely perturbed in the night' (easy enough to ascribe to his flatulence and breathing difficulties), for which he diets and takes purges and 'obtained sudden and great relief and had *freedom of mind restored to me*' (my italics)?[115] One important incident is particularly puzzling. Sometime in the first half of 1768, whilst Johnson was in Oxford helping Robert Chambers with the composition of the Vinerian law lectures, he was taken very seriously ill. We know about this event only from Johnson's retrospective comments. When he wrote to Chambers, who was then in Calcutta, fifteen years later, the memory was still vivid enough to be recalled as a landmark in his life. 'That dreadful illness which seized me at New inn Hall, left consequences which have I think always hung upon me. I have never since cared much to walk. My mental abilities I do not perceive it impaired.'[116] He had used the same phrase when writing to Bennet Langton in July 1774 – 'I have never recovered from the last dreadful Ilness.' It was obviously a crucial event: in his birthday meditation in September 1771 Johnson wrote 'For the last year I have been slowly recovering both from the violence of my last illness, and, I think, from the general disease of my life. My Breath is less obstructed, and I am more capable of motion and exercise. My mind is less encumbered ... ' At Easter 1772 he was less optimistic; 'I have yet got no command over my thoughts; an unpleasing incident is almost certain to hinder my rest. This is the remainder of my last ilness.'[117] Any serious illness is of course apt to leave behind it psychological consequences. Was this, perhaps, a stroke, or some sudden viral infection that exacerbated his breathing problems? (He spoke of a 'paralytick affection' to Lawrence.) Or was it a catastrophic mental collapse (how would that relate to walking?) In Johnson's accounts of his crises the medley of different languages deepens the mystery. At Easter 1776 Johnson wrote that his 'morbid melancholy and disturbance of mind' had in him 'its paroxisms and remissions.' His verb 'hung about me' in the letter to Chambers recalls Boswell's conventional diagnosis of 'the hypochondriacal disorder that was ever lurking about him'.[118]

And is it right to relate this illness to the diary entries which follow in the later months of 1768?

> I have now begun the sixtieth year of my life. How the last year has past I am unwilling to terrify myself with thinking. This day had been past in great perturbation. I was distracted at Church in an uncommon degree, and my distress has had very little intermission. I have found myself somewhat relieved by reading, which I therefore intend to practice when I am able. This day it came into my mind to write the history of my melancholy. On this I purpose to deliberate. I know not whether it may not too much disturb me.[119]

It is certain though that when Johnson spoke of his 'illness' he often had in mind his melancholy and depression of spirits. Both he and Mrs Thrale write of his mental condition as the condition of his 'health'. He wrote, too, of his 'disorders of body, and disturbances of the mind very near to madness', implying a reciprocally damaging relationship, perhaps. But – however tempting it is in the interests of narrative and diagnostic clarity – one must avoid presenting Johnson's physical illnesses as mere by-products of his psychological woes, as for instance does George Irwin when he describes Johnson's 'convulsions of the breast' and 'asthma' as 'typical psychosomatic illnesses'.[120] Psychoanalysis does have some explanatory power over aspects of Johnson's life, but it is dismaying too to find W. J. Bate writing of Johnson's jealousy of Mrs Thrale's attendance on her dying mother, and declaring, 'A part of him – the half-child part that from the beginning had been in competition with this woman of his own age for the attention of the daughter – began to develop symptoms that might deserve a comparable sympathy and concern from Mrs Thrale.'[121] These symptoms seem to be 'chronic bronchitis' and an inflamed eye. There are of course cases of this sort of thing in Freud.

But as soon as one investigates the symptoms of Johnson's melancholy, and especially the crisis of the sixties which resulted in his being taken care of by the Thrales, Johnson's medical history does become intertwined with the story of his moral and social life, and some form of psychoanalytic account becomes inevitable. The problem, which I touched on in the discussion of his strange movements, of just where to draw the boundaries round a person's medical history, is presented here in a particularly acute form. Does one exclude, for instance, from an account of his melancholy those private prayers in which Johnson asks for relief from 'vain terrours'? His manuscript diary contains many prayers which offer – in the manner of a devotional treatise – instructive models to be followed. Yet there is an element in them that is confessional: their form is certainly prayer but the overt content is self-laceration and self-reproach, and their deepest manifestation is of radical self-division. He complains of his sluggishness and idleness, his carelessness and disorder, berates himself for his failures to keep former resolutions, and pathetically resolves, again and again, to reform and order his life. In the midst of his prayers, petitions such as 'Deliver and preserve me from vain terrours' and 'Deliver me from the distresses of vain terrour' recur. It is notable that mention of such terrors is in the manuscripts almost invariably followed by words or lines which have been obliterated. (In two versions of a Prayer for Easter 1772 two and a half lines are suppressed after the words 'strengthen my mind, O Lord, deliver me from needless terrours').[122] The usual explanation of these terrors is that they are references to that 'fear of insanity which plagued him in his fits of melancholia', as the editors of his *Diaries* put it.[123] An alternative account suggests that they refer to his fear of damnation, since his passionate appetites and imaginations had, he felt, led to his corruption and loss of spiritual purity.[124] A more radical terror might have been that the opinions of the sceptics, the 'infidels' like Hume, which were gaining ground all around him, could easily be true, that there was no ultimately benevolent and ordered government of the world. Yet a fourth possibility is that these fears were essentially contentless, intense anxieties for which no adequate explanation presented itself to his conscious mind, and hence 'vain' and 'needless'. Johnson's religious scruples were perhaps both produced by and constitutive of his 'melancholy'.

Johnson experienced a second prolonged crisis in the early or mid sixties, which Boswell dated about Easter 1764. This time when 'he was so ill, as, notwithstanding his remarkable love of company, to be entirely averse to society' may be essentially the same illness as Mrs Thrale describes: 'In the year 1766 his health, which he had always complained of, grew so exceedingly bad, that he could not stir out of his room in the court he inhabited for many *weeks* together, I think *months*'.[125] She adds:

> Mr Thrale's attentions and my own now became so acceptable to him, that he often lamented to us the horrible condition of his mind, which he said was nearly distracted; and though he charged *us* to make him odd solemn promises of secrecy on so strange a subject, yet when we waited on him one morning and heard him, in the most pathetic terms, beg the prayers of Dr. Delap, who had left him as we came in, I felt excessively affected with grief, and well remember my husband involuntarily lifted up one hand to shut his mouth, from provocation at hearing a man so wildly proclaim what he could at last persuade no one to believe, and what, if true, would have been so very unfit to reveal.

With the 'attentions' of the Thrales the narrative of Johnson's problems cannot be segregated from aspects of his social life. His relationship with Mrs Thrale particularly is coloured by medical feeling, and not only because they shared an interest in medicine, and together shared the anxieties of the various family illnesses. When one examines the abundance of evidence of their relationship – Mrs Thrale's family diary, *Thraliana*, her *Anecdotes* of Johnson written up from it, Johnson's dozens of letters to her and hers in reply – one is in the presence of what one might call, noting the degree of conscious-ness of the participants, an early therapeutic friendship. His medical problems now become acknowledged as central to, even constitutive, of his life. Illness is no longer an aberration, an interruption of the fabric of social life: it is at the centre of the relationship.

From 1766 until after Henry Thrale's death in April 1781 Johnson stayed with the Thrale family in their house at Streatham for the better part of each week. Mrs Thrale became Johnson's confidante whilst he was in the house: whilst he was away, as on the trip to the Hebrides, he wrote to her regularly. In *Thraliana* she declared in 1779 'well does he contradict the Maxim of Rochefoucauld, that no Man is a Hero to his Valet de Chambre. – Johnson is more a Hero to me than to any one – & I have been more to him for Intimacy, than ever was any Man's Valet de Chambre'.[126]

The role Mrs Thrale assumed, though, was not so much valet as nurse – or warden. In the same passage of her journal she wrote: 'our stern Philosopher Johnson trusted me about the Years 1767 or 1768 – I know not which just now – with a Secret far dearer to him than his Life ... ' This 'secret' has often been associated, originally in 1949 by Katharine C. Balderston, the editor of *Thraliana*, with another note in the journal, in which Mrs Thrale writes 'Strange Connections there are in this odd World!' and adds in a footnote 'a dreadful & little suspected Reason for *ours* God knows – but the Fetters & Padlocks will tell Posterity the Truth'. It appears that when Mrs Thrale's effects were sold at auction in 1823 a padlock was indeed among them, with a note in her handwriting 'Johnson's padlock, committed to my care in the year 1768'.[127]

What 'truth' does the padlock tell? This is the most widely discussed of the mysteries that constitute Johnson's medical history. Chains and fetters are contemporary symbols of, and shorthand for, madness: it is plausible to assume that this is what Mrs Thrale assumed they would communicate to posterity. We know from other sources that Johnson feared insanity; perhaps he feared what he might do in such a state of misery and despair; perhaps in his extremities he wanted, perhaps he even liked, to be chained and locked up. Balderston had no doubt about the nature of the evidence she assembled. 'It belongs', she wrote, 'to the field of the clinical psychologist.'[128]

In the heyday of literary Freudianism, it was perhaps inevitable that the 'secret' would turn out to be a sexual one. Johnson, argued Balderston, had masochistic fantasies, which he sometimes called upon Mrs Thrale to enact with him. The centrepiece of her argument is a strange letter written in French which Johnson sent Mrs Thrale, conjecturally dated by Chapman to May 1773, five years after committing the padlock to her care, whilst he was actually staying with her, and evidently meant for secret transmission within the household:

> Most respected lady,
> Since while I am staying with you I must spend several hours each day in profound solitude, tell me whether you wish me to wander abandoned or to confine myself within certain prescribed limits. If you wish my very dear

mistress, you may simply leave me to whatever happens to come. The thing is done. You will remember the wisdom of our friend: *If I will do*, etc. But if it is not too much to hope that I may be worthy, as formerly, of the care and protection of a soul so amiable in its sweetness, so honourable for its nobility, grant me in a short note the right to know what is permitted me and what is forbidden. And if it seems best to you that I should remain in a certain place, I beg of you to spare me the necessity of constraining myself by taking away from me the power to leave the place where you want me to be. Which will not cost you more than the trouble to turn the key in the door twice a day. You must act absolutely as mistress, so that your judgment and vigilance may come to the rescue of my weakness.

As for the table, I hope everything from your wisdom and fear everything from your kindness. Turn your thoughts, most honoured Madame, that way. For you, it will not be at all difficult; you will be able to create a system ['une regime'] that is workable without noise and effective without danger.

Is it too much to ask of a soul as beautiful as yours, that mistress of others, it should become mistress of itself and overcome this inconstancy which so often has led it to neglect the enforcement of its own laws, to forget so many promises, and to condemn me to make so many reiterated solicitations that the memory horrifies me. One must grant or refuse; one must remember what one grants. I desire, my patroness, that your authority should always be palpable to me, and that you should hold me in the slavery that you are so well able to render happy. Permit me the honour of being, Madame, Your very obedient servant.[129]

This letter, suggested Balderston, 'is a pathological document, the product of a sick mind'. 'His dependence on her is supine, his subjection to her all but servile. He seems to crave this subjection as to a superior being, seeking and ensuing a "slavery", which she, and apparently she only, can "render happy." His one fear is that she will not make her rule severe enough.'[130] (One wonders what Balderston made of Elizabethan sonnets.)

A writer who only uses a foreign language occasionally is not in so much command of its idioms and tone as to prevent the possibility of misinterpretation.[131] The gallantry and compliment of this letter would probably have been rather toned down if it had been cast in English and English-speaking readers would have known exactly what to make of such formalities as 'I am Madame, Your most obedient and most humble servant.' Not being up with idioms can start hares. Peter Newton, the American psychologist from whose article I have borrowed the text of this translation, hints darkly that 'the part concerning a procedure for "the table" is the most densely obnubilated of the entire letter'.[132] (But Johnson is referring, I take it, to the household eating arrangements, and possibly to his need to be restricted in his diet.) The entire letter is capable of a perfectly ordinary reading. It is a plea for more clarity and consistency in the household affairs. Johnson wants to know what rules he is to obey at a time when Mrs Thrale is occupied in nursing her dying mother and there were numbers of ailing children, as well as builders, in the house.[133] Does she want him to keep out of the way? She has only to give him a consistent guide and he will obey. Of course the letter is also a plea – perhaps a rather infantile one – for attention from a woman who is busy with other cares but who has become established for Johnson in the role of nurse.

The climax of Balderston's evidence is another extract from Mrs Thrale's diary, now of 1779, six years after the letter. Mrs Thrale writes: 'And yet says Johnson a Woman has *such* power between the Ages of Twenty five and forty five, that She may tye a Man to a post and whip him if She will.' The marginal note on this is 'This he knew of him self was *literally* and *strictly* true I am sure'. 'At this point', Balderston writes, 'one is bound to inquire whether Mrs Thrale's role, beyond that of jailer and turnkey, was not also that of beater; and whether her allusion in the letter ("do not quarrel with your Governess for not using the Rod enough") was literal rather than figurative.'[134] More evidence of the same type could be adduced. In November 1772 Johnson was confiding to Mrs Thrale 'I use no exercises and therefore desire that no mortification may be spared to Madame, Your most obedient most humble servant.' Her letters pick up the hint: 'Return', she writes, 'to the Iron Dominion of Your Faithful and Obedient Servant.' The very passage of *Thraliana* which tells of the power of women over men suggests that Arthur Murphy, too, having been 'exhausted of *Love* by Miss Elliott the famous Courtezan,' is now the 'Slave' of a woman who 'holds her Prisoner fast' by 'Chains' (though she happens to be 'a modest Woman who keeps a Coffee House' and the chains are 'of Friendship only').[135] I cannot believe that anyone, let alone Johnson, who had been, perhaps still was, in the grip of a shameful obsession, would allude to it in this facetious way, and to the woman who was its object. How different is the remark in a letter of 27 June 1769, from Oxford, in which Johnson hopes that Mrs Thrale is 'well enough to resume your care for that which yet continues, and which your kindness may sometimes alleviate'. The obliqueness of that reference is what authenticates a real distress.

Yet those Johnsonians who have (correctly) argued against the more sensational of Balderston's readings can be seen creatively misreading themselves. The letter of Mrs Thrale which is assumed (but not known for certain) to be her response to Johnson's one in French is described by W. J. Bate as showing her 'completely aware' of 'what he is really craving ("care", "tenderness", "attention")'. More recently James Gray has argued convincingly that Johnson's letter is 'hardly the demand of a flagellant for more of the scourge and manacles, but rather the request of a troubled and disquieted guest for the restoration of order in the household'.[136] Both paraphrase and quote from Mrs Thrale's letter, but both entirely omit the phrases and sentence that I italicise:

What Care can I promise my dear Mr Johnson that I have not already taken? what Tenderness that he has not already experienced? yet it is a very gloomy reflexion that so much of bad prevails in our best enjoyments, and embitters the purest friendship. You were saying but on Sunday that of all the unhappy you was the happiest, in consequence of my Attention to your Complaint; and to day I have been reproached by you for neglect, and by myself for exciting that generous Confidence which prompts you to repose all Care on me, and tempts you to neglect yourself, *and brood in secret upon an Idea hateful in itself, but which your kind partiality to me has unhappily rendered pleasing. If it be possible shake off these uneasy Weights, heavier to the Mind by far than Fetters to the body.* Let not your fancy dwell thus upon Confinement and Severity. I am sorry you are obliged to be so much alone; I forsaw some ill consequences of your being here while my Mother was dying thus: yet could not resist the temptation of having you near me, but *if you find this irksome and dangerous Idea fasten upon your fancy,* leave me to struggle with the loss of one Friend, and let me not put to hazard what I esteem beyond Kingdoms, and value beyond the possession of them.[137]

What this 'hateful', this 'irksome and dangerous' idea exactly is, we are never going to be sure. It could simply be 'confinement and severity' – but in that case why does Mrs Thrale associate it with his 'kind partiality' to her? I will offer my own reading of the letter (it is not very different from Balderston's). For all its gentleness and tact, it seems clear she dislikes and is discouraging him from part of his behaviour. She seems to be protesting against his demand that she should do for him what he had best, in her view, do for himself, against making physical restraint (whether chains or locked doors does not matter) do the work of self-discipline and self-repression. She sees – she has understood from Johnson – that her role is essentially, though, not disciplinary but therapeutic: she understands that they are talking about a mental disease, that in one aspect of their friendship she acts as nurse or mother-substitute, and that the relationship they have established has created of Streatham a therapeutic space. Without having the terms for it, of course, she sees that Johnson has effected a transference-relation to her: and that this, in the circumstances, is 'dangerous'. Though in general 'her attitude', as Newton writes, is 'requisitely therapeutic',[138] she is not a therapist (still less an analyst). She has become an unwilling performer in Johnson's psychopathological drama, and since she has neither the concepts, the language, nor the time to deal with this her resource is to point out alternative kinds of therapy for Johnson's condition. In the last paragraph of her letter she says, for instance, 'Dissipation is to you a glorious Medicine, and I believe Mr Boswell will be at last your best Physician'.

Johnson was speaking from the heart when he wrote of some men's need for external authority in an anticipatory letter to Baretti of June 1761:

I do not wonder that, where the monastick life is permitted, every order finds votaries, and every monastery inhabitants. Men will submit to any rule, by which they may be exempted from the tyranny of caprice and of chance. They are glad to supply by external authority their own want of constancy and resolution, and court the government of others, when long experience has convinced them of their own inability to govern themselves.[139]

But it is not a monastery that is the best model for what Johnson and Mrs Thrale made of Streatham. In her recent accounts of the York Retreat, the Quaker hospital usually taken to mark the beginning of humane treatment of the insane in England, Anne Digby describes George Jepson, who became the Retreat's Superintendent in 1797 and who was the initiator of its 'moral management':

George Jepson's genius was to see the mad individual not as an object outside the boundaries of human reason . . . but as a man or woman whose disordered mind could be steadied by calm kindness. His object was not to categorize and condemn the mentally ill to an existence outside a normal, domestic routine. Instead, he placed them in a social setting except when his insight into their special needs indicated that they needed temporary seclusion from it. His overriding objective was to restore the self-esteem of patients through treating them with sympathy for their affliction, and respect for their individuality, and hence to build up their powers of self-control.[140]

When it became necessary, patients would be put into strait-jackets, though, or locked in their rooms. The regime that Johnson and Mrs Thrale devised was very similar. Like the Retreat, Streatham was a surrogate home. Mrs Thrale, filling the role of keeper or attendant, usually allowed Johnson the freedom of the house at all hours of the day and night, but on some occasions, presumably when he felt particularly disturbed, he would be 'in seclusion', in solitary confinement in his room, the theory being perhaps, as at the Retreat, that his mental state would benefit from the absence of sensory stimulation. On such occasions he occupied himself with lengthy and elaborate mathematical calculations. It was a combination of 'discipline' – confinement and restraint – with kindness and acceptance. Together then, Mrs Thrale and Johnson anticipated the 'moral management' of the insane (or those who thought themselves likely to become so) by some thirty years. There seems no reason to reject the general consensus that Mrs Thrale's 'requisitely therapeutic' attitude mitigated the symptoms of Johnson's melancholy, and possibly did more than, as Johnson put it, 'sooth', twenty years of a radically wretched life.

The last years of the friendship were lightened too, for Johnson, by the quite sudden remission of his asthmatic symptoms on the morning of June 18th 1779, when Johnson was staying in the country town of Ashbourne with John Taylor. Johnson commemorated its anniversary in his diary in 1780:

In the morning of this day last year I perceived the remission of those convulsions in the breast which had distressed me for more than twenty years. I returned thanks at Church for the mercy granted me, which has not continued a year.

During the same few days at Ashbourne Johnson received news of Henry Thrale's first stroke. Thus, as Johnson had written in the *Preface to Shakespeare*, 'is exhibited the real state of sublunary nature, which partakes of good and evil, joy and sorrow, mingled with endless variety of proportion and innumerable modes of combination ... in which the loss of one is the gain of another, in which, at the same time, the reveller is hastening to his wine and the mourner burying his friend.' The months June 1779 until Thrale's death in April 1781, months in which Thrale suffered one stroke after another, were for Johnson an *annus mirabilis*. His birthday meditation of 18 September 1780 begins with unusual cheerfulness, 'I am now beginning the seventy-second year of my life, with more strength of body and greater vigour of mind than I think is usual at that age'.

III

But, after the death of Robert Levet in January 1782, Johnson's own health began to 'totter'. His was not a 'slow decline' towards death, but a ferocious battle with a variety of disorders, conducted with every weapon of skill and intelligence he could command, and fought on one flank with his doctors themselves. The history of Johnson's last three years, for all its inevitable grimness, is at the same time a dramatic and even thrilling one. It centres round a series of extra-ordinary crises and equally extraordinary or even, as Johnson thought, 'miraculous', remissions. As Johnson's health got worse, so – in a perfectly natural fashion – his interest in it increased: he wrote long letters to Mrs Thrale in which scarcely any detail of his bodily state is omitted and after the final break with her in July 1784 he opened an even more minute diary of his daily condition. Besides this there are long letters to his doctors Richard Brocklesby and William Heberden, and – especially towards his end – many reports of observers and friends.

Against a background of gradually worsening breathing difficulties, and consequent insomnia (which he sometimes relieved by opium), as well as attacks of gout and toothache, there are these main crises: his aphasic attack on 16/17 June 1783, and his quick relief in about a fortnight; the sarcocele or painful swelling of the scrotum for which he was preparing for surgery in October 1783; his increasing oedema culminating in a period of intense illness in February 1784, which was relieved by the 'wonderful, very wonderful' remission of 19 February; the gradual return of oedema and intensifying 'asthma' relieved again on 13 August; and his dramatic attempt on the morning of 13 December 1784, the day he died, to seize more life by desperate surgery upon himself.

The most palpable and distressing symptom from which Johnson suffered in his last eighteen months was that his already large body – particularly his feet and legs – began to swell. This was oedema, or, as his contemporaries called it, 'the dropsy'. When Johnson's body was opened at the necropsy, his heart was found to be 'exceedingly large and strong, the valves of the aorta were beginning to ossify'.[141] His doctors could not have recognised that this enlarged heart was symptomatic of the circulatory disorder which probably linked the aphasic attack, the oedema and the congestion of his lungs. Johnson himself 'conceived the dropsy itself to be his disease'; the *fundi nostri calamitas*, the 'original and radical disease' as he wrote to his physician, Richard Brocklesby.[142] But Heberden's opinion was different; in his *Commentaries on the History and Cure of Diseases*, written the year before Johnson became his patient in 1783, he argued that 'A dropsy is very rarely an original distemper, but is generally a symptom of some other, which is too often incurable; and hence arises its extreme danger'.[143] He was, of course, correct. Oedema is not a disease in itself: the excessive buildup of fluid in body tissues or cavities is the consequence of an underlying disorder, usually congestive heart failure, in which increased pressure in the circulation forces fluid from the capillaries into the tissues.

Johnson first noticed that his legs had begun to swell in April 1783, but it is his stroke in June that is the first dramatic evidence of a failure in the circulation. The event is recorded briefly in Heberden's *Index Historiae Morborum*, his private case notes: 'Voice suddenly went in man aged 74, mind and limbs affected; voice almost restored within a few days. 17 June 1783.'[144] Johnson's own letter to Mrs Thrale, penned three days after the attack, is a valuable piece of medical evidence:

On Monday the 16. I sat for my picture, and walked a considerable way with little inconvenience. In the afternoon and evening I felt myself light and easy, and began to plan schemes of life. Thus I went to bed, and in a short time waked and sat up as has been long my custom, when I felt a confusion and indistinctness in my head which lasted, I suppose about half a minute; I was alarmed and prayed God, that however he might afflict my body he would spare my understanding. This prayer, that I might try the integrity of my faculties I made in Latin verse. The lines were not very good, but I knew them not to be very good, I made them easily, and concluded myself to be unimpaired in my faculties.

Soon after I perceived that I had suffered a paralytick stroke, and that my Speech was taken from me. I had no pain, and so little dejection in this dreadful state that I wondered at my own apathy, and considered that perhaps death itself when it should come, would excite less horrour than seems now to attend it.

In order to rouse the vocal organs I took two drams. Wine has been celebrated for the production of eloquence; I put myself into violent motion, and, I think, repeated it. But all was vain; I then went to bed, and, strange as it may seem, I think, slept. When I saw light, it was time to contrive what I should do. Though God stopped my speech he left me my hand, I enjoyed a mercy which was not granted to my Dear Friend Laurence, who now perhaps overlooks me as I am writing and rejoices that I have what he wanted. My first note was necessarily to my servant, who came in talking, and could not immediately comprehend why he should read what I put into his hands.

I then wrote a card to Mr Allen, that I might have a discreet friend at hand to act as occasion should require. In penning this note I had some difficulty, my hand, I knew not how nor why, made wrong letters. I then wrote to Dr Taylor to come to me, and bring Dr Heberden, and I sent to Dr Brocklesby, who is my neighbour. My Physicians are very friendly and very disinterested, and give me great hopes, but you may imagine my situation. I have so far recovered my vocal powers, as to repeat the Lord's Prayer with no very imperfect articulation. My memory, I hope, yet remains as it was. But such an attack produces solicitude for the safety of every Faculty.[145]

The consequences of the stroke are manifest in this letter, for the manuscript shows an unusual number of insertions and substitutions. For example, the word 'body' was first omitted in the antithesis 'however he might afflict my body he would spare my understanding'. So were important words in the next two sentences which he first wrote thus: 'This prayer that I might the integrity of my faculties I made in Latin verse. The lines were not very good but I knew not to be very good'. Johnson corrects these and fifteen other slips above the line, a graphic and moving illustration of his confession, 'My hand, I knew not why, made wrong letters'. Johnson's was not only a disorder of speech but a 'dysgraphic' one, in which patients have difficulty in expressing themselves in writing: a true aphasia, the loss of the faculty of language.[146]

William Heberden seems to have recognised that apoplectic patients sometimes have difficulty in writing as well as in speaking. In his *Commentaries* he says:

The inability to speak is owing sometimes not to the paralytic state of the organs of speech only, but to the utter loss of the knowledge of language and letters; which some have quickly regained, and others have recovered by slow degrees, getting the use of the smaller words first, and being frequently unable to find the word they want, and using another for it of a quite different meaning, as if it were a language they had once known, but by long disuse had almost forgotten ...[147]

Nevertheless, the apparently trivial but actually crucial symptom of handwriting difficulties was disregarded or repressed and treatment, in Johnson's case, proceeded on the premise that the disorder was some material malfunctioning at a particular site in the body – in this case the throat or tongue. In his second letter after the stroke, which requested Heberden's assistance, Johnson had written: 'I think that by a speedy application of stimulants much may be done. I question if a vomit vigorous and rough would not rouse the organs of speech to action.'[148] The treatment Johnson was subjected to (and subjected himself to) shows that his doctors shared his conception. They put a blister on his back (in order to draw the noxious humours away from his neck?) and one from each ear to the throat presumably to galvanise the vocal organs into action, or once again to draw the humours to the surface. Johnson insisted that the salve which would provoke the skin to blister be made according to his own prescription. Despite this and other 'stimulating' treatment, he recovered quite quickly and was well enough by 1 July to dine with his club. The wonder is that his attack was so slight and so brief: a month later Johnson could write 'I am very well except that my voice soon falters'.[149] As we have seen he thought his disorders were 'collected into this one dreadful effect'. Consistent with the premises of his treatment, Johnson shared the assumption of a monistic pathology, in which a single underlying condition – almost always thought of as a fluid substance, as in 'collected' – manifests itself as quite different illnesses at different times.[150]

But all this time he was harbouring another problem which soon became severe. On 10 July 1783 he went on holiday to Rochester in Kent and returned a fortnight later 'by water in a common boat, twenty miles for a shilling, and when I landed at Billingsgate I carried my budget myself to Cornhil before I could get a coach, and was not much incommoded.' On 20 July he wrote to William Cruikshank, the surgeon:

I have for twenty months had, if I judge rightly a Hydrocele. For twelve months it was totally without pain, and almost without inconvenience, but it has lately encreased so much that the water, if water it be, must be discharged. I beg to see You as soon as You can come, and hope your skill will be able to relieve me.[151]

Johnson's *Dictionary* defines hydrocele as 'a watery rupture': it was a testicular swelling. Cruikshank pierced the swelling early in August and found it to be not a hydrocele, but a 'sarcocele' or fleshy tumour. The trouble got so much worse that on 9 September Johnson, who was at Heale, near Salisbury, wrote to the well-known surgeon, John Mudge of Plymouth, asking his advice. 'I have a dreadful disease which nothing but Mr Pott's knife can remove, and the operation is not without danger', he wrote to John Taylor on 20 September. 'If the excision should be delayed there is fear of gangrene.' Johnson was afflicted with gout in his feet which delayed the operation. Mudge 'vehemently urges the excision, but tells me that the gout will secure me from every thing paralytick', he wrote, suppressing his doubts. An excision, without anaesthetics, at 74: no wonder Mrs Thrale was concerned. She sent reassurances: 'I think the Constitution is equal to all that is required of it'. Once more, Johnson escaped. The incision made by the surgeon had healed over superficially, but in late September or early October it burst open and Johnson was able to write to Mrs Thrale on 9 October that 'by very frequent effusions the tension is eased, the inflammation abated, and the protuberance so diminished as to incommode me very little'.[152] So the disease was left to nature to heal and little more is heard of it until Johnson's last days.

It had been a warm summer. As winter advanced, Johnson's letters become more melancholy. 'The old convulsions of the chest have a mind to fasten their fangs again upon me. I am afraid that winter will pinch me', he wrote. On 10 December returning, probably, from a meeting of the Essex Head Club, he suffered such an attack of breathlessness 'that Dr Brocklesby who came with me to my door, came, as he said, next day to see if I were alive'. From then on he was confined to the house until 21 April, which he counted was 'one hundred twenty nine days'.[153]

Besides his breathing difficulties Johnson was disturbed by the manifestly increasing dropsy. Now not only his legs but his 'lower parts' (3 January) began to swell. 'My legs and thighs grow very tumid' (12 January). His doctors told him that when warmer weather came and he perspired more, his 'watery disease' would evaporate, but he did not really believe them (9 February): in fact about this time he seems to have taken his treatment into his own hands, ordering a 'defensative' for his chest from Cruikshank on 13 February and, it has been discovered, taking other measures on his own initiative. In writing to Mrs Thrale Johnson is polite, if occasionally ironic, about his physicians' opinions. But there is known a fragment of a letter to John Taylor, old school friend and country parson, dated 22 March, in which Johnson comments that at this period 'The physicians pertinaciously told me I was not very near death, yet they did not think I ever should recover, but imagined my soul would for some time more or less inhabit an unweeldy bloated, half drowned body'.[154] It is not very difficult to deduce from the tone of this, I suggest, that Johnson in the part of the letter that is missing had explained why he had decided to act on his own account.

Johnson's conviction that the dropsy was his fundamental trouble was possibly confirmed because the one effective drug he took for it, squill, has some regulatory action on the heart, and hence relieved his breathing difficulties. In order to understand the events of February 1784 it is necessary to make a brief digression into the history of pharmacy. Squill is a precursor of digitalis, which in its pure form, as digoxin, is now used to control this disease. In 1775, William Withering first observed that the root of the foxglove was the active ingredient in a herb mixture which relieved a patient when prescribed by an old woman in Shropshire. Withering was told that the effects produced were 'violent vomiting and nausea' but he recognised its power as a diuretic. It was many years, though, before he learned to manage the administration of digitalis and to minimise its side effects. He gradually recognised that the drug's action is slow and sustained and therefore that titration – the exact measurement of doses so as to maximise its benefits and minimise its disadvantages – was a crucial factor in its administration. (Johnson, of course, tended to believe that it was only in large, even heroic amounts that drugs would work for him.) Learning to regulate the dose to control its toxic effects was a process of trial and error conducted on 163 recorded cases which took Withering ten years. It was only in 1785 that he published his famous *Account of the Foxglove*, the first scientific work on the treatment of a disease written in English. Some of the case-histories reported there illuminate Johnson's encounters with the squills. 'Case CVI' for example is a 'Mr S' of Birmingham, aged 61:

Hydrothorax and swelled legs. Squills were given for a week in very full doses, and other modes of relief attempted; but his breathing became so bad, his countenance so livid, his pulse so feeble, and his extremities so cold, that I was apprehensive upon my second visit that he had not twenty-four hours to live. In this situation I gave him the Infusum Digitalis stronger than usual, viz. two drams to eight ounces. Finding himself relieved by this, he continued to take it, contrary to the directions given, after the diuretic effects had appeared.

The sickness which followed was truly alarming; it continued at intervals for many days, his pulse sunk down to forty in a minute, every object appeared green to his eyes, and between the exertions of reaching he lay in a state approaching to syncope. The strongest cordials, volatiles, and repeated blisters barely supported him. At length, however, he did begin to emerge out of the extreme danger into which his folly had plunged him.[155]

This was in 1782. The crucial point about squill is that, like foxglove, the drug accumulates in the body: too much, and it becomes toxic. Like Mr S, Johnson disobeyed his doctors, with comparable consequences.

Squill is an onion-like plant that grows along the shores of the Mediterranean sea. Either in the form of dried powder, or compressed into pills, or steeped in wine or vinegar (as a 'decoction') it was prescribed as a diuretic and expectorant (it can still be found among the ingredients of proprietory cough medicines). Like digitalis, squill increases the force of ventricular contraction in the heart, regulates the heart's pumping action, and thus rids the tissues of superfluous or, as eighteenth-century writers called them, 'preternatural' fluids. The direct action on the kidneys is less important than its effect on the heart, which improves the circulation of blood through the kidneys and thus promotes their output of urine. Presumably squill, like digoxin, is absorbed quickly into the bloodstream but excreted very slowly. Its quality and hence its efficacy, as Johnson found, was apt to vary; its effects, as he also found, could be appalling.

The chronology is important here. On Tuesday 17 February Johnson wrote three brief letters, all of them suggesting that he was desperately ill, so ill that he hastened to make his will. He told Sir John Hawkins 'that he had the prospect of death before him, and that he dreaded to meet his Saviour'. He intended to spend the next day in appropriate religious exercise – fasting, humiliation, and prayer. But after almost a week of misery, his illness was suddenly relieved. Hawkins visited him on Saturday, 21st

and, upon entering his room, observed in his countenance such a serenity, as indicated that some remarkable crisis of his disorder had produced a change in his feelings. He told me, that, pursuant to the resolution he had mentioned to me, he had spent the proceding day in an abstraction from all worldly concerns; that, to prevent interruption, he had, in the morning, ordered Frank not to admit any one to him, and, the better to enforce the charge, had added these awful words, 'For your master is preparing himself to die'. He then mentioned to me, that, in the course of this exercise, he found himself relieved from that disorder which had been growing on him, and was becoming very oppressing, the dropsy, by a gradual evacuation of water to the amount of twenty pints, a like instance whereof he had never before experienced, and asked me what I thought of it.

I was well aware of the lengths that superstition and enthusiasm will lead men, and how readily some are to attribute favourable events to supernatural causes, and said, that it might savour of presumption to say that, in this instance, God had wrought a miracle; yet, as divines recognize certain dispensations of his providence, recorded in the Scripture by the denomination of returns of prayer, and his omnipotence is now the same as ever, I thought it would be little less than criminal, to ascribe his late relief to causes merely natural, and, that the safer opinion was, that he had not in vain humbled himself before his Maker. He seemed to acquiesce in all that I said on this important subject, and, several times, while I was discoursing with him, cried out, 'it is wonderful, very wonderful!'[156]

Johnson did not mention to Hawkins that five days previously he had taken, against his doctors' advice, a large quantity of squill powder. Johnson's first mention of squill in a letter is on 2 March, so this fact had never been suspected until a letter of Brocklesby to his friend Dr John Hope of Edinburgh, who had been consulted by Boswell about Johnson's health, was discovered by an American scholar, William W. Fee. Brocklesby wrote that

having nauseated his stomach with 5 or 6 grams of newly powdered Squills against Dr Heberdens and my advice for quantity we were obliged to intermit our administration altogether for a week, [this was the week during which Johnson felt so ill he was preparing to die] but whether the effects of them or from a spontaneous effort for his relief I know not, but within 5 days after he revolted against the taste of Squills, a sudden and unaccountable discharge of 22 pints of Urine came on in 24 hours and by taking 20 drops of Vinegar of Squills every night and morning ever since his excretions have surprisingly exceeded his liquids taken in and he is by this time entirely evacuated of all preternatural fluids in his legs and thighs as well as from his Chest . . .[157]

It might be that Johnson felt nauseated after he had taken the squill powder because of the resinous substances in the bulb which are highly irritating to the stomach, but it seems more likely that the nausea was caused by chemical action on the brain after the medicine had been absorbed into the bloodstream. Fee cites the work of Dr Francis Home, an eighteenth-century physician 'who deliberately gave his dropsical patients sufficient powdered squill to produce vomiting in the belief that the vomiting itself would effect a cure. Diuresis usually occurred on the fourth day of the administration of the drug when a therapeutic effect had been achieved, vomiting usually one to four days later when a toxic level had been reached.' In Johnson's case the initial toxic level was high (causing nausea and heart trouble) but it may be that over the few days 'the strength of the drug declined from toxic to therapeutic proportions'.[158] The diuresis certainly was, all the same, very wonderful. Johnson must have deduced that the squill was responsible since he kept on using it, sometimes again in massive doses. As the fragment of the letter to Taylor indicates, he did not repent defying his doctors.

The first entry in Johnson's medical diary *Aegri Ephemeris* or 'Sick-Man's Journal' is for 6 July 1784: 'Crura et femora tument' – 'shins and thighs swelling'. As McHenry writes, 'over the next five months, which are covered by the diary as well as in 19 letters to Brocklesby, there is a relentless battle between his dropsy and his diuretics and purgatives'.[159] The word 'battle' is right: now as in 1749 Johnson thought of illnesses as 'laying siege to life'. 'The Asthma attacks me often, and the Dropsy is watching an opportunity to return', he had written on 17 June to Mrs Thrale. 'The water has in these summer months made two invasions' he reported to Brocklesby (as in *The Vanity of Human Wishes* – 'Unnumbered maladies his joints invade' – a grim pun): later 'it keeps the truce'. Johnson's bottles of squill vinegar and diacodium are his 'weapons'; the squill pills are 'perfect bullets'.

Johnson's diary notes his medical condition each day in Latin; whether he slept well ('d.b') or – more frequently – badly ('d.m'); his bowel movements and the quantity of urine discharged, balancing this against his intake of fluids; his drugs, their quantity and discernible effects. Johnson was now an old and badly ailing man and there is, perhaps, an element of the hypochondria he so much despised in this diary: but like the detailed letters to Brocklesby, it strikes one much more as an act of scientific will. On 12 August he wrote to Brocklesby from Ashbourne (whence he had travelled to see what 'country air' could do for him) a report on another medicine:

You may remember that when I left London in my armamentarium medicum I took by your consent a bottle of Tincture of Cantharides which though you seemed to be a little afraid [of] it, you considered as having great powers to provoke urine, and such are I believe generally allowed it. Of this dangerous Medicine you directed me to begin with five drops.

I had once suffered by my disobedient excess in the use of squills, and I considered Cantharides as far more formidable; for a long time I did not venture them, but thinking a powerful medicine necessary, I began the use of them this Month.

August. 4. I took Tinct. Cantharid. in the morning 8 drops, in the evening,
10.

5.   In the morning 10 drops, in the evening 10.

6.   I neglected the account.

7.   In the day 60 drops, at night 20 more.

8.   In the morning, 20. afternoon. 30. Evening 30.

9.   In the morning at two doses. 80.

You see, dear Sir, that of this potent and drastick tincture I have taken 80
drops a day, for three days together, and You are expecting to be told the
consequence of my temerity, which You suppose to be punished with a
strangury, or to be rewarded with a salutary flood of water. But the truth is, a
very unpleasing truth, that this acrid and vigorous preparation, this *medi-
camentum anceps* has been as impotent as morning dew, and has produced no
effect either painful or beneficial. I have therefore for the present left it, and as
the water daily seems to encrease shall have recourse to squills, of which I
have a box, and hope that, as they are mingled with soap, their virtue is not
dried away.

On 10 August Johnson took 4 grams of squill, on the 11th 100 drops
of squill vinegar, on the 12th 240 drops in all, and recorded 'Urina
fluxit' on the 13th. He took 240 drops again that day and on the
fourteenth.[160] His asthma 'perceptibly remitted', though the dropsy
showed no marked improvement. Johnson thought the cause of his
easier breathing might be 'a catharsis and a day's abstinence'; but it is
probable that the squills in such large doses had some digoxin-like
effect upon his heart. He continued to take squills and on 30 August
could report 'My Water has lately run away, my Man tells me that
my legs are grown less; and my breath is much less obstructed. I think
the squils have been a very useful medicine'.

Still in the Midlands, at Lichfield in October, Johnson's condition
worsened. 'The water is now encreasing upon me', he wrote to
Boswell on 3 November. That day and the next he took a great
quantity of squill vinegar, in what must have been a desperate effort
to repeat the occurrence of February. He made himself violently ill,
vomited twice, and then repeated the dose.[161] But this time the drug
had no effect on his dropsy. His diary tells of his daily medical
condition up to 8 November with grim specificity. Often sleepless at
night, unable to breathe lying down, he rose early and sometimes
caught sleep in a chair for a couple of hours. He was frequently
drowsy from the diacodium and opium he took to obtain some ease.
The squills, for whatever reason, ceased to be effective, and his dropsy
inexorably increased. He made haste to return to London, where, he

supposed, more reliable and efficient drugs would be found. On his journey home, in mid-November, Johnson stayed for the last time with his old friend, the surgeon Edmund Hector. His dropsy was now risen to such a height that movement was difficult. Hector still lived in the house, No.1, the Square, Birmingham, that he had purchased in 1747. Ironically enough, on the opposite side of the Square stood No.10, which since 1775 had been occupied by William Withering, who, besides being Hector's cousin, was physician at the Birmingham General Hospital where Hector was consulting surgeon.[162] It seems almost incredible that digitalis, far more efficient than squill, was not talked of. Brocklesby's friend John Hope, the Professor of Botany at Edinburgh had been informed about the foxglove and it was used for patients in the Edinburgh infirmary. It appears in the *Edinburgh Dispensatory* for 1783. Was it never suggested to Johnson?

Always in search of new treatments, he had applied electricity, whose curative properties had been promoted by John Wesley among others, to his swelled legs and thighs on 12 July. (He had previously suggested this to Lawrence's daughter as treatment for the doctor's paralysed hands.[163]) He took rum to relax his breathing, and castor oil, suggested by Brocklesby, as a purge. He continued too to take large doses of squill vinegar in the country. On 16 August he had reported 'The squills I have not neglected, for I have taken more than 100 drops a day, and one day took 250'. The inadequacies of 'rural pharmacy' possibly misled him about the potency of the drug in such doses. On his return to London he was visited by George Steevens, who wrote:

In October, just before he came to London, he had taken an unusual quantity of squills, but without effect. He swallowed the same quantity on his arrival here, and it produced a most violent operation. He did not, as he afterwards confessed, reflect on the difference between the perished and inefficacious vegetable he found in the country, and the fresh and potent one of the same kind he was sure to meet with in town. 'You find me at present, says he, 'suffering from a prescription of my own. When I am recovered from its consequences, and not till then, I shall know the true state of my natural malady.' From this period he took no medicine without the approbation of Heberden.[164]

But there is certainly no mention of digitalis in Johnson's letters or journal.

In London, Johnson's condition continued to worsen and he

prepared himself for death. Sir John Hawkins reports that, on 7 December:

Dr Brocklesby came in, and, taking him by the wrist, Johnson gave him a look of great contempt, and ridiculed the judging of his disorder by the pulse. He complained, that the sarcocele had again made its appearance, and asked, if a puncture would not relieve him, as it had done the year before: the doctor answered, that it might, but that his surgeon was the best judge of the effect of such an operation. Johnson, upon this, said, 'How many men in a year die through the timidity of those whom they consult for health! I want length of life, and you fear giving me pain, which I care not for'.[165]

Taking the pulse was not yet part of medical routine; it was, in fact, as Johnson's reaction indicates, controversial. The essential disagreement among doctors was whether the frequency of the pulse or its quality (as Galen had held and many still believed) was the best guide to the patient's condition. Sir John Floyer – he who had sent the young Sam Johnson to be touched by the Queen – had initiated the revival of interest in pulse quantification in his 1707 work *The Physician's Pulse Watch*, and William Heberden was prominent among those who advocated numerical analysis of the pulse rate.[166] The effects of digitalis in slowing the pulse would almost certainly have been known to him. What was Brocklesby doing in taking Johnson's pulse? Was he monitoring the results of taking digitalis? In Heberden's *Index*, under the heading *Hydrops*, there is an intriguing single note which refers to Johnson and another patient:

Dropsy. anasarca yielded to purges, scarifying of thigh and vinegar of squill. Dr. Sam Johnson – and Wimberley, – when the dropsical corpse was cut into, the legs, thighs, and loins were distended with water, yet scarcely any was found in the belly. Dr. S. Johnson – was taken with the old cough, which had ended in asthma. Infusion of digitalis leaf, 2 ounces of leaf to eight ounces of water, taken in a spoonful every hour for 9 hours, and 5 ounces of urine were yielded without any nausea, but not without some stomach trouble. He died suddenly in the evening.[167]

Some time in these last days then, Johnson's doctors finally gave him digitalis, at this stage an experimental drug, the administration of which was full of uncertainty. How long before his death he was given it is unclear. In the *Account of the Foxglove*, published the next year, Withering recommends a dose of one dram (an eighth of an ounce) of dried leaves in an infusion, an ounce of the infusion to be given once in eight hours. Heberden's dose is thus excessive and dangerous.

Convinced that dropsy was his original and radical disease, Johnson sought more drastic measures. Brocklesby yielded to his plea for surgery and called in Cruikshank who 'apprehended that a mortification might be the consequence' of an incision. But the surgeon was willing to scarify or lance the surface of Johnson's legs, at which Johnson cried out 'Deeper, deeper; I want length of life, and you are afraid of giving me pain, which I do not value'. Or, as Hawkins has it, 'Deeper, deeper; – I will abide the consequence: you are afraid of your reputation but that is nothing to me.'[168]

Johnson took matters into his own hands in the last day of his life. William Windham relates circumspectly in his diary:

He had compelled Frank to give him a lancet, and had besides concealed in the bed a pair of scissors, and with one or the other of these had scarified himself in three places, two in the leg, etc. On Mr Des Moulins making a difficulty of giving him the lancet, he said, 'Don't you, if you have any scruples; but I will compel Frank ... ' He then made the three incisions above mentioned, of which one in the leg etc were not unskifully made; but the other in the leg was a deep and ugly wound from which, with the others, they suppose him to have lost nearly eight ounces of blood.[169]

The sarcocele had returned: when one remembers Cruikshank's unwillingness to cut into it, what the awkwardness of Windham's syntax conceals becomes plain: Johnson punctured his swollen testicle under the bedclothes. Frank Barber gave an account to Hawkins:

his master, being in bed, ordered him to open a cabinet, and give him a drawer in it; that he did so, and that out of it his master took a case of lancets, and choosing one of them, would have conveyed it into the bed, which Frank, and a young man that sat up with him, seeing, they seized his hand, and intreated him not to do a rash action: he said he would not; but drawing his hand under the bedclothes, they saw his arm move ...[170]

It was a heroic and terrifying act and almost too much for Johnson's friends – too much for his biographers, who prefer to emphasise the resignation of his last days: 'Whether we choose to call it reconciliation with God, or reconciliation with himself, the fact is there: calm descended at last ... '[171]

It seems clear that these final acts of Johnson were motivated by his own medical conviction that dropsy itself was his disease. Believing this, he was prepared to take any steps, however desperate and extreme they appear, which might bring relief. His doctors were acting on different premises. (It is a plausible reading of Heberden's case note that digitalis was not given to Johnson until the last day of his life: a possibility too, that the drug in such amounts contributed to his death.) As we shall see in the next chapter, Johnson thought to relieve his 'asthma' as well as other difficulties, by similarly direct surgical means, and was equally in conflict with the opinions of his physician. An essential aspect of this death-bed scene is that the patient himself was medically well-informed. Behind this case history is a perpetual struggle over power and initiative with his doctors. We notice the cabinet in the bedroom, and the case of lancets within it, and the fact that, even in his extreme condition, Johnson made two of his incisions 'not unskilfully'. How much did he know of medicine and surgery? That is a question it has been hard to suppress in this review of his medical history. How he learned medicine and what he learnt are questions I turn to in the next chapter.

2

THE PRACTICE OF PHYSIC

AS WE have seen, Johnson's medical history has attracted a good deal of attention during the last 200 years, and doctors specialising in a multitude of different ailments have written on his case. Little, though, has been written about his medical interests and beliefs. Occasional articles in medical journals have reminded us of Johnson's life-long interest in medicine and have cited some of his experiments and views,[1] but there has been no attempt to reconstruct the system of beliefs that lies behind Johnson's very frequent medical advice, and without this much of what he said and practised must remain unintelligible. This has been partly, no doubt, because until quite recently a medicine confident of its own onward progress has deemed superseded therapeutics and their rationales hardly worth remembering, and partly because, of all therapeutic practices those of the early and mid eighteenth century, that 'chaotic mixture' as the medical historian Erwin Ackerknecht calls it, of notions and procedures, has seemed most recalcitrant to investigation and perhaps least worth attempting to understand.[2] But to see Johnson in the midst of that 'chaos', that confused mixture of traditional procedures, empirical remedies and gropings towards a new more 'scientific' orientation may enable one not only to illustrate a comparatively neglected area of his intellectual interests, but to throw light – more generally – on the nature and constraining conditions of medical thinking in that era. 'Even the mind of Newton', Johnson observed in a review, 'gains ground gradually upon darkness.'[3] To understand, when a thinker was mistaken, what led him to his mistakes, what cogency and persuasive force prompted him to false conclusions, what specious assumptions dogged his steps, and to watch him as he frees his thinking, or finds that experience confounds his assumptions, is always interesting and may even be useful. Johnson, as I shall show, was educated in a medical school whose practices and beliefs are apt to seem to us absurd, if not grotesque, but, if only because it is an unwise assumption that the thinkers of the past were less intelligent than we are, there may be things to be learned from his engagement with it, none the less.

A very high proportion of Johnson's letters in the surviving correspondence touch on or discuss medical matters. Among them are some of the most earnest, most carefully considered he wrote. Naturally: they were addressed to friends whose well-being, whose continued existence even, urgently concerned him. Outside the letters Johnson's comments on therapeutics are rare (a suggestive fact in itself), but from these letters – and to a much lesser extent from reported comments in conversation – it is possible to reconstruct at least an outline of Johnson's probable views. As confirmatory evidence one may turn to the theories current in his day – not such a methodological leap as it sounds, since Johnson, as will be seen, grew up in a highly medicalised environment, and was closely associated, even worked with, at least two of the most prominent medical men of his time, whose views and prescriptions can still be examined in their surviving medical writings. Robert James and Thomas Lawrence, for all their differences, belonged to the same broad movement, as did other eighteenth-century physicians whom Johnson admired, Dr John Arbuthnot, for example. The relation of therapeutics to medical theory is of course problematic in every period; the example of William Harvey, who continued to treat patients according to Galenic notions long after he had discovered the circulation of the blood is notorious. But in Johnson's case those procedures and remedies that seem at first so bizarre, even horrifying, have a particularly clear relation to the supporting theory, and hence cease to be absurd.

Early eighteenth-century medicine is written as though in a foreign language. One can look up such terms as 'lentor of the blood', or 'epispastic' or 'spagyric' (to give three examples) in Johnson's *Dictionary*, but they make little real sense until one understands the system (or systems) of knowledge of which they are a part. When Johnson writes after Henry Thrale's 'apoplectic' seizure that it seems to him that the 'disorder, whether grumous or serous, must be cured by bleeding' his editor's note that 'the distinction . . . is roughly that between thick and thin' offers little real guidance in comprehending Johnson's diagnosis, nor does it help one to assess the quality of the advice he gives.[4] So often Johnson's medical interests have been thought of as amateur meddling, and a recurrent theme in biography of Johnson has been the charge of medical irresponsibility. The phrase 'dabbler in physick' suggests this. In her private journal Mrs Thrale wrote, 'Mr Johnson was however exceedingly attentive to his own health, and having studied Medicine pretty regularly I believe at some Period of his Life was tempted no little to the sin of Quackery.'[5] 'His death was accelerated by his own imprudence', wrote George Steevens; he 'must have shortened his own life by the bleedings that he underwent', echoed G. B. Hill.[6] The implication has survived in W. J. Bate's more recent discussion of Johnson's 'subjective' response to Henry Thrale's stroke. We must see what basis these insinuations have.

Of all the treatments which Johnson underwent himself and which are discussed or recommended in his letters, phlebotomy or bloodletting must be the most frequent. At various times in his life we know that Johnson took large quantities of drugs or medicinal substances – squill, musk, valerian, calomel, diacodium etc. – but in many exigencies it was to bleeding that he and his physicians had recourse. He was bled (in this, not unlike many of his middle-class contemporaries) for complaints as bewilderingly diverse as 'a cough and cold', (January 1761), an 'inflamed eye' (January 1773), flatulence (July 1775), but above all for acute difficulty in breathing and shortness of breath (February 1773, June 1775, January 1777 for example).[7] In mid-January 1777 difficulty in breathing led Johnson, after three sleepless nights, to consult his friend Thomas Lawrence, who ordered the loss of twelve ounces of blood. Johnson afterwards slept in a chair, but could not sleep lying down at night. He 'therefore did what the Doctor permitted in a case of distress. I rose and opening the orifice let out about ten ounces more. Frank and I were but awkward, but with Mr Levet's help we stopped the stream, and I lay down again, though to little purpose, the difficulty of breathing allowed no rest.' But after a third bleeding in four days, he was 'much better, at the expense of about thirty-six ounces of blood.'[8] This is not the only occasion he reports beneficial results – after sixteen ounces of blood had been taken in January 1782, he has 'an Elysian night compared to some nights past'. In the account of his case written for Heberden immediately after his stroke in June 1783 he wrote, 'I have been accustomed to bleed frequently for an asthmatick complaint'.[9]

Given this record of bleeding, it is startling to find Johnson remarking in a letter to Mrs Thrale of 8 May 1782:

Yesterday I was all so bonny, as who but me? At night my cough drove me to diacodium, and this morning I suspect that diacodium will drive me to sleep in the chair. Breath however is better, and I shall try to escape the other bleeding, for I am of the Chymical sect, which hold phlebotomy in abhorrence.[10]

'My physical friends are not able to give any precise meaning' to the phrase about the Chymical sect, wrote Chapman in his footnote on this letter. And it is difficult to make sense of this remark since only a few weeks earlier Johnson had written, 'This last phlebotomy has, I think, done what was wanted, and what would have been done at first with a little courage.' For a moment, I think, Johnson is parodying the mystical rhetoric of J.-B. van Helmont, a leader of the iatrochemical school of the seventeenth century who certainly 'held phlebotomy in abhorrence'. 'The strength or faculties', van Helmont declared, 'can never offend through abundance, not so much as in Methusalah: so neither doth good bloud offend through a too much abounding; because the vital faculties, and bloud are correlatives; Because according to the Scripture, the soul or vital spirit is in the bloud'.[11] Here is a notion – the 'Vital spirit' – that the new school of medicine that was dominant in the early years of the eighteenth century had vehemently discarded. Johnson is teasing Mrs Thrale who was often worried about the large amounts of blood he had taken from himself.

Phlebotomy is one of the two aspects of eighteenth-century medical practice most difficult for the twentieth-century reader to understand and appreciate. The other is the use of opium. In the case of opium, taken on its own or often in combination with other substances, Johnson's opinions and practice are entirely consonant with our ideas – far more so than those of many of his contemporaries. Sir John Hawkins claimed that Johnson took opium 'in large quantities' in the years after 1765, at first as 'relief against watchfulness,' later habitually, 'as a means of positive pleasure whenever any depression of spirits made it necessary. His practice was, to take it in substance, that is to say, half a grain levigated with a spoon against the side of a cup half full of some liquid, which as a vehicle carried it down.'[12] Hawkins' charge is easily refuted. Johnson's account of 'rheumatism in the loins' which he suffered at Oxford in 1770 implies perhaps that this was the first occasion that he had recourse to opium:

One night between the pain and the spasms in my stomach I was insupportably distressed. On the next night, I think, I laid a blister to my back, and took opium; my night was tolerable, and from that time the spasms in my stomach which disturbed me for many years, and for the two past harassed almost to distraction have nearly ceased. I suppose the breast is relaxed by the opium.[13]

Towards the end of the decade Johnson was using opium or diacodium, a syrup of marshmallow and poppy, to procure 'relaxation of the breast' regularly, if not habitually. In his last months, Johnson wrote a history of his taking of the drug, in order to quiet the fears of his friend John Ryland:

When I first began to take opium, my usual dose was three grains, which I found was in the opinion of physicians a great quantity. I know not however that it ever did me harm, for I did not take it often; yet that the demands of my constitution might not encrease, I tried to satisfy it with less, and the event is, that I have sometimes attained my purpose of appeasing spasms or abating chilness by half a grain . . . it is by frequent intermissions that so small a dose can preserve its efficacy.[14]

It is clear then that Johnson was very wary in his use of opium. His unwillingness to act without his doctor's permission is evident in a letter written to Lawrence's daughter in May 1782, after Lawrence had himself suffered a stroke. 'Please to ask the dear Doctor (for whom I pray) whether it be fit to still the cough now in its beginning with opium.'[15] Richard Brocklesby, Lawrence's successor, encouraged the use of opium, carefully managed, as is apparent in the letters he wrote to Burke, his life-long friend and patient, after Johnson's death.[16] Johnson, it is also clear, understood the concept of addiction and was very aware of the drug's dangers, which are emphasised in the long quotation from Hill's *Materia Medica* under Opium in the *Dictionary*: he writes frequently of his 'fear', his 'horrour' of opiates. 'I had the same terror of opium,' he wrote to Mrs Thrale in February 1784, 'and admitted its assistance only under the pressure of insupportable distress, as of an auxilary too powerful and too dangerous'.[17] At a time when a successful practitioner like Erasmus Darwin at Lichfield was prescribing opium 'with what now seems horrifying nonchalence', even to children,[18] Johnson's regulation of his dosage of one of the very few active drugs available deserves to be remarked as one instance where the thought about habituation that is so marked a feature of the *Rambler* essays brought tangible benefits.

But bloodletting is a different matter. Painful (one supposes), certainly unpleasant, inconvenient – for it normally required a surgeon and at least one assistant to be present – and without, to our minds, therapeutic results. What persuaded Johnson, of all eighteenth-century patients, that this was an invaluable resource? This question is the more intriguing because Johnson's critical acumen or scepticism was quite as great normally in the field of medicine as in morals or law or history. He was contemptuous of 'lotions', thought little of the Galenic 'alterative medicines' or cold bathing as remedies and subjected one of Dr Robert James's famous compound remedies to a devastating analysis when Brocklesby suggested it to him in 1783.[19] We can't be sure whether Johnson was bled more frequently than other patients of his time, but there is plenty of evidence that he was bled copiously (in 'heroic' amounts) and that he believed that it was only in such amounts that bleeding, for him at least, was effective. His faith in venesection is all the more striking because he was so careful and rational about its application. He reserved it for emergencies and urged that it not be used until other less drastic methods of evacuating bodily fluids had been tried and he was strongly against routine or periodic bleeding, for much the same reason that he guarded against the regular use of opium. He stressed the danger that regular bleeding might debilitate or exhaust the patient. Yet these cautions are cautions against the misuse of what he clearly considered a uniquely valuable therapeutic aid. We can perhaps understand why Johnson and his contemporaries used bloodletting (as well as purging, blisters and vessicatories) if we look into the school or schools of medical thought in which Johnson acquired his knowledge of the human body and its working.

Writing to Hill Boothby, in his most earnest manner in December 1755, he said 'Give me leave, who have thought much on Medicine, to propose to you an easy and I think a very probable remedy ... Dr Laurence has told me your case.' (He added 'I would not have you offer it to the Doctor as mine. Physicians do not love intruders, yet do not take it without his leave, but do not be easily put off'[20] an awareness of protocol which he did not always show in later years.) The tone of his discussion suggests that Hill Boothby, as an old acquaintance from his Midland days would be aware of his interest in and qualification to speak of medicine. Whether this is so or not, we can be reasonably certain, I think, that Johnson's medical education began whilst he was still a resident of his father's household.

Michael Johnson, besides bookseller in Lichfield and the surrounding towns, was in a small way a publisher. Ten works in all were printed for him. They range from Samuel Shaw's *Grammatica Anglo-Romana, Or, a Syncritical Grammar, Teaching English Youth the Latin Tongue by Few and Easie Rules* in 1687, to Sir John Floyer's *The Prophesies of the Second Book of Esdra*, in 1721.[21] His most substantial publication was also by John Floyer, the two-volume *The Touchstone of Medicines, Discovering the Vertues of Vegetables, Minerals, and Animals by their Taste and Smells.* Volume I appeared in 1687 and Volume II (Floyer in the Preface complains of 'The long neglect of the press') in 1691. Five years later Michael Johnson published *The Preternatural State of the Animal Humours* which is one of the half dozen or so medical works Samuel Johnson cites frequently in the *Dictionary.* In the same year as the second volume of the *Touchstone* finally appeared Michael had printed a pamphlet called *The Happy Sinner or the Penitent Malefactor, being the Prayers and Last Words of one Richard Cromwel*, which at first seems to belong to the evangelical rather than to the medical side of his business. But Cromwel was, as the title page announces, 'some Time a Souldier and Chyrugion in the late Duke of Monmouth's army' and the pamphlet contains 'His legacy to his County, of Choyce Physical and Chyrugical Receipts' including 'A very Extraordinary Receipt for the Worms' and 'Two several Receipts for that Troublesome Distemper the Wind Colick' as well as 'Directions to make Two Several Waters for the Eyes, with the last of which cured a Boy in Leichfield that had been blind Three Years'. All the ingredients for these wonderful remedies, so an Advertisement on the last page announced, 'are to be had at the Apothecaries, except the Queen of Hungarie's Water, which is sold of Michael Johnson, Bookseller in Leichfield'.[22]

Samuel Johnson spoke much later of his parent's 'trades' in the plural, and it is possible that Michael Johnson sold other drugs and chemicals besides the Queen of Hungary's water. His publishing record indicates his interest in medicine and an acquaintance, possibly close and certainly over an extended period, with Floyer, one of the late seventeenth century's most eminent physicians. And Floyer was not the only doctor in the small city known to Michael Johnson. In one of Floyer's other works, his second attempt to promote the efficacy of cold bathing as a 'both safe and useful' medical treatment in 1702, George Hector, 'an eminent surgeon in our town' is mentioned as the contributor of a case history. Hector is the 'man–midwife' who delivered Samuel Johnson in 1709, and the fact that the Johnsons employed a man is also evidence of Michael's comparative medical sophistication, since to do so was decidedly unusual until later in the century. At the time of his son's birth, Michael Johnson's lodger and the child's godfather was Dr Samuel Swinfen, who had taken his MD at Oxford in 1706 and practised in the city, so that like his son later, Michael Johnson shared his home with a 'practiser of physick'. It is easy to imagine Michael Johnson, Latin scholar, church-warden, and magistrate of Lichfield, in a small group of local intellectuals whose common interest in medicine was reinforced by antiquarian learning, and perhaps a shared Royalism and Toryism, as well as a spirit of enterprise.

One might think, knowing that Floyer recommended the scrofulous child be touched by the Queen, that he was a thoroughly old-fashioned physician, but this is far from the case. It is true that the mingling of Christian piety (or superstition) and medicinal remedies in *The Happy Sinner* can be paralleled in Floyer's work, but in most of his medical writings, his adherence to chemiatric and Galenic notions, and his loyalty to classical medicine, are combined, in an astonishing mixture, with independence of thought, a progressive interest in medical experimentation, and a quite free and eclectic pursuit of new medical ideas, a willingness, literally, to 'survey the world from China to Peru' for useful remedies and procedures.

In 1707, dedicated to Queen Anne, appeared *The Physician's Pulse Watch*, in the third part of which 'The Chinese Art of Feeling the Pulse is describ'd, and the Imitation of their practice of Physick, which is grounded on the observation of the Pulse is recommended'. His local patriotism stirred by Boswell's insinuation, during their visit in 1776, that the people of Lichfield appeared idle, Johnson declared, 'Sir ... we are a city of philosophers; we work with our heads, and make the boobies of Birmingham work for us with their hands.' Floyer caused Samuel Watson, a well-known watch-maker originally from near-by Coventry, to construct a portable instrument running for sixty seconds, which he carried about in a box so as to measure the rate of his patients' pulses accurately, and watches have had second hands on them ever since.[23] Unfortunately Floyer's thinking was interfered with by Galenic notions which made the magnitude or type of pulse as well as its rate criteria of the patient's condition. In 1602 Sanctorious (Santoria Santoria 1561–1636) had developed a cumbersome device for measuring the pulse, known as the pulsilogium. Floyer here and in other work is one of the conduits through which Sanctorius' pioneering introduction of quantitative experimental procedures into medical research entered the mainstream of English medicine.[24] Floyer did not only measure his patients' differing pulse-rates: he correlated pulse and respiration rates with such factors as age and sex, and so in his book 'for the first time in medical literature we meet with tabulated results'.[25]

In his *Treatise of the Asthma* (which Samuel Johnson borrowed from Lichfield Cathedral library in his old age)[26] Floyer gave the first detailed description of the change in the lungs now called emphysema, which he had in fact observed in the lungs of a broken-winded mare. For Floyer, as for Johnson and their contemporaries, the resulting difficulty in breathing was one form of asthma, but he differentiated it from the 'spasmodick' type from which he himself suffered every ten days or so. The Galenic notion of animal spirits permeates this work as it does his others. It is difficult in a brief quotation to convey the flavour of Floyer's writing, but the mixture of traditional ideas and experimental reasoning in this passage is typical:

And since Spirits [he means here 'strong liquors'] are so evidently Suffocating to Asthmatics (for Punch will immediately give me a Dysponoea), we may thence infer, That the Animal Spirits in the Asthma are too much rarify'd or expanded; and that whatsoever is contrary to Brandy Spirits, as Watry and Acid liquors, they will best agree with Asthmatics. And since this is by my Experience found to be true, I may infer . . . that the spirits and Humours are too much rarify'd in the Fits of an Asthma: This seems to me the true natural way of discovering the unknown state of humours in occult diseases; for that diet is most agreeable in every disease, which is contrary to that state of Humours which produce it; a cooling diet to rarefy'd Hot Humours, and a hot aromatic acrid Diet to a crude mucilaginous serous state.[27]

Later eighteenth-century doctors would treat the notion of 'animal spirits' with the contempt that is usually bestowed on a discarded rationale, but the idea that certain dietary substances are 'contrary' to corresponding disease states and therefore remedies for them, and the same broad categories for those diets (heating or cooling, for example), with all their attendant confusion between kinds of 'heat' and kinds of 'cooling' and between the action of substances inside and outside the body, continued to be used with confidence.

Besides his work on the pulse and asthma, Floyer wrote one of the first texts to deal specifically with the health of the aged, *Medicina Gerocomica; or, the Galenic Art of Preserving Old Men's Healths* (1724), when he was himself an old man. Even a work which seems to us as obviously wrong-headed as *The Touchstone of Medicines*, a treatise based on the nearly-medieval faith that the taste and smell of herbs and minerals gives us by God's direction an indication of their medicinal use, since they correspond to the same taste and smells in the humours of the body, is full of Floyer's enterprise and spirit of research. 'It is a great Shame to our Profession', he declares in the Epistle Dedicatory, 'That the Ignorant *Indians* should know more of *Plants* in their *Native Country*, and do greater Cures by Them, than our *Artists* can by Ours . . .' He lists a great many substances, and these, as his notebooks show, are only a selection of ones he has tried over the years. The presence of such an active pioneering spirit in Lichfield in the earlier eighteenth century suggests how deeply entrenched was that tradition of 'philosophical' enterprise in the city. Sir John Floyer is in many ways to his time what Erasmus Darwin was to the later years of the century, but unlike Darwin he has scarcely yet had his due.

The formative influence on Johnson's medical views was, almost certainly, another Lichfield citizen, Robert James, who knew the Floyer family, and who gave the local penchant for medical enterprise a new – and less reputable – form. Four years older than Johnson and for a while a school-fellow (at the Grammar School all the boys were taught in the same room), James matriculated at St John's College, Oxford, at the age of seventeen. Asked who would be the best source of information about his early life, Johnson replied, 'Doctor James can give a better Account of my early Days than most Folks, except Mr Hector of Birmingham & little Doctor Adams'.[28] James, as Johnson's life of the poet Smith makes clear, was often in company with David Garrick and Johnson himself at Gilbert Walmesley's house in Cathedral Close. 'My knowledge of physick', Johnson told Boswell, 'I learnt from Dr James . . . I also learnt some from Dr Lawrence, but was then grown more stubborn.'[29] James was obviously a very promising young man. He gained his BA at Oxford in 1726 and two years later became an extra-licentiate of the College of Physicians, and was granted his MD at Cambridge by royal mandate. Everything we know about him suggests a highly ambitious man, confident of his own abilities, unashamed of proclaiming them, determined to achieve success – which meant, for him, success in London. He is the physician as entrepreneur. If he achieved what he sought, it was partly because, in one way or another he co-opted the aid of three of the period's most brilliant literary talents.

He made his first bid for fame in a letter to Hans Sloane, President of the Royal Society, in 1731, in which he claimed to have found a new cure – mercury – for the bite of a mad dog. This claim was later published in the *Philosophical Transactions* and James became very tenacious of his right to his discovery. He published a first pamphlet on the subject in 1743, and, after his claim had been disputed, *A Treatise on Canine Madness* in 1760. The pamphlet is prefaced by a letter in Latin 'To Doctor Boerhaave' in which James informs the most eminent physician of the day of his discovery, and a testimonial letter, dated 1736, from 'J. Floyer', the older doctor's nephew. After practising in Birmingham, Lichfield and Sheffield James finally settled in London in the late 1730s.

Johnson arrived in London in 1737 and was soon working for Cave on the *Gentleman's Magazine*. In his first approach to Edmund Cave, proprietor of the *Magazine*, in November 1734, Samuel Johnson commended the journal's publication of 'loose pieces, like Floyer's, worth preserving'. (The piece in question is a letter of Floyer's giving another instance of a cure by cold bathing.[30]) In the issue for January 1739 appeared the first part of Johnson's first published work in the medical field, a life of Herman Boerhaave, Professor of Physick at Leiden, translated, or in parts paraphrased from the funeral eulogy of Boerhaave's friend Albert Schultens.

At the same time as his hack work for Cave, Johnson wrote anonymously for other masters. In February 1742 Robert James issued the first part of his massive *Medicinal Dictionary* for which as Johnson told Boswell, he 'had written, or assisted in writing, the Proposals ... and being very fond of the study of Physick, in which James was his master, he furnished some of the articles'.[31] Possibly Johnson and James together composed these paragraphs from his 'General Account of the Work':

PHYSIC is an art which every man practises, in some degree, either upon himself or others. Many Indispositions appear too trivial to demand the attendance of a Physician, and many Occasions require immediate Assistance: Men are, in the first Case, tempted by the Prospect of Success, and, in the second, obliged by Necessity, to depend upon their own Skill; and it is therefore their Interest to be so far instructed in Physic, as not to exasperate slight Disorders by an absurd Regimen and Medicines misapplied, nor suffer themselves, or others, to perish by sudden Illness or accident Disasters.

THAT almost every Family is furnished with general Axioms of Physic, to which every Case proves an Exception; and with Universal Remedies, by which no Distemper was ever cured; that Superstition, Prejudice, Ignorance and Mistake, have assigned to every Plant, and every Medicine, Qualities widely different from those which Nature has allotted them; and that Credulity, Obstinacy, and Folly, are hourly making Havock in the world; is obvious to the slightest observation.

To establish juster Notions in the bulk of Mankind, and introduce more useful Medicines into Families, has been charitably attempted, sometimes by familiar and easy Reasonings, and sometimes by collections of approved and well-proportioned Prescripts; but as the Endeavours of the scientific Writers have hitherto failed, for want of being sufficiently extensive; and as *good* Medicines are neither less liable than *bad* to be misapplied, nor less pernicious in unskilful Hands; we have endeavoured to supply all the Defects of those that have gone before us, and at once to familiarize the Knowledge, and reform the Practice, of Physic, by publishing A MEDICINAL DICTIONARY . . .[32]

One of Johnson's contributions to this 'sufficiently extensive' work of over six million words is the life of Boerhaave, slightly revised from the version previously printed in the *Gentleman's Magazine*, and with the addition of a commentary on Boerhaave's various works.

This 'Life' was in turn reprinted in the *Universal Magazine* for 1743. Three reprintings in such a short time shows how important − 'so loudly celebrated and so universally lamented throughout the whole learned world', as the Prefatory Note has it − Boerhaave was. There is no doubt that his work, partly because it summed up and systematised other knowledge, was crucially important to early eighteenth-century medical thinking and that Robert James did not escape his influence. A year after the *Medicinal Dictionary* was completed, James published a *Modern Practice of Physic* in two volumes, which, as the title page indicates, is a translation of 'Boerhaave's aphorisms with the commentaries of Dr van Sweiten, so far as was necessary to explain the doctrines laid down'.[33] This handbook, in characteristic fashion for James, reuses material from the *Dictionary*, which is itself directly derived from Boerhaave. The influence of the Dutch physician's celebrated system of medicine, which was 'more generally received than any former had been since the time of Galen' (as William Cullen wrote in his Preface to the work which was finally to give it the death blow in 1792[34]) is dominant throughout the *Medicinal Dictionary*, and can be discerned, not only in James' work but in the lectures of his successor as Johnson's mentor, Thomas Lawrence.[35] So to give an account of Boerhaave's work is actually to bring out some of the most widespread assumptions of medical thought in the period when Johnson was learning about medicine.

Boerhaave is, broadly speaking, an iatromechanist. The iatrome-chanist view of bodily structure and the causes of disease furnished a plausible explanation for clinical practices some of which had been long in use, such as cupping, blisters, purging, vesicatories, or the cantharides to which Johnson was subjected after his apoplectic seizure, and this, rather than any particularly novel discoveries or suggestions probably accounts for much of the appeal of the system. A translation of Boerhaave's influential 'Oration upon the Use of Mechanics in the Science of Physic' is included in the very extensive preface to the *Medicinal Dictionary*: it is praised in the biography of Boerhaave and presents a useful account of his views.

Boerhaave's system was built upon the foundation of the scientific discoveries of the previous century. The oration is founded upon the premise that 'the human body is of the same Nature with the whole Universe of Things which we contemplate', which turns out to mean the universe of Newtonian mechanics, which Boerhaave applies wholeheartedly to the phenomenon of the circulation of the blood, discovered by Harvey in 1628. Disease states are conceived, in strictly mechanistic terms, as some interference or interruption with the normal motions of the circulating fluids – and this interference, quite remarkably and crucially, is thought of as producing pathological variations in their quality as well as in their quantity. The body is envisaged as a structure of 'solids' – arteries, of many different orders of magnitude, which together compose more complicated glandular structures or 'vessels' – and the liquids or 'humours' (not to be confused with the Galenic or medieval humours, though evolving from these) which circulate through and around them.

Under the microscope, which Boerhaave acknowledges to be formative on his views, the blood had been seen to consist of solid particles of differing dimensions. This was because of the accidental circumstance that it was customary to dilute blood with a little water before examining it, thus causing haemolysis, but Boerhaave would know nothing of this. A red globule of blood, on standing, broke up into smaller yellow globules. These, in turn, vanished and 'pellucid' spherules, smaller still, remained. The microscopes in use were not powerful enough to reveal any still smaller particles, but reasoning by analogy, Boerhaave made bold to assume that they were.[36] These different stages in the composition of the blood were complemented by different dimensions in the 'solids' so that each kind of fluid was received only into arteries or vessels of appropriate size. Boerhaave elaborated a hierarchy of the containing vessels, of which the aorta was the largest and the nerve fibres the narrowest. The blood, originally in the aorta, is progressively refined:

The Artery ... emits cylindrical Tubes of so small a Diameter as not to admit the red Globules of the Blood, but only the thinner and colourless parts thereof; and hence you are furnished with a true idea of a lymphatic Vessel. The same Artery, again, at the same place, extends itself in a Trunk, which runs directly forwards, and, being larger than the Lymphatic Vessels, conveys the red and thicker part of the Blood, deprived of its thinner and serous part; and here is the genuine original of the Veins.[37]

The very finest, most subtle blood particles – those which Boerhaave had to hypothesise – refined in the cerebral cortex, became the 'nervous fluid' which is transmitted to every part of the body through a nervous system also conceived of as tubular.[38]

These tubes or canals, and the glands which they make up, are composed of fibres, and in a healthy body they are elastic: as the cardiac impulse impells the fluids through them, they distend from its pressure. But they also press back upon the humours, acting reciprocally upon them, and so restore themselves to a narrower capacity. This 'equilibrium or just balance between the quantity and impetus of the fluids & the resistance of the vessels', as James puts it, is the secret of health.[39] One recognises here the metamorphosis of an idea belonging to an earlier and discarded thought system, since equilibrium between the four humours was the key to health in Galenic medicine. In disease states, or senility, this balance is disturbed by physical abnormalities in the solids.[40] In children, too, the fibres may be too 'lax' or not elastic or compacted enough, and this makes them particularly vulnerable to a variety of maladies. Reassuring Mrs Thrale about her children in 1775, Johnson wrote, 'Miss and Harry are as safe as ourselves, they have outlived the age of weakness; their fibres are now elastick'.[41] But the fibres can also become too tough or rigid in old age – or through too much exercise. In fevers the diameter of the vessels may be lessened by spasms and the increased velocity of the fluids may generate 'heat' which will expand them. Then, James wrote, 'the redundant and raging blood, being denied a free Passage through the Blood vessels, is impetuously agitated hither and thither, and forced, as to improper Parts, thro' vessels whose diameters are naturally too small for the Admission of the blood, where it remains, becomes stagnant, and lays a foundation for dangerous inflammations'.[42]

This notion that the humours penetrate 'improper parts' and there cause obstructions is important for clinical practice. It explains why bloodletting could be considered appropriate treatment for Johnson's inflamed eye. Since the same physical laws prevail throughout the body – and Boerhaave is vehement in his scorn of the chemiatric theory of specific 'ferments' located in individual glands – it follows that a disorder that happens to be located in one specific site may, through medical intervention, be shifted to another, where its nature will not essentially change, though its symptoms may differ. So Johnson writes of a patient's 'scorbutick humour which I believe has fallen back upon his vitals.'[43] Gout, as we have seen, was a very widely accepted instance of a disease, (due to disordered nervous fluid), which has found, through mechanical causes – distance from the action of the heart and the weight of the body pressing upon the feet – a relatively innocuous site but which may produce a variety of more dangerous effects if it undergoes a 'revulsion' from the extremities to more 'noble' parts of the body. Thus Mrs Thrale, who held the orthodox view, was not pleased by Johnson's measures to get rid of it: 'my Fear is lest he should grow paralytick', she wrote, 'he will drive the Gout away so when it comes, and it must go *somewhere*.'[44]

By the same token, cures might be effected if the disorder, so often thought of as an obstruction, could be dislodged from a dangerous site to one less likely to cause trouble, on the surface or the extremities of the body. The efforts of physicians and surgeons were devoted to such means – setons, fontanels, vesicatories, cupping etc. – as were intended to 'derive' or 'discuss' diseased fluids away from the congested place. Purges and vomits too, might galvanise or shock the system and have the same desirable results. Obstruction becomes almost synonymous with disease (the psychiatrist William Battie, as we shall see later, was able to construct a theory of madness on the premise of obstruction), whilst in a healthy body there is space enough for the fluids to flow naturally through their appropriate canals: 'by the power of the heart and arteries', said Lawrence, 'the elements of the blood, condensed and mixed, form a liquid proper and suitable to permeate the smallest vessels. There will also be room everywhere in them for the liquid to be received easily. Hence there is due distribution of blood and a swift passage of nourishing moisture into their places . . .'[45] The anatomy of a 'well-formed man' thus behaved with as much decorum as its owner did in society and as often in eighteenth-century writing, medical and social metaphors are inextricably linked.

The mechanist view of the functioning of the body argued by Boerhaave had the attraction of being clear, systematic and comprehensive. But this theory alone cannot explain actual clinical practice, even if we were to imagine that the doctors accepted it without question, which is far from the case. Day to day therapeutics and preventive medicine were, in a sense, theoretically over-determined. Another concept from an older tradition played its part. The 'plethora', to use the definition of the term in the *Dictionary*, is 'that state in which the vessels are fuller of humours than is agreeable to a natural state of health'. 'Plethora' occurs when the body's natural and continuous manufacture of fluids is not relieved by their escape from natural outlets (for James and Lawrence haemorrhoidal bleeding was apparently considered one of these). In some constitutions the body continually manufactures too much fluid and then the surgeon must intervene. 'Prior, who bled me to day', wrote Mrs Thrale in her diary, 21 December 1781, 'thinks I shall die Apoplectick some Time for want of Bleeding; – so Johnson has always thought, & so I have always thought myself.[46] Diminishing the quantity of blood makes what remains more fluid and the circulation more active since it has more space in which to work. 'A suppression of the menses has soon been removed by opening a Vein in the Foot', writes Robert James, a sequence of events entirely in accordance with this medical theory.[47]

James himself is a vehement advocate of phlebotomy. He recommends it, for instance, in the treatment of breathing difficulties:

severe and violent Asthmas are produc'd by a Redundance of Blood and Humours, by their preternatural Thickness, or their conjestion in the Praecordia; for, when the Mass of Blood and Humours is too copiously and impetuously convey'd to the right Ventricle of the heart, it must, of course, be also more copiously carried to the Ramifications of the pulmonary Vessels; by which means, the elastic force of the inspir'd Air is, in consequence of the strong resistance of the blood, considerably impair'd. The Blood therefore which is not briskly enough propel'd thro' the pulmonary Vein, stagnates in its small Ramifications; and the fresh Supplies of blood, convey'd by the continued Pulsation of the Heart, distend and dilate the Ramifications of the Vessels: hence arise a Difficulty of Breathing, great Uneasiness, a Tremor and Palpitation of the Heart, together with an unequal, small, quick and frequent Pulse. This Asthma arising from a redundance of Blood, ought also to be distinguished by the Epithet Spasmodick.

79

The immediate remedy is clear:

Venesection never fails to lessen the Paroxysm, relieve the patient, and afford a due time for providing and exhibiting other Remedies . . .[48]

This extract typifies James' manner, both in those parts of the *Medicinal Dictionary* which are not excerpted from other sources and in his other works: he has (dare I suggest) all the confidence and dogmatism of a poor clinician. 'The more we know of the human Machine, the more simple it appears', he claims.[49]

I do not want to give the impression that James is a slavish follower of Boerhaave or his system. He speaks in an aside in his book on *Canine Madness* of 'theory, the precarious refuge of ignorance and inexperience . . .'[50] He was capable of making such a crucial criticism of Boerhaave's system as this, in his Preface to the *Medicinal Dictionary*:

It has happened very unfortunately for Physic, that the warm Imaginations of Theorists and Anatomists have represented to them many things in themselves extremely precarious, as certain Truths; and these have been warmly embrac'd as contributing to the Confirmation of some favourite Systems, which their Authors were determin'd to establish right or wrong . . .

Even *Boerhaave*, in the Oration made on Purpose to recommend Mechanics in Physic, deviates from his own Rules, and boldly supposes some things as certain, which would give him a good deal of Trouble to prove, if they should be denied. Thus, speaking of the ultimate Fibres of the Muscles, he represents them as minute Tubes inflated with Spirits. Now, the existence of these Spirits has never been demonstrated, and I believe never will. Whatever therefore is deduc'd from a Supposition of their Existence, is extremely precarious, and subject to infinite Controversy.[51]

Passages like this show what Johnson meant when he remarked that 'no man brings more mind to his profession' than James.[52] At the opening of his *Dissertation on the Gout and Rheumatism* James once more complains that the progress of medicine has been impeded by the dogmatic adherence of its professors to 'particular Systems of Theory and Modes of Practice'. But here his motives are suspect. He is pushing his own favourite remedies – mercury and antimony.

Actually, mercury's supposed remedial action could be explained in mechanist terms. Would not its weight and density slow the motion of the blood? But its admission to the pharmacopoea illustrates how chemical remedies and notions were superadded to the iatromechanist system and substances in fact were prescribed, just as they had been by older physicians, because they were 'contrary' to a particular diseased state of the body. 'The lenity of the humours is procured by drinking aqueous liquors; by a mild diet, by medicines gently diluting and obtunding; or, such as are in a singular and specific manner opposite to the prevailing acrimony', pronounces the *Modern Practice of Physic*.[53] The influence of the iatromechanist system can be discerned in or behind most eighteenth-century medical thinking, including Johnson's. But in the texts, and still more one would expect in practice, mechanist or physicalist concepts were interpenetrated by, augmented and confused by quite other notions, and many doctors admitted – some implicitly, others explicitly – that mechanics – what Heberden was to call disparagingly 'the general properties of dead matter' – could only give a woefully incomplete account of the living body.[54]

In the lectures of Thomas Lawrence, the Hippocratic notion of the healing power of 'Nature', for instance, mediated no doubt through the writings of Sydenham and Boerhaave, plays a crucial part. 'Nature', the inherent striving of the constitution for health, must be added, Lawrence insists, to undirected mechanical causes: it is an essential part of his explanation of convulsions, asthmatic fits and fevers. 'In plethorick people labouring under a thick state of the Fluids ... Nature endeavours by these violent involuntary motions, both to attenuate the thick Blood not easily circulable, and at the same time by straining the vessels to render them more Permeable.'[55] 'A Fever is an Extraordinary Exertion of Nature for some Good end'; though people may die through, 'if I may be allow'd to express myself so, an Omission of Nature in her Duty'.[56] In another interesting comment Lawrence invokes 'habit' alongside Nature. ''Tis well known to every body who has considered the motions of Nature with any kind of Care or Curiosity', he declares, 'that many distempers consist in the erroneous motions to which Nature has been habituated rather than to any real material cause.'[57] One does not easily find remarks like these in Robert James, who was a materialist – perhaps in every sense of the word.

Nor did Boerhaave's own system completely reject chemical treatments (it would scarcely have been so widely celebrated if he had). His 'insatiable Curiosity after Knowledge engaged him ... in the Practice of Chymistry'[58] but this pursuit, 'enchanting as it is' (Johnson remarks) had no influence on his medical theory. 'Chymical Art can afford Data, and determine their Conditions but will never supply us with Rules of arguing from them', he asserted in his 1703 oration.[59] He rejected with asperity the notion – not so far from the truth perhaps – associated with the names of such seventeenth-century physicians as Thomas Willis and J.-B. van Helmont, that the different secretions of the body are generated by specific chemical 'ferments' located in each gland. The scorn which many eighteenth-century medical writers direct against the iatrochemists must be a reaction to the extraordinary mystical rhetoric in which, for example, van Helmont expounded his theories, but it also has a social element: chemists, as Boerhaave implies, were 'sooty empirics', whilst the gentleman physician could claim a heritage of classical learning and an art that occupied a central place in man's understanding of this world. But at the same time many chemical treatments were very widely used. Their very name 'specifics' though may show that their adoption was thought of as quite separate from any general scheme of explanation.

And some medicines did seem to work. Samuel Johnson reviewed a book by Benito Geronimo Feijoo called *An Exposition of the Uncertainties in the practice of Physic*, a 'treatise intended to show the total inefficacy of physick to the restoration of health' in the *Gentleman's Magazine* for February 1751. It is true, Johnson concedes, in a remark of Hippocratian wisdom, that 'The effect of medicines with regard to the cure of particular diseases is indeed in a great degree uncertain, and they are frequently applied without success, because the disease is not sufficiently known, and the circumstances of the patient with respect to situation, habit, manner of life, and constitution are not regarded with sufficient attention'. But he goes on to declare that 'tho' medicines are sometimes applied without success, the effects of many are known and certain: Ipecacuana will vomit, manna will purge, and mercury will salivate; therefore whenever vomiting, purging or salivating are necessary of which in many cases there can be no doubt, it is evident that medicines may restore health'. Johnson certainly thought the investigation of new remedies as important as Sir John Floyer had. To Dr George Staunton, about to set sail for Guadeloupe in 1762, he wrote 'I do not doubt but you will be able to add much to knowledge, and perhaps, to medicine. Wild nations trust to simples; and perhaps, the Peruvian bark is not the only specifick which those extensive regions may afford us'.[60] A few years before, the *Literary Magazine* had shown a similar interest in the medicinal products of Jamaica, and many years later, Johnson was to urge that the Radcliffe travelling scholarships in medicine be used to explore remedies and practices beyond Europe.[61]

The best way of illuminating a medical theory and its relation to practice is to examine a doctor's handling of a particular case. It is fortunate, for us at least, that Johnson's medical beliefs are amply displayed in the series of letters, spanning nearly two years, he wrote to Mr and Mrs Thrale after the former had suffered an 'apoplectic seizure' on 8 June 1779. Mrs Thrale's letter giving the first news of the attack has not survived, but after an initial reply written on the mistaken premise that the attack was 'hysterical' and so presuming that all was already well, Johnson sent a series of concerned and earnestly argued letters to his 'Master' and 'Mistress' from Ashbourne and Lichfield (June to August) and from Bolt Court to Brighton, where the Thrales went in October. These letters make the usual reassuring gestures that friends make in these cases – instances of comparable attacks where the patient did very well etc. – but three distinguishing features can be singled out. There is, firstly, a characteristically Johnsonian feeling of horror at the unpredictable nature of the attack ('Time hovers o'er, impatient to destroy') and a consequently urgent awareness that, its causes not being understood, prevention of a recurrence was a difficult and anxious matter, in which professional experience would count a good deal. He urged the Thrales to go and see Heberden, and ask Heberden to consult with another doctor, Lawrence, if at all possible. Secondly, though, Johnson did not hesitate to give it as his own opinion that phlebotomy was the initial and diet and moderate exercise the supporting modes of prevention. Thirdly, the letters repeatedly insist that to keep a calm and cheerful state of mind was essential if the attack were not to recur.

The first of these hardly needs illustration. 'Such sudden violence is very dreadful, we know not by what it is let loose upon us, nor by what its effects are limited' (14 June). It was the more dreadful, Johnson thought at first, because there was no 'irregularity' in Thrale's everyday regimen, anything to make this 'seizure' explicable. The best he could suggest was that:

Chearfulness and exercise are your great remedies. Nothing is for the present worth your anxiety. Vivite laeti is one of the great rules of health. I believe it will be good to ride often, but never to weariness, for weariness is itself a temporary resolution of the nerves, and is therefore to be avoided . . .[62]

'Resolution' in eighteenth-century medical talk usually means healing, but here it must mean 'dissolution', one of the definitions given in the *Dictionary*. Johnson means that the nervous fibres (not, I think, the muscles) would be over-relaxed by too much exercise and so the harmonious balance between their strength and the force of the fluids would be destroyed. Riding was always recommended, on Sydenham's authority, as conducive to the enlivening of the circulatory system. But on 5 October, probably as a result of seeing Thrale again, and revising his opinion of the healthiness of his way of life, Johnson cautioned against exercise:

> It appears to me that Mr Thrale's disorder, whether grumous or serous, must be cured by bleeding; and I would not have him begin a course of exercise without considerable evacuation. To encrease the force of the blood, unless it be first diluted and attenuated, may be dangerous. But the case is too important for my theory.[63]

Chapman suggested that Johnson wrote 'any theory', but it is unlikely that Johnson would have offered any medical advice if he had no 'principles on which to reason'.[64] 'His' theory is actually identical with Robert James' who, under 'Apoplexy' in the *Medicinal Dictionary*, cites Sydenham's differentiation:

> The two most general causes of an apoplexy are *first*, a Plethora, or overfulness of Blood [what Johnson calls 'grumous' blood] *second*, a deficiency in vital powers, and a consequent redundance of viscid and serous humours.

The second of these types, apoplexy caused by 'extravagation of the Serum', is milder than the plethoric, in which the paralysis resulting from the attack is due to a 'bursting of the vessels in the brain'. In the milder type, only the serum passes through the pores of these vessels, interfering with 'the secretion of the subtle active Fluid' (i.e. the so-called 'nervous fluid') 'and by that means deprives one or other of the sides of all Sensation and Motion'. The logical course in both cases was to reduce the amount of the circulating fluids and Thrale was, accordingly, bled.

But on 21 February 1780 he had another attack. It is recorded in Mrs Thrale's diary:

> Another Stroke of the Apoplexy or Palsy or some dreadful Thing! poor Mr Thrale! and with such a Desire of Life too – how it shocks one! but Sir Richard Jebb has saved his Life; Heberden left us in our Distresses very

ungenteely: Jebb is the Man for Medical, as Lord Chatham for Political Courage; he bled his Patient *usque ad Deliquium* & he is now once more in Possession of Life Intellect and Limbs![65]

The outcome of Jebb's drastic treatment would have confirmed Johnson's conviction, which was Robert James's too, that bloodletting had to be copious to be effective. On 20 April he was telling John Taylor that 'the quantity of blood taken from you appears to me not sufficient. Thrale was almost lost by the scrupulosity of his Physicians, who never bled him copiously till they bled him in despair; he then bled till he fainted, and the stricture or obstruction immediately gave way, and from that instant he grew better.'[66] In August, when Thrale probably suffered yet another stroke, Johnson wrote consolingly to Mrs Thrale: 'You are at least doing, what I was always desirous to have you do, and which when despair put an end to the caution of men going in the dark, produced at last the good that has been obtained. Gentle purges, and slight phlebotomies are not my favourites, they are pop-gun batteries, which lose time and effect nothing . . .'[67]

If 'exercise and carelessness' was the keynote of Johnson's advice in the early stages of Thrale's illness, 'caution and resolution' was the call later. In those early months of 1780 Johnson was himself dieting. He dined every second day on vegetables only and urged Thrale to follow suit. 'A thin, slender, cool, regular Diet', according to John Arbuthnot's *Practical Rules of Diet* which Johnson had used in the *Dictionary*, is 'proper' in a regimen which seeks to avoid an apoplexy, but Johnson could have found the advice in a number of places.[68] George Cheyne's *Essay of Health and Long Life* recommends the practice which he now took up, of an exclusively vegetable diet 'a Day or Two in the Week'.[69] But Thrale did not. 'I have no notion of health for a man whose mouth cannot be sewed up', cried his wife. Throughout the spring and summer Johnson wrote. He reiterated that it was only by adhering to some rule that Thrale could survive:

> The chief wish that I form is, that Mr Thrale could be made to understand his real state, to know that he is tottering upon a point, to consider every change of his mental character as the symptom of a disease, to distrust any opinions or purposes that shoot up in his thoughts; to think that violent Mirth is the foam, and deep sadness the subsidence of a morbid fermentation; to watch himself, and counteract by experienced remedies every new tendency or uncommon sensation . . .[70]

This elaborate and formally cadenced sentence is in Johnson's most solemn manner. The iatrochemist's concept of 'a morbid fermentation' is borrowed to give an air of grave medical learning to these directions. Johnson is marshalling all the authority belonging to the sage author of *Rasselas* and the *Rambler* behind his advice to a friend.

When one reviews these letters to the Thrales (there are at least ten of lengthy and considered advice) W. J. Bate's comment that faced with his friend's illness Johnson 'forgot what he knew of medicine' seems astonishing. Bate suggests that Johnson was so frightened at the prospect of losing Thrale that 'in complete subjectivity' he gave his friend only the sort of advice he was continually giving himself – 'that most of our troubles are created by our own minds, and what we need above all are "diversions" to get us out of ourselves'.[71] An element of subjectivity can probably be hardly avoided in any advice to a friend, and after all our most earnest suggestions will be based on our own experience, but to convict Johnson of irresponsibility here one would have to show that his suggestions were offered negligently or were without a theoretical basis. Far from being depressed and obsessed by death at this date, as Bate implies, Johnson felt better than he had done for years, and his letters of mid-1779 up to Thrale's death in April 1781 leave an impression of more energy and buoyancy than the others of any earlier period. At any rate it was not only Johnson who claimed that his advice was correct: 'Mr Shaw will maintain, that he and I saved my Master' (14 August 1780). 'Every thing that I have told you about my dear master has been true,' Johnson wrote later that month, 'Every thing that I have ever proposed for Mr Thrale has been found right in the event'.[72]

It is obvious that Johnson had no qualms about his qualifications to offer medical advice whether or not this brought him into conflict with professional physicians. Heberden, who left Mr Thrale so 'ungenteely' without bleeding him, was notably cautious about the efficacy of phlebotomy in such cases, but Johnson seems to have had no reservations and recommends it, in exigencies, as wholeheartedly to his other correspondents as he does to the Thrales. Whilst on scientific matters always curious and open-minded, Johnson was certainly not gullible (an instance: he teases Mrs Thrale about the reputed virtues of Bath water, so loudly touted in the eighteenth century[73]). Iatromechanic theory made sense: it gave a clear and plausible rationale for a procedure which had been in use for centuries. Could it have been this alone that stood behind Johnson's conviction of its effectiveness? Or did the theory reinforce his subjective experience of its value? But to stress the authority and cogency of Boerhaavian theory and its possible influence on Johnson's views is to enter the fascinating but dangerous area of the 'placebo effect'.

To discuss Johnson's belief in phlebotomy under this rubric, as so often with 'psychological' explanations, is really to pre-empt the issue. Obviously, Johnson's 'horror of vacuity' played its part. When the onset of illness is felt as an ambush, an attack, a seizure, aggressive forms of response, not 'pop-gun batteries', are likely to be psychologically attractive. The association of ideas in this advice to Taylor of June 1773 may be significant: 'do not lye down without struggle or resistance. I have by some uncommon necessity been blooded five times this year, and I think have always been the better ...' Johnson, like us all, expected to receive benefit from any medical intervention whose general efficacy he believed in and the fact that bloodletting brought the patient to the centre of a circle of physician, surgeon and assistants may also be relevant. The attention of others, like their letters, may 'operate as cordials' as Johnson surely knew.[74] Yet all such explanations, of course, leave us unsatisfied.

'Johnson must have shortened his life by the bleedings that he underwent', wrote Birkbeck Hill. 'Today we know that Johnson felt better after a bleeding despite it, not because of it', two recent writers on Johnson's medical interests have declared.[75] This seems to be orthodox contemporary opinion, but as Marie Boas Hall has pointed out, it is often quite extraordinarily difficult to find out whether the therapeutics of previous centuries worked.[76] Bleeding has been used at least since the time of Hippocrates, and yet now that we have other means to attain the end it served, previous treatments tend to be dismissed as obviously ineffective. The question here is not whether Johnson's theory was mistaken. It is a question of whether or not he was mistaken about his actual physical condition, before and after phlebotomy. He was, as we saw, perfectly able, even when hard-pressed by disease, to subject the 'dangerous' Tinture of Cantharides to a personal clinical trial. However formidable the drug's reputation, he was clear that it had no useful result – in fact no result at all – for him. Can we believe that he consistently mistook his own improvement after bleeding?

Johnson's own subjective conviction that phlebotomy mitigated his asthmatic symptoms brought him into conflict with Thomas Lawrence, whose lectures make clear his belief – perfectly sound according to the monistic premises of iatromechanist thinking – that gout and asthma were interrelated and that gout had a potentially relieving effect on asthma. 'The Gout falling upon the Head causes Apoplexys, Lethargies, and other Drowsy oblivious disorders, Falling upon the Breast it produces according to the parts affected and the Activity of Nature in attempting its discussion, an Asthma, a Pleurisy, or a Peripneumony' he said. 'Gouty matter repell'd brings on a difficulty of breathing, which disease entirely goes off whenever Nature drives it back again to the extremities.' In his eloquent Latin letter to Lawrence of March 1782, Johnson points out, on the contrary, that once, when the gout was particularly fierce, he had suffered simultaneously in the foot and the chest. He therefore begs and beseeches Lawrence not to forbid bloodletting and for the bleeding to be done without timidity or caution. Unwilling to act without his doctor's blessing, his convictions were in direct conflict with his physician's own deeply held beliefs. When he was bled, he reported great relief and sound, dreamless, sleep.[77]

Treatments that seem successful for one disorder are often unwarrantably extended to others. I suggest that it is very possible that Johnson's breathing difficulties were relieved by bleeding, even though we may remain sceptical about its efficacy in Thrale's case, or for an inflamed eye. Lester King has recently insisted that in several conditions, high blood pressure and lobar pneumonia, for instance, venesection would bring relief, if only temporarily.[78] 'Vascular conjestion in the lungs can place a burden on the right side of the heart. Any disproportion between the volume of blood and the ability to pump it may improve after venesection. So too with the difficulty in breathing that for Hippocrates served as one indication for blood-letting.'[79] In one of the very rare modern trials of phlebotomy, reported in 1975, despite the presumptions and expectations of the research team, 'Eight of the 11 phlebotomised subjects noted symptomatic improvement following the procedure while none of the controls did'.[80] The researchers could find no explanation for the responders' relief of their dispoenic symptoms and only suggest vaguely that perhaps their 'internal cues' were more sensitive than the measuring instruments available. So perhaps the usefulness of bleeding still remains an open question. It was still practised until the First World War for some complaints, particularly for the circulatory disorders associated with acute respiratory symptoms, as in Johnson's case.[81]

Johnson's medical education probably began then, whilst he was still in Lichfield, reading voraciously among the stock of his father's shop. On a foundation – we may assume – of classical and Galenic learning was built, under the tuition of James, a knowledge of and (with reservations) adherence to the dogmas of contemporary medicine, with its emphasis on the body as a unitary system of mechanical processes. His medical education was informal (so was that of many other practisers of physic), but he certainly felt qualified, as we have seen, to offer detailed medical advice even to the extent of 'intruding' upon the opinions of qualified practitioners. 'It does not appear from your doctor's prescription that he sees to the bottom of your distemper. What he gives you strikes at no cause', is typical of remarks in his letters to John Taylor.[82] A letter of advice to Mrs Thrale a couple of weeks later ends, 'I think you will in a week have reason to praise your Physician'.[83] Undoubtedly he means himself. As an amateur practitioner, Johnson was convinced that gout was not a prophylactic, and that the loss of substantial amounts of blood relieved difficulties in breathing. Neither his contemporaries nor medical historians have been willing to believe him but it is surely very probable that he was right.

3

TRANSACTIONS OF THE MEDICAL
WORLD

Fortune of physicians

JOHNSON'S KNOWLEDGE of medicine, then, often brought him into conflict with the professional opinions of his physicians. His medical learning may have been unique among eighteenth-century amateurs, but he was of course far from the only 'dabbler' in medicine who took it upon themselves to dictate treatment:

We had been at Bath but a day, when, on the arrival of the post, Madam proved so very wise, as to show me a letter from Dr. Jebb, afterwards Sir Richard, in which she was pretty bluntly reprimanded for her playing the physician with her children, and earnestly entreated at the same time to forbear giving her daughter what she termed *tin pills* . . .

In the act of giving me the Doctor's letter to read, See, See, said Madam with a pert promptitude that always formed one of her chief characteristics, see what fools these physicians are! They presume to know better how to manage children than their mothers themselves![1]

Baretti's libellous account of Mrs Thrale clearly implies that it would be thought scandalous for her to take the treatment of her children out of the hands of Jebb. We have no way of knowing whether eighteenth-century ladies often treated their doctors in this fashion, or how much eighteenth-century patients obeyed and how much they disregarded their medical advisers, or whether self-medication was less or even more prevalent than today.[2] The amazing success of John Wesley's *Primitive Physic* with its folk and sometimes lethal 'remedies' suggests that among the poorer classes it was almost universal, but that might well be expected, given that physicians' fees were well beyond the pockets of all but the genteel and the rich.[3] Among the educated classes in touch with the orthodox medical profession it is very likely, I think, that medical knowledge was quite widespread. The nature of that knowledge – which derived essentially from Hippocratic and Galenic sources, supplemented by Sydenham and Boerhaave – was after all far from esoteric. What is more, since medicine was systemic – conceiving of illness as a malfunctioning of the patient's whole constitution, not as specific and localised internal lesions each with its own complicated aetiology – its principles, once grasped, were easy to apply to whatever particular affliction oneself or one's dependants suffered. All one's ingenuity could then be lavished on devising novel combinations of drugs.

It is time to sketch the social aspects of the medical world in the mid eighteenth century, the context in which Johnson, as a journalist, wrote many pieces of medical interest. Pharmaceutical and physiological knowledge, for the first decades of the century at least, was stagnant. Whilst the pressures on physicians to accede to the whims of their wealthy patients may account at least partly for this inertia, as Jewson has argued in a famous paper,[4] it is also likely that during this period those patients – or some of them – were becoming better informed. Medical learning, by which I mean orthodox medical learning, based on the classics and as practised by the College of Physicians, was becoming popularised: in particular the cloak of Latin which served to preserve the mystery and prestige of a profession which all too often had little of practical value to offer, was gradually drawn away.[5] Naturally, those physicians like Robert James who were agents of the popularisation were afflicted with some insecurity and accompanied their efforts with attacks upon quacks and old women.[6] One of the justifications of their enterprise offered by James and other compilers of medical handbooks like William Buchan was that their works would enable the reader to defend himself against 'ignorant pretenders' and upstart empirics. Buchan's *Domestic Medicine* (1769) is the most significant of these popular works.[7] Robert James' *Medicinal Dictionary* started out, at least, as an earlier attempt at a similar diffusion of useful knowledge. In the pompous prose of the Proposals which Johnson wrote with him, a moral as well as pragmatic justification is offered for the enterprise since 'It is doubtless of importance to the Happiness of Mankind, that whatever is generally useful should be generally known; and he therefore that *diffuses* Science may with Justice claim, among the Benefactors to the Public, the next Rank to him that Improves it.' But another paragraph is eminently Johnsonian in its outbreak of passionate indignation at those who would oppose the spreading knowledge, or who, like Bernard Mandeville, cast doubt on the motives of amateur doctors:

THERE was a time, when those whom Providence had blessed with Leisure, Affluence and Dignity, did not think it any Diminution of their Characters to attend the necessities of the Indigent, and alleviate the Miseries of the Diseased. And how little they have deserved from Mankind, who have laid out their Rhetoric, and their Wit, in representing this kind of Charity as ridiculous, useless and pernicious, is apparent, from the melancholy Condition of Multitudes, who, disabled by Sickness from their daily Employment, languish and perish without Assistance. Had this Charity been better directed and the *Warmth of Benevolence* assisted by the *Light of Knowledge*, it had perhaps never sunk into Neglect; its Success would have defended it from Contempt, and Levity and Inhumanity would have been afraid to attack it. If it should ever revive, it may perhaps, hereafter, exert a more beneficial Influence, and we shall have this great Satisfaction, That our Endeavours have enabled Virtue to assume its natural Dignity, and to set at Defiance the Insolence of the Proud, the Thoughtless and the Cruel.

Johnson was to call William Heberden, whose help he called for after his stroke in 1783, 'ultimus Romanorum, the last of the learned physicians'.[8] Learned himself, Johnson was also, as luck would have it, a participant in that early 'laying open' of medical knowledge to those without the acquaintance of the classical languages. The times had changed. Sydenham had written his major works, including the *Medical Observations* of 1676 in English, but it had been thought necessary for them to be turned into Latin for publication. This was accordingly done by Dr John Mapletoft, and in the process their individualistic emphasis was toned down, and a 'strong dash of classical erudition added instead'.[9] In 1742, it became necessary for this process to be reversed. Dr John Swan, a Staffordshire physician who was also among the contributors to Cave's *Gentleman's Magazine*, published an English translation of the works of Sydenham. Johnson, out of personal involvement or as one of Cave's regular staff writers, contributed a prefatory 'Life of Dr Sydenham'. Later in the century the appearance of medical items translated from the *Journal des Savants* in a magazine with which Johnson was connected is evidence of how far Latin had been dislodged from its position as the international language of medicine – a change which accompanied changes in the composition of the profession and the development of experimental techniques in medical research.

The pages of the *Gentleman's Magazine* during the time that Johnson wrote for it reveal another significant aspect of the early eighteenth-century medical world. In the August 1738 issue one item is 'Dr Mortimer's Account of A Remedy for the Bite of a Viper'. In the next month's issue appears a letter reporting another medical secret, 'Dr Boerhaave's Receipt for an Ulcer in the Bowels'. Dr Boerhaave would only take a fee of half a guinea for a consultation, says the writer, and goes on to congratulate himself, like one of Swift's Moderns, on his own magnanimity in disclosing the prescription:

As I believe this Prescription of much greater Value than ten Times such a trifling Sum, especially to that part of the World who suffer by too free a Use of the Bottle; and as they can never more enjoy the Advantage of his personal Advice, I look upon the making it publick as a Matter of some Merit . . .

    Your constant customer,
    R.J.[10]

Other issues of the *Magazine* reported cures for the gout, cures for the dropsy and an interesting letter signed 'Amasius', the pen-name of John Swan, pleaded for a law to enforce public disclosure of 'Mr W—d's medicines', in the public interest. But the secret medicine that occupies most space in the *Gentleman's Magazine* is Mrs Stephens' 'Medicines for the Stone'. In this famous case, David Hartley was the instigator of a campaign, first to propagate the virtues of Mrs Stephens' nostrum by means of dozens of testimonial letters, and secondly by soliciting subscriptions to a fund which would reimburse the lady for her loss in making her valuable secret public. The appeal met with success. The Duke of Leeds, the Countess of Huntingdon and the Bishop of Salisbury were among those who brought the sum subscribed to nearly two thousand pounds. But Joanna Stephens would not reveal the secret for less than five thousand. Her friends sought a grant from Parliament, a Parliamentary commission – in what must be one of the first involvements of the legislature in medicine – was set up to examine the question of the lithontriptic's efficacy: twenty of its twenty-two members (which included Hartley as well as the pioneering scientist Stephen Hales and the distinguished surgeon William Cheselden) signed a certificate vouching for the 'Utility, Efficacy and Dissolving Power' of the medicines. In June 1739 the *Magazine* was able to report a 'full discovery'. Despite the testimony of physicians and philosophers, of bishops and barons, Mrs Stephens' solvent powder was found to consist of powdered and calcined egg-shells and snails, for which she duly took the sum granted by the Government for her secret.[11]

One turns to magazines like the *Gentleman's* for insight into the medical life of the period because there were no professional medical journals. It seems likely that the formal exchange of medical information was minimal, since any promising new compound or drug tended to be thought of as a trade secret, to be jealously guarded by its owner. Nor is there any professional or public scrutiny, let along testing, of these reported remedies or 'cures' or systems of treatment. Jewson puts it mildly when he writes that 'controversy was not conducted according to the canons of the scientific method'.[12] The atmosphere was not critical: testimonies and publicity, fashion and fruitless rivalry took the place of impartial assessment and made the advancement of knowledge uncertain.

So was professional success. In his life of Aegineta, a physician of the seventh century, Johnson remarks, 'That reputation of every kind is capriciously distributed cannot but be frequently observed; nor is it less usual for Authors, than for Men of every other Class, to be recompensed for their Endeavours in a Manner disproportioned to their Merit.'[13] The state of medical knowledge in the early and mid eighteenth century probably made it even more of a lottery whether professional skill and knowledge led to a doctor's success or not, for lottery it certainly seems in Johnson's famous comments in the *Life of Akenside*:

> At London he was known as a poet, but was still to make his way as a physician; and would perhaps have been reduced to great exigencies, but that Mr Dyson, with an ardour of friendship that has not many examples, allowed him three hundred pounds a year. Thus supported, he advanced gradually in medical reputation, but never attained any great extent of practice, or eminence of popularity. A physician in a great city seems to be the mere play-thing of fortune; his degree of reputation is, for the most part, totally casual; they that employ him know not his excellence; they that reject him know not his deficience. By any acute observer, who had looked on the transactions of the medical world for half a century, a very curious book might be written on the 'Fortune of Physicians'.

Johnson might well have had in mind the contrasting careers of his two early friends Robert James and Richard Bathurst. 'My *dear dear* Bathurst, whom I loved better than ever I loved any human creature', he cried to Mrs Thrale whilst telling an anecdote of his youth.[14] Sir John Hawkins associates Richard Bathurst's career with Johnson's remarks in the *Life of Akenside*. 'Dr Richard Bathurst', he writes, 'was a native of Jamaica, and the son of an eminent planter in that island, who coming to settle in England, placed his son in London, in order to qualify him for the practice of physic.'[15] Bathurst took the degree of MB at Peterhouse in 1745, after an initial sojourn in London. It was whilst Bathurst was attending the anatomical lectures given by Dr Frank Nicholls at St Thomas's Hospital in the 1730s that according to the biographical account of Thomas Lawrence in the *Gentleman's Magazine* in 1787 he and Lawrence met and became friends.[16] It was Bathurst who introduced Lawrence to Johnson.

'He possessed the qualities that were most likely to recommend him in his profession; but, wanting friends, could make no way in it', says Hawkins. He seems to have found friends, in the more modern sense, among London's journalists and hack writers. Piecing what evidence we have about his time in London together it seems likely that he was often in need of help, mostly financial. Boswell says, on Anna Williams' authority, that Johnson dictated the essays in the *Adventurer* signed 'T' to Bathurst, who wrote them down and collected the two guinea payment. Johnson is said to have smiled at the report that he did not *write* them.[17] There exist some detailed Proposals for a *Geographical Dictionary* along the lines of Johnson's earlier proposals with James (both insist on the importance of the naming of authorities, for instance, so that the reader can check on the accuracy of the information provided), which Johnson dictated to Bathurst probably in the early fifties.[18] The Proposal was sent to the printer Strahan, whom Johnson tells, 'The Undertaker, Mr Bathurst is a Physician of the University of Cambridge of about eight years standing, and will perform the work in such a manner as may satisfy the publick. No advice of mine will be wanting, but advice will be all that I propose to contribute unless it should be thought worthwhile that I should write a preface, which if desired I will do and put my name to it.'[19] The project was probably designed to capitalise on Bathurst's experiences as a traveller but the scheme came to nothing. Bathurst eventually in September 1754 picked up the post of physician to the most recently founded charity hospital, the Middlesex, housed in a row of dwellings off Tottenham Court Road, and with beds for only fifteen patients in a quarter 'abounding with poor objects'. (One can imagine it.) It was 'supported by precarious donations', Hawkins remarks, and in its early years physicians and man-midwives resigned in quick succession. A new site was acquired in 1754 and a new hospital for sixty-four patients opened in 1757, but by this time Bathurst too had resigned his position.[20] As we shall see, Johnson later made yet another attempt to involve Bathurst in a literary project but in 1757 the doctor left

London for the Barbadoes, a disappointed man, having 'never opened his hand to more than one guinea.'[21] He died in 1762 at the Havannah. All that remain of him are two letters written to Johnson from Jamaica in 1757, a few essays and an article. He is the one person, apart from his family and Hill Boothby, whom Johnson remembers in his prayers.

'We might well wonder', writes Geoffrey Holmes, 'what qualities were called for in a physician of the Augustan age to secure the astonishing rewards reaped by such professional tycoons as Sloane, Richard Mead or John Radcliffe.'[22] The answers he suggests are good public relations and luck – as well as hard work. Robert James never made it to the heights achieved by these giants of the previous generation but his career suggests that hard work as well as enterprise went into the making of his success. He published a number of books, including translations of Bernardini Ramazzini's *Treatise on the Diseases of Tradesmen*, a pioneering work on occupational disease, and Simon Paulii's *Treatise of Tobacco, Tea, Coffee and Chocolate*, even before his patenting of a 'fever powder' in 1747. Along with Dr Thomas Dover's powders, this became probably the most successful of eighteenth-century patent medicines (202 preparations were listed by the *Gentleman's Magazine* in 1748) and survived, so it is said, to be included in Queen Victoria's medicine chest, and to be thrust down the throats of little boys like Ernest Pontifex at the slightest sign of fever.[23] It has generally been assumed that with the success of the powders Johnson's and James' paths diverged, and Johnson's biographers since Boswell have not cared to dwell on their hero's contacts with a schoolfriend whose dealings were at least slightly shady. James' partner in the manufacture and marketing of the powders was John Newbery the publisher (as Jack Whirler, who has his fingers in so many pies that he cannot spare time enough for any of them the subject of an affectionate satiric sketch in the *Idler* 19), father-in-law of Christopher Smart and landlord, for a time at least, of Oliver Goldsmith. Both of these writers contrive to publicise the fever powders, Smart in the dedication (to James) of his poems, and Goldsmith in the story *Goody Two Shoes* (published by Newbery) where the heroine's father dies miserably in the first sentence because 'he was seized with a violent Fever in a Place where Dr James's Powder was not to be had'.[24] Goldsmith's own miserable death in 1774 was convincingly ascribed by the apothecary William Hawes to his being in a place where Dr James' powders could be had all to readily.[25] James was still visiting Johnson in 1773 when they discussed the condition of Mrs Salusbury, Hester Thrale's mother, who seems to have been James' patient. James, true to his mechanist lights, wished that the 'Cancerous humour' from which she suffered 'would return to the breast again'.[26] On his visit to London in 1775 Dr Thomas Campbell heard a story of Johnson and 'Dr James, who is, it seems, a very lewd fellow, both *verbo et facto*. James it seems in a coach with his whoor, took up Johnson and set him down at a given place. Johnson, hearing afterwards what the lady was, attacked James when next he met him, for carrying him about in such company.' 'Damn the rascal', Johnson is reported to have said, 'he is past sixty, the ——.' In another version of the story, 'James apologised by saying that he always took a swelling in his stones if he abstained a month etc – Damn the rascal, says Johnson, he is past sixty: the swelling would have gone no farther'.[27] In any case in this story the carriage is at least as notable as the 'whoor': that symbol of the metropolitan doctor's success which James – giving a lift to his eminent literary friend – had conspicuously achieved.

In the medical world of the 1830s and 40s, despite the power of the College of Physicians (a power one might say, unkindly but truly, used primarily not to encourage research but to exclude those who had not followed the orthodox routes of qualification from the profession and its privileges), there is little discussion of any aspect of medicine that would count in our eyes as rational. A good deal of what little there is comes from the pen of Johnson, who, initially in the pages of the *Gentleman's Magazine*, is the medical journalist, as well as the political journalist, of the period. He does not directly survey or discuss medicines or treatments. But within studies mostly biographical and historical he shows what a critical and rational approach to medicine might be like. What he wrote was, as we shall see, hack work, produced in haste, to the orders of others, but in a context where the most eminent professionals could endorse Mrs Stephens and her medicines it demonstrates qualities of independent judgement which align it with the experimental approach to medicine that was emerging in those same years.

The first of these writings, the 'Life' of the great Dutch physician and teacher Herman Boerhaave, which is spread over four numbers of the *Gentleman's Magazine* in 1739, raises at once a question that is central to the discussion of Johnson's medical journalism. This piece, like most of Johnson's other biographical studies of medical figures, is a translation, in this case from the Latin commemorative eulogy of Boerhaave's friend and colleague Albert Schultens, *Oratio academica in memoriam Hermanni Boerhaavii.*[28] To what degree then can it be relied upon as evidence of Johnson's views – as distinct from evidence of his interest in medicine? Richard Schwartz, among others, has argued that it makes little difference. 'The fact', he declares, 'that he often depended on these sources for factual material in no way invalidates the resulting works as mines of information concerning his own attitudes.'[29] Yet, given especially that Johnson himself issues so many warnings about the necessity of scepticism in a historian, it might be as well to reserve judgement. Certainly, the emphases of this 'Life' are ones that will recur constantly through Johnson's writings on the lives and activities of physicians, so that (for instance) it could well be imagined that he was learning from as well as concurring with Boerhaave and his disciples. Briefly, the 'Johnsonian' themes in the life are these: an emphasis on clinical observation and experimental knowledge as the foundations of medicine, with Hippocrates and Sydenham as the great exemplars; a scorn of mere book-learning, with the rider that knowledge and study of the classics of medicine is of course necessary; attacks on the iatrochemists and Descartes; and a strongly personal response to imagined pain.

But though these features will recur in Johnson's medical writings, most of them would not have surprised the *Gentleman's Magazine*'s readers. They were orthodox positions for the time. Many of the remarks that have been quoted as evidence of Johnson's own opinions may simply be a reflection of Boerhaave's, since Boerhaave himself shared the Baconian and Newtonian standpoint of Sydenham as well as many of his contemporaries. Such a remark as 'The History of his Illness can hardly be read without Horror' strikes a truly Johnsonian note but it is in fact a translation of Schultens' words 'Atrocis Morbi Historiam ...' The discussion of the jargon of chemical writers 'who seem generally to have affected not only a barbarous but unintelligible Phrase ... either because they believed that mankind would reverence most what they least understood, or because they wrote not from Benevolence but Vanity, and were desirous to be praised for their Knowledge, though they could not prevail upon themselves to communicate it' also sounds Johnsonian, but attacks on iatrochemists as 'airy dreamers' are commonplace in this decade. More specifically characteristic of Johnson (though having its source in Schultens) is the emphasis in the 'Life' on the great physician as exemplar of human virtue, as moral hero. This biography suggests, as had Bacon, that the real impediments to the advancement of knowledge are human vices. Records of the arduous work which lay behind Boerhaave's famous clinical and diagnostic skills should be preserved, it is claimed, since 'men are generally idle and ready to satisfy themselves, and intimidate the industry of others, by calling that impossible which is only difficult'. Boerhaave's greatness, on the other hand, is indistinguishable from his moral stature:

> Yet so far was this great Master from presumptuous Confidence in his Abilities, that, in his Examinations of the Sick, he was remarkably circumstantial and particular. He well knew that the Originals of Distempers are often at a Distance from their visible Effects; that to conjecture, where Certainty may be obtained, is either Vanity or negligence; and that Life is not to be sacrificed, either to an Affectation of quick Discernment, or of crowded Practice, but may be required, if trifled away, at the Hand of the Physician.[30]

It is a far cry from the great Dr Boerhaave, *communis Europae preceptor*, to the humble Robert Levet. But if the medical profession, as this 'Life' declares, 'must undoubtedly claim the second Place among those which are of the greatest Benefit of Mankind', Johnson suggests implicitly here, as in the poem which commemorates Levet, that the good doctor's clinical accomplishment – what in one sense is his strictly medical skill in the observation and diagnosis of the signs of disease – is the focus of personal discipline, indifference to the various lures of vanity, which makes it a moral matter as well.

Soon after followed 'A Panegyric on Dr MORIN by Mr Fontenelle' (*Gentleman's Magazine* 1741), a translation by Johnson, to which he added besides the title, two characteristically dissenting footnotes. In 1742 he wrote the 'Life' of Sydenham already mentioned. In 1743 he worked with James on the Proposals for James' great enterprise, the *Medicinal Dictionary*. Far from being a brief sketch or outline like many others Johnson wrote these comprise a comprehensive set of desiderata for a medical encyclopaedia which are clearly the result of long thought on the subject. They stress the importance, in 1743, of separating medical and pharmaceutical knowledge from tradition, myth and folklore and so of a comparative and critical approach to the enormous body of received information. The object of the *Dictionary* is not merely to gather together or summarise the existing material: it is to clear up confusion and to distinguish the really useful from among the mass of received so-called knowledge. What Johnson was proposing was an analysis of medical knowledge, the establishment of a coherent base for intelligent and rational practice. From 1747 to 1755 he is engaged on his own *Dictionary*, but in 1756 he becomes involved, probably in an editorial capacity, with the *Literary Magazine*, predominantly a political organ, but, like most magazines of the age, with a strong coverage of medical and scientific news. For this journal, he writes at least a dozen reviews on medical, para-medical and scientific topics, reviews which include some of his best work.

All this writing is unsigned, but running through it is a set of recurrent preoccupations which make it possible to think of it as amounting to one corpus of work and so to assign dubious or contested pieces to their author. The two footnotes to the Fontenelle 'Life' of Morin give an indication of its flavour. As Morin grew older, he augmented his very frugal diet with an extra ounce of wine a day. Fontenelle adds, admiringly, that 'his Weakness encreasing, he was forced to encrease his Quantity of Wine, which yet he always continued to adjust by Weight.'[31] Johnson's footnote makes clear what he thinks of this example:

> The practice of Dr Morin is forbidden, I believe, by every Writer that has left rules for the Preservation of Health, and is directly opposite to that of Cornaro, who, by his Regimen repaired a broken Constitution, and protracted his Life without any painful Infirmities or any decay of his intellectual Abilities to more than a hundred Years; it is generally agreed, that as Men advance in years, they ought to take lighter Sustenance, and in less Quantities, and reason seems easily to discover that as the concoctive Powers grow weaker, they ought to labour less.

If Johnson speaks here as a medical authority, in his second note on the 'Life' he writes more ruefully as a hack. 'Among his papers', says Fontenelle, 'was found a Greek and Latin Index to Hippocrates, more copious and exact than that of Pini, which he had furnish'd only a Year before his Death. Such a Work required the Assiduity and Patience of a Hermit' – a claim the translator takes leave to doubt. 'This is an instance of the Disposition generally found in Writers of Lives, to exalt every common Occurence and Action into Wonders. Are not Indexes daily written by Men who neither receive nor expect very loud Applauses for their Labours?'[32] Readers of the *Lives of the Poets* will recognise here a familiar note. 'Distrust is a necessary qualification of a student in history', Johnson wrote in 1742.[33]

The 'Life' of Sydenham expresses a tension that is to run through all Johnson's medical writings in the next decades. On the one hand there is a commitment to the new scientific spirit of empirical research, and on the other is loyalty to classical and theoretical learning. Sydenham is a man who has 'excelled in science', Johnson writes in his laudatory introductory paragraphs. He endorses Sydenham's 'contempt of pernicious methods supported only by authority, in opposition to sound reason and indubitable experience' as the source of good practice in medicine.[34] Yet mixed with this is a passionate emphasis on Sydenham's learning and scholarship. Without learning, the physician who relies on experimental knowledge may grow 'wise only by murder'. Sydenham 'could not but know', Johnson claims, 'that he rather restored than invented most of his principles, and therefore could not but acknowledge the value of those writers whose doctrines he adopted and enforced'.[35] Thus it is possible to read this *Life* in diametrically opposite ways. Richard Schwartz argues that Johnson's sympathy with Sydenham's empirical research is reflected in his adoption of analogous methods in the life itself. Johnson speaks of Sydenham's youthful mind 'struggling with rustic prejudices, breaking on trifling occasions the shackles of credulity, and giving proofs in its casual excursions, that it was formed to shake off the yoke of prescription and dispel the phantoms of hypothesis'. 'He enters into the spirit of the methodology which he approves and recommends', writes Schwartz,[36] by interrogating the received evidence about Sydenham's life and reinterpreting it. Johnson suggests the notion that Sydenham scorned theory and scholarship has been generally received because of 'that self-love which dazzles all mankind'. 'If it be . . . remembered', he writes, 'how much this opinion favours the laziness of some, and the pride of others; how readily some men confide in natural sagacity, and how willingly most would spare themselves the labour of accurate reading and tedious enquiry, it will be easily discovered how much the interest of multitudes was engaged in the production and continuance of this opinion, and how cheaply those of whom it was known that they practised physick before they studied it, might satisfy themselves and others with the example of the illustrious SYDENHAM.' On the other hand, Thomas Kaminski reads this impassioned defence of scholarship and learning as an unwillingness to accept the main thrust of Sydenham's work, and argues that 'Johnson either could not see or would not accept the principle underlying Sydenham's comments to Blackmore – that all authority untested by experience is suspect, making bedside practice the only effective way to learn medicine'.[37] The conflicts that are latent in this biography – championship of learning with scorn of mere authority, commitment to useful knowledge with hatred of mere experimentation – run through the writings in which Johnson handles medical topics in the following years. But the most prescient aspect of this account of Sydenham's life is that Johnson sees it as an earnest warning against 'the dangerous experiments of the ignorant and presumptuous'.

The very incomplete catalogue of Johnson's library published after his death shows that he owned, besides more modern medical writers such as Paracelsus, Borelli (an iatromechanist) and Boerhaave, the works of the classical physicians Hippocrates of Cos, Galen, Aurelius Cornelius Celsus, and Oribasius.[38] None of these is among the biographies that Johnson contributed to James' *Medicinal Dictionary*, though 'The *History* of Physicians being an Account of the Lives, Writings and Characters of the principal Authors in Physic, will be inserted in the Work, as their Names occur in the Alphabet', promise the Proposals James issued in 1743. Whether Johnson was the sole author of these Proposals is doubtful.[39] James' 'discovery' of mercury as a cure for rabies is given a puff, which is suspicious. But it would be difficult not to attribute to Johnson this description of the general design of the work:

MANY MEDICINAL DICTIONARIES have been already written, some by men whose only praise was Assiduity and Labour; others, by such as added Learning to their Industry: and some, perhaps, by those to whom an impartial Critic would have allowed neither the Wages of Labour, nor the Laurels of Science, who have transcribed Truth and Error without Distinction, have been too ignorant to lop off the Superfluities of their Predecessors, and too lazy to supply their Defects.

OF these Writers, the best, equally with the worst, have proceeded upon a Scheme which our Design resembles in nothing but in persuing, like them, the Order of the Alphabet. They endeavour to explain the *Terms* only; we, together with the *Terms*, the *Science* of Physic. They enable their readers to *Name* Distempers which we instruct them to *cure*. Their Attempts were indeed useful, and are therefore to be mentioned with Gratitude; the knowledge of Words must necessarily precede the Study of Science; this knowledge they undertook to facilitate and have succeeded so well, that often nothing can be added to the Accuracy of their Explications; and such Passages we have carefully translated without the weak Ambition of concealing the benefit by unnecessary variations.

Scholarship, research and antiquarian learning are clearly going to be necessary to the enterprise, but knowledge will not be assembled without the exercise of 'Distinction'. 'As the compilers of *Dictionaries of Science* have, either from Negligence or Vanity, for the most part, omitted to support their Assertions by Authorities, their collections have necessarily this Defect, that their Credit can rise no higher than that of the Compiler and are therefore of little Use in Questions of Importance'. The information the *Medicinal Dictionary* brings together, the Proposals insist, will not be information for its own sake. Always the criterion will be its usefulness in actual clinical practice. To attain its ends, the *Dictionary* would need a combination of scholarly learning and an acute instinct for practical usefulness. (And perhaps James and Johnson together were not entirely mistaken in thinking that they had the right qualifications.) The proposal for the *Materia Medica* is admirably comprehensive:

THE *Materia Medica* of the Antients lies, at present, in great Confusion; Many Plants, and even Animals, were called by different Names by the *Greeks* in different Ages, and even at the same times in different parts of Greece. This Variety of Names has so much obscured the Authors who have written on the *Materia Medica*, that it has not been unusual for Botanists to lose their Time searching for a Plant mentioned by some of the Antients, when they have been well acquainted with it by another Name.

NOR has only Labour been wasted by this Perplexity, but Life itself often endangered; for great Virtues being attributed to some Plants by the Antients, is has frequently happened, that Physicians, deceived by the Name, have used plants of very different Qualities. No care has therefore been omitted, that might contribute to disentangle the Confusion of this Part of physical Learning, by collecting the different Names of the same Things, and distinguishing different things too frequently mentioned by the same Name, as far as proper Authorities could be found to support Our opinion. And, in order to give the Curious an Opportunity of making further Improvements in this Article, the sum of what *Theophrastus*, *Dioscorides*, *Pliny*, the *Rei Rusticae Scriptores* etc., have said of Particular Plants, Minerals, and Animals, will be given, and tempered with the Accounts of more modern Authors.

In the event, the *Materia Medica* sections of the *Dictionary* like the rest, are compilations of extracts from earlier authors, brought together with little or no attempt at criticism. The ideals of the proposals do not even begin to be carried out in James' Preface – which might suggest that the ideas about what the Dictionary should attempt were largely Johnson's. His contribution to the work itself is slight: the translations from Daniel Le Clerc and Bernard le Bovier de Fontenelle that have been attributed to him are more likely to be by another hand. The Life of Boerhaave was revised and reprinted in the *Dictionary*, but only one other biography (of Alexander, often known as Trallian from his birthplace) and, less certainly, one or two more, can be attributed to him with any confidence, not, one must admit, a large contribution to a work of over six million words.

The writer of the Life of Actuarius in the *Dictionary* (who may have been Johnson) speaks of 'Books, which have always been found fallacious and uncertain Guides.' Other remarks suggest that the author has gone back to the original texts, in the spirit of the *Life* of Sydenham. Aegineta, for example, we are told, 'appears upon a careful Examination, not to be so implicit a Transcriber as he is generally represented; but to have considered the Practice of the Antients attentively, and to have admitted or rejected it upon just Consideration. He sometimes dissents from Galen, and once ventures to hint his Disapprobation of the Doctrine established by Hippocrates himself.'[40] But, alas, this remark is itself a virtual transcription. The impression of first hand research is an illusion. The biography of Aegineta mentions 'the opinion of Dr. Freind' and turning to John Freind's *History of Physick* (1725–6) we find these remarks on Aegineta:

> But let us consider this author a little more distinctly, notwithstanding some have represented him in so mean a figure, as if nothing of moment were to be found in his writings. I shall confine my self only to his *sixth* Book: in which I will venture to say, he is much more than a *bare* collector ... he is so far from being a mere copier, that he sometimes dissents from *Galen*, and seems to prefer a more modern experience to his ... Nay, he is so far from blindly following the ancients, that he is not satisfied with what *Hippocrates* himself says, about setting a broken nose; but subjoins a more modern practice, which he seems to prefer.[41]

There is nothing in the Life of Aegineta, in fact, which does not derive from Freind. Johnson (if it is he) has rewritten Freind's informal and occasionally rambling account, (for his book is 'a discourse written to Dr Mead'), condensing and sharpening it, but except for the moralist's remark about the capriciousness of reputation, already quoted, this is all he has done.

The Life of Alexander is even more revealing. This seems to be the most warmly written of the biographies, claiming as it does that Alexander is 'the only writer of the later Ages who has ventured to form his own Plan, or who can claim the Character of an original Author', but this claim, it turns out, is also paraphrased from Freind.

Every fact in the Life, everything which derives from a first-hand reading of Alexander's texts is Freind's. This is true of passages which one might have taken as particularly characteristic of Johnson's scepticism, as this for instance:

He is strongly inclined to believe whatever has been told of the Efficacy of Medicines, and seems never to suspect either Weakness or Imposture. Nor is the Power of Medicines the only Object of his Credulity, which extends even to the Efficacy of Amulets and Charms, and mentions some Remedies of this sort for the Ague, Stone, Gout and Colic. Those whose Reverence for Antiquity produces in them a Regard even for the Follies and Superstitions of antient Times, may here gratify their Curiosity with a Quotation from Ostanes, one of the old Persian Magi.[42]

Freind writes that Alexander

seems to be a strong believer in the force of all his drugs. There is another foible too, which I must not forget, his *superstition*, and the faith he has in *Charms* and *Amulets*, much beyond what one would expect from a man of his good judgment. He endeavours to give some reasons for it, and pleads the *precedent* of *Galen*; there are several instances of his being addicted to *Magick*; and he is the only Physician, perhaps, who ever quoted *Ostanes*, one of the oldest of the *Persian Magi*. However, whether this proceeded from the humour of the times, or the weakness of old age, the credulity should be overlooked. I shall just take notice, that he mentions these sort of remedies only in *Agues, Stone, Colick and Gout* ...[43]

Johnson, it is true, reinterprets and comments on the material he takes from Freind. Thus Freind is surprised by Alexander's omission of the disorders of women, but Johnson suggests that this would have interfered with the integrity of his plan; Freind does attempt mildly to excuse Alexander's superstitions, but Johnson says – without mentioning Freind – that to do this is 'to produce Testimonies in Favour of Folly'. For all the derivativeness of their material, the judgements are in Johnson's own language, and to that degree made his own. One needs to remind oneself, not for the first time perhaps, that Johnson was a journalist, writing under pressure, making do with the materials at hand and doing the minimum that would suffice to make a presentable job. But, except for the first of the lives, Actuarius (which does seem based on a first-hand reading of Actuarius's discourse on urines, as well as upon Freind), none of these pieces carries into effect the methodological precepts the Proposals proclaim.

There is one, apparently trivial, feature that may identify Johnson's anonymous writing. The word 'perhaps' is common enough in scholarly writing; it is used for instance by John Freind in the passage just quoted. It signifies caution or (sometimes, perhaps) insecurity on the writer's part about the claim he is advancing. But Johnson's characteristic use of 'perhaps' is rather different: it is often used to preface a judgement which is quite the reverse of cautious or restrained – clinching, dogmatic, in fact. 'The slanders of these Men', he writes in the life of Actuarius, 'are Infections, against which it would be more for the Interest of the World to find an Antidote, than against any Contagion of Disease; and *perhaps* a Remedy, of resistless and never failing Efficacy, may always be found in a Generous Confidence in God, a Steady Conduct, with Respect to those with whom we converse, and a vigilant Attention to our Words and Actions'[44] (my italics). This 'perhaps' is rhetorical, a kind of delusory breathing space for the reader before a crushingly weighty proposition is delivered. Johnson's 'perhaps' does not always work in the same or in a similiar way, of course: occasionally it seems to function simply as irony. 'His Discourse upon the animal Spirits, is perhaps neither more nor less intelligible than modern Treatises on the same Subject' he writes in the same life. And 'perhaps' in a weak or neutral form occurs in the concluding sentence of Alexander: 'Whatever might have been his Character as a Man, he has deserved as a Writer much more Applause than he commonly receives, and perhaps he is in Merit the next of the Greek Authors to Areteus and Hippocrates' – and 'perhaps' in this case covertly acknowledges that this is Freind's but not necessarily Johnson's view.[45] The rhetorical or falsely concessive 'perhaps' though can be a useful guide through the obscurities of Johnson's anonymous journalism.

Johnson signed the contract for his *Dictionary* in June 1746. It was published nine years later. 'Perhaps' is frequent there too, but only in the etymologies, as for instance of pox: '... of the same original, perhaps, with *powke* or *pouch*'. Johnson shows no similar hesitation in his definitions of medical, surgical and anatomical terms in the *Dictionary*. In fact for the definitions of many medical terms he relied on the authority of John Quincy's *Lexicon Physico-Medicum: or, a New Medicinal Dictionary* ('collected', as the title page of the first edition in 1719 announces, 'from the most eminent Authors, and particularly those who have wrote upon Mechanical Principles') which reached its sixth edition in 1747. For almost all accounts of herbs and drugs he used John Hill's *A History of the Materia Medica* (1751).

Quincy's name appears very frequently in the *Dictionary*, but in addition his lexicon is used for many definitions without acknowlegement, and therefore this work too is an unreliable index of Johnson's medical knowledge. Thus the definitions of abdomen, alterative, antedote, apoplexy, cathartick, chronic, emollient, gland, oedema, muscle, palsy etc. are attributed to Quincy but ague, apoplexy, carotid, catheter, coma, hemiplegy, palpitation etc., which are substantially Quincy's definitions with occasional slight emendment, are not. Even quite lengthy definitions, as of plethora, are taken word for word from Quincy. Johnson himself seems to have supplied the definitions for words which Quincy defines by lengthy anatomical discussions, such as brain, skin or heart (many columns of iatromechanical theorising in Quincy: in Johnson 'the muscle which by its contraction and dilation propels the blood through the course of circulation, and is therefore considered the source of vital motion') and to have modified, in the interests of elegance or propriety, several others, for example atheroma, catheter, or deobstruent. In the first definition of mad – 'disordered in the mind; broken in the understanding; distracted; delirious without a fever' – only the last phrase is Quincy. Johnson also supplied most of the definitions of the professional divisions of medicine, such as chirurgeon, barber, or empirick, in the process avoiding Quincy's violently anti-chymical bias. But it is not possible to see the *Dictionary* as embodying anything like a considered Johnsonian intervention in current medical debate.

In the compiling of the *Dictionary*'s illustrative quotations Johnson used as sources only seven strictly medical works, three of them by John Arbuthnot (*Essay concerning the Effects of Air on Human Bodies*, 1733, *Essay concerning the choice of Aliments*, 1735, and *Practical Rules of Diet*, 1736). He also – probably because he had it in his possession – used the book by Floyer published by Michael Johnson, *The Preternatural State of the Animal Humours described by their sensible qualities*, (1696), Gideon Harvey's *Morbus Anglicus; or the Anatomy of Consumptions*, (1st edition, 1676), and two works of surgery, Richard Wiseman's *Eight Chirurgical Treatises* (first published as *Several Chirurgical Treatises* in 1676) and Samuel Sharp's *A treatise of the Operations of Surgery*, first published in 1739.[46] Johnson though often illustrates words with a primarily medical significance from non-medical writers. Thus 'contagion' is illustrated by Shakespeare, 'humour' by Milton, 'lungs' by Dryden and Shakespeare. 'Marrow' is defined from Quincy and supported by illustrations from Shakespeare,

Bacon, *Hudibras* and Addison. Conversely, he uses his medical and surgical sources not just for medical or 'philosophic' words ('bedpost' and 'pearl', for instance, are illustrated from Wiseman). Sharp's *Surgery*, described as 'a book otherwise elegantly written', is found fault with for a false use of 'precariousness'. Floyer for 'slippery' uses 'slippy' which Johnson calls 'a barbarous provincial word'. The personal or idiosyncratic elements in the *Dictionary* tend inevitably to be exaggerated in any selection of definitions: so it seems important to say that the vast majority of the medical definitions are straightforward and orthodox, useful as a guide through the terminology of early and mid-eighteenth-century medical writings, but rarely involving any critical reflections upon past or present medical practice. It seems to me difficult to argue that either the definitions or the choice of quotations represent a particular medical school or point of view.

In his recent study of the *Dictionary*, though, Robert de Maria remarks on its 'largely satirical characterisation of the three professions' declaring, for instance, that it contains 'much satire on medical practice. Temple dismisses the whole art when he says "It is best to leave nature to her course [14] who is the sovereign physician in most diseases."'[47] This is a strained interpretation of Temple's Hippocratian remark, I think. One may question too whether 'satire' is appropriate to a work of compilation and definition, and which contains, necessarily, so many heterogeneous expressions of opinion. Johnson's very next definition of 'course' is 'catamenia' illustrated by Harvey, 'the stoppage of women's courses, if not suddenly looked to, sets them undoubtedly into a consumption, a dropsy, or some other dangerous disease' which implies a different view of medical intervention. Definition 10 quotes Wiseman to the same effect: 'The glands did resolve during the course of physick, and she continueth very well to this day.' Quotations under 'chirurgeon' also suggest that medical intervention is often necessary, even when everything seems to be going well. 'When a man's wounds cease to smart only because he has lost his feeling, they are nevertheless mortal, for his not seeing the need of a chirurgeon'. 'Nature could do nothing in her case without the help of surgery . . .' begins the quotation from Wiseman under the word 'chirurgical'. Under 'patient' Addison is quoted as saying 'A physician uses various methods for the recovery of sick persons; and though all of them are disagreeable, his patients are never angry'. Doubtless a hunt through the *Dictionary* would turn up many other instances: but why go on? Selection from its vast resources may appear to prove Johnson adopting many positions, but I doubt whether his quotations can be taken as a wholly reliable guide to his own opinions. Through its quotations the *Dictionary* does of course transmit a good deal of traditional scepticism about the profession, as well as praise for it. It will not be chance though that under 'leech', an old term for doctor, Johnson quotes Gay's praise of the physician who is its chief medical source:

> A skilful leach
> They say, had wrought this blessed deed;
> This leach Arbuthnot was yclept.

After the *Dictionary* was published in 1755, Johnson became connected with a short-lived publication called the *Literary Magazine*. The nature and extent of his contributions to this in 1756–7 have always been even more of a mystery than his work for Robert James. 'He engaged also to superintend and contribute largely to another monthly publication, entitled "The Literary Magazine or Universal Review"; the first number of which came out in May this year [1756]', writes Boswell. 'What were his emoluments from this undertaking, and what other writers were employed in it, I have not discovered. He continued to write in it, with intermissions, till the fifteenth number; and I think that he never gave better proofs of the force, acuteness and vivacity of his mind, than in this miscellany, whether we consider his original essays, or his reviews of the works of others'.[48] He lists twenty-six reviews said to be by Johnson some of which, like the articles on Admiral Byng, 'Hanway's Eight Day's Journey, and Essay on Tea', and 'A Free Inquiry into the Nature and Origin of Evil', Boswell says, 'I know he avowed'. The others are attributed 'from internal evidence'. Birkbeck Hill 'had no doubt' that Johnson, in addition, wrote the review of 'A True Account of Lisbon since the Earthquake', in the first number, but L. F. Powell thought this 'very doubtful'. Courtney and Nichol Smith attribute several more pieces to Johnson, and Bloom in *Samuel Johnson in Grub Street* lists over thirty pieces by Johnson. Donald Greene suggested that in addition to those reviews listed in Courtney, Johnson probably reviewed several other books, including two significant books on electricity, 'The Subtle Medium Proved' by Richard Lovett and 'Observations on a Series of Electrical Experiments by Dr. Hoadly and Mr Wilson'.[49] Greene argued that Johnson's contributions almost filled some numbers of the magazine, and that there was therefore no doubt that he was its editor. Donald Eddy in his monograph on the *Magazine* declines to accept these attributions by Greene, but suggests six more pieces previously unmentioned, including 'Mr Bower's Escape from Macerata' are by Johnson.[50]

Johnson might have enjoyed these latter-day disputes. Boswell was always keen to get from him a list of his works but he liked to evade the question. 'I once got from one of his friends', Boswell writes, 'a list, which there was pretty good reason to suppose was accurate, for it was written down in his presence by this friend [Bishop Percy] who numerated each article aloud, and had some of them mentioned to him by Mr Levett, in concert with whom it was made out; and Johnson, who heard all this, did not contradict it. But when I showed a copy of this list to him, and mentioned the evidence for its exactness, he laughed, and said, "I was willing to let them go on as they pleased, and never interfered"'.[51] (Boswell claims to have later got a revised and accurate list from Johnson, but if so Johnson did not include, or forgot, many items from the *Magazine*.) The same spirit of mystification can be detected in a letter which Johnson wrote to Robert Chambers at Oxford, 31 July 1756, thanking him for a contribution. 'I shall take care to send you the monthly [number] gratis, if you contribute to it. But you must not tell that I have any thing in it. For though it is known conjecturally I would not have it made certain.'[52]

This ambivalence has not simply provided puzzles for editors and scholars. It is intrinsic to the tone and flavour of the *Magazine*. Johnson had been a journalist in literary London for almost twenty years when 'he assumed or submitted to the office of a reviewer' as Sir John Hawkins puts it. He had succeeded in the great enterprise of the *Dictionary*: and the *Rambler* series, whilst not a great success financially, had immensely increased his reputation. His prestige was high, his style easily recognisable, imitated and parodied. The reviews in the *Literary Magazine* sometimes preserve that almost complete neutral anonymity usual in eighteenth-century reviewing. At other times the voice of the reviewer becomes a more evidently individual one and even emerges as an 'I' – stepping forward as a personality with views and experience of his own, freely giving them play over the material he is reviewing. While the decorum of anonymity is not broken, a personal experience is brought to bear; and in such instances the reader is free to assume that the authority speaking is Samuel Johnson. For instance there is a note in the second issue of the magazine on a letter about supposedly ancient characters cut on a stone found when the Black Swan Inn in Holborn was demolished. 'The curious author of the foregoing paper', the editor writes, 'seems a little misled by a desire too frequent among inquirers into past times, a desire to exalt every thing into remote antiquity. Whatever was meant by the numbers of this stone, they certainly do not intend the year in which it was thus engraved. The shape of the figures is modern, very modern. The numeral character of *four* was as lately as the fifteenth century of another form, as this exact inspector of the dates of old books very well knows ...'[53] After a long quotation in another review praising the fertility of the Ohio Colonies, Johnson writes: 'Upon these pompous paragraphs let a man whose course of life has acquainted him very little with American affairs venture to make a few observations'. Sometimes, as Greene says, reviews by (or attributed to) Johnson almost fill the *Magazine*. These different reviewing modes, sometimes moving or oscillating between the candid or impatient or ironic 'I' and the formal, neutral, summarising 'we', within the same review, stamp the pieces in the *Literary Magazine* with their unique quality.

The *Literary Magazine* was predominantly a political journal, but as Johnson's introductory preface 'To the Public' makes clear – and as the subsequent contents show – scientific discovery and innovation and particularly 'physiological discoveries' are important emphases:

Our regard will not be confined to Books; it will extend to all the productions of Science. Any new calculation, a commodious instrument, the discovery of any property in nature, or any new method of bringing known properties into use or view, shall be diligently treasured up wherever found ... We hope to find means of extending and perpetuating physiological discoveries, and with regard to this Article, and all others, intreat the assistance of curious and candid correspondents.

The *Literary Magazine* was not alone in this decade in offering scientific information to its readers. Both major magazines, the *London* and the *Gentleman's*, 'printed mathematical questions and solutions, remedies for every thing from snake bite to consumption and meteorological accounts. Charts and drawings of flora and fauna, lists of prizes to be granted by the society for the Encouragement of Arts, Manufactures and Commerce, and case histories submitted by physicians filled the pages of both major magazines', writes R. D. Spector.[54] Exactly the same miscellany is the *Literary Magazine*'s formula. What makes the difference is Johnson's distinctively sceptical, abrasive questioning of the scientific procedures or philosophical arguments in the books the *Literary Magazine* picks up for review.

Arthur Murphy remembered that his editorship of the *Literary Magazine* 'engrossed but little of Johnson's time. He resigned himself to indolence, took no exercise, rose about two, and then received the visits of his friends.'[55] Among the friends whose assistance Johnson obtained on the *Magazine* was Richard Bathurst, who contributed an article (signed 'R.B.') 'On the Inconveniences and Disorders arising from Strait lacing in Stays' to the first issue. Bathurst compares the bodies of European women distorted by what he calls 'these murdering machines' of stays to the bodies of 'children of naked people in Africa and America' of whom he speaks, he says, from 'my own experience'. In the second number of the *Magazine* is a review of *Physiological Essays* by Robert Whytt, long and detailed and informed (far more demanding than the usual medical contributions to the *Gentleman's Magazine*) which one would guess to be by a surgeon or physician, who may again be Bathurst. Certainly the author is someone close to the editor for he speaks of carrying out the 'professed design' of the magazine to take notice of all 'improvements in every art and science'. It is possible too, that Bathurst had something to do with the various geographical and natural history items which, after political commentary, take most space in the magazine: he had, after all, travelled widely and intended to publish a Geographical Dictionary. Another medical item in an early issue of the magazine, 'An Account of Worms in Animal Bodies' by Frank Nicholls, is reprinted from the *Philosophical Transactions* of the Royal Society. Nicholls had been Bathurst and Lawrence's old teacher. His anatomical lectures in the thirties, so a contemporary reported, had achieved 'a celebrity never attained by any other before or since. The novelty of his discoveries, the gracefulness of his manner, and the charms of his delivery, attracting to him, not only the medical people in every line, but persons of all ranks, and all professions, who crowded upon him from every quarter'. Though his fame was eclipsed by Hunter and Cheselden, Nicholls was still the King's physician until 'turned out' in favour of a Scotsman by Bute in 1760. Johnson told Boswell that he had 'somewhere or other' given an account of Nicholls' *De Anima Machina* (1751), but this has never been found. I suspect that it lies concealed as a 'digression' contained in Lawrence's Latin *Medical Lectures (Praelectiones Medicae)* of 1758.[56]

Another old familiar of Johnson puts in an appearance in the

Magazine's pages. In the tenth number a review of a book purporting to offer 'an easy short and certain method of treating persons bit by mad animals' ends with an attack on the *Critical Review* whose authors, it is claimed, 'have stepped out of their road to rob Dr James of the honour of his invention of curing this disorder by means of mercury'. The tone of this note – 'People should learn to read before they write. Had these gentleman ever read the philosophical transactions they might have known that this discovery was made by Dr *James* in the year 1731 . . .'[57] – suggests that if this is not James himself it may be his fellow proprietor in the fever powders, the man who, Murphy remarks, got Johnson his job on the *Literary Magazine*, John Newbery.

Johnson himself reviews only one book which can be thought of as directly on a medical or 'physiological' topic. This is Dr Lucas' 'Essay on Waters'. Indirectly, or incidentally, in the course of reviews on topics as diverse as Newton's metaphysics, the use of ventilators in ships, electrical experiments, the history of Aleppo, the drinking of tea and the origin of evil, he remarks on many matters which come within the compass of the medical world. The piece on the 'Essay on Waters', like all of these other reviews on scientific topics, is concerned to critically assess the validity of the author's conclusions, whether these are inferred from experiments or arrived at through reasoning. Thus Johnson, though admitting that 'to discuss it fully would require more time than I am willing to bestow on it', shows that an experiment cited by Lucas is worthless, since no measurements are taken and there are no adequate controls. 'So useless are these trials, which an elegant writer has lately degraded to their proper rank by the name of *bruta experientia* unless theory brings her light to direct their application.'[58] (The writer was Thomas Lawrence.) After giving a long extract concerning Lucas's recommendation for the use of medicinal baths the impersonal reviewer – 'we shall venture the following remarks' – relaxes into his alternative mode, in the famous words:

It is incident to physicians, I am afraid, beyond all other men, to mistake subsequence for consequence, to use the fallacious inference *post hoc*, ergo *propter hoc*. 'The old gentleman' says Dr Lucas, that uses the cold bath, 'enjoys in return an uninterrupted state of health'. This instance does not prove that the cold bath produces health, but only, that it will not always destroy it. He is well with the bath, he would have been well without it. I have known, every man has known, old men scrupulously careful to avoid cold, who enjoyed in return an uninterrupted state of health.

The caution not to bathe with a full stomach is just, though it is violated every summer day without hurt.

The rules about the posture to be used in the bath, and the directions to forbear to speak during the action of the water, are refinements too minute to deserve attention, he is past much hope from baths to whom speech or silence can make any difference ...[59]

These remarks on physicians are followed in the *Magazine* by two pieces by medical men – 'An Account of Worms by Frank Nicholls, M.D. Med. Reg. F.R.S.', already mentioned, and 'A Proposal to restore the hearing when injured from an obstruction of the *Tuba Eustachiana*. By Mr Jonathan Wathen, surgeon in Devonshire Square', also taken from the *Philosophical Transactions*. This piece cites six cases, five out of whom found relief from a procedure to cleanse the Eustachian tubes through the nose. It is, as one might expect, rather more convincing than most of the 'cures' or remedies reported on anecdotal evidence in the magazines: there, anecdotal evidence seems always to be thought sufficient to establish the reality of a 'cure'. So it is worth pointing out that Johnson's comments on Lucas imply the principle of the controlled trial, first made use of by James Lind on board the *Salisbury* in 1747 to demonstrate the efficacy of lemon-juice against scurvy.

The next piece in this issue (No. 5, 15 August – 15 September 1756) of the *Literary Magazine* is one of the items over which there is dispute. It begins 'Electricity is the great discovery of the present age, and the great object of philosophical curiosity. It is perhaps designed by providence for the excitement of human industry, that the qualities of bodies should be discovered gradually from time to time'. A long and interesting extract from Lovett's book follows, which includes an account of a primitive battery. Also disputed is the next review 'Observations on a series of Electrical Experiments' By Dr Hoadly and Mr Wilson', which includes these sentiments:

[T]o create a matter so different from all other matter so as to gravitate only toward itself, is perhaps one of the arts of a philosopher unwilling to be silent when he has nothing to say. Surely the *primum mobile* with the cycles and epicycles afforded solutions with which importunity might be equally silenced and curiosity equally satisfied.

If we apply the rule-of-thumb clue to the detection of Johnson's style already mentioned – 'perhaps' prefacing a resoundingly definite pronouncement – we shall readily ascribe this piece to him. Hoadly and Wilson assume the existence of 'aether', which (says the reviewer), 'is perhaps but *materia subtilis* with a new name', solely upon the authority of Newton. With these remarks one can compare the accepted review of Newton's *Four letters* to Dr Bentley:

> Let it not be thought irreverence to this great name, if I observe, that by *matter evenly spread* through infinite space, he now finds it necessary to mean *matter not evenly spread*. Matter *not evenly* spread will indeed convene, but it will convene as soon as it exists. And, in my opinion, this puzzling question about matter is only, how *that could be that never could have been*, or what a man thinks on when he thinks on nothing.[60]

The evidence of Johnson's scientific acumen and medical knowledge in these reviews then, is incidental and fragmentary. Another instance in the *Literary Magazine* is the long review of *The Natural History of Aleppo* by a doctor, Alexander Russell, which includes a long paraphrase of Russell's account of the Aleppo disease, and its treatment, with the characteristic remark on a therapeutic recommendation 'the vertues of rue to resist infection [are], I fear, imaginary'. Johnson's comments on practical medicine are confined to such brevities and asides as these. Yet there is no doubt that medical issues, in the broadest sense, occupied some of his most earnest thinking in these mid century years.

Charity and cruelty

Johnson's most famous pieces in the *Literary Magazine* are his reviews of the philanthropist Jonas Hanway's *Journal of an Eight Days Journey ..., to which is added an essay on Tea, considered as pernicious to health, obstructing industry, and impoverishing the Nation*, and his review of the littérateur Soame Jenyns' *On the Nature and Origin of Evil*. The review of Hanway's book has some medically interesting things to say about the practice of drinking tea, but it is more significant because of Johnson's comments, more or less incidental, on Hanway's favourite charity, the Foundling Hospital. The review of Soame Jenyns is very well known, but it shows differently in this context, revealing in the course of its parodies of Jenyns' propositions just how deeply Johnson had responded to current medical developments. No. 17 of the *Idler*, an essay published less than a year later, underlines how thoroughly Johnson's disturbance was informed by knowledge of contemporary physiological practices. The two reviews show different faces of the journalist Johnson, and I shall use them to discuss his response to the two most significant features of the contemporary medical world: the proliferation of charity hospitals and the rise of experimental physiology, phenomena that were ultimately connected, since the hospitals were to be the laboratories of the new medical science. Together with *Idler* 17, they enable one to present Johnson as informed witness, on the one hand, to the growth of charity in its medical guise; on the other to the medical guise of cruelty.

One of the most well-known of the *Idler* essays, No. 4 (6 May 1758) is a discourse on the charity of the present age, which, as Johnson suggests, has been exemplified above all in the foundation of hospitals. He was looking back on three decades of philanthropic activity. 'The most apparent and pressing miseries incident to man have now their peculiar houses of reception and relief', he declares. 'Between 1719 and 1750, five new general hospitals were founded in the Metropolis, along with nine in the country, a figure which reached thirty-one by 1800', writes David Owen, the historian of English philanthropy.[61] The London hospitals were the Westminster (1719), Guy's (1725), St George's (1733), the London (1740), and the Middlesex (1745). They were founded largely through the efforts of individuals, by whom, as Johnson later remarked to Boswell, 'the rest are driven on'.[62] One such determined promoter was Dr Thomas Talbot, to whom Johnson lent a hand in the writing of his *Address to the nobility, gentry and clergy of the County of Hereford*, his third attempt to muster up support for the building of a county Infirmary. There Johnson notes that the building of a hospital is a project 'which all the maxims of wisdom, and all the duties of charity conspire to recommend'.[63] The hospitals were paid for by voluntary contributions, and as *Idler* 4 makes clear, they were envisaged as hospices as much as infirmaries. Contributors were 'nobility, gentry and clergy'; patients or inmates were members of the servant or labouring classes. As the plans of purpose-built hospital buildings make plain, the chapel was often the focal point of the design.

To follow the arguments and petitions which led to the establishment of the Exeter hospital in 1741 (which occupy many pages in the *Gentleman's Magazine* during the years of Johnson's connection with the journal) is to see clearly just how mixed were the motives which led to such foundations. In the 'Historical Chronicle' for September 1741 is an account of the laying of the Hospital's foundation stone, the fervour of which reminds one of the atmosphere in Blake's poem in *Songs of Innocence* about the children of the charity schools, 'Holy Thursday', half a century later (and raises the same suspicions):

A very great Number of Gentlemen *of every Party*, Benefactors to the Hospital, met together at the *Chapel House* of *St Peter*, from whence they walk'd in solemn Procession, attended by the City Musick, to *Southernhay*, where a Party of Soldiers was drawn up, who favoured them with Three Volleys of Small Arms ... There were several Thousand People, who had the Pleasure of seeing the Solemnity, and there was not one Murmur heard. Every Heart was full of Joy, too great to be express'd, and which can be imagin'd only by those who delight in the Happiness of their *Fellow Creatures*. The Air was filled with the Universal Shouts of the Multitude. The *Rich* rejoiced exceedingly that they were to be the happy Instruments of so great a Blessing to their Country, and the *Poor* echo'd back their Acclamations of Joy with Blessings upon their Pious and Generous Benefactors. Such a Day of Gladness has not been known here for many Years ...[64]

At the same time some of the impulses that led to the foundation of the hospitals were scientific and medical. There is no doubt that some members of the profession understood that the Hospital would serve as a laboratory for the advancement of scientific medicine.[65] As Talbot's *Address* puts, it, 'It is moreover, expedient to have a variety of disorders collected together, for the instruction of young students; who, by attending the practice of learned and experienced physicians and surgeons, in such hospitals, gain more knowledge in a few months than by private business can be obtained in several years ...'[66] Poor patients might be better cared for in the hospital than at home, though that was by no means certain; but only in the hospital could the profession act freely and pursue the advancement of knowledge freed from the whims and interference of the wealthy patron-patient. (It was, of course, a social advantage for a doctor to have a place on the board of a hospital.) Literally hundreds of doctors were 'Boerhaave's men'. (Among them was that Thomas Attwood of Worcester whom Johnson's parents consulted about his eye troubles – and Boswell's uncle John.) At Leyden or Utrecht English and Scotsmen had been taught by methods far more advanced and efficient than the traditional lectures at Oxford or Cambridge – they had learned medicine at the bedside of the patient. These men naturally brought back to England a belief in the value of bedside consultation and training which for most of them could only be achieved as it was in Holland in the public hospital.[67] As the London Hospital Sermon for 1754 put it 'the art of Healing is improved ... by frequent Occasions for able Professors to consult, and ingenious Candidates to learn from them, to the common Advantage of all Ranks of Men'.[68] Thus charitable, benevolent, scientific and as far as the profession was concerned, self-interested motives were blended. And middle-class eagerness to subscribe to such institutions had a good deal to do, too, with fears – widespread in the early eighteenth century – that the population was declining, and to the demand for labour.[69] Modern historians stress that the hospitals were agencies of social control: places, certainly, where the sick might be healed, but equally importantly where the poor might be taught their duty to their betters and where the Gospels might be propagated. The Foundling Hospital or, to give it its correct name, the Hospital for the Maintenance and Education of Exposed and Deserted Young Children, which (after overcoming objections that it would encourage vice and illegitimacy) opened its doors in 1741 was not a hospital in the modern sense. (The first for Sick Children – Great Ormond Street – was not opened until 1853.) The foundling infants were baptised on the Sunday after admission with such names as Michael Angelo, Clarissa Harlowe and John Milton. (The initial practice of naming the children after the Governors had been found to cause embarrassment.) By the middle of the century, the Foundling Hospital was London's most fashionable charity, but children were still turned away from its doors.[70] The Governors' application for Parliamentary support was granted in 1756 (it coincided with the outbreak of the Seven Years War and the fear that the future might not provide sufficient food for powder). There followed the years of the General Reception: infants flooded in, overwhelming the Hospital's resources, at the rate of a hundred or more a week. In November 1756 Samuel Johnson accompanied some ladies on a visit to the wards, and commented on what he found there in the course of his review of Hanway's book in the *Literary Magazine* for May 1757.

Before looking at these comments, let us consider Johnson's response to Hanway's main argument. The persona of the reviewer is mischievous and relaxed, but Johnson does attend to Hanway's arguments about tea with careful analysis. Hanway claims, for instance, that 'The Chinese use little green tea, imagining that it hinders digestion and excites fevers'. 'How it should have either effect', Johnson replies, 'is not easily discovered, and if we consider the innumerable prejudices which prevail concerning our own plants, [a point made in the Proposals for the *Medicinal Dictionary*] we shall very little regard those opinions of the Chinese vulgar, which experience does not confirm.' Hanway denies that the crews of Chinese ships are saved from scurvy, as was reported, by drinking tea: the reviewer replies, 'About this report I have made some enquiry and though I cannot find that these crews are wholly exempt from scorbutic maladies; they seem to suffer them less than other mariners in any course of equal length. This I ascribe to the tea not as possessing any medicinal qualities, but as tempting them to drink more water, to dilute their salt food more copiously; and perhaps to forbear punch, or other strong liquors': cogent enough reasoning, but showing that Johnson was apparently ignorant of James Lind's work. Yet the second edition of Lind's *Treatise on the Scurvy* is reviewed in the next number of the *Magazine*, as is his *Essay on the most effectual means of preserving the health of seamen.*[71] This can only mean that, if Johnson had taken the role of editorial supervisor for the earlier issues of the magazine, he had relinquished it by this time, April – May 1757. If Johnson's information was correct, the diminished incidence of scurvy among the tea-drinking Chinese may have been due to their habit – one Hanway notes and recommends – of 'drinking it sometimes with acids'.

Among the other mischiefs of tea, Hanway claims it is an emetic. 'He afterwards quotes Paulli to prove that tea is a *dessicative and ought not to be used after the fortieth year.* I have then long exceeded the limits of permission, but I comfort myself, that all of the enemies of tea cannot be in the right. If tea be dessicative according to Paulli, it cannot weaken the fibres, as our author imagines; if it be emetic it must contringe the stomach, rather than relax it.' But when Hanway joins to his attack on tea a diatribe against 'spiritous liquors' Johnson's tone changes and the impersonal editorial 'we' becomes the endorser of a statement in his most solemn manner. Paradoxically though, this impersonal address can be read as a veil thrown over a more shameful confession than that of drinking tea:

From tea the author digresses to spiritous liquors, about which he will have no controversy with the *Literary Magazine*, we shall therefore insert almost his whole letter, and add it to our testimony, that the mischiefs arising on every side from this compendious mode of drunkenness are enormous and insupportable; equally to be found among the great and the mean; filling palaces with disquiet and distraction, harder to be born, *as it cannot be mentioned*; and overwhelming multitudes with incurable diseases and unpitied poverty.(my italics)[72]

Perhaps behind this lies the memory of Tetty Johnson, 'always drunk and reading romances in her Bed' according to Robert Levet. Tetty had died in 1752.

Throughout the review Johnson insists that tea has no 'medicinal qualities'. He calls it a 'watery luxury', 'an insipid entertainment': 'it neither exhilarates the heart nor stimulates the palate'. He was, of course, mistaken. Tea, at least drunk in the quantities he drank it, often a dozen cups at a time (though eighteenth-century tea cups were smaller than ours) is a stimulant and a diuretic. Less well-known than these properties is the fact that it contains a rare alkaloid, theophylline, which is not found, for instance, in coffee. Theophylline stimulates heart muscle and relaxes involuntary muscles like the muscles of the bronchial tubes. Synthetic compounds of this substance ('aminothyll-ine') have been used widely in more recent years to relieve bronchial spasm. Just conceivably, then, Johnson's addiction to tea, rather than exacerbating his indigestion, as is sometimes claimed, may have brought him this side-benefit.

Hanway, already interested in the Foundling Hospital, of which he became a life Governor the following year, declares that, whatever dreadful abuses occur in the workhouses, in the hospital the children are guarded from both tea and gin. Johnson now switches into the personal mode: 'I know not upon what observation Mr Hanway founds his confidence in the governors of the *Foundling Hospital*', he writes, 'men of whom I have not any knowledge, but whom I intreat to consider a little the minds as well as bodies of the children'. The reviewer's previously established good-humour and open-minded-ness make his next comment the more biting: 'I am inclined to believe irreligion equally pernicious with gin and tea, and therefore think it is not unseasonable to mention, that when a few months ago I wandered through the hospital, I found not a child that seemed to have heard of his creed or the commandments. To breed up children in this manner, is to rescue them from an early grave, that they may find employment for the gibbet; from dying in innocence, that they may perish by their crimes.' *Idler* 4 was insistently to set the foundation of the hospitals, of their various kinds, within a Christian context. No ancient civilisation had provided a model for such benevolence; only the light of Revelation could have prompted charity which was more than casual or occasional. It would follow logically that the hospitals themselves could not educate or reclaim except through the agency of the gospels. Johnson's comment, and the fuss it caused, indicate forcefully that, whilst the foundation of the hospitals was certainly in one sense a manifestation of Enlightenment secularism, their socially reclamatory function was perceived as quite central.

Johnson's criticism of the religious education of the children of the Foundling Hospital was picked up and reprinted in two London newspapers, the *London Chronicle* and the *Gazeteer*. Its authorship was obviously known for it was ascribed to 'a truly good Man and very able Writer'.[73] The Governors of the Hospital seem to have been very sensitive to an allegation that might put the continuance of Parliamentary support – still in its first year – in jeopardy, and they were determined to find out who this author was. They ordered their solicitor to visit the offices of the two newspapers and the *Literary Magazine* and to insist on the disclosure of the reviewer's name.

The publisher of the *Magazine*, Richardson, refused to cooperate. He steadfastly 'denied that it was in his power to disclose the Author'. Meanwhile, Hanway, in characteristic fashion, had rushed into print with a letter to the *Gazeteer* of 26 May. He seems to have defended himself from every possible charge a paranoid imagination could have detected in Johnson's review and to have included some threat that its author should 'consult [his] safety when [he] talks of corporations'. The Governors of the Hospital took steps, in the face of Richardson's intransigence, to carry out that threat. They ordered their solicitor to consult with the Attorney General and seem to have envisaged a criminal prosecution for libel. Since the Hospital was now supported both by the King and Parliament, 'a charge that the Governors were breeding up children in irreligion might', as Ruth McClure writes, 'be interpreted by a judge as seditious because it reflected on an agency of the King's government'.[74]

Johnson's *Reply* to Hanway, which was published in the *Literary Magazine* of 15 May – 15 June 1757, may have been instigated by the journal's proprietors, for it is the only time he is known to have replied to criticism. But if so, and if 'the threat of a lawsuit for libel was hanging over his head' no sign of anxiety or appeasement is detectable in the piece.[75] Johnson explicitly defends himself, repeats his allegations, and declares he has witnesses, concluding

He has, however, so much kindness for me, that he advises me to consult my safety when I talk of corporations. I know not what the most important corporation can do, becoming manhood, by which my safety is endangered. My reputation is safe, for I can prove the fact; my quiet is safe, for I meant well; and for any other safety, I am not used to be very sollicitous.[76]

And just to prove the point, the rest of the *Reply* is a devastatingly mock-serious apologia which contrives to make Hanway, the Governor of the Hospital, who keeps horses to his carriage, appear preposterously self-important, whilst his antagonist, the journalist, availing himself of the privilege of anonymity, nimbly and easily scores unanswerable points against him. Johnson is perfectly in control and sure of his ground, perhaps because he knew that he spoke, in this instance, for an unimpeachable establishment position.

The case, it is usually agreed, is startlingly different with Johnson's review of what the *London Magazine* called 'a very little but a very wicked book'[77], Soame Jenyns' *A Free Inquiry into the Nature and Origin of Evil*, the second part of which appeared in the same number of the *Literary Magazine*, though Jenyns was merely a literary gentleman and Hanway may have had the power of government behind him. This review is printed in three instalments over the three issues of the magazine in 1757 (the divisions seem quite arbitrary).[78] It is the last Johnson contributed to the *Magazine*, in some important respects a summation of his work on the journal and the most significant of these writings on medical or paramedical topics. The review is a product of hack journalism. Unstructured, repetitious, written against the clock (the reviewer speaks of 'the present haste of this extract') the piece eloquently bespeaks the conditions, medical, social and economic, under which it was produced.

Its roughness is part of its effectiveness. The manner is that of one who is hard-pressed both by the difficulty of the topics under discussion, and by the conditions under which these harrowing problems must be discussed. In contrast to the urbane irony of the Hanway review the first paragraphs are angry, abrupt and rude: 'When this speculist finds himself prompted to another performance, let him consider whether he is about to disburthen his mind or employ his fingers, and if I might venture to offer him a subject, I should wish that he would solve this question, why he that has nothing to write should desire to be a writer?' It becomes clear, though, that this antipathy to Soame Jenyns partly deflects another kind of disturbance or dismay in the writer. After a long quotation from Jenyns on the chain of being has been transcribed, a rather different reaction is defined. 'This doctrine of the regular subordination of beings, the scale of existence I have often considered', Johnson writes, 'but always left the enquiry in doubt and uncertainty.' Pausing after a critical analysis of the logic of the chain of being he says 'To these meditations humanity is unequal'. As still more taxing issues are thrown up by Jenyns' material this note of personal incapacity or distress comes to predominate in whole paragraphs of the review, which has far more discussion and commentary in proportion to extracts than other eighteenth-century reviews, as if the reviewer were compelled, however reluctantly, to face and elucidate dilemmas he finds almost insupportable and to disclose the most painful parts of his own history. 'That hope and fear are inseparably or very frequently connected with poverty and riches, my surveys of life have not informed me' may just manage to preserve a magisterial irony, but instances of reluctant involvement begin to tell a different story. 'This author and Pope perhaps never saw the miseries which they imagine thus easy to be borne'; 'the compensations of sickness I have never found near to equivalence, and the transports of recovery only prove the intenseness of the pain'; 'I cannot forbear to observe, that I never yet knew disorders of the mind increase felicity ...'

'I am always afraid of deciding on the side of envy or cruelty', he writes again. 'The privileges of education may sometimes be improperly bestowed, but I shall always fear to withhold them, lest I should be yielding to the suggestions of pride, while I persuade myself that I am following the maxims of policy; and under the appearance of salutary restraints, should be indulging the lust of dominion, and that malevolence which delights in seeing others depressed.' To some extent here Johnson is modelling, demonstrating what an appropriate scrupulousness on these issues might be like. The twists of the syntax, however, catching the mind in the act of self-deception, vividly embody the treacherous alternatives from which it suffers.

I do not mean to reproach the author for not knowing what is equally hidden from learning and from ignorance. The shame is to impose words for ideas upon ourselves or others. To imagine that we are going forward when we are only turning round. To think that there is any difference between him that gives no reason, and him that gives a reason that by his own confession cannot be understood.

Here, too, the anger and impatience is inseparable from anguish and frustration. Johnson is bullying Jenyns, but at the same time the abrupt truncated syntax gives dramatic expression to a mind locked in the prison of repetitive, fruitless questioning. In passages like these the review demonstrates, perforce, the reviewer's mental suffering. This is important, since the reality of pain, of suffering, is what is at issue.

Jenyns' Olympian point-of-view – that evil in the part is necessary to the good of the whole – does not recognise the reality of that suffering which its purpose is to explain. In its blindness, its lack of experience but especially of imagination, his philosophy is cruel: and it is the implicit cruelty, I think, not the complacency or conservatism or even the intellectual confusion of this elegant piece of *belles-lettres* which maddens Johnson.

The review's context is significant in a number of ways. The leading article of *Magazine* No. 10, January – February 1757, is 'An Account of Robert Francis Damiens, who attempted to stab Lewis XV as he was stepping into his coach', which ends in a gruesome recital of the infamous punishments inflicted on the would-be assassin: 'The art of torturing is now arrived to a very refined species of cruelty', says the writer, apparently with approval, 'lest this wretch should have taken poison, an emetic was instantly given him; and every artifice that can both prolong his life and at the same time give him the most exquisite pain is studied by the physicians. Thus does this abominable madman remain to be excruciated in every manner human wit can devise.' One of the ghastly and prolonged tortures devised for Damiens was 'that he should be dragged to the place of execution, and on a scaffold have his flesh torn off with red hot pincers from his breasts, arms, legs and thighs . . .' As Donald Greene has pointed out, this horrifying image embedded itself in Johnson's imagination, to come to the surface again as he angrily refutes Jenyns' complacent picture of what living in poverty means: 'The poor indeed are insensible of many little vexations which sometimes embitter the possessions and pollute the enjoyment of the rich. They are not pained by casual incivility, or mortified by the mutilation of a compliment; but this happiness is like that of a malefactor who ceases to feel the cords that bind him when the pincers are tearing his flesh.' Johnson's indignation and anger at Jenyns' bland ignorance and complacent self-sufficiency here combine with a horrified memory of torture – torture devised by physicians – to produce a scathing metaphor in which the suffering of the writer whose imagination has borne the image is as strong an ingredient as the suffering of those he depicts.

This horror at the possible perversions of medical and philosophic experimentation is the main imaginative ingredient in the review of *A Free Inquiry*'s most powerful passage. Jenyns ventures to suggest that there are beings higher in the scale than ourselves, who bear the same relation to us, as we do to the animals, and who in Johnson's paraphrase 'may deceive, torment, or destroy us for the ends only of their own pleasure or utility'. Johnson then develops this hint:

> I cannot resist the temptation of contemplating this analogy, which I think he might have carried further very much to the advantage of his argument. He might have shewn that these *hunters whose game is man* have many sports analogous to our own. As we drown whelps and kittens, they amuse themselves now and then with sinking a ship, and stand round the fields of Blenheim or the walls of Prague, as we encircle a cock-pit. As we shoot a bird flying, they take a man in the midst of his business or pleasure, and knock him down with an apoplexy. Some of them, perhaps, are virtuosi, and delight in the operations of an asthma, as a human philosopher in the operations of the air-pump. To swell a man with a tympany is as good sport as to blow a frog. Many a merry bout have these frolic beings at the vicissitudes of an ague, and good sport it is to see a man tumble with an epilepsy, and revive and tumble again, and all this he knows not why. As they are wiser and more powerful than we, they have more exquisite diversions, for we have no way of procuring any sport so brisk and so lasting as the paroxysms of the gout and stone which undoubedly must make high mirth, especially if the play be a little diversified with the blunders and puzzles of the blind and deaf. We know not how far their sphere of observation may extend. Perhaps now and then a merry being may place himself in such a situation as to enjoy at once all the varieties of an epidemical disease, or amuse his leisure with the tossings and contortions of every possible pain exhibited together.

The rhetorical expansion of the original conceit expresses the writer's savage relief at being freed for a moment from the tormenting and perplexing issues he has been forced to think about. An exercise of imaginative power, a release, a strange pleasure ('I cannot resist the temptation . . .') fills out this analogy. Parallel examples come quickly and easily to a mind that relishes seeing how neat the analogy can be made to seem. The accumulated instances thus bestow upon the notion that human beings are the play-things of a capricious and cruel will a kind of momentary but appalling plausibility, whilst the grammatical structure of the sentences, approaching the same topic from a different direction each time, conveys a sense of mastery that replicates, whilst it parodies, the predatory ingenuities of these gods. At the same time, the imagining of so much pain, in so much detail, for whatever purpose, is painful, and the effect of that pain is to intensify the writer's savage anger towards Jenyns. Penetrating it all is an unconscious knowledge that pain begets cruelty, and this in a mind as scruptilous as Johnson's augments its disturbance.

More sober, more sage pronouncements follow, and then the idea returns obsessively:

[A] set of beings unseen and unheard, are hovering about us, trying experiments upon our sensibility, putting us into agonies to see our limbs quiver, torturing us to madness, that they may laugh at our vagaries, sometimes obstructing the bile, that they may see how a man looks when he is yellow; sometimes breaking a traveller's bones to try how he will get home, sometimes wasting a man to a skeleton, and sometimes killing him fat for the greater elegance of his hide.

This is an account of natural evil which though, like the rest, not quite new is very entertaining, though I know not how much it may contribute to patience.

The phrase 'trying experiments upon our sensibility' suggests how much Johnson's horror had been aroused by the experiments implied in Whytt's *Physiological Essays*. The writer's imagination – once given the hint – is fertile with examples of human suffering so bizarre, so unearned, that it cannot resist shaping and expressing them, releasing at the same time its hatred of the insignificant object that has caused its own suffering. But this indulgence precipitates a sense of exhaustion and futility, a weakly dis missive ending to the paragraph, and the final threadbare irony of 'very entertaining'.

In these passages of the review the text presents graphic images of physical pain, whilst its broader movement, its shifts and turbulences of feeling, its angry rhythms simultaneously communicate mental torture. It is partly the pain of filling one's imagination with such horrors, but more deeply it is the pain of finding that one is left 'in doubt and uncertainty'. The disarray communicates the devastating effect that being forced to confront both horrors and the metaphysical problems they focus has upon the writer's composure. The review of *A Free Enquiry* thus occupies an exceptional place among Johnson's paramedical writings. Much more of his work touches on or discourses upon suffering: this piece may well be said to portray it. *The Rambler*, *Rasselas* and the letters, for instance, discuss many painful matters but they do so in a manner which is sober and purposive, in rhythms and cadences which communicate reassurance, and whose firmly ordered sentence patterns and controlled ironies imply a structured, comprehensible world. There are memorably temperate statements in the review but its central significance in the Johnsonian canon is inseparable from its fracturing of that composure, its exposure of his vulnerability, anger and torment, and the painfully unresolved questions that lie beneath the sage gravity of his usual public persona.

Naturally readers, too, are disturbed in different ways. 'However famous the Jenyns review may be, it must be noted that the display of outrage in the piece is somewhat uncharacteristic, particularly the shrill *ad hominem* attack on a writer whom one would expect Johnson to overlook as unworthy of his time and energy', writes Richard Schwartz in a book devoted to discussion of the piece.[79] If one situates the review within its context, it is possible to understand Johnson's antipathy to Jenyns more clearly. His work on the *Magazine* (and elsewhere) shows his to be a mind passionately devoted to scientific truth, as Schwartz himself has shown, continually aware of the caution and diligence its pursuit entails and valuing truth because of its usefulness in the service of mankind. To such a mind empty speculation is anathema, and speculation – easy, seductive, offering the gratifying illusion of thought – is what Soame Jenyns' work contained. Johnson's attack, which has offended so many scholarly ears polite (another writer calls it 'overly zealous') is vehement partly because Jenyns' piece is a representative antithesis of the work the *Literary Magazine* hoped to publicise. Jenyns contrasts with, for instance, the 'pious' and 'candid' author of *Collateral Bee-Boxes; or a new, easy, and advantageous method of managing Bees*, reviewed in the first number, 'willing to communicate his knowledge for the advantage of others, and careful to learn before he presumes to teach', who spent forty years perfecting his project, or the more famous Stephen Hales, the review of whose *An Account of A Useful Discovery* begins, 'This is another of the labours of a life spent in the service of mankind'.

In some ways in fact the review is a conscious summation and valediction to Johnson's work on the *Literary Magazine*. 'Of the productions of the last bounteous year, how many can be said to serve any purpose of use or pleasure', he exclaims: it was precisely a year since Johnson had begun work as reviewer on the *Magazine*. Its first issue, announced for February, was delayed for months until it appeared undated in May 1756. Johnson was ill during December 1755 'with a cough so violent that I once fainted under its convulsions'; during January and February an inflammation in his good eye made it almost impossible for him to read or write. He was attended by Dr Lawrence, who was also treating Johnson's beloved friend Hill Boothby, but she died on 16 January, and Johnson was grief-stricken. The paucity of letters for these months is eloquent. Two that he did write are to Samuel Richardson, one appealing to him, the other thanking him for a loan.[80] On 16 March Johnson was arrested for a debt of five pounds, eighteen shillings. 'Poverty', as he writes in the review, 'in its easier and more tolerable degree, is little more than necessity of labour, and, in its more severe and deplorable state, little more than inability for labour'. The review is a powerful and disturbing work then because Johnson's personal condition as well as his intellectual dilemmas are unwillingly expressed through it. Of all Dr Johnson's writings it is the one which represents him most fully in the position of the patient.

Johnson and vivisection

The Soame Jenyns review, as Leopold Damrosch remarks, 'has to a remarkable degree resonances throughout his other writings'.[81] One of these is certainly *Idler* 17, which is as disturbing as and more puzzling than the review. Disturbing, in this instance, because it concerns vivisection, the use of living animals in laboratory experiments, a subject that arouses violent passions and intense controversy from that day to this, because the essay vividly depicts the sufferings of the animals, and because of the essay's impassioned revulsion and indignation. Puzzling, because the actual sources of that outrage are unclear in the essay itself and have remained obscure despite the fact that it has been frequently reprinted and so widely referred to as to have become a classic of 'anti-vivisection' literature.[82]

The *Idler* essay first appeared, like the others in the series, on the front page of a newspaper called the *Universal Gazette*, on Saturday, 5 August 1758. The readers of the paper, accustomed to the lightweight, relaxed style that Johnson adopted for the series, each shorter than his earlier *Rambler* and *Adventurer* essays, must have been disconcerted when its whimsical opening commentary, first on the weather and then on the foibles of amateur scientists, suddenly became intensely serious:

> The Idlers that sport only with inanimate nature may claim some indulgence; if they are useless, they are still innocent: but there are others, whom I know not how to mention without more emotion than my love of quiet willingly admits. Among the inferior professors of medical knowledge, is a race of wretches, whose lives are only varied by varieties of cruelty; whose favourite amusement is to nail dogs to tables and open them alive; to try how long life may be continued in various degrees of mutilation, or with the

excision or laceration of the vital parts; to examine whether burning irons are felt more acutely by the bone or tendon; and whether the more lasting agonies are produced by poison forced into the mouth, or injected into the veins.

It is not without reluctance that I offend the sensibility of the tender mind with images like these. If such cruelties were not practised, it were to be desired that they should not be conceived; but, since they are published every day with ostentation, let me be allowed once to mention them, since I mention them with abhorrence.

Mead has invidiously remarked of Woodward, that he gathered shells and stones and would pass for a philosopher. With pretensions much less reasonable, the anatomical novice tears out the living bowels of an animal, and stiles himself physician, prepares himself by familiar cruelty for that profession which he is to exercise upon the tender and the helpless, upon feeble bodies and broken minds, and by which he has opportunities to extend his arts of torture, and continue those experiments upon infancy and age, which he has hitherto tried upon cats and dogs.

These hateful practices, Johnson says, have been defended as necessary to the pursuit of knowledge, but the truth is, he declares

that by knives, fire and poison, knowledge is not always sought, and is very seldom attained. The experiments that have been tried, are tried again; he that burned an animal with irons yesterday, will be willing to amuse himself with burning another tomorrow. I know not, that by living dissections any discovery has been made by which a single malady is more easily cured. And if the knowledge of physiology has been somewhat encreased, he surely buys knowledge dear, who learns the use of the lacteals at the expense of his humanity. It is time that universal resentment should arise against these horrid operations, which tend to harden the heart, extinguish those sensations which give man confidence in man, and make the physician more dreadful than the gout or stone.[83]

This essay was reprinted in the *Gentleman's Magazine* for August under the heading 'On the Practice of Dissecting Animals'.

Johnson's style, in the *Idler* as elsewhere in his essays, is a generalising one. No particular doctors are named, as no particular hospitals were named in *Idler* 4, yet the essay is filled with clues which suggest that Johnson had specific targets in mind, and perhaps specific memories of reported experiments. The piece is informed with an outrage that obviously relates to some fairly recent provocation, and the obvious implication of the declaration that these experiments are 'published every day with ostentation' is that Johnson and his contemporaries were bombarded with reports of such experiments, though none seem to have been reported in the *Universal Gazette* itself. But the clues are nevertheless very confusing, and seem to take us in different directions. Johnson speaks of 'the inferior professors of medical knowledge' and of 'anatomical novices', phrases themselves not easy to reconcile. Nor do anatomical novices usually 'publish with ostentation'. The body of the essay charges these experimenters with causing terrible sufferings, merely, like the gods in the review of *A Free Inquiry*, for their own amusement and 'sport'. But at the same time Johnson writes as if he is aware that some of these experiments, at least, are made in the name of physiological research. The reference to 'the use of the lacteals' is particularly puzzling. The Yale editors of the *Idler* are silent on the point, though the reference to Mead is footnoted. Russell Brain, in a well-known essay, first published in 1934, suggested that Johnson's attack was directed against the brothers William and John Hunter,[84] who were currently engaged in research on 'the use of the lacteals', but this is unlikely, as I shall argue.

It should be pointed out, though, that this is not the only place in his works where Johnson attacks animal experimenters.[85] In the notes to Shakespeare's *Cymbeline*, published in 1765, but very likely compiled some years earlier, and possibly contemporary with the *Idler* piece, Johnson singles out Cornelius' rebuke to the Queen (who proposes to try the force of poisons on 'such creatures as / We count not worth the hanging') in Act I, scene v:

> Your highness
> Shall from this practice but make hard your heart.

and writes

There is in this passage nothing that much requires a note, yet I cannot forbear to push it forward into observation. The thought would probably have been much amplified, had our author lived to be shocked with such experiments as have been published in later times, by a race of men that have practiced tortures without pity, and related them without shame, and are yet suffered to erect their heads among human beings.[86]

The *Idler* began on 15 April 1758, presumably when Johnson thought himself in sight of the end of his labours on Shakespeare. The *Proposals* for a new edition of Shakespeare's plays had been issued on 8 June 1756, and Johnson in the early months of 1758 was sanguine about its imminent completion. Curiously enough, his work on

Shakespeare is more or less contemporaneous with his involvement in the *Literary Magazine*. As he lay incapacitated in those winter months Johnson could not have been cheered by the news that another new monthly periodical – one destined to be ultimately far more successful than the *Literary Magazine* – had appeared on the scene. This was the *Critical Review*, produced by a group of writers, including Dr Thomas Armstrong, presided over by Tobias Smollett, and the first number of which is dated March 1756. As it happens, both these journals offer clues in the search for the provocation behind *Idler* 17.

Tobias Smollett, of course, was a doctor. Originally of the University of Glasgow, where he was apprenticed to an apothecary, he purchased his MD from Marischal College, Aberdeen, for the sum of £28 Scots in 1750. More importantly, he was on friendly terms, since his arrival in London, with some of the most notable medical men of the day, including William Smellie, and both the Hunter brothers. He seems also to have been acquainted with Dr Thomas Lawrence.[87] Given the interests of its founders, it's not surprising that reviews of medical books feature prominently in the pages of the *Critical*: and given Smollett's temperament it is not surprising that these reviews often provoked replies and the magazine was often embroiled in medical disputes.

One of the controversies that raged in the *Critical Review* was occasioned by the notice (very probably by Smollett) of a book published by Alexander Monro Jnr., of Edinburgh, on the lymphatic veins. 'This elegant Latin treatise', the review begins, 'owes its origin to some experiments on live animals which [Monro] made at Edinburgh four years ago.'[88] Monro claimed to discover that the lymphatic veins 'perform the office of absorbent vessels thro' the whole body'. Yet, replies the reviewer, 'Dr Hunter has read public lectures in anatomy eleven years: and in every course' (as can be confirmed 'by the testimony of above an hundred unexceptionable witnesses') declared his belief that the lymphatics were a system of absorbing vessels. He presents what reads very like a direct transcript of Hunter's lecture notes, in which the argument is that the correspondences between the lacteal and the lymphatic systems is so great that the likelihood is they function alike, and 'there is no difference but the name'.

In the late seventeenth century Bartholin and Rudbeck had independently each demonstrated the ubiquity of lymphatics in the human body. Frederick Ruysch (1638–1731) also advanced knowledge of the lymphatic vessels.[89] In the words of James' *Medicinal Dictionary*, Mr Ruysch 'had asserted, that the Resistance he felt upon blowing into the lymphatic Vessels, gave him Reason to believe, that these Vessels were furnished with Valves, which, he confess'd, he had not seen, but said, he was not singular in his Judgment as to that Particular'. Challenged to prove their existence, Ruysch 'actually found those Valves, to the Number of above two thousand, and gave incontestable proofs of the Reality, of that which he had before advanced as a Conjecture only'.[90] As early as 1701 Martin Lister and William Musgrave performed experiments to discover the function of the lacteal vessels. By the time Hunter was lecturing it was generally allowed that the lacteals were the absorbing vessels of the alimentary canal. There was therefore no need to learn, in Johnson's phrase, 'the use of lacteals'. What was controversial in 1757 was whether the close analogy of the lymphatics to the lacteal absorbents, in their valvular structure and mode of termination, meant that they functioned analogously to the lacteals as absorbents, and if they absorbed, whether or not the red veins absorbed too. As Hunter remarks, 'The lacteals were discovered, traced, and their use ascertained from the circumstance of a manifest and particular colour, in their contents . . .' but it was difficult to replicate this experiment with the lymphatics.

The review of Monro appeared in September 1757. The dispute about procedure continued with a letter from Monro Senior, in November, insisting that though Hunter might announce the doctrine, Monro had provided experimental proof and, in December, an article headed 'Facts relating to the dispute between Dr Hunter and Dr Monro' dated 'Nov. 23 1757' and signed by William Hunter. There Hunter repeats his claim that ever since 1746 he had advanced the doctrine of the lymphatics being the system of absorbing vessels. He gives a list of medical men who attended his lectures who will testify in his favour. His essential point is that his lectures constituted 'publication': 'you will observe that there can be no dispute that I was the first who published this doctrine about the lymphatics and that Dr Alexander Monro, jun. was the first who printed it'.[91]

The dispute dragged on with another letter, this time from Dr Donald Monro, and another reply from Hunter in December. In July 1758 the *Critical Review* summarised Mark Akenside's Gulstonian Lecture on the Lymphatics published in that year's *Philosphical Transactions:* in October it noticed a pamphlet (probably by Akenside) attacking Monro's claims and remarked, perhaps rather wearily, that 'The truth is, this discovery may have been made by a great many different people, without any intercourse one with another.'[92] William Hunter did not take up the challenge to publish (in the more modern sense) his work until in 1762 his *Medical Commentaries* Part 1 appeared, 'containing a plain and direct answer to Professor Monro, Jnr'. Much of this is filled by testimonial letters. One from 'Mr Watson, reader of anatomy, and surgeon to the Middlesex Hospital', writes of the lectures, from 1748, 'You told us – You had traced the lymphatics from the *Testis* of a dog into the thoracic duct – You informed us, the lymphatics might be demonstrated either by blowing into the artery, or by making a ligature on the emulgent veins of a living dog . . .'[93] Henry Watson, Surgeon, is listed alongside Bathurst as one of the staff of the Middlesex Hospital in a brief note in the *Gentleman's Magazine* of January 1757. This is one of the routes then, by which Johnson could have got to hear of the Hunterian experiments. Another could have been through another of his friends, the unlicensed practitioner, Robert Levet, who attended William Hunter's lectures, though this was probably later in the century (see chapter 6).

Otherwise, though both authors 'publish with ostentation' and claim to have performed experiments, they are not described in print, certainly not in the detail that might explain his horrified reaction. But William Hunter moved quickly to verify his position on the non-absorbency of the veins. His brother John, the surgeon and anatomist, was still at Covent Garden, running the anatomy school there, and 'at this time', William later reported, ' was deeply engaged in physiological inquiries, in making experiments on living animals, and in prosecuting comparative anatomy with great accuracy and application. It is well known that I speak of him with moderation when I say so. He took the subject of absorption into his consideration, and from all his observations was inclined to believe that in the human body there was one, and but one, system of vessels for absorption.' William Hunter quotes John Hunter on these experiments, made in the presence and with the assistance of himself and seven others, of which the first begins

Animal First. – Experiment 1. on the 3rd November 1758, I opened the belly of a living dog. The intestines rushed out immediately. I exposed them fully; and we observed the lacteals filled with a white liquor at the upper part of the gut and mesentery; but in those which came from the ilion and colon the liquor was transparent.[94]

When William Hunter moved to Great Windmill Street in 1757 John remained at Covent Garden with the anatomy school. We know that pupils were sometimes brought in to assist with experiments, and there is evidence enough that Hunter used dogs and cats, as well as sheep, rabbits and asses in his research. According to Ernest Gray, 'Before he died Hunter had dissected at least five hundred species of animals'.[95] Johnson's reference then may suggest a rather hazy notion of just what the purposes of Hunter's experiments were rather than his 'being in touch with a physiological research actually in progress'. Johnson's medical acquaintances were likely to be rather old-fashioned in their knowledge and views. Another type of experiment described by Johnson – that to discover 'whether the more lasting agonies are produced by poison forced into the mouth, or injected into the veins', on the other hand, may well reflect some hearsay knowledge of what John Hunter was doing. He certainly 'conducted a series of experiments to determine the effects of the introduction of foreign materials into the circulation. He made intravenous injections of a great variety of substances, including salt, vinegar, nitric acid, opium and gin. He concluded that "many substances thrown into the blood produce more violent effects in this way than when taken into the stomach, and even cause immediate death".'[96]

Nor is there evidence that Johnson knew of a paper read to the Royal Society on 2 March 1758 by 'Edward Wright M.D.' on *An Experiment, by which it appears, that salt of steel does not enter the Lacteal vessels*:

An ounce and a half of salt dissolved in a sufficient quantity of water, filtrated and mixed with about a pound of bread and milk were forced down the throat of a dog that had been kept fasting for 36 hours. An hour after he had swallowed this mixture, having secured him in a supine position, as is usual in such experiments, we opened the abdomen, and observed the lacteal vessels, like white threads, running along the mesentery in a very beautiful manner. Upon slitting open part of the small guts, we there found a good deal of the mixture ... we found it necessary to open the thorax, and tie the thoracic duct a little above the receptacle, which, from the ligature, soon became turgid, the animal being alive and warm and the chyle still continuing its course towards the thoracic duct. Having cut open the receptacle, we easily collected a sufficient quantity of chyle ...[97]

Possibly Johnson had some hearsay knowledge of similar experiments: the bland and unperturbed manner of Wright's piece implies they were common.

But another aspect of *Idler* 17 makes it almost certain that neither the Hunters nor research on the lacteals were Johnson's main target. This is the sentence: 'it is not without reluctance that I offend the sensibility of the tender mind with images like these'. In the sense of 'quickness and acuteness of apprehension' the term sensibility was current long before Johnson wrote. About the same time as Johnson's piece, according to the OED, sensibility comes to mean also 'readiness to feel compassion for suff'ring'. It is possible that the word struck Johnson as a telling one to use here because sensibility was precisely what the experiments he had in mind were about, sensibility not merely of the 'tender mind', but of the animal body.

A colleague of Monro at the University of Edinburgh, Robert Whytt, was engaged in another controversy, more consequential but no less acrimonious, and which persisted throughout the decade, and was frequently reported, with Albrecht von Haller, the most important of Boerhaave's pupils. The controversy was over which parts of the body were endowed with sensibility and which with irritability. Galen had long ago proposed that all sensibility was bound to the nervous system, and that the muscles were brought into action by the nerves. 'Irritability' was recognised by Glisson (1597–1677) who proposed the term. For Haller an irritable part was one which contracted to the touch; a sensible part was one whose stimulation was either consciously noticed, in a human subject, or caused signs of unrest in an animal. From 1746 onwards he submitted all parts of the body to a long series of experiments to discover which were sensible to stimulation and from 1751, as he writes, 'I have examined several different ways, a hundred and ninety animals, a species of cruelty for which I felt such a reluctance, as could only be overcome by the desire of contributing to the benefit of mankind'.[98] In the course of these experiments Haller pricked, cut, tore, scraped and burned the animals' tendons and ligaments, as well as pouring various acids and corrosives on them. His most controversial conclusion was that the tendons, as well as other parts such as the *periosteum* of the bones, and the membranes of the brain, 'are neither capable of sensation, nor pain'.[99]

Haller's views were challenged by Robert Whytt, most notably in his *Physiological Essays*, published in 1756, which received widespread publicity. The *London Magazine*, for example, ran extracts from it for four issues, from January to April 1756; the *Monthly Review* prefaced its substantial account in January with a review of Haller's dissertation; as we have seen, the *Literary Magazine* gave it a serious review in May. One of Whytt's main arguments was drawn from Hippocrates' dictum that 'a greater pain drives out a less':

When the thorax of a living animal is laid open, it does not seem to receive any additional pain by pricking or cutting its heart; no new convulsions are produced; nor any change in the body, except perhaps a quicker repetition of the motion of the heart: does it follow from this that the heart is without feeling? No, surely: but only that, after the torture suffered by laying open the thorax, the new pain produced by wounding the heart is too small to make any impression upon a dying and half insensible animal.[100]

Whytt ascribed nerves, and therefore sensibility, to the tendons: experiments on living animals, though not detailed, are implied on every page of his argument. There were other disagreements, particularly over what parts of the body possessed the property of irritability. Haller, for instance, had allowed that the lacteals possess irritability: Whytt argued that if this were so (as he agreed) all the lymphatic vessels must also possess it – implying that he accepted the Hunterian view that the lymphatics and the lymphs made up the one absorbing system. Experiments were also performed to test whether opium induced an anaesthetic effect. To this end opium was sometimes given by mouth or injected. Whytt's *Observations on Irritability* recounts, for instance, how a medical student, 'Mr Robert Ramsey', injected opium into a wound made in the abdomen of a small dog, an experiment first carried out by Mead.[101]

Haller's significance lies partly in his recourse to experimental method. Remarking that he had discovered 'several truths contrary to the opinions generally received', near the opening of his book, he adds, 'This last reason had obliged me to be very exact in my proofs, because I was fully persuaded that an opinion so little foreseen would at first appear improbable, and only gain assent by the clearest conviction. For this reason I was obliged to repeat and multiply my experiments ... for I am persuaded that the great source of error in physic has been owing to physicians, at least a great part of them, making few or no experiments, and substituting analogy instead of them.'[102] And so Haller suggests that only replication of his experiments can afford grounds for challenging his conclusions: 'Physicians, anatomists, and surgeons, who are of another opinion, will I hope pardon me for differing so widely from them, and defer condemning me till they have compared the experiments upon which that opinion is founded.'[103] It seems likely that Haller and those who followed him were the main objects of Johnson's wrath.

Haller had claimed that the achilles tendon and the patella were insensible and Richard Brocklesby was one who undertook to verify his experiments. His paper, 'An account of some Experiments on the Sensibility and Irritability of the several parts of Animals' was published in the *Philosophical Transactions* for 1755 (1756). We can be almost certain that Johnson had seen this piece since in the *Transactions* it follows the paper on the *Tuba Eustachia* and immediately precedes Frank Nicholls's *Account of Worms in Animal Bodies*, both of which the *Literary Magazine* took up and reprinted in its early issues.[104] Brocklesby's paper was scathingly treated in the *Critical Review* where the reviewer (presumably Smollett) declared 'Hallers' doctrine of irritability was so well established, that it required no further confirmation; or if any student doubted the truth of his experiments, he might have satisfied himself in private, without disgusting the public with a recapitulation of barbarous executions, which were productive of no new phenomena. Where then was the importance of the inquiry? – One would imagine that Dr. Brocklesby had directed and superintended those barbarities, on purpose to have an opportunity of promulgating his own aversion to cruelty, in the preamble of his letter ...'[105]

Johnson's *Idler* essay accuses those who experiment on living animals with causing suffering merely for amusement's sake. It is certain that he was right in saying that such experiments were 'tried', and 'tried again' partly because, for the obvious reason adduced by Whytt, clear results were very difficult to obtain. Introducing 'An Observation of the Insensibility of Tendons' in the *Medical Observations and Inquiries* of 1771 William Hunter himself declared that 'the attention of the public has been very generally attracted to the dispute; *experiments have been made without end and without mercy ...*' (my italics). Yet observation had 'so often contradicted observation' that the question was still unresolved.[106] Johnson fears too that animal experimentation may lead the physician to 'exercise upon the tender and the helpless, upon feeble bodies and broken minds' the tortures he has tried previously upon cats and dogs. George Qvist has argued convincingly that John Hunter's famous venereal inoculation experiment of 1767 was not performed, as myth has it, on Hunter himself. But if this is so it must mean that the experiment was performed upon another human subject, who in Qvist's words, 'could well have been one of the many destitute outcasts of subnormal mentality who roamed the streets of London at this time.'[107]

Johnson's concern is not only with the animal victims; it is with the consequences for the doctor's relationship to his patients: the repetition of such experiments brutalises those who, for whatever reason, initiate them. This preoccupation with the destructive effects of all habituation is one of the most marked features of Johnson's moral writings and very striking in such *Rambler* essays as no. 89, not to speak of its crucial importance to the case of the astronomer in *Rasselas*. Johnson may have been alerted more particularly to the dangers of doctors becoming what we now call sadistic by the publicity given to the tortures of Damiens, tortures supposed to have been invented by the physicians and surgeons of the court who, in the words of the *Monthly Review*, 'communicated the result of their *profound* and *humane* studies for prolonging the pain and for rendering it the most excruciating that could be'.[108] As Andreas-Holger Maehle and Ulrich Tröhler have pointed out, it is also an extension of the theological view of Aquinas, that cruelty to animals might lead to cruelty to humans.[109]

It is clear then that Johnson's claim that experiments on animals were 'published every day with ostentation', though a rhetorical exaggeration, has a good deal of truth in it. The use of living animals in medical research probably reached a (temporary) peak in the middle years of the eighteenth century. The procedures that had led to Harvey's discovery of the circulation in 1628 had vindicated Bacon's proposal that animals be substituted for humans in the furtherance of anatomical study, and in the later years of the seventeenth century members of the Royal Society, like Christopher Wren and Robert Hooke, had also performed experiments on dogs. In the transition from a medicine which could account for the processes of the body only, in Heberden's phrase, by the properties of dead matter, and which confused *in vitro* processes with *in vivo* ones, early physiologists like Floyer and Stephen Hales had begun the modern understanding of the body's properties and functioning. The Hunters and Monro were engaged in a competition to reveal what William Hunter later called 'the greatest discovery, in both physiology and pathology, that anatomy has suggested since the discovery of the circulation'.[110] The topics in dispute between Haller and Whytt were equally momentous. Haller's *Dissertation* has been called a classic, 'an outstanding document of indefatigable experimentation and clear reasoning'.[111] Many others, including the students of these doctors and surgeons, 'anatomical novices', were undoubtedly involved in replicating and verifying these experiments and their conclusions.

Johnson's *Idler* remains the most powerful – though not the only – eighteenth-century protest against these 'hateful practices'.[112] It is an example of Johnson's imaginative capacity to 'present an evil to his mind', and his valuation of that capacity as an index of common humanity.[113] The intense compression brings together in a single paragraph appalling details from experiments conducted in pursuit of widely different scientific ends. It is probably the moral dilemmas his protest raises as well as the inherent content of the essay itself that has led most Johnsonian critics to evade or neglect giving it the attention in the Johnsonian canon it deserves.[114]

In the course of his work as a journalist, then, Johnson wrote much that is evidence for his medical interests and knowledge, but since most of this work *is* journalism, done at the behest of men like Edward Cave or Robert James, it is evidence so indirect and fragmentary that only its persistent scepticism makes it notable. Yet there is no doubt that medical issues, in the broadest sense, preoccupied some of his thinking in these years when the hospital movement was gaining momentum and medical research on living creatures widely practised. Current medical research is a latent subject in his most famous review, and in *Idler* 4 and 17, as well as less formally, in other reviews, he forcefully intervened to comment on the current medical scene. His stress was always on the important link between the practice of medicine and the virtue of charity: he was appalled (and perhaps percipient) at the possibilities of medical experimentation, whilst at the same time being broadly in sympathy with its underlying purposes and philosophy. In the forties and fifties, he worked alongside medical men – Swan on Sydenham, James on the *Medicinal Dictionary*, Bathurst and probably others on the *Literary Magazine*. If not a participant, he was certainly, as he implies in the *Life of Akenside*, an acute observer of the medical world.

This had its effect on other parts of his writing. In the life of Actuarius, the physician is quoted as saying that slanders are 'infections', which 'it would be more for the Interest of the World to find an Antidote than against any Contagion or Disease'. This is, of course, a commonplace metaphor. But Johnson often exploits with more purposiveness and invention the capacity of medical language to extend to moral matters, and to intensify the gravity of the mood.

Idler 17, as I have suggested, turns upon a kind of pun on the word 'sensibility'. And we find Johnson using medical metaphors to good effect when he advises Henry Thrale that 'violent Mirth is the foam, and deep sadness the subsidence of a morbid fermentation', or when he describes the course of grief in language drawn from the eighteenth-century physician's view of the body in writing to Dr Lawrence on the occasion of his bereavement. 'He that outlives a wife whom he has long loved, sees himself disjoined from the only mind that had the same hopes, and fears, and interest ... The continuity of being is lacerated. The settled course of sentiment, and action is stopped, and life stands suspended and motionless till it is driven by external causes into a new channel.'[115] In these instances his correspondents would certainly have picked up the resonances of these phrases.

But medical language and metaphor permeate Johnson's serious work very extensively:

> Unnumbered maladies his joints invade
> Lay seige to life and press the dire blockade ...

'Blockade' is a pun, since disease is so frequently associated with an obstruction at the perceived disease site. 'What is certain', writes W. F. Bynum in a review of eighteenth-century medical historiography, 'is that the language of disease was much more widely understood than it was to become in the nineteenth century.'[116] When Johnson uses medical metaphors then he is employing a generally appreciated language to give pungency and force to his discussion of moral and social matters. *The Rambler* was produced in the midst of the years I have covered in this chapter – and in its numbers Johnson's medical interests are shaped into a new form.

4

MEDICINE AS METAPHOR

'JOHNSON'S MEDICINE looks backward', declared W. K. Wimsatt.[1] He was discussing the evidence of Johnson's medical interests contained in the *Rambler* series of essays, written and published between 1750 and 1752, whilst Johnson was also engaged on the *Dictionary*. The only medical writers mentioned there by name are Hippocrates, Celsus and 'old Cornaro'. Boerhaave, 'the learned, the judicious, the pious Boerhaave', is, it is true, cited, but as a moral rather than as a medical hero; William Harvey is mentioned, too, but that is part of a joke about 'a late writer' who 'has put Harvey's doctrine of the circulation of the blood into the mouth of a Turkish statesman, who lived near two centuries before it was known even to philosophers or anatomists'. (*Rambler* 140), which writer, of course, was Johnson himself, in the tragedy *Irene* (1749).[2] But Johnson's medical knowledge may be detected in the *Rambler* all the same, beneath that grandeur of generality which characterises Johnson's prose in this enterprise. No. 85, for example, which is in praise of health and exercise, remarks that 'very learned treatises have been produced upon the maladies of the camp, the sea, and the mines' and contains the following paragraph:

With ease, ... if it could be secured, many would be content; but nothing terrestrial can be kept at a stand. Ease, if it is not rising into pleasure, will be falling towards pain; and whatever hope the dreams of speculation may suggest of observing the proportion between nutriment and labour, and keeping the body in a healthy state by supplies exactly equal to its waste, we know that, in effect, the vital powers unexcited by motion, grow gradually languid; that as their vigour fails, obstructions are generated; and that from obstructions proceed most of those pains which wear us away slowly with periodical tortures, and which, though they sometimes suffer life to be long, condemn it to be useless, chain us down to the couch of misery, and mock us with the hopes of death.[3]

'Obstructions' are not unknown to classical medicine, but as we have seen, occupy the key position in iatrophysicalist accounts of the body that they do here. The 'dreams of speculation' which seek an exact balance between nutriment and wastage must suggest the experiments of Sanctorius who, by means of his famous 'statical chair', applied Galilean principles of measurement to biological matters (and thereby introduced quantitative experimental procedures into medical research). Sir John Floyer, among many later experimenters, tried to determine the results of different diets and amounts of exercise on his own health.[4] Of eighteenth-century physicians, both George Cheyne and John Arbuthnot discuss the possibility of arriving at a diet in which quantity of nutriment shall be exactly proportionate to labour whilst discussing the role of exercise in facilitating digestion and a due motion of the circulating fluids.[5] Johnson's deliberately vague and old-fashioned term, 'the vital powers', seems to operate very much like the circulation.

Yet Wimsatt is right. There is little direct evidence of Johnson's contemporary medical knowledge in the essay series. The reason for this has to do with the *Rambler*'s conscious – and enormously ambitious – design. The editors of the Yale *Rambler* point out in their Introduction how few citations from the Bible the series contains and how many (60 per cent) are from classical Greek or Latin authors.[6] This might imply what I believe is the case: that Johnson in the *Rambler* is, among other things, attempting to rival the ancient moral philosophers and to supply a gap in their work first identified by Francis Bacon, whose writings he had read or was reading for the *Dictionary*. Discussion of the variety of moral philosophy associated with the Stoics was central to Johnson's ambition, for in order to establish his own position he needed above all to attack the ground that they, in the sphere of moral exhortation, particularly occupied.

The Rambler may be short on particular medical references and information, but it is certainly long on medical metaphors. 'The motif of disease and its remedy or prevention is one of the most persistent', Wimsatt noted.[7] 'Frequently a *Rambler* paper takes for its subject some intellectual malady like procrastination or idleness or envy and ponders a remedy', writes Max Byrd.[8] The 'motif' occurs for the first time, humorously, in *Rambler* 2, which is a self-admonishing reflection upon the tendency of writers to lose themselves in dreams of future fame:

Those who have proceeded so far as to appeal to the tribunal of succeeding times, are not likely to be cured of their infatuation; but all endeavours ought to be used for the prevention of a disease, for which, when it has attained its height, perhaps no remedy will be found in the gardens of philosophy, however she may boast her physick of the mind, her catharticks of vice, or lenitives of passion.

I shall, therefore, while I am yet but lightly touched with the symptoms of the writer's malady, endeavour to fortify myself against the infection, not without some weak hope that my preservatives may extend their virtues to others, whose employment exposes them to the same danger.

(He goes on to cite 'the sage advice of Epictetus the Stoic'.) Variations on the metaphor of the 'physic of the mind' occur in a host of subsequent essays in which 'intellectual maladies' or 'mental diseases' are examined. The metaphor is in fact closer to a structural principle than a 'motif' in a significant number of essays, for these are organised in ways that resemble the presentation of the material in a medical handbook. In the Proposals for the *Medicinal Dictionary*, for example, it is promised to illustrate 'the great Hippocratic Art of CURING DISEASES' by 'exhibiting under every Distemper' firstly, select cases of those who died of the disease, 'by which the immediate Causes of Diseases and the Concomitant Symptoms, may with most certainty be discovered'; then

2. An accurate Description of the Disease, in which the Symptoms that are peculiar to it, and distinguish it from all other Distempers, will be diligently remarked.

3. The Prognostics, being Directions for judging whether the Disease is likely to terminate in Health, Death, or some other Distemper.

4. The Method of Cure, both in regard to Regimen and Medicine, as laid down by the principal Authors ...

A distinct sequence of essays in the *Rambler* displays a similar pattern of diagnosis, prognosis – sometimes a form of spiritual death – and 'method of cure'. Human passions or dispositions: anger (11), affectation (20), anxiety (29), sorrow (47 and 52), profligacy (53), peevishness (74), curiosity (103), envy (183) – to give some examples – are described, distinguished from passions with similar conditions or results, and their probable consequences examined. Jonathan Swift will typically run vices together in a comprehensive denunciation of human iniquity: 'Begging, Robbing, Stealing, Cheating, Pimping, Forswearing, Flattering, Suborning, Forging, Gaming, Lying, Fawning, Hectoring, Voting, Scribling, Stargazing, Poysoning, Whoring, Canting, Libelling, Free-thinking ...'[9] The enormous difference in degree between these offences is banished by the vehement momentum of this cavalcade. Johnson's effort in the *Rambler* is consciously directed, rather, to the separation of one vice, or condition, from neighbouring vices that may be mistaken for it. His is an attempt not just to castigate but to probe into, explore and describe just what the experience of envy or anger is, just what troubles the over-rigorous or the day-dreaming or the anxious person breeds for themselves and others. The various species of human failings are defined, the vicious separated from the more venial. The model of medicine is instrumental in his doing this. He is, in effect, constructing an elementary nosology of intellectual maladies, in which the symptoms of vices are defined, their courses over time described, and remedies, 'avoiding that dangerous and empirical morality which cures one vice by another' (183), proposed.

Peevishness, for example:

No disease of the mind can more fatally disable it from benevolence, the chief duty of social beings, than ill-humour or peevishness; for tho' it breaks not out in paroxysms of outrage, nor bursts into clamour, turbulence and bloodshed, it wears out happiness by slow corrosion, and small injuries incessantly repeated. It may be considered as the canker of life, that destroys its vigour and checks its improvement, that creeps on with hourly depredations, and taints and vitiates what it cannot consume ...

This troublesome impatience is sometimes nothing more than the symptom of some deeper malady. He that is angry without daring to confess his resentment, or sorrowful without the liberty of telling his grief, is too frequently inclined to give vent to the fermentations of his mind at the first passages that are opened, and to let his passions boil over upon those whom accident throws in his way ... (*Rambler* 74)

The metaphor or conceit is sustained by the 'philosophic' diction. The metaphors of 'fermentation', 'corrosion' and 'canker' foster the impression that the diagnosis has scientific status and precision.

Not all of these *Rambler* essays are about what we should strictly call vices – some are about human propensities which can readily become destructive if allowed to develop unchecked:

Sorrow is not that regret for negligence or error which may animate us to future care or activity, or that repentance of crimes for which, however irrevocable, our Creator has promised to accept it as an atonement; the pain which arises from these causes has very salutary effects, and is every hour extenuating itself by the reparation of those miscarriages that produce it. Sorrow is properly that state of mind in which our desires are fixed upon the past, without looking forward to the future, an incessant wish that something were otherwise than it has been, a tormenting and harassing want of some enjoyment or possession which we have lost, and which no endeavours can possibly regain ... (*Rambler* 47)

This definition of the disorder is followed by a critical survey of methods of treatment. 'Some have thought, that the most certain way to clear the heart from its embarrassment is to drag it by force into scenes of merriment. Others imagine, that such a transition is too violent, and recommend rather to soothe it into tranquillity.' The medical parallel is kept lightly before us in these analogies to treatment by purgative medicines or baths and emollients, and is confirmed in the essay's final prescription that 'The safe and general antidote against sorrow is employment'. *Rambler* 74 illustrates its account of peevishness with a portrait of a peevish woman, 'Tetrica', and Johnson's use of such figures, though obviously indebted to works of moral exhortation, like William Law's *Serious Call*, has parallels in medical texts. James's 'Proposals' promise, for instance, 'SELECT Cases in confirmation of the Doctrine laid down, which will be collected not only for the Information of the Reader, but with some regard to his Entertainment'.

'Physic of the mind' is, as Johnson implies when he introduces the phrase, a traditional metaphor of moral philosophy. It is connected with the very origin of ethics which was a discipline modelled on medicine. Hippocrates, in fact, is an important figure in ancient thought not just as a pioneer of medical diagnosis but because of the philosophical implications of his work. Galen actually argued that Plato and Aristotle were indebted to him for the essences of their philosophies, and this, whilst obviously a gross exaggeration, does contain a grain of truth. It is to the prior achievement of Hippocratic medicine that Aristotle turns in the first pages of the *Nichomachean Ethics* as he seeks a powerful bulwark in his argument with those members of Plato's academy who conceived ethics upon the model or paradigm of mathematics. Hippocratic medicine stood as a luminous example of a field of human inquiry which is not the less a science for being concerned with the individual and content with imprecision.[10] The analogy of moral philosophy and medicine had first been suggested by Plato in the *Phaedrus*, but in picking it up and developing it, Aristotle turns it against Platonic conclusions. For him, as Werner Jaeger remarks, the applicability of the medical analogy 'rests on the fact that both the art of the physician and that of the ethical philosopher always deal with individual situations and with practical actions'.[11] The supreme and universal good of Plato is not useful and is in fact ignored by many practitioners of particular good, Aristotle says, just as the physician is not interested in health itself but in the well-being of the individual patient. The focus of Aristotelian ethics is a result, in effect, of the thought of Hippocrates.

Aristotle does not merge the discipline of the ethical philosopher with that of the Hippocratic physician, as later writers tended to do. The example is useful, indeed essential, in defining the nature of his project, but Aristotle does not take the comparison so far as to conceive of the ethical philosopher as standing in the same relation to his subject as the physician does towards his patient. In other words, the ethical philosopher is not concerned with healing or with the offering of remedies, and Aristotle hardly conceived of human nature as in want of a 'cure'. Aristotle keeps the two disciplines parallel – and apart. Despite his emphasis on practical application he is less concerned with specific advice and moral instruction than with defining the nature of his subject and its specific methodology.

This at least is the charge levelled against him in Francis Bacon's *The Advancement of Learning* (1605). Whilst the ancients give excellent descriptions of the virtues, Bacon complains, they neglect 'how to attain these excellent marks and how to frame and subdue the will of man to become true and conformable to these pursuits'.[12] In his formulation of just what is needed Bacon too uses medicine as an appropriate analogy. The reason for the neglect of moral instruction, he suggests, is that 'men have despised to be conversant in ordinary and common matters', and (quoting Virgil's *Georgics*) he says, 'these Georgics of the mind, concerning the husbandry and tillage thereof, are no less worthy than the heroical descriptions of virtue, duty and felicity'. 'Cultivation' of the mind is the defining metaphor for this putative endeavour until in section 22 of the Second Book he cites 'that aphorism of Hippocrates *Qui gravi morbo correptio dolores non sentiunt, iis mens aegrotat*' ('Those who are sick without feeling pain, are sick in their minds'). Hence, his thought seems to run, medicine is needed for the mind as well as for the body. 'And if it be said, that the cure of men's minds belongeth to sacred divinity, it is most true: but yet moral philosophy may be preferred unto her as a wise servant and humble handmaid.' From this point in his argument Bacon keeps the two analogies of agriculture and medicine in tandem. 'The husbandman cannot command', he says, 'neither the nature of the earth, nor the seasons of the weather; no more can the physician the constitution of the patient, nor the variety of accidents. So in the culture and cure of the mind of man . . .' Once again, Bacon suggests that moral philosophy should examine what is possible to different men, given their differing temperaments and circumstances, just as 'the knowledge of the diversity of grounds and moulds doth to agriculture, and the knowledge of complexions and constitutions doth to the physician; except we mean to follow the indiscretion of empirics, which minister the same medicine to all patients.' He continues

Another article of this knowledge is the inquiry touching the affections; for as in medicining of the body, it is in order first to know the divers complexions and constitutions; secondly, the diseases; and lastly, the cures: so in medicining of the mind, after knowledge of the divers characters of men's natures, it followeth in order to know the diseases and infirmities of the mind, which are no other than the perturbations and distempers of the affections.[13]

Bacon, in fact, does not diagnose the diseases and infirmities of the affections: his outlined programme, carried out in part in the *Essays*, concentrates on positive enabling discussion – what practical and useful hints there are that will enable us to contrive 'use and advantage' from our intellectual resources.

Johnson, then, inherited the metaphor of 'intellectual maladies'. The posture of the moralist as physician of the mind was a familiar one to adopt. But – as Johnson points out in one of the *Rambler* essays himself – postures that are at first adopted tend to become, in course of time, part of one's carriage, naturalised into one's demeanour. Johnson, it might be thought, also inherits Bacon's intellectual programme, with the important difference that, the medicine of humours or complexions having fallen into disrepute, he pays little attention to the differing constitutional characteristics of groups of men and women and concentrates instead on the isolation and diagnosis of specific, but universal, intellectual maladies. But, if so, is this programme carried out with Baconian earnestness? Does this metaphor, so insistently present in the *Rambler*, become anything more than a metaphor, a loose analogy, momentarily entertaining and delighting the mind? Is it anything more significant than a conceit, and a rather worn-out one at that? Paul Fussell describes the typical attitude of the 'Augustan humanist' towards metaphor: 'To the humanist, metaphor, which operates like rapid or almost instantaneous simile, does not actually assert that "a *is* b". Tenor and vehicle are never thought to interfuse; regardless of closeness or resemblance, the two terms of a comparison remain ultimately distinct', and so it may be with *The Rambler*.[14] In his book on Bacon, Brian Vickers argues that in *The Advancement of Learning*, Bacon, on the other hand, 'thought in images'. 'If we could pick out one aspect from the second book,' he writes, 'it would be his continued and possible increasing tendency to allow vehicle to precede and even displace tenor, that is to think in images.'[15] 'The themes of health, sickness and medicine ... run so deep in Johnson's mind,' as Wimsatt remarked, 'that here it is not easy to distinguish the literal from the figurative.'[16] I should like to raise here the question of what Johnson's use of this metaphor actually means, in other words to inquire into the level of seriousness of these images of the moral life as illness, of the moral essayist as physician of the mind.

In Act I of *The Cherry Orchard* Gayev murmurs, 'You know, if a lot of cures are suggested for a disease, it means the disease is incurable. I've been thinking and puzzling my brains, and I've thought of plenty of ways out, which means there aren't any.' His doctor creator has put an ancient medical axiom into his mouth. There is perhaps no need to take some of the *Rambler*'s medical comparisons – like the correspondence suggested between the fragility of the body and marriage in *Rambler* 45 – too seriously. The many jocular or half-facetious references to 'epidemical infections' and the 'contagion' of various follies seem designed partly to achieve that lightening of the tone which Johnson seems to have thought appropriate to the essay (described in the *Dictionary* as 'a loose sally of the mind'). Even more elaborate instances, like *Rambler* 95, for example, in the form of a letter from 'Pertinax', could be thought largely facetious. It begins

Sir
   There are many diseases both of the body and mind, which it is far easier to prevent than to cure, and therefore I hope you will think me employed in an office not useless either to learning or virtue, if I describe the symptoms of an intellectual malady, which, though at first it seizes only the passions, will, if

not speedily remedied, infect the reason, and, from blasting the blossoms of knowledge, proceed in time to canker the root.

Pertinax's intellectual malady is sophistry, which is presented specifically throughout the essay by analogy with fever. 'Vitiated' initially by his father's training, he is placed 'where everyone catches the contagion of vanity, and soon began to distinguish [himself] by sophisms and paradoxes.' The sophist's activity is presented as careering headlong out of control of his own judgement, until, like a fever, it reaches a crisis ('I shuddered at my own corruption') in which it is resolved. Hereafter, Pertinax 'prescribed a new regimen' to his understanding, 'forebore to heat his imagination with needless controversies', and is thus able to claim in the letter's last paragraph: 'By this method I am at length recovered from my argumental delirium, and find myself in the state of one awakened from the confusion and tumult of a feverish dream.' The correspondences are ingenious and amusing, but the skill and wit of Johnson's medical parallel does not disguise that what is actually described is an intellectual condition, the result of bad early training, sustained by worldly success, and reformed at last by conscious recognition and voluntary effort.

In his review of *A Free Inquiry* Johnson's attention focuses on the unpredictable nature of corporeal evil. 'Many a merry bout have these frolic beings at the vicissitudes of an ague, and good sport it is to see a man tumble with an epilepsy, and revive and tumble again, and all this he knows not why', he writes. These frolic beings have precisely what we lack – power over our physical sufferings. Yet, on the other hand, the moral realm seems to be founded on a premise that is difficult to reconcile with this view (or perception) of physical evil. Here – in the discourse of the moralist – to behave in certain ways leads more or less directly to certain consequences, and the purposive exposure of these dispositions or 'vices' depends upon the assumption that the reader's recognition of them is the first stage in the activation of his or her moral will. The moralist would have no motive in writing if the 'remedies' for these evils were not, conceivably, within our power. 'The only end of writing is to enable the readers better to enjoy life or better to endure it: and how will either of these be put more in our power by him who tells us we are puppets, of which some creature not much wiser than ourselves manages the strings?' Johnson had asked. For the moralist, human beings exercise free will: but can free will be exercised over contagions and infections and the fragility of the human constitution? The distinction is not, of course, as clear-cut as I am making it, since the endeavour of medicine is certainly to include bodily evils within the order of things. 'It was a principle among the ancients', Johnson remarks in *Rambler* 85, 'that acute diseases are from heaven, and chronical from ourselves.' Preventive medicine, from Hippocrates onwards, has entered moral ground in so far as it has sought to establish connections between condition–generating behaviour and bodily pain. But fundamentally, I think, a strain, a gap in the analogy is always threatening to appear. Johnson's habitual metaphors for illness (not Johnson's alone of course) which define its onset as an 'attack', a 'seizure' an 'invasion' can only deepen our sense of a conflict between the medical metaphor for moral vices and the facts of the moralist's enterprise.

Johnson, then, may present himself as one of those who 'have undertaken the arduous province of preserving the balance of the mental constitution' (*Rambler* 47), on the analogy of the Galenic physician preserving the balance of the four bodily humours, but the tradition which sees the moral philosopher as an analogue of the physician conflicts with an equally strong emphasis in moral philosophy on the role of the will. And so, many of the medical metaphors are emptied of force and do not signal any therapeutic insight. The example of the obsessively house-proud Erephile, 'embittered by age and solitude', in *Rambler* 112, concludes, 'Peevishness is generally a vice of narrow minds and ... proceeds from an unreasonable persuasion of the importance of trifles. The proper remedy against it is to consider the dignity of human nature and the folly of suffering perturbation and uneasiness from causes unworthy of our notice.' The portrait of Erephile cogently suggests a woman frustrated and imprisoned in the only role – that of housekeeper – allowed her, and that it is her bitterness and disappointment with life which give rise to her 'moral' fault. Johnson's remark in a letter to John Taylor that 'It does not appear from your Doctor's prescription that he sees to the bottom of your distemper. What he gives you strikes at no cause', might be applied here.[17] The lack of psychological insight leads to the prescription of a form of will-power, when it is the exertion of her will that symptomises Erephile's disorder.

The metaphor (if it is right to call something a metaphor which is reduced to so shadowy a presence as this), is made even less convincingly therapeutic by the fact that it is sometimes used with an obviously punitive intention. Medicines are rarely pleasant to take. Remedies and cures, especially if they take the form of surgery, can seem almost as appalling – and notoriously were in the eighteenth century as appalling – as the evils they confront. It often seems that the metaphors of pains and remedies ask to be understood within a greater metaphor of man's fall. The plainest statement of what Wimsatt called 'physical evil as the badge and punishment of our fallen state' is in Elizabeth Carter's *Rambler* 44.[18] 'Beings conscious of a frame of mind originally diseased', she writes, 'must use the regimen of a stricter self-government. Whoever has been guilty of voluntary excesses must patiently submit both to the painful workings of nature, and needful severities of medicine, in order to his cure.' Johnson rarely uses such a disciplinarian tone as this, which is based on the assumption that illnesses are deserved by their sufferers' mismanagement of their bodies. (Thus Rolleston wrote that Johnson's gallstone was the 'penalty' for his erratic eating habits).[19] But, like the idea of a 'stricter regimen', the phrase 'physic of the mind' has an admonitory touch that 'medicine' alone does not quite convey, since 'physic' for Johnson and his contemporaries usually means purges and vomits. Medical treatment then lends itself to the moralist's purposes because it can be construed as a penance, a blend of remedy and severity, of promised cure and present punishment.

Yet there are at least three ways in which the medical metaphor is central to Johnson's enterprise. Firstly, his conviction of the universality of human nature, announced so uncompromisingly in the *Preface* to Lobo's *Voyage to Abysinnia*: 'that wherever human nature is to be found, there is a mixture of vice and virtue, a contest of passion and reason', is supported by the universality of human anatomy and physiology. This is the real point behind that characteristic opening of a *Rambler* essay which, as Wimsatt noted, makes 'a formal statement of some melancholy physiological principle' and then extends this to the moral or intellectual sphere.[20] Secondly, the medical parallel facilitates or develops (it is not easy to tell which comes first) a crucially important and original feature of Johnson's moral thought. This is his conception of the moral life in time, or, as one might put it, of the progressive course of moral disease. Swift is a useful comparison again. For him, it is an index of the corruption of the times that women of 'tainted reputation', as he remarks in *A Project for the Advancement of Religion and the Reformation of Manners* (1709), are received politely in public assemblies, though of course whores would not be. This, he says, 'looks like a sort of compounding between Virtue and Vice; as if a Woman were allowed to be vicious, provided she be not profligate: as if there were a certain Point, where Gallantry ends, and Infamy begins; or that an hundred criminal Amours were not as pardonable as Half a Score.'[21] Swift argues in the *Project* that the 'several pernicious vices frequent or notorious among us, that escape or elude the punishment of any law we have yet invented, or have had no law at all against them; such as atheism, drunkenness, fraud, avarice, and several others' can be, and ought to be, 'remedied' (he uses this term) by various forms of legal censorship and coercion. Johnson, on the other hand, would argue that whilst there is an inexorable logical continuity between (say) 'gallantry' and 'infamy', between a propensity to a certain behaviour and a vice, it is precisely this unfolding over time which offers the opportunity for inner remedy. The 'certain point' at which an apparently innocent tendency like day-dreaming, or fastidiousness, or grief 'turns over' and becomes a vice – becomes morbid – cannot be detected, but that this point of transformation exists is central to Johnson's conception of the moral life. Because vicious tendencies progress over time, becoming less and less controllable, until they eventually master the person who at first 'indulged' them, they are open to the moralist's intervention. One is always travelling towards or away from vice in Johnson's essentially dynamic conception. A static moral life, a life consumed by some overwhelming preoccupation, is not in a state of poise or exemption: it is stagnant, and that too is a morbid condition. In both cases, motion, action, the disruption of a tendency or an inclination is what the moralist can effect. His role is thus very close to a physician's or surgeon's, the timing of whose interventions is always of such momentous importance.

Habituation thus becomes a crucial concept in Johnson's picture of the moral life. Many *Ramblers* anticipate the emphasis on habit that is of such importance in Johnson's account of the mad astronomer in *Rasselas*, which I shall discuss in the next chapter. 'We are in danger from whatever can *get possession* of our thoughts to obstruct the way that leads to happiness . . .'(*Rambler* 7 – my italics) Pertinax's intellectual error or folly, persisted in by him, develops or progresses in the course of time until it seems to acquire a life or motive force of its own, and usurps initiative from the self. 'My fallacies began to operate upon my own mind', writes Pertinax. They have become involuntary. In other essays, tendencies of the mind, if persisted in, become a kind of unconscious, or (to avoid anachronism) a kind of parasite, dictating to their host thoughts or behaviour unsanctioned by, but not on the other hand exactly forbidden by the will. *Rambler* 11 speaks of the consequences of the frequent indulgence of anger 'which a man, by often calling to his assistance, will teach, in a short time, to intrude before the summons, to rush upon him with resistless violence, and without any previous notice of its approach.' This transfer of power from, as it were, one part of the self to another is dramatised in the *Rambler* by sentences in which the conscious or volitional self is both subject and object. In *Rambler* 17 as ambition is kindled in the mind 'we represent to ourselves the pleasures of some future possession and suffer our thoughts to dwell attentively upon it, till it has wholly engrossed the imagination, and permits us not to conceive any happiness but its attainment, or any misery but its loss'. Here the easy sequence of verbs 'we represent . . . suffer our thoughts . . . engrossed . . . permits' suggests how smoothly and stealthily this destructive transference is enacted. *Rambler* 47 on the 'affection of the breast,' sorrow, suggests that

. . . it too often happens that sorrow, thus lawfully entering, gains such a firm possession of the mind, that it is not afterwards to be ejected; the mournful ideas, first violently impressed, and afterwards willingly received, so much engross the attention, as to predominate in every thought, or darken gayety, and perplex ratiocination. An habitual sadness seizes upon the soul, and the faculties are chained to a single object, which can never be contemplated but with hopeless uneasiness.

Here the metaphors cluster together to suggest the plight of those incarcerated by reason of insanity. 'All sorrow that lasts longer than its cause is morbid, and should be shaken off as an attack of melancholy, as the forerunner of a greater evil than poverty or pain', Johnson was to write to Mrs Thrale.[22]

A more complex example is *Rambler* 112, about fastidiousness.

Sensibility may, by an incessant attention to elegance and propriety, be quickened to a tenderness inconsistent with the condition of humanity, irritable by the smallest asperity, and vulnerable by the gentlest touch. He that pleases himself too much with minute exactness, and submits to endure nothing in accommodations, attendance and address, below the point of perfection, will, whenever he enters the croud of life, be harassed with innumerable distresses, from which those who have not in the same manner increased their sensations find no disturbance.

As with sorrow, it is the cultivation of a tendency, itself quite innocuous, which bestows upon it the power ultimately to inflict suffering. 'In things which are not immediately subject to religious or moral considerations, it is dangerous to be too long or too rigidly in the right.' What turns normal conditions into pathological ones, changing them from passive to active, and transforming the soul upon which they seize from actor to patient, is something apparently quite simple, their unnatural continuance over time. Johnson has a consistent repertoire of metaphors – corrosion and cankering (which, says the *Dictionary*, 'seems to have the same meaning and origins with cancer') and their variations are the most important – the function of which is to represent the destructively transformative action of vicious tendencies over time. Sorrow is 'a kind of rust of the soul . . . it is the putrefaction of stagnant life . . .' The most telling language, though, is that of addiction. The day-dreaming student is seized by a 'frigid and narcotic infection' which 'like the poison of opiates, weakens his powers without any external symptoms of malignity'. So parallel are the processes of habit in the moral sphere and of addiction in the physical, in fact, that the simile tends to lose all sense of artifice, tenor and vehicle tend to merge and distinction between mind and body ceases to have much point. The persuasive force of the metaphors then is to authenticate the moralist's assumption of the physician's role.

There is a third sense in which medical metaphors are alive and meaningful in the essays. Terms such as 'corruption', 'depravation' and 'degenerate' which are borrowed from physical processes are commonly used in moral discourse to convey disgust and repudiation. In Johnson's *Rambler* there is a pattern almost the reverse of this. Language which belongs to the realm of physical evil is habitually used of mental or moral evil, with the result that 'vice' tends to be amalgamated with or be dissolved into descriptions of suffering. 'The passions of little minds, acting in low stations, do not fill the world with bloodshed and devastation, or mark by great events the periods of time, yet they torture the breast on which they seize', he writes in *Rambler* 66. Vanity, the passion under examination here, is thought of, in Johnson's habitual manner, as coming from outside the self, and the syntax turns the harbourer of the vice into its victim. It is not merely that, as *Rambler* 76 remarks, 'no man was yet wicked without secret discontent': Johnson's language often identifies the wickedness with the discontent, as in the description of suspiciousness a few issues later. 'It is said, that no torture is equal to the inhibition of sleep long continued; a pain, to which the state of that man bears a very exact analogy, who dares never give rest to his vigilance and circumspection, but considers himself as surrounded by secret foes, and fears to entrust his children, or his friend, with the secret that throbs in his breast, and the anxieties that break into his face.' (79) In *Rambler* 17 he suggests that the moralist may 'set the heart free from the corrosion of envy, and exempt us from that vice which is, above most others, tormenting to ourselves, hateful to the world, and productive of mean artifices and sordid projects' (a view of envy shared by Bacon and John Stuart Mill among others). We hear too, of 'fear, the most overbearing and resistless of all our passions' (17), or 'the fruitless anguish of impatience' (32), 'the gulfs of insatiability' (38), the dreamer poisoned by opiates (89), the vicious man attacked by internal 'arrows of reproach' (76). Resentful anger, too, is in Johnson's eyes a form of anguish:

He that willingly suffers the corrosions of inveterate hatred, and gives up his days and nights to the gloom of malice, and perturbations of stratagem, cannot surely be said to consult his ease. Resentment is an union of sorrow with malignity, a combination of a passion which all endeavour to avoid, with a passion which all concur to detest. The man who retires to meditate mischief, and to exasperate his own rage; whose mind never pauses from the remembrance of his own sufferings, but to indulge some hope of enjoying the calamities of another, may justly be numbered among the most miserable of human beings ...

At the height of his 'infection' Pertinax, the sophist, does not enjoy that dizzying sense of his own importance which controversialists do in Swift. Rather

I had perplexed truth with falsehood, till my ideas were confused, my judgment embarrassed, and my intellects distorted. The habit of considering every proposition as alike uncertain, left me no test by which any tenet could be tried; every opinion presented both sides with equal evidence, and my fallacies began to operate upon my own mind in more important enquiries. It was at last the sport of my vanity to weaken the obligations of moral duty, and efface the distinctions of good and evil, till I had deadened the sense of conviction, and abandoned my heart to the fluctuations of uncertainty, without anchor and without compass, without satisfaction of curiosity or peace of conscience; without principles of reason, or motives of action...

When moral evils so consistently reveal themselves as sufferings, the stance of the moralist as physician becomes rather more plausible.

Descriptions of suffering, in *The Rambler*, are not confined to those pieces which explictly allude to the format of medical writings. In many essays, apart from those shaped as medical histories, human miseries, whatever they are, take on the pungency and virulence of physical suffering. In *Rambler* 6, for instance, a rather cool and detached commentary on the notion that changing one's place of residence will make one happy suddenly produces a comparison to

> those that suffer under the dreadful symptom of canine madness, termed by physicians the hydrophobia or 'dread of water.' . . . These miserable wretches, unable to drink though burning with thirst, are sometimes known to try various contortions or inclinations of the body, flattering themselves that they can swallow in one posture, that liquor, which they find in another to repel their lips.

This analogy is startling in its terribleness, yet Johnson introduces it with the disarming 'Who can look upon this kind of infatuation, without reflecting . . .?' Sometimes images of torture are accompanied by a grim kind of humour, as in the reinterpretation in *Rambler* 163 of the myth of Tantalus:

> 'I saw,' says Homer's Ulysses, 'the severe punishment of Tantalus. In a lake whose waters approached to his lips, he stood burning with thirst, without the power to drink. Whenever he inclined his head to the stream, some deity commanded it to be dry, and the dark earth appeared at his feet. Around him lofty trees spread their fruits to view; the pear, the pomegranate and the apple, the green olive, and the luscious fig quivered before him, which whenever he extended his hand to seize them, were snatched by the winds into clouds and obscurity.'
>
> This image of misery was perhaps originally suggested to some poet by the conduct of his patron, by the daily contemplation of splendour which he never must partake, by fruitless attempts to catch at interdicted happiness, and by the sudden evanescence of his reward, when he thought his labours almost at an end. To groan with poverty, when all about him was opulence, riot and superfluity, and to find their favours which he had long been encouraged to hope, and had long endeavoured to deserve, squandered at last on nameless ignorance, was to thirst with water flowing before him, and to see the fruits to which his hunger was hastening, scattered by the wind.

In yet another *Rambler* people who have lost their money are said to be 'torn in pieces' by the 'vultures which always hover over fortunes in decay'.

The latent meaning of these sometimes almost gratuitous metaphors is the omnipresence of suffering and it suggests an imagination laden with memories of pain. It is possible to relate the frequent appearance of such metaphors not only to Johnson's reading in medicine, but to the conditions of his private life that no doubt led to this interest. *The Rambler* nowhere directly expresses Johnson's experience of illness. What happens rather is that in these essays Johnson recasts and reconfigures his illness symptoms into an acceptable public mode of moral discourse. He refocuses private illness meanings into stabilised and detached public metaphors of disease. In other words, whilst the writer sets himself up as physician, and as we shall see, inserts himself into a specific tradition of moral discourse in which the writer figures as a doctor, the metaphors of his text betray his condition as patient. His harrowing experience of the conditions that are metaphorised into the ills he designs to 'cure' is what underwrites his authority as a sage.

Having presented so insistently the sufferings of various human conditions, Johnson turns naturally, in a complementary series of essays, to the general question of remedy. But there was already in existence a body of thought, influential and revered, which dealt with precisely this question, and which Johnson could not help but discuss if he wanted to clear the way for attention to his own prescriptions. A whole series of *Rambler*s therefore alludes to, or specifically mounts a critique of the stoic philosophers of the first century AD (*Rambler*s 2, 6, 29, 32, 47, 52, 89 etc.). In the writings of the first-century Latin tragedian and moralist Seneca, the younger, one finds in fact close anticipations of Johnson's specific handling of the parallel between the moralist's and the physician's enterprise. Like Johnson, Seneca suffered from ill-health, particularly asthma, all his life (Caligula spared him on the assumption that the sickly philosopher would probably soon die off anyway) and perhaps as a result of this, medical parallels and analogies are endemic in his work. In his essays, such as that *On Tranquillity*, and in the *Letters to Lucilius*, the medical parallel utilised by Plato and Aristotle is first notably turned in Johnson's way.

For Seneca, as for other later classical philosophers, the claim that their work had practical utility was urgent. Deprived of political power by Nero in AD 62, Seneca travelled about southern Italy, composing the letters to Lucilius in the few years before, on the emperor's orders, he and his wife with him, took their own lives in AD 65. The letters have been called 'specimens of an activity of moral consultancy, real or imaginary, which Seneca wants us to regard as his substitute for the life of political action'.[23] In an endlessly reiterated comparison Seneca claims to be the physician who can heal the ills of a man's soul as a doctor heals those of his body. In one of the first of the letters, defending himself from the charge of purposelessness, he writes, for instance, that he is 'working for later generations, writing down some ideas that may be of assistance to them. There are certain wholesome counsels, which may be compared to prescriptions of useful drugs; these I am putting into writing; for I have found them helpful in ministering to my own sores, which, if not wholly cured, have at any rate ceased to spread ... '[24] The essay *On Tranquillity* is organised as a prescription for the 'complaint' of Serenus, who asks the philosopher for 'any remedy by which you can put a stop to this vacillation of my mind'. The claim of the moralist to be a physician is kept constantly before the reader by repeated parallels between the mind and the body, and by moral injunctions drawn from medical and physiological experience. 'Just as some sores long for the hands that injure them, and delight in being touched, and whatever irritates the foul itch of their bodies is grateful; in like manner I should say that those minds, in which passions break out like bad sores, consider toil and trouble a pleasure' Seneca writes. 'As in time of pestilence, we must be careful lest we sit near persons who are already seized and burning with the disease, because we shall incur danger and be poisoned by their very breath; so in choosing the character of our friends we must endeavour to choose those who are least impure. It is the beginning of disease for healthy bodies to come in contact with the sick.'[25]

Johnson's friend, colleague on the *Gentleman's Magazine* and contributor to the *Rambler*, Elizabeth Carter, published in 1758 a translation of the sayings of another stoic, the slave Epictetus (AD 55–135).[26] In her Introduction Carter makes an assessment of stoicism from the Christian point-of-view, comparing its 'excesses' with those of the rival school of Epicurians. 'The stoical excess was more useful to the Public', she writes, 'as it often produced great and noble Efforts towards that Perfection, to which it was supposed possible for Human Nature to arrive. Yet, at the same time, by flattering Man with false and presumptuous Ideas of his own Power and Excellence, it tempted even the best to Pride'.[27] Johnson, who was one of Elizabeth Carter's many subscribers, would have concurred with what he read there. No Christian could accept the stoic 'boast' that overcoming vulnerability is within the unaided power of man, yet this did not mean that one could have no sympathy at all with their endeavour. Johnson's exasperation with, even contempt for, such claims is obvious enough. *Rambler* 150 opens, like several others, with disparaging remarks directed at the stoics. Their attempts at consolation resemble 'the practice of physicians, who, when they cannot mitigate pain, destroy sensibility, and endeavour to conceal by opiates the inefficacy of their other medicines'. Yet the very adoption of this metaphor, I suggest, already concedes the similarity between their field of practice and his own: the stoics are simply a rival school. Johnson goes on to make an explicit acknowledgement, borrowing one of Seneca's favourite metaphors, that 'the antidotes with which philosophy has medicated the cup of life, though they cannot give it salubrity and sweetness, have at least allayed its bitterness and contempered its malignity; the balm which she drops on the wounds of the mind abates their pain, though it cannot heal them', and the essay that follows is essentially a commentary on Seneca's *On Tranquillity*. It is misleading to suggest that because, logically, 'Christian-stoicism is a contradiction in terms' Johnson could not have to some extent shared the stoic position.[28] The premise of stoic philosophy, that life is compounded of pain, and the aim and the endeavour of the stoic philosophers, to suggest means by which its pain could be alleviated, are the same as his. In Seneca's use of the medical parallel not only is moral philosophy analogous to medical practice, but, since vices are 'sores', the 'sage' becomes a compassionate doctor. Common as medical metaphors are in later philosophy – common as they are in all discourse – Seneca and Johnson are linked by the frequency and consistency with which they assume this role. Moral philosophy is not for them as it was for Bacon an instrument of mental eugenics; it is offered as a balm for 'wounds'. The moralist becomes one who seeks for the means of alleviating pain. Nor does this mean only the offering of consoling reflections. Seneca and Johnson's approach more nearly resembles the search for mental techniques by which not painful experience, but more specifically, painful or obsessive thoughts, may be managed or controlled.

Seneca concludes his Epistle 53 to Lucilius with this typical flourish:

The wise man's life spreads out to him over as large a surface as does all eternity to a god. There is one point in which the sage has an advantage over the god; for a god is freed from terrors by the bounty of nature, the wise man by his own bounty. What a wonderful privilege, to have the weakness of a man and the serenity of a god. The power of philosophy to blunt the blows of chance is beyond belief. No missile can settle in her body; she is well-protected and impenetrable. She spoils the force of some missiles and wards them off with the loose folds of her gown, as if they had no power to harm; others she dashes aside, and hurls them back with such force that they recoil upon the sender. Farewell.[29]

Rambler 32 is Johnson's most thorough and earnest statement of his disagreements with the stoics on 'the art of bearing calamities'. His famous words adopt and modify Seneca's proud metaphors:

> The cure for the greatest part of human miseries is not radical, but palliative. Infelicity is involved in corporeal nature, and interwoven with our being; all attempts therefore to decline it wholly are useless and vain: the armies of pain send their arrows against us on every side, the choice is only between those which are more or less sharp, or tinged with poison of more or less malignity; and the strongest armour which reason can supply, will only blunt their points, but cannot repel them.
>
> The great remedy which heaven has put into our hands is patience, by which, though we cannot lessen the torments of the body, we can in great measure preserve the peace of the mind, and shall suffer only the natural and genuine force of an evil, without heightening its acrimony, or prolonging its effects.

Johnson's revision of Seneca merges his metaphors with ones drawn from the Christian tradition. For instance, the phrase 'involved in corporeal nature and interwoven with our being' reiterates Milton's description of our fallen condition in *Areopagitica*, in which 'the knowledge of good is so involv'd and interwoven with the knowledge of evill', though Johnson's 'corporeal' gives the verbs a characteristic palpability.[30] And whilst borrowing Seneca's conception of philosophy or reason as a shield warding off the arrows of outrageous fortune, Johnson revivifies the metaphor in a single word, 'tinged'. The peculiar memorable force of his prose resides in the combination of a syntax which asserts that the powers of the will or reason are drastically curtailed, with a balanced, controlled cadence which comfortingly implies that strength is present and of some avail, none the less.

Johnson at the close of this essay makes what, taken in isolation, could look like a routine Christian gesture towards the necessity of patience, 'a settled conviction of the tendency of every thing to our good'. In the body of the essay he proposes a quite different conception of patience which conflicts with both Christian and stoic quietism, one much more in line with his actual practice in dealing with his physical ills. 'Patience and submission are very carefully to be distinguished from cowardice and indolence. We are not to repine, but we may lawfully struggle; for the calamities of life, like the necessities of nature, are calls to labour and exercises of diligence.' Activity and motion are intrinsic to Johnson's conception of 'patience'. His metaphors for diseases of the soul, as we have seen, are metaphors often enough of inertia, of abeyance of the will. Sorrow, he declares, 'is the putrefaction of stagnant life, and is remedied by exercise and motion'. So no wonder Johnson has little sympathy with the stoic ideal of 'apathia', remarking in a typical comment in *Rambler* 47, 'An attempt to preserve life in a state of neutrality or indifference, is unreasonable and vain ... we may surely endeavour to raise life above the middle point of apathy at one time, since it will necessarily sink below it at another.'

Johnson, of course, has internalised the legacy of Newtonian mechanics. Metaphors of force, of motion, of attraction and repulsion, of momentum and balance, make up the very fabric of his prose. It is partly for this reason that the 'remedies' he proposes coincide with, or parallel, the teachings of earlier medical writers on the management of physical disease. Sometimes, as Sydenham, Cheyne and other physicians had before him, Johnson simply recommends physical exertion or exercise as a remedy for mental distress. More interestingly, he sometimes seems to carry the idea of motion as itself curative into the mental realm. A typical statement is, 'Active employment or public pleasure, is generally a necessary part of this intellectual regimen, without which, though some remission may be obtained, a complete cure will scarcely be effected'. The mind works in just the same way as the body, Johnson surmises, and the same physical laws apply to the one as to the other. A medicine which saw the body largely in dynamic or even hydraulic terms, and therefore treated its disorders with means intended to effect drastic changes in its distribution of solids and fluids is carried over, by metaphor, into the realm of mental 'remedies'. Just as 'obstructions' were to be dislodged by exercise or by abrupt shocks, or 'peccant matter' moved from a site within the body to some less dangerous place on its surface and there released, so Johnson's prescriptions tend to envisage some form of physical reorientation within the mind. Day-dreaming, that curse of scholars, may be cured, he suggests, by 'close application to some new study, which may pour in fresh ideas, and keep curiosity in motion'

(89). 'Sorrow is a kind of rust of the soul, which every new idea contributes in its passage to scour away' (47). It helps the melancholic, Johnson suggests, to 'take a survey of the world, to contemplate the various scenes of human distress' for this 'furnishes a new employment for the mind and engages the attention on remoter objects' (52). 'The attention is dissipated by variety, and acts more weakly upon any single part, as that torrent may be drawn off to different channels which, pouring down in one collected body, cannot be resisted.' Behind the metaphor is perhaps the conception of iatromechanical 'discussion', the drawing off into different channels of the body's vitiated fluids. 'Austerities and mortifications are means by which the mind is invigorated and roused, by which the attractions of pleasure are interrupted, and the chains of sensuality broken', Johnson writes in *Rambler* 110. 'Austerity is the proper antidote to indulgence; the diseases of the mind as well as body are cured by contraries, and to contraries we should readily have recourse if we dreaded guilt as we dread pain.' Treatment 'by contraries' is a piece of ancient medical lore at least as old as Galen: but the contrary that Johnson has in mind here is really analogous to iatromechanics, since it consists in 'a change of life'. There may be limits to Johnson's conception of psychological remedies, but in many ways these simply reflect the corresponding conceptual limitations of the physiological medicine from which he was deriving his parallels.

Yet many of the *Ramblers* touch on topics nowadays dealt with in psychological therapy, in its many guises. Extreme groundless anxiety is examined in *Rambler* 29 for example; sorrow settling into habitual melancholia and psychic inertia in *Rambler* 40; obsessive or neurotic behaviour in 89. Johnson's 'remedies' for these maladies do not promise complete cures. They rest, too, on the premise that the will of the sufferer is still sound, that he or she can still be recalled to the principles of 'right reason'. Johnson, of course, understands this limitation of his practice. Essay after essay stresses that its intervention will only have any salutary effect on the earliest symptoms of a mental or emotional disease, when for instance 'the pain of repressing them is less pungent' (38). Otherwise they become 'radicated by time' (89), and, in time, as I have argued, Johnson's metaphors show them to become inaccessible to the will or the reason. Medical metaphors begin, in the *Rambler* essay series, as forms of conceit. Words like 'acrimony', 'affection', 'fermentation', 'mortify', or 'obstruct' all probably would convey for the series' first readers a freight of medical significance and so tend to bestow a complex resonance (half witty, half medically grave) upon the Rambler's voice. But the conceit becomes something more than this in Johnson's adoption of the inherited comparison between moral philosophy and medical counsel. It becomes an essential way of expressing his conception that human emotional life is largely a matter of suffering and that therefore the moralist who addresses its illnesses or diseases becomes, perforce, a kind of physician.

One could claim then, that in the *Rambler* Johnson generates by metaphorical transference the role of psychological physician. No such function, no such role had previously existed (in England, at any rate). True, as Bacon wrote, 'the poets and writers of histories' were 'the best doctors of this knowledge' of the mind, but their comments were random, unsystematic, embedded in works with their own dramatic or narrative ends. Here for the first time is a writer who addresses himself to the ills of the mind, under the aegis of a metaphorical framework which legitimises his activity as a form of therapeutics. The systematic employment of the medical metaphor not only shapes the essays, it also proclaims Johnson's essential ends. He examines the mind, not to further intellectual endeavour, to maximise its capacities, as had Bacon, nor to scarify and denounce its evil ingenuities as did earlier moralists and sermon writers, but firstly, to isolate and define its various maladies, and secondly to offer help to those who suffer from them. A generation brought up on the sociological, psychological and medical 'case-history' may find his discussions severely restricted by the mode in which they are presented, but there is some evidence that his contemporaries recognised the nature of his achievement and understood its significance. Partly because the Rambler promised no miraculous cures, no invulnerable defences, and in fact drew attention to the limits of his medicinal power, carefully circumscribing the occasions on which his remedies could be effective, he was to be believed. His credibility or authority, so crucial in any paramedical transaction, may partly be ascribed to this, but also perhaps to the sober and impersonal detachment with which his style invested these dissections of morbid conditions. Boswell, at least, pays tribute to *Rambler* 54 as 'occasionally very medicinal to the mind' and he goes on to adopt Johnson's own metaphor in the famous and heartfelt tribute he pays to the enterprise as a whole. 'I venture to say, that in no writings whatever can be found *more bark and steel for the mind*, if I may use the expression'.[31] Johnson had succeeded in using his private experience of suffering as metaphors, and in the process had converted himself from patient into doctor.

The *Rambler* was the foundation of Johnson's contemporary reputation, as the ten collected editions before his death in 1784 testify. The prestige and authority acquired by the 'sage' of these moral essays was to be drawn upon many times by Johnson in his later years when he was asked for psychological advice or comfort. If these essays anticipate, as I have been implying, a psychotherapeutic approach to the inner life, it must be noted that it was many years before such a role could become anything remotely like a professional one. But I shall argue in the next chapter that a few years later Johnson nevertheless made an important contribution to the history of psychiatry that those professionally engaged in the treatment of the ills of the mind acknowledged and made use of – that unlike the *Rambler* essays, offers a study in convincing detail of an individual psychological 'case'.

5

THE HISTORY OF A MAN OF LEARNING

THE MORAL climax to *Rasselas* (1759) is the chapters (40–4 and 46) describing the astronomer. The young prince, who has been searching for the ideally happy way of life, one day declares that he intends 'to devote himself to science, and pass the rest of his days in literary solitude'. 'Before you make your final choice', replies Imlac, the poet, philosopher and man of the world who is his mentor, 'you ought to examine its hazards, and converse with some of those who are grown old in the company of themselves. I have just left the observatory of one of the most learned astronomers in the world, who has spent forty years in unwearied attention to the motions and appearances of the celestial bodies, and has drawn out his soul in endless calculations.'[1] Imlac then tells the history of his acquaintance with this astronomer of Cairo: how he first visited him, how they gradually became more intimate, how Imlac's admiration grew until he 'thought him the happiest of mankind, and often congratulated him on the blessing that he enjoyed'. But the astronomer has evidently some secret anxiety, and one night when they are sitting together 'in the turret of his house', in the darkness, he declares: 'Hear, Imlac, what thou wilt not without difficulty credit. I have possessed for five years the regulation of weather, and the distribution of the seasons ...' Imlac, with great respect, asks him how long he has possessed this power, and he replies that it originated in a fancy: 'About ten years ago, said he, my daily observations of the changes of the sky led me to consider, whether, if I had the power of the seasons, I could confer greater plenty upon the inhabitants of the earth':

'One day [he declares] as I was looking on the fields withering with heat, I felt in my mind a sudden wish that I could send rain on the southern mountains, and raise the Nile to an inundation. In a hurry of my imagination I commanded rain to fall, and, by comparing the time of my command, with that of the inundation, I found that the clouds had listened to my lips.'[2]

This occasion, five years ago, has been led up to by five years of fantasising in which the astronomer 'sat days and nights in imaginary dominion'.

The story of Imlac's acquaintance with the astronomer and the later development of their friendship is accompanied by passages in which Imlac expounds to Rasselas and his companions, his sister the Princess Nekayah and her maid Pekuah, a theory about the origins and development of insanity. Johnson is represented in Richard Hunter and Ida MacAlpine's monumental compilation *Three Hundred Years of Psychiatry, a History presented in Selected English Texts*, and in Stanley Jackson's recent *Melancholia and Depression, From Hippocratic Times to Modern Times* by this speech of Imlac:[3]

'Disorders of intellect, answered Imlac, happen much more often than superficial observers will easily believe. Perhaps, if we speak with rigorous exactness, no human mind is in its right state. There is no man whose imagination does not sometimes predominate over his reason, who can regulate his attention wholly by his will, and whose ideas will come and go at his command. No man will be found in whose mind airy notions do not sometimes tyrannize, and force him to hope and fear beyond the limits of sober probability. All power of fancy over reason is a degree of insanity; but while this power is such as we can controul and repress, it is not visible to others, nor considered as any depravation of the mental faculties: it is not pronounced madness but when it becomes ungovernable, and apparently influences speech or action.

To indulge the power of fiction, and send imagination out upon the wing, is often the sport of those who delight too much in silent speculation. When we are alone we are not always busy: the labour of excogitation is too violent to last long, the ardour of enquiry will sometimes give way to idleness or satiety. He who has nothing external that can divert him, must find pleasure in his own thoughts, and must conceive himself what he is not, for who is pleased with what he is? He then expatiates in boundless futurity, and culls from all imaginable conditions that which for the present moment he should most desire, amuses his desires with impossible enjoyments, and confers upon his pride unattainable dominion. The mind dances from scene to scene, unites all pleasures in all combinations, and riots in delights which nature and fortune, with all their bounty, cannot bestow.

In time some particular train of ideas fixes the attention, all other intellectual gratifications are rejected, the mind, in weariness or leisure, recurs constantly to the favourite conception whenever she is offended with the bitterness of truth. By degrees the reign of fancy is confirmed; she grows first imperious, and in time despotick. Then fictions begin to operate as realities, false opinions fasten upon the mind, and life passes in dreams of rapture or of anguish.[4]

It is this theory, not Johnson's narrative of the astronomer, which, by and large, has been received into the history of psychiatry: whether it is original or not can be seen if we set it in the context of the ideas about insanity current in his day.

There are two main approaches to problem of insanity in the mid eighteenth century. One group, the philosophers of mind, discussed madness as the false association of ideas; the other, the professional physicians, attempted to apply the premises of their physicalist training to the exploration of mental aberrations. The picture is complicated because several of the philosophers – Berkeley, Mandeville, David Hartley and most importantly John Locke – were doctors or amateur doctors themselves. Of the professional physicians who wrote on insanity the most successful and significant was William Battie, physician to St. Luke's Hospital, whose work *A Treatise on Madness* was published in 1758, not long before Johnson began work on *Rasselas* in January 1759. Battie's is a professional work in the sense that it draws upon wide clinical experience with insane or disturbed patients, it is intended for fellow physicians, and it goes about its business in a rigorously methodical or deductive manner. It is not, like earlier works in this field, a self-help handbook, or a discourse on such genteel disorders as melancholy, hypochondria or the spleen. Battie proposes a theory of insanity, categorises insanity into two main types, and argues that cases in the second – 'consequential' – insanity, are open to cure. The *Treatise on Madness* is a great contrast to *Rasselas*, but Battie's argument is worth reviewing because it gives such a clear view of what a progressive and enlightened mid eighteenth century physician thought about insanity.

Battie begins from the premise that insanity is a disorder of sensation and perception. The origin of sensation and perception being the nerves, madness must be caused by interference with their proper composition or internal functioning. In what seems to be a reliance upon Boyle's corpuscular philosophy he suggests that whatever changes take place in the nerves must be due to rearrangement of their medullary or inner particles, and that this, in turn, can only be due to some external force – 'which force necessarily implies impulse and pressure'. Battie says that he cannot say how this 'pressure upon the medullary substance contained in the nerves' actually produces 'delusive ideas', but he affirms that autopsies of those who have died insane abundantly confirm this hypothesis of compression and obstruction in the brain.

Battie was, of course, trained as an orthodox physician. (He was made President of the College of Physicians in 1764 – the only psychiatrist ever to hold the position.) By claiming that the inner workings of the 'nervous substance' cannot be known, and by transferring his attention to the 'external causes', he succeeded at one stroke in bringing insanity into the same explanatory system as other disorders in the eighteenth century. Whatever the immediate cause of insanity, its proximate cause is compression of the material substance of the nerves brought about by the distention of neighbouring vessels, exercising abnormal force upon the substance of the nerves, and thus causing them to malfunction: insanity is resolved into a disorder of the body conceived of as a hydraulic system. The forcible propulsion of fluids, the distention or constriction or obstruction of pipes, channels and vessels, 'the sudden intrusion of improper fluids into smaller canals': here is the familiar landscape of the eighteenth-century body now offered as an explanation of delusive sensation. Hence there is nothing specially unique about the site or locus of madness. Battie obeys the unitary consequences of iatromechanism in full. 'The same sanguinary or serous obstructions' he writes, 'are capable in any other nervous part of the body of exciting false ideas as well as in the brain'.[5]

But what, in turn, precipitates these 'obstructions'? In answering this question, Battie links his theory to the traditional view of the remoter causes of insanity and to the traditional typology of the insane. There are two main causes: 'Tumors by Fluxion', and 'Tumors by Congestion'. The first suffices to explain the 'repeated observation that Madness frequently succeeds or accompanies Fever, Epilepsy, Child-birth, and the like muscular disorders; and that the tumultuous and visibly spasmodic passions of joy and anger are all at least for a time maniacal'.[6] The second form is far more serious:

As for Tumors by Congestion ending in Madness, that is to say those loads of fluids which gradually overcharge the vessels contiguous to the nerves, and by compressing a sufficient quantity of medullary matter create delusive sensation as effectually as does inflammation or any sudden distention of the same vessels: such gradual or chronical congestions are frequently, tho' not always, an effect of a very different sort of muscular constriction, easily distinguishable from the former by its manner of invasion and continuance.

For this spasmodic action of the muscular fibres is very gentle at first, and so far from alarming either the patient or his friends, that for some time it is very little attended to or even discernible. But what it wants in violence is more than made up by its obstinate duration and increase: inasmuch as it seldom remits, and is with great difficulty relieved by art.[7]

Furthermore, pressure upon the nerves may be due to weakness or 'laxity in the overloaded vessels themselves', a laxity caused by neglect of exercise, or by 'premature, excessive or unnatural Venery' or, in a striking descent from the attitude of philosophic objectivity to the familiar Augustan contempt for the virtuoso, prolonged study:

And from hence we may account for the chimaerical dreams of infirm and shattered Philosophers, who after having spent many days and nights without closing their eyes in unwearied endeavours to reconcile metaphysical contradictions, to square the circle, to discover the Longitude or grand Secret, have at last fallen half asleep, and who by excessive attention of body have strained every animal fibre, and may without a metaphor be said to have cracked their brains.[8]

Battie's book provoked an intemperate, anti-intellectual, but nevertheless quite shrewd reply by Dr John Monro, physician to Bethlem Hospital, his ire aroused by Battie's opening remarks about the secrecy which had hitherto surrounded the treatment of the insane. It received a notice by Smollett in the *Critical Review* and was read by both Johnson and Boswell. Smollett's review accepts and endorses the iatromechanism of its author. 'By the bye', he writes, 'we are surprised that our author, in enumerating the causes of madness, has omitted a lentor and viscosity of the blood ... Such a fluid circulating with difficulty through the tender vessels of the brain, will certainly distend these vessels, so as to occasion an extraordinary pressure on the medullary substance; and this pressure will be apt to produce either the *melancholia* or *mania*.'[9]

It is interesting to compare Battie's iatromechanism with a more conventional account of madness, and there are good reasons for choosing as an example Robert James' *Modern Practice of Physic* of 1746 which is representative in including 'melancholy' among physical disorders and not the less representative for being badly confused. Among the 'causes' of melancholy which James (following Boerhaave) cites is 'all things which fix, exhaust, or disturb, the nervous fluid of the brain' (Battie treats this 'chimaera' as he calls it, of the 'nervous fluid' with contempt.) But other 'causes' have certain resemblances to Battie's theory. Melancholy, from which madness 'differs only in degree', is linked to 'that disorder of the blood and humours, which the ancients called black bile', but the specific nature of the disorder is, once again, compression. Not, in James' account, of the medullary substance, but of the blood. 'This disorder has, for its material cause, the earth, and the inspissated oil, of the blood, united and compacted together':

if the matter of the disorder ... is rendered more dense, tenacious and incapable of motion, it will necessarily be forced into the hypochondriac vessels, as is obvious from the nature of this humour, the situation and condition of these vessels, and the known laws of hydraulics. Hence it will gradually remain, be accumulated, and become stagnant there.[10]

James (or his source) is uncertain whether these 'obstructions' in which the essential cause of melancholy lies, are 'the cause, or the effect, of a perverted imagination', and although his account of the causes of insanity is quite different from Battie's he seems to agree that scholars are particularly vulnerable. Its preconditions are: 'every thing which expels the more moveable and fluid, and fixes the other parts of the blood; violent exercise of the mind employed almost day and night on one and the same object; obstinate watchings, violent commotions of mind, in the way of mirth and sorrow ...'[11]

Since Battie classifies madness into different species, he is able to resist the notion that there is any specific or general remedy for the condition. Instead, he emphasises the importance of management and regimen, stressing the necessity of removing the patient from his usual surroundings. He is sharply critical of the practice at Bethlehem Hospital of allowing spectators into the wards:

The visits therefore of affecting friends as well as enemies, and the impertinent curiosity of those, who think it pastime to converse with Madmen and to play upon their passions, ought strictly to be forbidden.[12]

He makes one recommendation which Johnson was later to remember and endorse. The madman's employment 'should be about such things as are rather indifferent, and which approach the nearest to an intermediate state (if such there be) between pleasure and anxiety'.[13] But since, as Boswell dryly remarked, his book is 'sufficiently corporeal',[14] his diagnosis of the causes of madness as varieties of constriction and pressure necessarily involves him in proposing physical remedies. In the case, for instance, 'when delirious pressure from the nervous substance, more particularly that contained in the abdomen, is gradual or chronical, if such gentle evacuants, tho' often and properly repeated, prove unable to lessen or relieve the stagnating matter ... it becomes absolutely necessary to shake with violence the head and hypochondria by convulsing the muscular fibres with emetics rougher purges and errhines. For such spasmodic action communicates a vibrating motion to the solid fibres of the whole body ...'[15] Hence though Battie's theory of madness differs from the more traditional one in James, the remedies suggested tend to be more or less the same.

The intention of cure being 'to remove those obstructions which are either the cause or the effect of a perverted imagination' it follows that a violent physical impact may be the surest way to dislodge them. If madness results from gradual muscular constriction, perhaps 'an alternate motion of muscular fibres artificially excited in some other part of the body' may relieve it. Various forms of shock treatment may be serviceable in the case of 'fixed nervous Sensation as in obstinate muscular constriction', 'it being a known observation ... that no two different perceptions can subsist at the same time any more than the two different species of morbid muscular action, viz *the convulsive and the constrictive*'. But before one castigates as 'barbarous and cruel' the treatment given by eighteenth-century doctors to the insane, one needs to understand the premises behind it.[16] 'Unexpected precipitation into the sea' which James says is the 'principal remedy' for madness, may be a traditional but is not a wanton cure. The nineteenth-century 'moral managers' of the insane found such treatments horrifying partly because their iatromechanistic theoretical justification had been utterly forgotten. Battie writes sensibly and humanely in fact about the caution needed in applying the traditional 'remedies', bleeding, blisters, vomits etc. This, and his emphatic statement that it is better to do nothing rather than to do harm, was obviously influential in creating a more enlightened climate for the discussion of insanity in the later eighteenth century. In fact, the *Treatise on Madness* may be said to have initiated serious discussion of the subject.

Battie's remarks upon cure were to be far more influential than his theory. But that theory was generated by the need, which affected everyone who wrote about madness, to forge a connection or to build a bridge, between the observable, social or sociological position of the afflicted person, and his or her crazy notions. Just how did these (generally agreed) conditions, long study, particularly of abstruse matters, religious obsession, deep grief (etc.), produce in certain cases such bizarre symptoms? The answer to this question, it is worth remarking at this point, was bound to be delayed until the symptoms themselves had been more closely observed and more accurately described, but an important approach to the problem was offered from a different direction by the philosophers, and particularly by two with medical experience, John Locke and David Hartley.

Locke puts his finger upon this crucial issue as early as 1677/8 in journal entries which anticipate some of his thinking about the nature of insanity in Book 2 of *An Essay Concerning Human Understanding*. In the *Essay* he makes what Hunter and McAlpine call his 'classical distinction between the mental processes of "Idiots" and those of "Mad Men"':

> In fine, the defect in Naturals, seems to proceed from want of quickness, activity, and motion in the intellectual faculties, whereby they are deprived of reason; whereas madmen, on the other side, seem to suffer by the other extreme. For they do not appear to me to have lost the faculty of Reasoning; but having joined together some ideas very wrongly, they mistake them for truths; and they err as men do that argue right from wrong principles: for by the violence of their Imaginations, having taken their fancies for realities they make right deductions from them . . .[17]

In the Journal Locke distinguishes between the faculties of memory and imagination. Madness, he thinks, occurs 'when the mind takes one for t'other its own imagination for realitys and in this (it seems to me) madness consists and not in the want of reason'. This may explain the tendency of madness to result from prolonged study:

Hence one may also see how it comes to passe that those that thinke long and intently upon one thing come at last to have their minds disturbed about it and to be a litle crackd as to that particular. For by repeating often with vehemence of imagination the Ideas that doe belong to or may be brought in about the same thing a great many whereof the phansy is wont to furnish, those at length come to take soe deepe an impression that they all passe for cleare truths and realitys though perhaps the greatest part of them have at several times been supplied only by the phansy and are noething but the pure effects of imagination. This at least is the cause of great errors and mistakes amongst men even when it does not wholly unhinge the braines and put all government of the thoughts into the hands of the imagination as it sometimes happens, when the Imagination by being much imploid and getting the mastry about any one thing usurps the dominion over all the other facultys of the minde in all other, *but how this comes about or what it is gives it on such an occasion that empire how it comes thus to be let loose I confesse I cannot guesse.* (My italics)[18]

As Leslie Stephen remarked, Locke 'raises great questions without solving them', and never really answers this one.[19] In the *Essay* his attention is not upon madness, but on that false association of ideas which may make a normal man seem, in one particular, insane. 'A man who is very sober, and of a right understanding in all other things, may, in one particular, be as frantick as any in Bedlam'. This may happen suddenly, or it may be the effect of 'long fixing his Fancy upon one sort of Thoughts' but the explanation Locke profers is little more than a descriptive metaphor: it is that, for him, 'incoherent Ideas have been cemented together so powerfully, as to remain united'.[20] This pseudo-physiological explanation in fact disguises the really active agent, which is unnamed and invisible.

In chapter 33 of his second Book he examines that unreasonableness in men usually called prejudice, but which he considers a more serious 'taint' and argues that it comes from the same root and 'to depend upon the very same cause' as madness.[21] He gives many examples of the persistence of 'wrong connections' which continue to operate in the mind long after they were originally forged and in defiance of the acknowledged voice of reason:

Instances of this kind are so plentiful every where, that if I add one more, it is only for the pleasant oddness of it. It is of a young gentleman, who having learned to dance, and that to great perfection, there happened to stand an old trunk in the room where he learned. The idea of this remarkable piece of household stuff, had so mixed itself with the turns and steps of all his dances, that though in that chamber he could dance excellently well, yet it was only while that trunk was there, nor could he perform well in any other place, unless that, or some such other trunk, had its due position in the room . . .[22]

Locke devotes only one paragraph to the question of how these false connections are made:

This strong combination of ideas, not allied by nature, the mind makes in itself either voluntary, or by chance; and hence it comes in different men to be very different, according to their different inclinations, education, interests, etc. Custom settles habits of thinking in the understanding, as well as of determining in the will, and of motions in the body; all which seems to me to be but trains of motion in the animal spirits, which once set a-going, continue in the same steps they have been used to, which, by often treading, are worn into a smooth path, and the motion in it becomes easy, and, as it were, natural. As far as we can comprehend thinking, thus ideas seem to be produced in our minds; or, if they are not, this may serve to explain their following one another in an habitual train, when once they are put into their tract, as well as it does to explain such motions of the body.[23]

This explanation is a strange blend of abstract and physiological concepts. Trains of motion occur ('trains' are defined in Johnson's *Dictionary* as 'series, consecution either local or mental') which, like a stop-watch or a pendulum, or (more likely) a mechancial toy, are 'set a-going'. This toy 'continues in the same steps' (it is a walking toy), but attention slips away from the toy itself to the path which is the consequence of its 'treading' and which is 'worn smooth' by its continued (mechanical?) action. Does this happen inside the animal spirits? Where does the path lead to? The language leaves it quite unclear whether what occurs in the 'animal spirits' is meant to be a physiological reality or whether Locke is employing these terms merely as metaphors. And in the midst of this there are the 'animal spirits' themselves, which are also a metaphor but which are assumed, as generations of Galenists had assumed they were, to be reality.

David Hartley's account of madness shows a similar entanglement of metaphor and (supposed) physiology. In his *Observations on Man* (1749) he takes over the notion of madness as false association of ideas from Locke, and supplies a physiological mechanism to explain how this takes effect. Essentially his explanation consists of attributing physical properties to mental ideas. Ideas may, in certain circumstances, become 'magnified'; the 'vibrations belonging' to them may increase, and, if the nervous system is already disordered, then 'unnatural associations are too much cemented'. Locke's notion 'incoherent Ideas have been cemented together' is still half a metaphor: Hartley wants us to believe it actually happens. Like Battie, Hartley appeals to the autopsy as evidence:

In dissections after madness the brain is often found dry, and the blood vessels much distended; which are arguments, that violent vibrations took place in the internal parts of the brain, the peculiar residence of ideas and passions; and that it was much compressed, so as to obstruct the natural course of association.[24]

Hartley's theory depends entirely upon the sudden violence of these vibrations. He therefore has to supply a new explanation for the well-known tendency of scientists and philosophers to go mad.

'Inquiries after the philosopher's stone, the longitude, etc' lead to madness, not because of the protracted study associated with them, (though, he says, madness 'is of the same kind' with 'the prejudices and opinionativeness which much application to one set of ideas only occasions'), but because men are prompted to them – rather implausibly – 'by strong ambitions, or covetous desires'.

A later explanation of insanity combines Locke and Hartley. It is due to 'that tendency . . . vibrations in the medullary substance which when once excited, have to continue'.[25] This emphasis in Locke was most influential. The crucial source of the disorder in his account and in many writers (though not Hartley, who substitutes violence) who follow him, is repetition, continuance, or duration over time. It is repetition, or continuance, which accounts for the crucial transformation lying at the heart of the distinction between mere eccentricity and madness, the transformation of a voluntary to an involuntary process. How do ideas or fancies which we first entertain, come in the end to entertain, or to torment, us? The answer, for those who followed Locke, is their persistence over time. 'It matters not', writes Dr Mead, the most famous physician of his day, 'whether the ideas be true and real, or false and imaginary, provided the mind has been long intent upon them . . .' 'The instrument of all these motions, both of the mind and the body', he thinks, 'is that extremely subtile fluid of the nerves, commonly called animal spirits . . .'[26] George Cheyne offers an alternative physiological mechanism whilst at the same time including – or perhaps one should say 'including out' – the same essential explanation:

> The Chronical Passions, like chronical Diseases, wear out, waste and destroy the Nervous System gradually. Those Nerves which are necessary for considering, brooding over and fixing such a Set of Ideas on the Imagination, being constantly employ'd, are worn out, broken and impaired . . .
> . . . Some of these Passions, as Love, Grief and Pride, when very intense and long indulg'd, terminate even in Madness. The Reason is . . . because long and constant Habits, of fixing one Thing on the *Imagination*, begets a ready Disposition in the Nerves to produce again the same Image, till the thought of it becomes spontaneous and natural, like Breathing, or the motion of the Heart, which the Machine performs without the consent of the Will; . . .[27]

A passion, or idea, or image, innocent or neutral enough in itself becomes, over time, vicious or pathogenic. Over time it is 'indulged' and becomes a habit.[28] If insanity is the result of 'excessive intention of the mind, and thoughts long fixed on any one object', 'excessive attention of the body', 'obstinate watchings', or 'the frequent and uncurbed indulgence of any passion or emotion' (to cite the formulations of four different eighteenth-century physicians), it is clear that the doctor has an ethical as well as a medical duty to perform. This disorder, so bizarre and perplexing in its manifestations, originates in a moral fault – or rather in behaviour which becomes morally suspect by virtue of its repetition over a long period of time. Serving as an 'explanation' this aspect of the disorder's genesis draws its sting, domesticates it, situates it firmly within the universe of rational cause and effect. The mechanisms of the various theories of madness are really only means whereby this moral cause can be plausibly converted into its psychological performance.

Johnson's astronomer is evidently a relative of those who cracked their brains pursuing abstruse mathematical and scientific inquiries. He too has become ill as the result of bad habits contracted in his isolation. Time again takes the crucial role:

In time some particular train of ideas fixes the attention ... By degrees the reign of fancy is confirmed; she grows first imperious and in time despotick ...[29]

Johnson's is a purely psychological account. His distinction – even from the philosophers – is to refuse the temptation to insert an intermediary concept between the inception of the habit and its outcome. No vibrations in the medullary substance, no compression of the nerves, no pinguious blood, no nervous fluid, no subtle animal spirits are brought in to give a spurious scientific cogency to the analysis. There simply is no explanation: 'In time ... fictions operate as realities ...' This, the crucial moment, passes silently, without attention or comment. But it is not an oversight or an inadvertence. What Johnson's account stresses is precisely what the psychiatric approaches were designed to suppress: the dreadful apparent spontaneity of this transformation in mental life. 'Few can attain this man's knowledge', Imlac gravely rebukes his listeners, 'and few practise his virtues; but all may suffer his calamity. Of the uncertainties of our present state, the most dreadful and alarming is the uncertain continuance of reason.'[30]

There is an obvious divergence between the psychiatric endeavour to find causes (as the first step towards finding cures) and the prevailing endeavour (if one were to isolate it as this) of Johnson, to foster a more sympathetic attitude to the insane. To assume as a premise that the cause of insanity is frighteningly unknown, though we may avoid circumstances that tend to bring it into effect, is no starting point for a project devoted to the scientific understanding of the disorder. But several factors make this distinction between the two enterprises too simple. Psychiatry is no different from other branches of medicine in its dependence upon observation. Locke only restates Hippocrates when he writes in a letter to Richard Morton of 1692:

I fear the Galenists four Humours, or the Chymists Sal, Sulphur and Mercury, or the late prevailing Invention of Acid and Alcali, or whatever hereafter shall be substituted to these with new Applause, will upon Examination be found to be but so many learned empty Sounds, with no precise, determinate Signification. What we know of the Works of Nature, especially in the Constitution of Health, and the Operations of our own Bodies, is only by the sensible Effects, but not by any Certainty we can have of the Tools she uses, or the Way she works by. So that there is nothing left for a Physician to do, but to observe well, and so by analogy argue the like Cases, and thence make to himself Rules of Practice.[31]

General theories, says Locke, are 'that Romance way of Physick'. The eighteenth-century psychiatric writers neglect observation for theory: what is more, they are governed by the prejudice that a physiological 'explanation' is more valid or more convincing than a psychological one. So – victims of their very haste to explain – they produce in their 'vibrations', their 'nervous fluid', their 'delirious pressure' even Locke himself with his 'animal spirits', 'but so many learned empty sounds'. The science of Battie or Hartley is little more than a rigorous – or at least a determined – deductiveness from their own physiological postulates.

This science may be read in an infernal sense. When mechanical concepts are introduced they segregate the mad subject from the writer, a segregation intensified, most clearly in Battie, by the insistently foregrounded apparatus of logic and reasoning. The display of system, the tabulation of 'species of insanity' one meets with in later works of the century such as Erasmus Darwin's *Zoonomia* or Thomas Arnold's *Observations on Insanity*, may be the beginning of a genuine nosology, but they also serve the same need: to put as large a distance as possible between oneself and one's material. It is as if the student of madness were striving to convince himself that the theory he develops is not the product of his own inner fantasy. The thought is never far away. Monro suggests that Battie's 'metaphysical enquiries' should be proposed 'to the academicians of Bethlem, where it is amongst the *senior recluses* only that I can expect to find any one who is able to resolve them all.'[32] Even though Battie, remembering *Rambler* 32, writes 'Uneasiness is so interwoven in the very frame of mortals', he too is capable of this kind of insult, saying that theorists (of a different school) 'deserve' the 'suspicion of insanity'.[33]

Johnson's account is not less cogent than those of his contemporaries, but it is much more tentative, and the ground of its appeal is not to logic or rationality but to common experience: 'He who has nothing external that can divert him, must find pleasure in his own thoughts; for who is pleased with what he is?' The tendency is to align the writer with the symptoms he describes, to imply that the thought-processes he traces are universal ones, known to him as well as to others. At the same time, Johnson does advance a theory. The astronomer has become ill – or at least so it seems – as the result of his prolonged study. But if Johnson takes from the common stock this age-old notion that 'over much study' as Burton called it, makes one mad, he changes its emphasis. Implicitly self-confessional material is introduced to elucidate what actually happens in the mind of the student. 'When we are alone, we are not always busy . . .' Isolated and deprived, the scholar takes refuge in compensatory fantasies. It is not, therefore, his concentration but his relaxation that is the origin of the bad habit. Yet Johnson concurs with his contemporaries in locating the origins of madness in a habit, a habit 'indulged' until the favourite conception 'fixes' itself in the mind, and what was previously at the command of the will becomes obsessive and involuntary. Like them, Johnson sees normality and insanity as a continuum – a continuity drawn over time from a moral fault to its inevitable psychological punishment.

Much as they laboured to construct plausible theories of the origins of madness, and for all their experience with inmates, Battie and his contemporaries rarely seem in their writings to have observed the insane subject with any attention; they were content with largely traditional and stereotyped accounts of what a mad person was like (someone obsessed with religious guilt, for instance, someone raving and violent). Battie distinguished between different insanities and so moved towards the depiction of the individual case, but neither in his work nor in any writer prior to Johnson is the history of a patient's disorder through different phases given any but the most cursory attention. To quote Locke once again, 'Nicely to observe the History of Diseases, in all their Changes and Circumstances, is a Work of Time, Accurateness, Attention and Judgement'. 'An accurate history of the several kinds of madness from these physicians, who are much conversant with this distemper, is greatly wanted . . .', wrote Hartley in 1749.[34]

Johnson's achievement was to conceive of the study of the insane man as a narrative of his insanity, and to depict – as part of the madman's condition – the story he tells himself about its genesis, and the story of his interaction with others. This originality is what is stressed in the tributes that were paid to *Rasselas* by later eighteenth-century psychiatrists, John Haslam for example. Haslam, Apothecary to Bethlehem Hospital, is much the most literate and intelligent later eighteenth-century writer on insanity, as well as being a 'master of clinical description' himself.[35] His book *Observations on Madness and Melancholy* is pervaded by the influence of Johnson. Its epigraph is 'Of the uncertainties of our present state, the most dreadful and alarming is the uncertain continuance of reason'. He treats the older notion, that madness is a result of 'too great or long continued exertion of the mental faculties, as in the delirium which often succeeds long continued and abstract calculation' with contempt, substituting instead a half-paraphrase from *Rasselas*. 'The indulgence in those reveries which keep the imagination on the wing and imprison the understanding' he says, 'is likely to promote it'.[36]

Haslam's citation of *Rasselas* celebrates Johnson's understanding of just how plausible the madman can appear, and thus demonstrates, as Haslam says, how treacherous is the term 'lucid interval':

To those unaccustomed to insane people, a few coherent sentences, or rational answers, would indicate a lucid interval, because they discovered no madness; but he, who is in possession of the peculiar turn of the patient's thoughts, might lead him to disclose them, or by a continuance of the conversation, they would spontaneously break forth. A beautiful illustration of this is contained in the Rasselas of Dr. Johnson, where the astronomer is admired as a person of sound intellect and great acquirements by Imlac, who is himself a philosopher, and a man of the world. His intercourse with the astronomer is frequent; and he always finds in his society information and delight. At length he receives Imlac into the most unbounded confidence, and imparts to him the momentous secret. 'Hear, Imlac, what thou wilt not, without difficulty, credit. I have possessed, for five years, the regulation of weather, and the distribution of the seasons . . .'[37]

'Beautiful' is as much a professional as an aesthetic judgement: it celebrates the precision and finesse, the sheer inwardness with the demeanour of the mad that Johnson shows. This judgement is echoed by Thomas Arnold, who emphasises the clinical status of the whole history, saying, 'Though I can produce nothing better than poetical authority for this instance, yet as it is perfectly consonant to what I myself have experienced to be fact, I have ventured to set it down as such ... The whole story, and the observations upon insanity which accompany it, are as just, and philosophical, as they are elegant.'[38] It is an amazing confession that, nearly forty years after Hartley, professional psychiatry had still no better case studies than Johnson's fictional one. The account of the growth of the astronomer's disorder, the picture of his behaviour, is so convincing in fact, that many have suggested that the portrait must have been drawn from someone whom Johnson knew or had known.[39]

'What gives Johnson's fictional insight that madness is bred by imagination its special poignancy is the fact that it is clearly autobiographical', writes Roy Porter, and many readers intuitively agree with him, supported in their conviction by the many diary entries, such as those which Porter quotes, detailing Johnson's ceaseless struggle with 'vain imaginations'.[40] 'He had studied medicine diligently in all its branches', wrote Mrs Thrale, 'but had given particular attention to the diseases of the imagination, which he watched in himself with a solicitude destructive of his own peace.'[41] But besides worrying about his own habits of mind, Johnson had many opportunities of observing the eccentricities of others. One of the most significant stresses in the astronomer study – that madness may pass undetected in the world – came home to him early. Reporting a story of his father's always locking the front door of his dilapidated workshop, though anyone might easily walk in through the back, Mrs Thrale has Johnson say, '*This* ... was madness, you may see, and would have been discoverable in other instances of the prevalence of imagination, but that poverty prevented it from playing such tricks as riches and leisure encourage.'[42]

The very first time that Johnson and Boswell spoke privately together their talk was on this topic. It was 24 May 1763 and Johnson was living in rented and rather squalid rooms at No. 1 Temple Lane. 'Madness', Boswell reports Johnson saying,

frequently discovers itself merely by unnecessary deviation from the usual modes of the world. My poor friend Smart shewed the disturbance of his mind, by falling on his knees, and saying his prayers in the street, or in any other unusual place. Now, although, rationally speaking, it is greater madness not to pray at all, than to pray as Smart did, I am afraid there are so many who do not pray that their understanding is not called in question.[43]

It is an astonishing coincidence that on the other side of the wall, in the Temple, unknown to either of them, William Cowper was probably dwelling.[44] He was at this very time preparing himself with increasing anxiety for a position as Clerk of the Journals of the House of Lords, anxiety that was soon to drive him to suicide attempts and eventually to a private asylum at St Alban's. His 'terrors on this occasion arose to such an astonishing height', wrote his biographer William Hayley, 'that they utterly overwhelmed his reason.'[45]

'Madness has many mansions', according to Rochester. Christopher Smart's insanity had little enough in common with Cowper's, or with Johnson's melancholy, though Johnson tended to align himself with Smart's case. 'He insisted on people praying with him', he told Charles Burney, 'and I'd as lief pray with Kit Smart as anyone else. Another charge was, that he did not love clean linen; and I have no passion for it'.[46] If the public point here is that the behaviour of the insane and those considered robustly normal have much in common, the private thought is that perhaps insanity too is shared.

The lives of these two men were intertwined quite closely in the years before the writing of *Rasselas*. Their main connection might well have been the publisher John Newbery. Like Johnson's father, Newbery was a bookseller who also sold medicines. He was Smart's publisher, his father-in-law, and it seems clear, took charge of him when his symptoms of mental illness first appeared.[47] He may have referred Smart to his partner Dr Robert James. In 1756 Smart was certainly confined to Newbery's residence in Canonbury House, Islington, a mansion in which Goldsmith also lodged. On his recovery from this illness, Smart published a *Hymn to the Supreme Being on recovery from a dangerous fit of illness*, a poem prefaced by an effusive letter of gratitude to James who had attended him. The letter also defends the Fever Powders 'against the impotent attacks of those whose interest interferes with that of Mankind', an echo of the polemic in James' *Dissertation on Fevers* of 1748.[48] Treatment evidently included doses of the powders. From the poem itself it seems that the illness was as much a mental as a physical collapse: 'When death stood o'er me with his threat'ning lance', Smart writes, 'reason left me in the time of need, / And sense was lost in terror or in trance'.[49]

'This was the third time', Smart declares to James, 'that your judgment and medicines rescued me from the grave, permit me to say, in a manner almost miraculous'.[50] But alas, James' treatment did not prevent a relapse, and Smart in June 1756 was removed from Newbery's and confined to a private asylum.[51] In May 1757 he was handed over to William Battie at St Luke's Hospital. There his diagnosis must have been 'original' rather than 'consequential' madness, for he was discharged incurable in May 1758. His poverty being extreme, his friends sought to do what they could. David Garrick arranged a benefit performance of two plays, *Merope* and *The Guardian*, an event which took place on 3 February 1759. It was announced in the *Public Advertizer* on Wednesday, 17 January: 'For the benefit of a Gentleman, well known in the literary world, who is at present under very unhappy circumstances.' This was the same week, as it happens, that Johnson is said to have been writing *Rasselas*.

Another poet who might well have been in Johnson's thoughts was William Collins. Johnson had known Collins since he first came to London as 'a literary adventurer' about 1744. In the later years of the decade 'his life was assailed', writes Johnson in his biography, 'by ... dreadful calamities, disease and insanity'. 'His disorder was not alienation of mind, but general laxity and feebleness, a deficiency rather of his vital than his intellectual powers', Johnson says in 1781, and his judgement is corroborated by more modern scholars.[52] Whatever the specific causes of his condition Johnson again saw its affinities to his own. 'I have often been near his state', he wrote to Joseph Warton in December 1754, 'and therefore have it in great commiseration.' In April 1756 Johnson again wrote to Warton:

What becomes of poor dear Collins? I wrote him a letter which he never answered. I suppose writing is very troublesome to him. That man is no common loss. The moralists all talk of the uncertainty of fortune, and the transitoriness of beauty; but it is yet more dreadful to consider that the powers of the mind are equally liable to change, that understanding may make its appearance and depart, that it may blaze and expire.[53]

This carefully composed elegiac sentence is echoed in Imlac's declaration that 'Of the uncertainties of our present state, the most dreadful and alarming is the uncertain continuance of reason.'

But it is obvious that there are few close correspondences between either Smart's or Collins' cases and the astronomer's. Collins' madness was accompanied by progressive physical disability: Smart had bouts of frantic exhilaration, his drunkenness was as notorious as his praying; his illness was manifested in behaviour that was publicly sensational: he prayed in St James' Park and routed all the company. In this respect he conformed to his contemporaries' expectations. 'All agreed that it was the essence of lunacy to be visible, and known by its appearance', writes Porter, reviewing eighteenth-century cultures of madness. For 'Burton's or Boswell's contemporaries',

madness gave itself away. The mad looked quite peculiar. They went near-naked, tore their clothes or dressed fantastical, their hair festooned with straw. They acted oddly: now motionless, withdrawn: now preternaturally violent. They gobbled strange foods, such as vermin and dung, or refused to eat. They moved and gesticulated incessantly, apparently never sleeping, racked by tics and convulsions. Some bayed at the moon, or howled like dogs. Others tried to kill themselves. Altogether they were sub- or anti-human.'[54]

It is this traditional notion of the madman as beast or brute (a notion that was reflected in the often brutal treatment meted out to the insane) that the astronomer's story confronts, and against this background that its emphasis on the 'uncertain continuance of reason' has its shocking force. All Johnson's stress is upon the similarities between the state of madness and 'normal', socially accepted, behaviour. The dramatic structure of the chapters depends upon the contrast between the astronomer's public reputation – 'his integrity and benevolence are equal to his learning', says Imlac – and the sudden revelation of his inner life. The astronomer is guarded in demeanour, perfectly sober and reasonable in conversation. He is slow and reluctant to communicate his belief in his powers to Imlac, and when he does communicate his secret, the confession is accompanied by signs of guilt and anxiety. His obsession consumes and torments him, but he passes for a normal, in fact a supremely admirable, man.

One seeks for models among Johnson's acquaintances for this portrait, because there seem to be no precedents for this in fiction or medical texts. But there are brief instances in the literature on insanity which may have offered hints towards the construction of the astronomer's obsession, as well as towards its accompanying emotions. Richard Brocklesby's *Reflections on Antient and Modern Music, with the application to the cure of diseases* (1749), for instance, gives an account of the onset of insanity which has some resemblances to Johnson's (as well as to Locke's). The insane person, Brocklesby writes, at last come[s] to dwell upon the same subject so long, till the mind has imposed a sort of mechanical necessity on the organs that excite this idea, still to go on in the same manner; hence it sometimes happens, the person shall strive with his utmost efforts to get rid of that particular thought, yet it will in spite of his endeavours rush upon his mind, and dwell with him continually, sometimes the whole external face of things is changed . . .[55]

But rather than give examples from his own observation, Brocklesby, like Thomas Arnold, falls back upon a classical instance:

A woman, mentioned by TRALLIAN [de arte Medica, Lib. i, cap. xvii] continually held up her middle finger, on which she imagined she was supporting the whole world, and was in perpetual anxiety lest she should suffer her finger to give way, and destroy the world, with its inhabitants . . .[56]

Similarly the astronomer's responsibilities demand 'unremitted vigilance'. He declares 'If the task of a king be considered as difficult, who has the care only of a few millions, to whom he cannot do much good or harm, what must be the anxiety of him, on whom depend the action of the elements and the great gifts of light and heat!' Supreme power, that is also unending punishment: that is the paradox of the insane obsession.

But if there are passing mentions of guilt and anxiety in the literature as an accompaniment or constituent of insane delusions, there are no precedents for the central and extended attention Johnson gives to this aspect of the astronomer's experience. Nor are there formal precedents for another fundamental aspect of Johnson's presentation, his allowing a madman a voice. It is the astronomer in fact who initiates the whole discussion of madness, when he breaks his silence and makes his disclosure to Imlac in chapter 45: it is the astronomer who, in revealing his delusion, reveals that he has 'reasoned long against his conviction': it is the astronomer's voice which speaks of the 'fear, disquiet and scrupulosity' that accompanies this conviction (chapter 46) and later tells of his struggles against the inveterate persuasion that rushes upon his soul. This madman is endowed with self-reflection, self-consciousness, and a self-knowledge that tragically approaches completeness: Johnson even has him say, 'I sometimes suspected myself of madness'. This dramatic presentation of the astronomer's experience sets up some conflicts with the theory of insanity Imlac expounds. Some of the nuances of his speeches in fact suggest interpretations more consonant with later developments in the history of psychology.

The astronomer is presented initially as merely a representative figure, by profession a philosopher or scientist (not a poet or man of letters), and when he is first mentioned by Imlac he belongs obviously with the clinical stereotypes of the textbooks. He has 'spent forty years in unwearied attention to the motions and appearances of the celestial bodies, and has drawn out his soul in endless calculations'. He is one 'whose thoughts have been long fixed upon a single point', sufficient clue to Johnson's readers that he was destined for madness, even if the hint is lost upon Rasselas and his party. The stereotype is modified, given light and shade, as the figure's behaviour is dramatised: 'He would sometimes,' says Imlac, 'gaze upon me in silence with the air of a man who longed to speak what he was yet resolved to suppress. He would often send for me with vehement injunctions of haste, though, when I came to him, he had nothing extraordinary to say. And sometimes, when I was leaving him, would call me back, pause a few moments and then dismiss me.'[57] This series of symptomatic actions thus formally presents evidence of mental conflict. The astronomer has evidently something on his mind, and these preliminaries leave us to wonder whether its outbreak into speech would be a good or a bad sign.

In an earlier episode of *Rasselas* the schism between the public self of another 'sage', the stoic philosopher, and his private sufferings is marked by the entry of the prince into a darkened inner room, the 'misery's darkest cavern' of the poem on Levet. The astronomer's impulse to disclosure finally triumphs whilst he and Imlac are sitting in darkness (and faces, though Johnson does not say as much, cannot be seen):

'At last the time came when the secret burst his reserve. We were sitting together last night in the turret of his house, watching the emersion of a satellite of Jupiter. A sudden tempest clouded the sky, and disappointed our observation. We sat a while silent in the dark, and then he addressed himself to me in these words: 'Imlac, I have long considered thy friendship as the greatest blessing of my life. Integrity without knowledge is weak and useless, and knowledge without integrity is dangerous and dreadful. I have found in thee all the qualities requisite for trust, benevolence, experience and fortitude. I have long discharged an office which I must soon quit at the call of nature, and shall rejoice in the hour of imbecility and pain to devolve it upon thee.'

'I thought myself honoured by this testimony, and protested that whatever could conduce to his happiness would add likewise to mine.'

'Hear, Imlac, what thou wilt not without difficulty credit. I have possessed for five years the regulation of weather, and the distribution of the seasons:

the sun has listened to my dictates, and passed from tropick to tropick by my direction; the clouds, at my call, have poured their waters, and the Nile has overflowed at my command; I have restrained the rage of the dog-star, and mitigated the fervours of the crab. The winds alone, of all the elemental powers, have hitherto refused my authority, and multitudes have perished by equinoctal tempests which I found myself unable to prohibit or restrain. I have administered this great office with exact justice, and made to the different nations of the earth an impartial dividend of rain and sunshine. What must have been the misery of half the globe, if I had limited the clouds to particular regions, or confined the sun to either side of the equator?' (chapter 41)

The circumstances that surround this announcement make it a confession. Imlac is the first person, in five years, in whom the astronomer has felt enough confidence to broach his secret. But what does the astronomer's speaking really mean? In one sense – the most obvious – he is seeking to legitimise his obsession, to find his convictions corroborated in the outside world, to capture Imlac's collaboration: in this sense it is an outbreak of disease. In another, the breaking of silence puts the delusion at risk, and implicitly calls for help. When he is getting better, the astronomer reinterprets this moment; 'I now see', he declared, 'how fatally I betrayed my quiet, by suffering chimeras to prey upon me in secret; but melancholy shrinks from communication, and I never found a man before, to whom I could impart my troubles ...[58] Imparting his troubles, is not, on the face of it, though, what he does here. What he speaks is mad, but speaking at all is a sign of sanity.

Imlac is placed in a difficult position by this doubleness of purpose. He must not sacrifice by too evident a scepticism the privileged position the older man accorded him – that would be to sacrifice all hope of curative intervention. But if he seems to collaborate with the delusion, that too puts an obstacle in the road to recovery. Imlac's tentative, brief questions leave much unstated, but their caution prepares for the explicit discussion of attitudes towards the insane that is the subject of the following chapter (44). In effect, Imlac's questions make use of that always precarious resource, the distinction between the disease or delusion and the person who harbours it. He is respectful, addressing the astronomer as 'Sir' (he is called 'thou' in reply): 'Why, Sir, do you call that incredible which you know, or think you know, to be true?' – a question whose skill consists in its offering the astronomer the possibility of different selves, one of which is potentially aware of his disorder.

But the astronomer is an eighteenth-century scientist, a watcher of the skies, an observer *par excellence*. He knows that on these grounds he has no case, and he is ready with an answer: 'I know too well the laws of demonstration to think that my conviction ought to influence another, who cannot, like me, be conscious of its force.' The speech becomes more emotional in its rhythms, more obviously ego-centered, as he shifts his ground from Enlightenment 'demonstration' to quasi-Romantic 'feeling'. 'I, therefore, shall not attempt to gain credit by disputation. It is sufficient that I feel this power, that I have long possessed, and every day exerted it.' The imperious quality of his speech – as befits one who rules the welfare of the world – continues in the dictatorial sentences that follow one another in chapter 43, 'The astronomer leaves Imlac his directions.' So Imlac acquiesces, and there follows the abstract discussion of 'the dangerous prevalence of Imagination' and an interlude in which the young travellers talk with an old man before the story returns to the astronomer in chapter 46. This break in the narrative shows more attention to dramatic effect than Johnson is sometimes given credit for: at the end of the intervening chapter the princess and her lady retire because 'the madness of the astronomer hung upon their minds', an effect that the delay, the suspension, of the astronomer's story also has upon the reader.

'Surely this man is happy!' exclaims the princess on first hearing of the astronomer and his reputation. The irony is that he is, in fact, dreadfully unhappy. Many eighteenth-century writers would have been capable of thinking up a madman who believes he controls the climate. But Johnson puts at the forefront not the delusion itself, but the astronomer's suffering: the compulsion, and the guilt and anxiety which always accompany it. If he is temporarily absent from his station, 'some painful sentiment pressed upon his mind', when he carries out his great office he is burdened with scruples: he must ensure that the world receives a due proportion of sunshine and rain, yet his good intentions are frustrated by his failure to harness the winds. Though his powers are God-like, he fears persecution from a yet stronger power: if 'The great charge with which I am entrusted' is neglected, he cries, 'how dreadful is my crime!' He worries too about who is to follow him – 'the care of appointing a successor has long disturbed me.' Around the basic obsession or delusion are gathered a whole cluster of – as we would say – neurotic anxieties and fears.

Powerful as he thinks he is, the astronomer describes his condition as being in the grip of stronger powers. There is a remarkable passage in Bernard de Mandeville's *Treatise of the Hypochondriak and Hysterick Passions* which describes vividly what the astronomer too experiences:

'tis Heaven to me when I think how perfectly well I am; but then how miserable on the other side again is the thought, of harbouring some where within me, tho' now I feel it not, a vast enormous Monster, whose Savage force may in an instant bear down my Reason, Judgement and all their boasted strength before it. It is inconceivable that when I perceive my Affliction coming upon me, I should be so sensible as I am, that the dangers I dread, and the sorrows I foresee, are only chimeras, mere Falsities, and nothing but the Impositions of a Distemper; and yet, as it increases, sink underneath the weight of it, tho' armed with so much Resolution against it. I know it, I resist it, yet I can't overcome it . . .[59]

Johnson's metaphoric language is less powerful than Mandeville's, but it too stresses the frightening and degrading experience the sufferer undergoes. 'This contemplation fastened on my mind', laments the astronoker, and later he declares, 'If I am accidentally left alone for a few hours . . . my inveterate persuasion rushes upon my soul, and my thoughts are chained down by some irresistible violence'. 'I am like a man habitually afraid of spectres, who is set at ease by a lamp, and wonders at the dread which harrassed him in the dark, yet, if his lamp be extinguished, feels again the terrours which he knows that when it is light he shall feel no more.'

Fancy 'grows first imperious, and in time despotic', reiterates Imlac in his account of the genesis of insanity, 'false opinions fasten upon the mind, and life passes in dreams of rapture or of anguish'. Johnson's metaphors imply that there are forces in the mind with independent agency, that these are primitive, bestial, predatory, latent with dreadful power. But the implications that reside in this language are not brought to the point of conceptualisation. Lockean associationism conceives of different faculties or agencies of the mind, but does not conceive of them as having sources of power unavailable to other faculties. 'All symptoms give the impression of a something that seems to break in upon the personality from an unknown source – a something that disturbs the continuity of the personality and that is outside the realm of the conscious will', agrees a more modern psychologist.[60] The 'complexes' are 'autonomous', says Jung, 'they offer resistance to the conscious intentions and come and go as they please.'[61] 'Symptoms', says Freud, 'give the patient himself the impression of being all-powerful agents from an alien world, immortal beings intruding into the turmoil of mortal life.'[62] But though this sense of a foreign presence, a spectre, is a consistent part of the astronomer's experience, Johnson's account or analysis of insanity gives no explanation for it or its origins. It is simple enough for the modern reader to read the astronomer's descriptions of an apparently external force as reports, in effect, of the unconscious. The sage's anxiety is for him, and for Johnson, explained by the burdensomeness of his task, but a modern reading of such a case would suggest that it is on the contrary connected to an inner reality hidden from him. Its presence would be the sign that the real pressures behind his fantasy were not being directly expressed in it. Such an interpretation might go on to suggest that the astronomer's guilt attaches to his original, hidden, fantasy, or to his 'indulgence' in it, but has been transferred in his conscious mind to its symptoms. The process of repression has split it from its original cause and attached it to another idea which is then mistaken for it. The primordial fantasy has become distorted into a fantasy of power (or perhaps of power of a different sort) at the same time as the emotions have been transformed, in ways for which analogies would be found in the phobias, from pleasure to 'fear, disquiet and scrupulosity'. The super-ego, to adopt later Freudian terminology, though, has not been deceived: it can read that code which to the ego is baffling, and thus punishes the obsessive fantasy as much as it would punish the original idea of which the fantasy is a symptom. Such an explanation of the astronomer's misery is of course not remotely like anything that Johnson's account gives a hint of: I offer it only to underline the suggestion that the 'unremitting anxiety' which accompanies the delusion, as well as the process of 'going mad' itself, is not explicable in the terms that Johnson had available to him, and to suggest how far he is from the Freud to whom he has been so often compared.[63]

What account of the astronomer's guilt Johnson gives is in Imlac's remarks in chapter 46. 'When melancholick notions take the form of duty', he says, 'they lay hold on the faculties without opposition, because we are afraid to exclude or banish them.' The astronomer's duties are carried out under the eyes of a jealous, punishing god, but this assumption is too deeply engrained in Johnson's thought to be made explicit here. Imlac's discussion seems to escape from the point in another respect: the astronomer's are not merely melancholic notions, they are obsessive convictions. He really believes he has supernatural powers, his scruples and dutifulness are merely its accompaniment or consequence. Yet Imlac's earlier remarks about the origins of insanity do contain some insight that can be applied illuminatingly to the astronomer's particular case. Why does his delusion take this form? Not, as common sense would reply, that having so much to do with the skies, his dreams naturally concern them. Rather the question is, why are these dreams of power?

When we are alone we are not always busy; the labour of excogitation is too violent to last long; the ardour of enquiry will sometimes give way to idleness or satiety. He who has nothing external that can divert him, must find pleasure in his own thoughts, and must conceive himself what he is not; for who is pleased with what he is? He then expatiates in boundless futurity, and culls from all imaginable conditions that which for the present moment he should most desire, amuses his desires with impossible enjoyments, and confers upon his pride unattainable dominion. The mind dances from scene to scene, unites all pleasures in all combinations, and riots in delights which nature and fortune, with all their bounty, cannot bestow.

In time some particular train of ideas fixes the attention, all other intellectual gratifications are rejected, the mind, in weariness or leisure, recurs constantly to the favourite conception, and feasts on the luscious falsehood whenever she is offended with the bitterness of truth.[64]

The motive force, so Johnson's account suggests, is the desire of pleasure, and the mechanism, to use a Jungian term, is compensatory. There is an antithesis, a balance between the fantasy and the reality – between 'the lusciousness of falsehood' and 'the bitterness of truth'. The astronomer's delusion of power can then be thought of as a compensation for his actual powerlessness. When he has emerged from belief in his gifts, Imlac's concluding advice is 'keep this thought always prevalent, that you are only one atom of the mass of humanity, and have neither such virtue nor vice, as that you should be singled out for supernatural favours or afflictions'. For the astronomer, the surrender of his delusion is almost a confession of his life's failure. 'I have passed my time in study without experience', he says sadly:

'in the attainment of sciences which can, for the most part, be but remotely useful to mankind. I have purchased knowledge at the expence of all the common comforts of life; I have missed the endearing elegance of female friendship, and the happy commerce of domestick tenderness. If I have obtained any prerogatives above other students, they have been accompanied with fear, disquiet and scrupulosity; but even of these prerogatives, whatever they were, I have, since my thoughts have been diversified by more intercourse with the world, begun to question the reality.'[65]

There is undoubtedly sympathy with this figure, but hidden within the chapters on the astronomer is also a critique of the pursuit of useless knowledge. Johnson's commendation of Raphael's reproof of Adam's curiosity after the planetary motions in the *Life of Milton* is only one place in his work where he criticises the search after 'star-knowledge', in John Hardy's phrase, rather than the cultivation of self-knowledge. More importantly, and more perceptively, the chapters provide a parodic extrapolation and reversal of the Enlightenment fantasy (see, for example, *Robinson Crusoe*) that it might be possible to appropriate the natural world completely to the purposes of man.[66] To subjugate Nature to the rule of Reason is a common urge, of which the astronomer's dreams are one version, and Johnson's own enterprises are another. The hubristic desire for total control over the natural world is a madness, like Xerxes' in the lines of Juvenal long known by heart to Johnson before he translated them as:

> ... Madness fires his Mind
> The Waves he lashes and enchains the Wind.

Such mad ambition is not unknown to scholars, moralists and lexicographers. In *Adventurer* 137 attention is given to the claim that 'no age was ever made better by its authors, and that to call upon mankind to correct their manners, is like Xerxes, to scourge the wind and shackle the torrent'. More significantly, in the closing passages of the Preface to the *Dictionary*, Johnson speaks of his early hopes that his enterprise might fix the language, and that it was in his power 'to change sublunary nature'. 'I have indulged expectation which neither experience nor reason can justify', he confesses, and declares that 'to enchain syllables and lash the wind are equally the undertakings of pride'.[67] The day-dreams of benevolent power of the astronomer, 'the regulator of the year', are thus not so very different from the day-dreams of Samuel Johnson, the regulator of the language, and these chapters castigate them just as the chapter of *Rasselas* about the Arab who is bored to death with his harem, might well be thought to castigate Johnson's fantasies of life in a seraglio.[68] Johnson saw that his own dreams and ambitions had the seed of madness in them. The turret of the astronomer is a metaphoric transposition of the attic at Gough Square.

In chapter 46 the Princess and Pekuah, her maid, visit the astronomer who 'was pleased to see himself approached with respect by persons of so splendid an appearance' and Johnson's case history begins to approach the question of cure. Pekuah's 'conversation took possession of his heart': he wants to see more and more of them, and so they invite him to the house of Imlac, 'where they distinguished him by extraordinary respect'. 'From this time the astronomer was received into familiar friendship, and partook of all their projects and pleasures: his respect kept him attentive, and the activity of Rasselas did not leave much time unengaged.'

This may be linked with Johnson's later and more famous remark to Boswell in 1777 that 'a madman loves to be with people whom he fears; not as a dog fears the lash; but of whom he stands in awe'.[69] Superficially this resembles such commonplaces of mad-doctor's doctrine as Thomas Willis's statement that 'indeed for the curing of Mad people, there is nothing more effectual or necessary than their reverence or standing in awe of such as they think their Tormentors.'[70] But this is an argument for brutal treatment to subdue the animal wildness of the insane, as Willis continues, 'Furious Madmen are sooner, and more certainly cured by punishments and hard usage, in a strait room, than by *Physick* or Medicines'. Johnson's position is completely misunderstood if it is assumed that he is speaking in favour of hard usage of the mad. On the contrary, his ideas about therapy resemble those to be announced by the humanitarian guardians of the insane over half a century later. The Quaker, Samaul Tuke, at York, found the patients' 'desire for esteem' a powerful agent towards their management and cure: 'This principle in the human mind which doubtless influences in a great degree, though often secretly, our general manners; and which operates with peculiar force on our introduction into a new circle of acquaintance.'[71] The astronomer is now mingling with personages of whom he stands in awe and he naturally wishes to aquit himself well with them. Johnson's theory, like that of those who supposedly revolutionised the treatment of the insane in the first decades of the nineteenth century, is that as a result of this his mind will have less time and energy to spend on its own problems and delusions and they will therefore diminish. Rasselas, his sister and her maid surround the astronomer with just such a 'fictional family' as the managers of early asylums created to subdue the manifestations of insanity in their patients. Since this theory and the institutional treatment it promoted have come under attack for substituting inner compulsions, inner guilts, inner chains, for the external restraints previously employed by mad-house keepers,[72] it is worth pointing out that Johnson's stress is on the contrary fact, the compulsion, the loss of liberty felt by the madman when he is governed by his delusion. Mental or spiritual freedom was precisely what he lost in his madness, for he was 'chained down', not literally, as the inmates of Bedlam were, but by his thoughts. In comparison, mingling with others, and keeping the thoughts of his common mortality, as Imlac advised, 'always prevalent', he is 'set at ease'. But Johnson would certainly not have supported later nineteenth-century reformers' calls for institutional confinement of the insane: as his comments on Smart's case ('I did not think he ought to be shut up. His infirmities were not noxious to society') and the whole drift of the astronomer's history suggest he believed that madness frequently passes undetected and without destructive effect. It was through mingling with ordinary society, by submitting to the current of the world, that it might be alleviated, if not cured.

In his suggested therapy, then, as in his attitude to the insane, Johnson is extraordinarily advanced beyond contemporary theorists, though some keepers of asylums, like Dr Nathaniel Cotton at St Albans, to whom Cowper recorded his gratitude, probably showed similar kindness towards their charges.[73] In other respects Johnson's astronomer has much in common with his contemporaries. He is a scholar, whose madness has arisen from too much concentration on one subject over too long a period of time, and the theory by which Johnson explains it owes much to Locke. But Johnson parts company with the medical and philosophical discourse on madness in his stress on the apparently normal outward appearance of the madman, on madness's private, secret reign, with its frightening corollary that madness is something we may all suffer from. The astronomer is literate, highly articulate, highly self-aware: but these qualities cannot save him from being possessed by insane delusions. Johnson's notion that the astronomer's fantasy is one of superhuman power is certainly consistent with traditional ideas of madmen's fantasies; but again he brings a new dimension by stressing the anxiety, the guilt and unhappiness that are the delusion's accompaniments. Finally, the cure he proposes is one which his contemporaries were beginning to explore. Prompted partly by Battie's work, private and later public asylums increasingly stressed the sequestration of the troubled in mind, and removal from their families. The palliative, if not radical, remedy for the astronomer is, too, simply a change in his outer circumstances – not sequestration, in his case, but company. Imlac may adopt a kindly, sometimes interrogative role that resembles the therapist rather than the 'mad-doctor', but the astronomer undergoes no version of the 'talking cure': his new friends do not encourage him to dwell on his fantasies, or on his own past life. Instead the stress is on escape from himself, activity and diversion.

Johnson's depiction of the astronomer's 'case', this 'history of a man of learning' is very different from the medical case history as conceived by his contemporaries. Not until the later nineteenth century was the patients' account of their experience thought to be so relevant to understanding their disorder. Johnson's presentation, sometimes consciously imprecise, and certainly less dogmatic, than those of his contemporaries writing within an avowedly medical tradition, is in effect more cogent. His avoidance of explanatory physiological concepts suggests an awareness of the balance between observation and theory appropriate to a certain stage of scientific development more percipient than the essentially pre-emptive theories current in his time. The writings of philosophers and physicians differ from Johnson's not in being less fictional, less fanciful, less metaphoric: they are riddled with metaphor, but unconsciously and therefore destructively so. Johnson's fictional case history is at least as important and probably had significantly more impact upon emerging ideas about the insane (as well as showing more intimate knowledge of them) than most of the professional work of his time. The narrative of the astronomer's case, as well as Imlac's theory, then, is an important contribution to psychiatric history. It is a latter-day confirmation of Francis Bacon's view that, where 'medicining of the mind' is concerned, the poets and writers of histories are 'the best doctors of this knowledge'.[74]

6

DR ROBERT LEVET

IN HIS *Dissertation on the Gout and Rheumatism* of 1745 Robert James explained why he included no detailed prescriptions:

I esteem it a high Injury to Society to furnish Empirics with Materials to destroy Mankind, by their Misapplication. By Empirics I mean all those whose Consciences permit them to trifle with the Healths, and play with the lives of Men, without proper education to form their Judgments, and duly qualify them for so arduous an Undertaking; who dare to affront Providence, by daily premeditated Murders, for the narrow consideration of improving a private Fortune . . .

Diagnosis and prognosis, James declares, have scarcely been improved beyond their sources in Hippocrates and his followers, and he warms to the attack:

Now those whose Education have not qualify'd them for reading the Sources from whence the most essential Parts of Physic are derived, and who have never heard of, and much less perused their best Copyers, are not very likely to be aquainted with the principal Doctrines of Physic. Hence in the Chambers of the Sick, instead of Predictions, we so frequently hear of Nervous Fevers, Nervous Symptoms, Animal Spirits, and all that unintelligible Jargon, and unmeaning Impertinence, which is too frequently made the Asylum of Ignorance, and the Refuge of Quackery and Imposture, to the infinite Reproach of true Physic and the scandal of the Healing Art.[1]

James' comments reflect the orthodox and academic medicine of the period in their stress on classical learning as well as on the doctor's reasoning from sound 'doctrines' of physic. The dominant tradition of English medicine made logic more important than observation and held that theory derived its force more from internal consistency than empirical verification. There was a related tendency to undervalue practical experience and to look down upon those whose knowledge or practice of medicine involved them in actually examining patients.

James obviously sees the relationship between the formally educated, qualified physician and other practitioners in adversarial terms;
throughout the century the words 'empiric', 'irregular' or 'quack'
designate with contempt those who dare to set up as doctors without
having attended university and acquiring there the appropriate
classical and theoretical training. In London, the bastion of this
position was the College of Physicians, which with its sister corporations, the Corporation of Surgeons (separated from the barbers in
1745) and the Society of Apothecaries, attempted to control the
profession and to impose a tripartite division, almost a caste system,
upon its members. At the top were the fellows of the College, scarcely
ever numbering more than fifty, and those doctors to whom, after
passing an examination, it granted a licence to practise within
London, and its extra-licentiates, doctors licensed to practise outside
the seven-mile limits of the city.[2] Graduates of Oxford and Cambridge could also practise, even those whose degrees had been given –
as, incidentally, Robert James' had been – by royal mandate,
sometimes without having carried out an appropriate course of study.
Next came the surgeons, including increasingly as the century wore
on, the 'man-midwives', who some thought scarcely gentlemen since
their job would involve more physical contact with the patient than
simply feeling his or her pulse. The apothecaries acted in many ways
as medical advisers to the poor, though they were forbidden by law to
charge a fee for consultation.

In actuality, both in London and especially outside the city, these
divisions were impossible to sustain. The country doctor, or the
doctor based in a county town whatever his formal qualifications,
found himself undertaking surgery, usually minor and routine, and
supplying as well as prescribing medicines for his patients.[3] Medicine,
after all, was a business. The type of practice had to be tailored to the
needs of the patients, the availability of resources, the proximity of
rival practitioners etc. Some of these rivals would no doubt be
officially unqualified or 'irregular', not to mention the very numerous peasant or folk doctors who, perhaps like Silas Marner, gained a
reputation for healing powers on the basis of a traditional knowledge
of one or two active herbs.[4] Many clergymen and gentry, there is
literary evidence in plenty to suggest, would have prescribed fairly
systematically, and as well as these there were the itinerant practitioners, not all of them quacks, who travelled from town to town,
offering to cure disorders, cancers or venereal disease.[5] When we

consider the variety of medical practice it becomes very difficult to substantiate a hard-and-fast division between orthodox and unorthodox medicine, or to use this division as an index to the probable nature or standard of practice. A dissenting minister, James Clegg of Chapel-en-le-Frith in Derbyshire took up the practice of medicine, having learned the rudiments from a physician in near-by Macclesfield. When he was threatened with prosecution he bought an MD from Aberdeen and became, by this process, a 'legitimate' physician.[6] 'Sir' John Hill, one of the most notorious quacks of the mid eighteenth century (though he made important contributions to botanical knowledge and Johnson used him in the *Dictionary*), similarly got his degree from one of those universities, as Sir John Hawkins sourly remarked, which would scarce refuse one to an apothecary's horse. And John Mudge, called by Boswell 'the celebrated physician', whom Johnson consulted by letter about his sarcocele in 1783, was actually an irregular; he obtained his MD at King's College, Aberdeen, only in 1784, when he was over sixty.[7]

The diffusion of medical practice and knowledge throughout the kingdom was recognised, if in an ambiguous manner, in a work such as William Buchan's *Domestic Medicine* (the first of many editions appeared in 1769), which steers its way carefully between maintaining the necessity of professional medical assistance and at the same time plausibly offering help and advice to the middle classes who, it implicitly acknowledges, act as physicians for their families and servants.[8] Much earlier, the proposals for the *Medicinal Dictionary* make it clear that it is at least partly aimed at readers who practise medicine as a branch of charity. Not much is as yet known of the ordinary literate person's knowledge of medicine in the eighteenth century, since medical historians have tended to concentrate so much on official medicine and the lives and achievements of a few star names. But there were, then as now, lots of publications aimed at the medical self-help market.[9]

It is as hard to find out much about the lives and therapeutic practices of the unlicensed doctors. Unlike the official physicians, they kept no records of consultations. They were sometimes employed by the overseers of the poor and given the deferential title of 'Dr' in the accounts of payment, but they must frequently, even more often than qualified doctors, have received their fees in the form of payment in kind. They probably lived from hand to mouth. The itinerant quacks have at least left behind them the newspaper advertisements in which their healing powers and their royal patrons are touted. But the lives of these obscure men, never meeting the junctures of official power, must have almost entirely perished, leaving no memorial behind.[10]

Robert Levet is one who would have gone into the dark with the rest but for his friendship with Samuel Johnson. The two men first met at about the same time (1746) that James was thundering against empirics. Levet may have lived with Johnson before 1762, but certainly for about twenty years he was an inmate of Johnson's household, occupying the garret at Bolt Court. One night in January 1782, when Johnson was with Mrs Thrale, he was musing alone in his room about his future and he resolved (so he later told Boswell) that, if he were to set up house elsewhere, he would at all events try to retain Levet's companionship. In the morning the servant, probably Frank Barber, brought him word of Levet's death. Johnson wrote that day to Thomas Lawrence:

Sir,

Our old friend Mr Levett, who was last night eminently cheerful, died this morning. The man who lay in the same room hearing an uncommon noise got up: and tried to make him speak, but without effect, he then called Mr Holder the apothecary, who though, when he came, he thought him dead; opened a vein but could draw no blood. So has ended the long life of a very useful, and very blameless man.[11]

Lawrence was retired by this time, but still being consulted almost daily by Johnson, who was suffering a particularly severe bout of asthmatic trouble. In the following spring Johnson was reciting to his friends and giving out copies of his famous memorial verses on Levet. Eventually the poem found its way into print in the *Gentleman's Magazine* for August 1783:

On the Death of Dr ROBERT LEVET,
by Dr. JOHNSON

Condemn'd to hope's delusive mine,
    As on we toil from day to day,
By sudden blasts, or slow decline,
    Our social comforts drop away.

Well tried through many a varying year,
    See LEVET to the grave descend;
Officious, innocent, sincere,
    Of ev'ry friendless name the friend.

Yet still he fills affection's eye,
  Obscurely wise, and coarsely kind;
Nor, letter'd arrogance, deny
  Thy praise to merit unrefin'd.

When fainting nature call'd for aid,
  And hov'ring death prepar'd the blow,
His vig'rous remedy display'd
  The power of art without the show.

In misery's darkest caverns known,
  His useful care was ever nigh,
Where hopeless anguish pour'd his groan,
  And lonely want retired to die.

No summons mock'd by chill delay,
  No petty gain disdain'd by pride,
The modest wants of ev'ry day
  The toil of ev'ry day supplied.

His virtues walk'd their narrow round,
  Nor made a pause, nor left a void,
And sure th'Eternal Master found
  The single talent well employ'd.

The busy day, the peaceful night,
  Unfelt, uncounted, glided by,
His frame was firm, his powers were bright,
  Tho' now his eightieth year was nigh.

Then with no throbbing fiery pain,
  No cold gradations of decay,
Death broke at once the vital chain,
  And forc'd his soul the nearest way.

Johnson's friends and biographers were inclined to disapprove of Johnson's friendship with Levet. Hawkins described him as 'one of the lowest practitioners in the art of healing that ever sought a livelihood by it'. Mrs Thrale called him 'that odd old surgeon whom [Johnson] kept in his house to tend the out-pensioners'. Boswell wrote of 'his humble friend Mr Robert Levet, an obscure practiser in physick amongst the lower people'.[12] All three were amused, even slightly scandalised, at Johnson's respect for his friend's abilities. 'Johnson', wrote Hawkins, 'whose credulity in some instances was as great as his incredulity in others, conceived of him as of a skilful medical professor, and thought himself happy in having so near his person one who was to him, not solely a physician, a surgeon, or an apothecary, but all.'[13] Boswell was particularly amused on Good Friday 1773, breakfasting with Johnson on tea and cross buns, to hear Frank, the negro servant, refer to 'Doctor Levet'. There is no doubt that Johnson did value Levet's abilities highly. Writing to Thomas Cumming, a Quaker acquaintance who was desperately ill, in May 1774, for instance, he says 'I have been talking of your case with my Friend Mr Levet, who has had great practice, and of whom I have a very high opinion'. He urges Cumming to move to Clerkenwell, where Levet might visit him, and adds encouragingly, 'Ther[e] is a man now living whom Mr Levet restored from ulcerated lungs after many Physitians had deserted him'.[14]

After Johnson's death an anonymous correspondent to the *St James Chronicle* supplied an account of Levet's life, which was reproduced, after some 'mistakes' had been corrected, in the *Gentleman's Magazine* of February 1785. Among other things this gives the following details of Levet's medical education:

Mr Levett, though an Englishman by birth, became early in life a waiter at a coffee-house in Paris. The surgeons who frequented it, finding him of an inquisitive turn, and attentive to their conversation, made a purse for him, and gave him some instructions in their art. They afterwards furnished him with the means of other knowledge, by procuring him free admission to such lectures in pharmacy and anatomy as were read by the ablest professors of that period. Hence his introduction to a business, which afforded him a continual, though slender maintenance. Where the middle part of his life was spent, is uncertain. He resided, however, above twenty years under the roof of Johnson, who never wished him to be regarded as an inferior, or treated him like a dependent. He breakfasted with the doctor every morning, and perhaps was seen no more by him till midnight. Much of the day was employed in attendance on his patients, who were chiefly of the lowest rank of tradesmen. The remainder of his hours he devoted to Hunter's lectures, and to as many different opportunities of improvement as he could meet with on the same gratuitous conditions. 'All his medical knowledge', said Johnson, 'and it is not inconsiderable, was obtained through the ear. Though he buys books, he seldom looks into them, or discovers any power by which he can be supposed to judge of an author's merit.'

This is a rather different history than we would guess from Johnson's poem, with its reference, for instance, to Levet's 'narrow round' and 'single talent'. (Neither Johnson nor Mrs Thrale had travelled abroad before their brief visit to Paris and Northern France in September 1775. Neither could speak French with any fluency.)

After Levet's death, Johnson wrote for information to Hull, his birthplace. He received back a three and a half page letter from John Thompson from which Hawkins drew the additional information that Levet

lived with his parents till about twenty years of age. He had acquired some knowledge of the Latin language, and had a propensity to learning, which his parents not being able to gratify, he went to live with a woolen draper at Hull: with him he stayed two years, during which time he learned from a neighbour of his master somewhat of the practice of physic: at the end thereof he came to London, with a view possibly to improve himself in that profession; ... having saved some money, he took a resolution to travel, and visited France and Italy for the purpose, as his letters mention, of gaining experience in physic, and, returning to London with a valuable library he had collected abroad, placed one of his brothers apprentice to a mathematics-instrument maker, and provided for the education of another. After this he went to Paris, and, for improvement, attended the hospitals in that city. At the end of five years he returned to England, and taking lodgings in the house of an attorney in Northumberland court, near Charing cross, he became a practicer of physic.[15]

These accounts suggest a man who without any formal apprentice-ship acquired varied experience over a long period. He evidently knew some Latin; in Paris he attended both public lectures and the hospitals; his second stay in Paris lasted five years; later, back in London, he kept up his education by attending the lectures of 'Hunter', in all probability William rather than John Hunter.[16] 'Those who communicate literature to the son of a poor man, consider him as one not born to poverty, but to the necessity of deriving a better fortune from himself. In this attempt, as in others, many fail, and many succeed', wrote Johnson, defending the access of the poor to education against the snobbish Soame Jenyns. When we read these accounts of Levet's various attempts to aquire a medical education for himself we are prompted to speak, I think, not so much of Levet's single talent as of his determination, his single-minded devotion, despite all the obstacles of his social position and comparative poverty, to his vocation.

It is a paradox that in pre-Revolutionary France Levet was able to pick up that training in his chosen profession which the caste system of London medicine would certainly have denied him. Europe was at peace in the 1730s, France prospered under Cardinal Fleury, and Paris was the pre-eminent medical centre of Europe. According to contemporary accounts, foreign physicians and students came to Paris in large numbers to attend the public lectures in medicine and to attend the hospitals 'where access was easy for them.'[17] There were at least six opportunities for instruction in anatomy in Paris at this period: the School of Medicine, the School of Surgery or St Côme, the Jardin du Roi, the Collège Royal, in the major hospitals, and by private lessons. At three places, the Jardin Royal or Jardin du Roi, the School of Medicine and St Côme, the lecture-demonstrations were public. At the end of the seventeenth century crowds of four to five hundred people had regularly attended Pierre Dionis' demonstrations at the Jardin du Roi. Admission was by sealed ticket given to *garçons chirurgiens*, the apprentices to master surgeons. Later, in the 1720s, such lectures became fashionable and under Joseph-Guichard Duverney, as many as 140 foreigners attended in a single year. In 1724, a Royal Edict created and endowed five teaching chairs, including anatomy and surgical operations, at St Côme.[18] These, too, were public courses.

In London, by contrast, there were few large public hospitals. When, in the thirties and forties, the charity hospital movement began, the policy of their Boards of Governors was at first to exclude pupils and apprentices. Whether or not instruction in Paris was given, in the Boerhaavian manner, at the bedside, it is certain that in the hospitals lectures and demonstrations were held in which students could gain direct experience of anatomy and surgery. In 1720, for instance, the Hotel Royal des Invalides, the Military hospital of Paris, founded a 'practical school of anatomy and surgery'. The stress on 'practical' is significant. Students in Paris, as Toby Gelfand has shown, regularly dissected cadavers and acquired firsthand anatomical knowledge. And, according to a contemporary English observer, probably the surgeon, John Harrison, students, including foreigners, could attend the Paris hospitals free of charge.[19]

Robert Levet's five-year stay in Paris – which must have been in the late thirties – would have provided him with significant opportunities for instruction in a centre which was the best, most active and admired in Europe. Surgery, and especially obstetrics, was in the process of being remade into a scientific knowledge. Johnson remarked that 'All his medical knowledge, and it was not inconsiderable, was obtained through the ear'. The information that Levet picked up from lectures and demonstrations in Paris and later built on by attending William Hunter's lectures, may well have been some of the most advanced of its time.

During the first half of the eighteenth century it became common for enterprising young surgeons to supplement their income by organising private anatomical courses, often in their own homes, and it was these private courses that gave students the opportunity for dissection. When William Hunter, who visited Paris in 1743–4, began his own private course in London in 1746, this was the model he followed.[20] His advertisements stressed that anatomy would be taught in the 'Paris manner', a claim that accurately reflected the prestige of Parisian anatomy and physiology at the time, and heralded the innovation, for courses in England, that practical instruction would be given.[21] It was largely through the efforts of William Hunter and his brother John that London overtook Paris in this field over the next half-century.

William Hunter's career crossed with Thomas Lawrence's. In 1740–1, apprenticed to a surgeon, William Hunter attended the course in Anatomy and Physiology held 'at the corner of Lincoln's Inn Fields, near Clare Market' by Frank Nicholls, which he later called 'by far the most reputable that was given' in London.[22] When Nicholls retired, in 1741, his course was taken over by Lawrence, his friend and pupil, who had earlier been appointed to succeed him as Anatomy lecturer at Oxford, though Lawrence apparently did not begin lecturing until 1743. Hunter, it seems, had hoped to succeed Nicholls, and when Lawrence announced that his lectures would include instruction in Nicholls' method of preparing subjects for dissection he made haste to announce that his lectures would include the same material. In Oxford, Lawrence had been forced to give up the unequal struggle to gain an audience, owing to the success of his upstart rival as Anatomy lecturer Nathan Alcock. A similar fate awaited him in London. According to Hawkins, a grateful patient, Lawrence

had many hearers, till Hunter, a surgeon, arrived from Scotland, who, settling in London, became his rival in the same practice, and having the advantage of Dr Lawrence, in his manner of enunciating, together with the assistance and support of all his countrymen in this kingdom, and, moreover, being a man whose skill in his art was equal to his pretensions, he became a favourite with the leading men in the practice of physic, and in a few winters drew to him such a resort of pupils, as induced Dr Lawrence to give up lecturing, and betake himself to the general exercise of his profession.[23]

Hunter 'reduced the pompous oratorical mode of lecturing to the simple and familiar description':[24] Lawrence, whose 'vacuity of countenance' gave one no intimation of his gifts, was besides a thoroughly old-fashioned doctor, if his insistence that Latin was the only fitting vehicle for medical treatises is anything to go by. Mrs Thrale tells a touching story of Johnson's last visit to Lawrence when both old men were very ill, 'one from difficulty of breathing, the other from paralytic debility'. So that Johnson could consult Lawrence, 'they fairly sate down on each side a table in the Doctor's gloomy apartment, adorned with skeletons, preserved monsters etc., and agreed to write Latin billets to each other'.[25] The 'monsters' were in all probability the anatomical preparations Lawrence would have used in lecturing. Nicholls and Lawrence had taught anatomy in about thirty sessions, but it was Hunter's practice to deliver over one hundred. As his reputation and numbers of pupils increased, the lectures were augmented still more until they were far more comprehensive than the term 'anatomy lectures' indicates:

They embraced anatomy, physiology and pathology and also courses in operative surgery and mid-wifery. The autumn course of 1775 ... consisted of 112 meetings, which is probably about the average, and extended over about three and a half months ... The importance of these courses can hardly be over-estimated; with the exception of chemistry and materia medica, they were the whole of what may be described as the science part of a medical education in those days.[26]

William Hunter's courses were held, as the memoir of Levet suggests, in the afternoons. Like their French prototypes they became fashionable, and Burke, Adam Smith and Gibbon were among the famous non-medical people who attended. According to the reminiscences of one doctor, William Wadd, 'at the period when Garrick was in his zenith' Hunter rescheduled his lectures from the evening to 2pm so that those who wished could take in both his performances and those of the great actor.[27] But Hunter's courses were scarcely 'public' in the sense that they were free. Certainly, 'The door is ... open to every person whose curiosity prompts him to be present' at the first lecture, Hunter's advertisements advised. Thereafter Hunter charged originally three, later possibly seven guineas, though after a student had completed one course he might attend subsequent ones free. If Levet attended on 'gratuitous terms', as the *Gentleman's Magazine* contributor implies, it is possible that his attendance was only casual or occasional, and that Johnson, who we know procured other favours from Hunter, procured Levet this one, too.[28] William Hunter has not gone down in history as a generous or charitable man, to say the least.

It will have been noticed that Levet's contemporaries do not agree in their descriptions of his occupation, his trade or profession – whichever it was. 'Physician in ordinary', was Arthur Murphy's term. 'A necessary man, a surgeon', Mrs Thrale once called him. 'Mr Levat, I suppose sir', she cheekily asked Johnson on another occasion, 'has the office of keeping the hospital [she seems to have meant Johnson's ailing household], in health? For he is an apothecary.'[29] Hawkins' description 'not solely a physician, a surgeon or an apothecary but all' has already been given. We can assume, I think, that Levet supplied drugs for his poor patients; those who could scarcely afford to pay their doctor would not have been able to afford apothecary's fees as well. The remark that his patients 'were chiefly of the lowest class of tradesman' is interesting too. Levet's patients might not have been then the totally destitute, for these might have been in the care of the Overseers of the poor. We may imagine Levet scraping a living between the very poor and the lower middle classes who could afford a surgeon or apothecary. It was a time when London seems to have been well supplied with official and licensed practitioners of medicine.[30] One characteristic of Levet that caused some amusement to Johnson is notable too. 'Johnson would observe, he was, perhaps, the only man who ever became intoxicated through motives of prudence. He reflected, that if he refused the gin or brandy offered him by some of his patients he could have been no gainer by their cure, as they might have had nothing else to bestow on him. This habit of taking a fee, in whatever form it was exhibited, could not be put off by advice or admonition of any kind. He would swallow what he did not like, nay what he knew would injure him, rather than go home with an idea, that his skill had been exerted without recompence.'[31] Levet's behaviour in other words was a way of laying hold of status: he took payment, of whatever kind, to remind his patients that he was, to use a modern term, a health care professional. It also, of course, ministered to his patients' self-respect.

One of the few weapons available to the College of Physicians in its fitful forays against unlicensed doctors throughout the century was to instruct its members to refuse to co-operate or consult with unqualified men. It is fascinating, therefore, to find the ex-President of the College, through Johnson's agency, doing just that (though Levet of course, as a surgeon-apothecary, or whatever, was not a rival physician.) Levet carried out minor surgery and prescribed drugs to Johnson's household on Thomas Lawrence's instructions. On one occasion at least, in January 1777, Levet came to the rescue when a bleeding which had been ordered by Lawrence failed to stop. Johnson's letter to Lawrence announcing Levet's death is sufficient evidence of the respect and friendship uniting the three men. It suggests that medical relations during the century were a good deal more complicated than the propaganda of the likes of Robert James would lead one to think.

Most upper and middle class patients of the time clearly recognised the distinctions between the different categories of practitioner, and indeed insisted on them.[32] Johnson's friends and biographers are no exception. Johnson himself, we happen to know, was perfectly well informed about them. In February 1775 he wrote to Thomas Lawrence for clarification, on Boswell's behalf, of whether it could be held invidious to call a man 'Doctor of Medicine' rather than 'Physician' in England. A Doctor Memis or Menis had brought a court case against the Royal Infirmary of Aberdeen which had given him this title in its charter (the grounds being presumably that the title implied that he was not officially qualified), and Boswell was appearing for the defence.[33] He wrote the same day to Boswell:

> I consulted this morning the President of the London College of Physicians, who says, that with us, *Doctor of Physick* (we do not say *Doctor of Medicine*) is the highest title that a practicer of Physick can have; that *Doctor* implies not only *Physician*, but teacher of physick; that every *Doctor* is legally a *Physician*, but no man, not a *Doctor*, can practice Physick but by *licence* particularly granted. The Doctorate is a licence of itself.[34]

Moreover, Johnson, as Chapman noted, 'is, as a rule, punctilious in the use of titles.'[35] Yet Johnson's poem commemorating Levet, an unlicensed practitioner, an 'empiric', was entitled, on its first appearance, 'On the Death of *Dr* Robert Levet' – an open defiance, it might seem, of professional protocol. The poem's subsequent history confirms that this was how it was perceived. In all of the numerous magazine reprintings of the poem during Johnson's last year this title is reproduced exactly, but in the posthumous *Works* of 1787 it becomes 'On the Death of Mr Robert Levet', with (in later editions) the explanatory sub-heading, 'A Practiser in Physic'. Johnson's poem addresses itself in part to 'lettered arrogance', but lettered arrogance it seems was not so easily placated.

'Mr', of course, is a courtesy title too. Sometimes we hear of Mr Frank Barber. These questions of social protocol are not merely extrinsic to the poem but germane to its whole nature. It everywhere acknowledges that it belongs to a context where social distinctions, professional arrangements, etiquette, loyalties and class feeling constitute invisible expectations and constraints. The poem may thus tell us a good deal about both Levet's practice and about medical conditions of the time, and so I think it does. But it does not yield this information easily, nor is it on the surface. Attempting to analyse the poem as an historical document involves first confronting or negotiating certain aspects of Johnson's conscious poetical method. His poems eschew detail and particularity in conformity with deeply held convictions. Writing of Samuel Butler's *Hudibras* Johnson declares that 'the manners, being founded on opinions, are temporary and local, and therefore become every day less intelligible and less striking'. 'All poems describing manners require notes after fifty years', he said with some disapproval. His conception of human nature, his theory of poetry and his practice of poetry are all consistent, and all what we may call a-historical. His premise is that human nature is uniform, not only 'from China to Peru' not only from high to low but throughout historical time. 'The interests and passions, the virtues and vices of mankind, have been diversified in different times, only by unessential and casual varieties', he wrote in *Adventurer* 95; 'such is the constitution of the world, that much of life must be spent in the same manner by the wise and the ignorant, the exalted and the low. Men, however distinguished by external accidents or intrinsick qualities, have all the same wants, the same pains and . . . the same pleasures' (*Idler* 51). As the word 'constitution' implies, Johnson's thinking on this matter is often based on an analogy with the human anatomy; as all men and all women share the same anatomical characteristics, so their differences are 'casual' and 'inessential', external and – Johnson declares – much less important.

Poetry, Johnson argues, should address itself to, and elicit a response from, essential human nature – that part of present and future readers which might be thought independent of historical times and circumstances. If it is to succeed in this it obviously should not entangle itself with contemporary manners and social conditions, for 'poetry' as Johnson writes in *Rambler* 36, 'cannot dwell upon the minuter distinctions, by which one species differs from another, without

departing from that simplicity of grandeur which fills the imagination; nor dissect the latent qualities of things, without losing its
general power of gratifying every mind by recalling its conceptions.'
It 'has to do rather with the passions of men, which are uniform, than
their customs, which are changeable.' His view is consistent
throughout his career. It appears again, for instance, in his famous
judgement of Gray's *Elegy* ('The Churchyard abounds with images
which find a mirrour in every mind, and with sentiments to which
every bosom returns an echo' – a remark made, in completing the
Lives of the Poets, not a year before composing his own elegy for
Levet.)

As we might expect then, the poem is written in language which
seems plain, general, even stereotypical. But its apparently generalised
language is very different from the common run of eighteenth-
century commemorative verses, including Gray's *Elegy*, however
much Johnson's poem conforms to the conventional format of such
poems. Compare it with one of its prototypes, the memorial verses
'On the Death of Dr Cheyne' published after George Cheyne's death
in 1734:[36]

> Of Virtues, common to the Race
>   Of Mortals he possest;
> Yet heighten'd with uncommon Grace,
>   They stood his own confest.
>
> Discreetly wise, and temperate,
>   Where Folly keeps her Court;
> And Luxury in pompous State
>   Enjoys her feastful Sport.
>
> Learned, yet affable, and free,
>   His Treasures to dispense,
> With unaffected Modesty,
>   Sound Judgment, manly Sense.
>
> Learned yet humble and devout
>   He grateful spent his Days;
> And studiously his Gifts laid out
>   In the great Giver's Praise.
>
> Like him beneficently kind,
>   Nor Impotent to save;
> To Rich and Poor an equal Friend
>   Like Baiae's balmy Wave.

> Fee'd, or unfee'd, by Rich or Poor,
>   He all his Art employ'd
> With artless Remedy to cure,
>   And give what he enjoy'd
>
> Health, which, by him, by all confest,
>   To Temperance we owe;
> The cheapest, easiest, safest, best
>   Physician here below ...

The writer of lapidary verses naturally has limited resources. Both doctors employed their 'art' for the advantage of the poor, both were 'friends' to their patients. In both poems there is a strong stress on the physician's own temperate life. The doctors are seen – not surprisingly – as carrying out God's work. In both poems predictable adjectives for the good doctor are linked with adverbs which (in the case of the Levet poem successfully) attempt to give them more precise life. The Cheyne poem ends with Death's 'impartial Dart' striking 'sure', perhaps a shadowy anticipation of Johnson's poem's ending with Levet's death 'the nearest way'. Johnson's poem seems obviously to belong to the same conventional mode, but in fact language which appears at first general or conventional almost always reveals a certain edge of wit or exactitude that makes it particularly telling. An obvious example of the poem's relative sophistication is the first stanza:

> Condemn'd to hope's delusive mine,
>   As on we toil from day to day;
> By sudden blast or slow decline,
>   Our social comforts drop away.

That 'dropping away' can be felt as either a sudden dreadful fall, or a gradual slide down a slope. But since 'blast' is an attack of contagious disease and 'decline' is the commonly accepted phrase for a wasting illness the language fuses 'physick' with physics. This apparently slight poem contains many other verbal ingenuities.

Cheyne was one of the early eighteenth century's most famous doctors, Fellow of the Royal Society, and a prolific, vigorous writer. Philosophically an iatromechanist, his attention to what he called 'my own crazy carcase' led him to the authorship of many books on regimen, including the very widely read treatise on *The English Malady, or a Treatise of Nervous Diseases of all Kinds* (1733) which Johnson recommended to Boswell.[37] Like Samuel Johnson, for most of his life Cheyne abstained from drinking spirits or wine, and vehemently defended the innocence of tea. His 'low' diet of vegetables, fruit and milk was widely followed. Levet, on the other hand, was decidedly 'obscure': the publication of memorial verses in his praise in the *Gentleman's Magazine* may have been an act of some significance. When the poem first appeared, 'Dr Johnson' was appended to the title; its readers would have known that this was a tribute by a man who was the age's foremost intellectual and sage. They would therefore have been keenly conscious of those differences between Johnson the writer of the poem and Levet its subject which might obviously impede or inhibit the sincerity of the poet's tribute to his friend. Some of the social conditions the poem arises from and addresses are underlined by Mrs Thrale's responses.

Its appearance in the *Gentleman's Magazine* came more than a year after Mrs Thrale had first written it down in her memorandum book, *Thraliana*:

Streatham 18: [April 1782.] Doctor Johnson has been writing Verses on his old Inmate Mr Levett he tells me: that poor Creature was 84 or 85 years old this Winter, when after an uninterrupted Series of Health he died suddenly by a Spasm or Rupture of some of the Vessells of the Heart. He lived with Johnson as a sort of *necessary Man*, or Surgeon to the wretched Household he held in Bolt Court; where Blind Mrs Williams, Dropsical Mrs Desmoulines, Black Francis & his White Wife's Bastard with a wretched Mrs White, and a Thing that he called Poll; shared his Bounty, & increased his Dirt. Levett used to bleed one, & blister another, & be very useful, tho' I believe disagreable to all: he died while his Patron was with me in Harley Street – & very sorry he was – in his way of being sorry – & he wrote these Verses ...[38]

Mrs Thrale's facts are unreliable, but one thing emerges clearly: her disdain for Johnson's household extends, in this private notebook, to Johnson himself. Her note slips revealingly into the antithetical cadence of early Augustan satire: they 'shared his Bounty, and increased his Dirt' – which turns, in the manner of Pope or Dryden, Johnson's 'bounty' into the lordliness of an upstart, and by equating it with 'dirt' makes it discreditable to both parties. 'Dirt', as in Pope or Swift, is an index of the rather less than human status accorded this household.

In her *Anecdotes*, published after Johnson's death, Mrs Thrale's account of Bolt Court is more circumspect. She speaks of his nursing 'whole nests of people in his house, where the lame, the blind, the sick, and the sorrowful found a sure retreat from all the evils whence his little income could secure them'. Her other reference to Levet occurs when she writes about Johnson telling anecdotes of his wide acquaintance among the poor:

When he raised contributions for some distressed author, or wit in want, he often made us all more than amends by diverting descriptions of the lives they were then passing in corners unseen by any body but himself and that odd old surgeon whom he kept in his house to tend the out-pensioners, and of whom he said most truly and sublimely, that

> In misery's darkest caverns known
> His useful care was ever nigh ...[39]

'In corners unseen by any body' is certainly one interpretation of Johnson's moving phrase. Mrs Thrale has some difficulty getting her act together on the subject of Johnson's charity: on the one hand it is so thorough-going and so exemplary that it implores a passing tribute; on the other, she cannot rid herself of a feeling that it is all rather disgusting. Her tone thus vacillates between uneasy humour and a transparently false sanctimony.

Her difficulties illustrate some of the problems of finding harmonious tones which bridge the gradations of a manifestly hierarchical society, gradations apparent in Johnson's poem itself. Readers of it in the *Gentleman's Magazine* were referred to Levet's obituary notice in a previous number, which reads:

In Bolt Court, Fleet Str, at the house of his friendly patron Dr. Johnson, Mr. Rob. Levet, a very useful, skilful and charitable practitioner in physic, in full possession of every power both of body and mind, though supposed to have been 80 years old. He was born near Hull in Yorkshire.[40]

The main difference between this and the draft of the notice that Chapman prints among Johnson's letters is the rather curious phrase, 'his friendly patron'. When Johnson himself writes about Levet he speaks of him usually as a 'friend', 'a very old and loyal friend'. Is the obituary compiler uneasy with the word 'patron' or with the word 'friend'? Partly, one supposes, under the influence of Johnson's definition of 'patron' in the *Dictionary* ('commonly a wretch who supports with insolence, and is paid with flattery'), the term falls out of use during this period, so that in *Emma* (1816) the yeoman farmer Robert Martin is said by the squire, Mr. Knightley, 'to consider me as one of his best friends'. Many years later, in 1857, Mrs Clennam asks her seamstress Little Dorrit what friends she has and Amy replies,

'Only you and Mr Clennam'. It is apparent that the term 'friend' is commonly understood in the broad sense that includes patronage.[41] These nuances of meaning in the word are put to use in the poem's second stanza:

> Well tried through many a varying year
> See Levet to the grave decend,
> Officious, innocent, sincere,
> Of ev'ry friendless name the friend.

The wit of the last line involves two shades of meaning in the word 'friend' being brought together and played off against each other. The formal phrase, 'a friendless name' refers to a public quality; it means someone without influential connections, someone who cannot call upon a patron for support or protection. By delaying 'friend' to the end of the line, the poem's syntax infuses the word with new warmth and depth of meaning – a meaning to be contradistinguished from the resonances of 'friendless name'. Levet's friendship, 'innocent' and 'sincere', it implies, involves no touch of patronage or condescension. The praise itself is delicately judged, especially delicate and meaningful in a world, which the poem takes note of, where the opposite is usually the case. In the next stanza, the third, one can glimpse such constraints of convention, as they bear down upon the poet and his subject:

> Yet still he fills affection's eye,
> Obscurely wise, and coarsely kind;
> Nor, letter'd arrogance, deny
> Thy praise to merit unrefined.

'He had no learning', says Sir John Hawkins, in his account of Levet, 'and consequently was an unfit companion for a learned man.' Johnson's respect for Levet is undermined by Boswell, even whilst he repeats Johnson's words: 'such was Johnson's predilection for him, and fanciful estimation of his moderate abilities, that I have heard him say he should not be satisfied, though attended by all the College of Physicians, unless he had Mr. Levet with him'.[42] Boswell, like Mrs Thrale, was of aristocratic descent and comfortably off; Johnson cannot but have been aware that the gentle-folk, successful artists and tradespeople with whom he spent literally half his life, did not understand and were perhaps hostile to his friendships with the more humble. But 'affection's eye' is the poet's and he is addressing himself, as much as his readers, when he calls on 'letter'd arrogance' to put aside its snobbish preconceptions and squeamishness and pay tribute to Levet. It is as if the poem acknowledges a slight inhibition in the poet, which is a reflection of anticipated resistance within the tradition and the audience of polite literature, or as if the poet must expose a division within himself, between his 'affection' and his social or intellectual loyalties. The lines recall Gray's

> Let not Ambition mock their useful toil,
>   Their homely joys, and destiny obscure;
> Nor Grandeur hear with a disdainful smile,
>   The short and simple annals of the poor.

But in Johnson's case the address to 'letter'd arrogance' is more militant. One does not need to suppose that 'letter'd' is particular rather than general – that Johnson might have had in mind the letters MD – to feel that in turning the self admonition outwards to a putative reader the poem effects a successful transition to a more politically edged mode. There are similarities with the concluding passages of Johnson's life of another friend, Richard Savage, and its impassioned scorn of those whose affluence and refinement lead them to look down on a man whose life was not so comfortable as their own. The next stanza of the poem continues the praise of Levet:

> When fainting nature called for aid
>   And hov'ring death prepar'd the blow,
> His vig'rous remedy display'd
>   The power of art without the show.

Levet's practice demonstrated the skill, the courage and quickness of an accomplished surgeon or physician. That is obviously the meaning of the first half of this last line. But what does 'without the show' imply? The term 'art' is closely associated with the professional guild, corporation or company, a group of men solely empowered by charter to practise a particular craft or skill. Each medical corporation had its own constitution, arms and privileges. The line is not simply neutral, descriptive of Levet's own demeanour, but may involve a reflection upon the 'show', in the first place the armorial bearings, the gold-topped cane and all the other trappings of the official medical corporations. It certainly defends Levet from the condescending attitudes that are epitomised in Hawkins' remark that 'his external appearance and behaviour were such, that he disgusted the rich, and terrified the poor'.

If this is so, then specific, locally charged references are latent in the seeming orotund grandeur of the lines. This is even more true of the next stanza, the fifth:

> In Misery's darkest caverns known
>   His useful care was ever nigh,
> Where hopeless anguish pour'd his groan,
>   And lonely want retir'd to die.

In one reading, like the Dungeon of Giant Despair, the caverns are metaphors for that misery we call 'deepest': 'Suffering is permanent, obscure and dark', Wordsworth was to write. The phrase 'dark caverns' is one of those expressions which attempts to communicate or search out through the use of a metaphor the pain of a pathological mental state whose essence is the absence of the power of articulation, of energy, will and hope. The cavern suggested may be that cavern which is the human skull. Yet here Levet's 'useful care' is 'nigh'. This certainly implies that the caverns have geographical reality, are places which one can approach. 'Caverns' must also then describe the actual dwelling places of the poor, must subliminally remind the reader that Levet's patients might literally live underground in darkness, in the basements and cellars of London's slums. The darkness that surrounds Levet and his patients is actual, then: but on a third level of meaning it is, once again, metaphysical. 'We have histories of diseases, but not of health, biographies of doctors but not of the sick', writes Roy Porter, lamenting as so many recent medical historians do, our lack of knowledge of the patient, especially the poor patient.[43] The images of mines and caverns in the poem co-operate with the 'obscurity' that surrounds Levet to suggest the invisibility of these poor patients and their doctor to the eye of history, or to the official records of society, compiled by its articulate self-conscious possessors of tradition and authority. These patients have, the poem goes on to suggest, erased themselves from notice and from history. As 'self-respecting' poor, they have chosen to withdraw from the public stage and die in isolation. Levet visits

> Where hopeless anguish pour'd his groan,
>   And lonely want retir'd to die.

(Or, in the version which Johnson repeated to Boswell: 'And labour steals an hour to die'.) The phrase 'pour'd his groan' implies not merely the inarticulacy of the acutely suffering, but – 'poured' in the 'cavern'

– that the suffering is unrecognised, unheard, wasted; 'steals' suggests that the death of a poor labourer is merely recognised as an aberration in the official schedule of a working day.

The poem goes on to praise Levet's devotion to his vocation in terms which again involve some reflection upon the actual habits of other doctors:

> No summons mocked by chill delay,
> No petty gain disdain'd by pride
> The modest wants of evr'y day
> The toil of ev'ry day supplied.

'The physician scorns to touch any metal but gold' declared a contemporary.[44] The refusal of physicians to attend unless their fees could be paid was, rightly or wrongly, a matter of common indignation. John Wesley, for example, defending his right as an unlicenced doctor to practise, wrote

Ought I to have let one of those poor wretches perish because I was not a regular physician? to have said, 'I know what will cure you, but I am not of the College: You must send for Doctor Mead?' Before Doctor Mead had come in his chariot the man might have been in his coffin. And when the doctor was come, where was his fee? What! he cannot live upon nothing![45]

Dr Mead in his chariot is a figure of eighteenth-century medical mythology. In contrast to this caricature, Johnson's phrase 'chill delay' suggests, in a peculiarly intimate fashion, how a physician's professional self-regard might result not in obvious inhumanity but in a wounding condescension from someone whose office is to heal. The lines condense what Johnson says in *Rambler* 145, about society's attitude to manual labourers:

Yet though the refusal of statues and panegyric to those who employ only their hands and feet in the service of mankind may be easily justified, I am far from intending to incite the petulance of pride, to justify the superciliousness of grandeur, or to intercept any part of that tenderness and benevolence which, by virtue of their common nature one man may claim from another.

The verb 'mock'd' in 'no summons mock'd by chill delay' suggests, with particular force, the violation of a common bond.

One further prototype of this poem is certainly to be found in the lines about his father that conclude Pope's *Epistle to Dr. Arbuthnot* (1735):

> Stranger to civil and religious Rage
> The good Man walk'd innoxious thro' his Age.

This apparently conventional metaphor becomes revivified in the Levet poem, for specific references are again fused with conventional tropes. When Johnson celebrates Levet's virtues he calls up memories of the particular way Levet attended his patients. Unlike a successful member of the College, a gentleman travelling in his carriage, Levet's 'virtues *walk'd* their narrow round'. Levet did literally walk back and forth across London to his patients. ('Here is Mr Levet just come in at four-score from a walk to Hampstead, eight miles in August', wrote Johnson in a letter of 1780.) The notion of Levet as pedestrian – in several ways – becomes, as it is explored and developed via the rhythm, the core of the poem.

Pope's tribute to his father continues:

> No Courts he saw, no Suits would ever try,
> Nor dar'd an Oath, nor hazarded a Lye.
> Un-Learn'd, he knew no Schoolman's subtle Art,
> No Language, but the Language of the Heart.
> By Nature honest, by Experience wise,
> Healthy by Temp'rance and by Exercise:
> His Life, tho' long, to sickness past unknown,
> His Death was instant, and without a groan ...

One's dominant consciousness, reading these lines in their place in the satire, is of the unbridgeable distance between its speaker, Pope, and his father. The poet has shown himself by turns exasperated, perturbed, angry, exuberant, magisterial, savage, but always involved in contestation with others. Nothing could be more unlike the 'innoxious' private and retired existence of his father. Whilst praising him, the lines express nostalgia for a life to which – as the poem has made abundantly clear – the poet's own nature is radically unsuited. There is therefore sentimentality mingled with the pathos of the concluding lines;

> Oh grant me thus to live and thus to die!
> Who sprung from Kings shall know less joy than I.

Because there is no explicit 'I' in the Levet poem, and no explicit relationship between the poet and his subject, there is less danger of insincerity. And it is precisely the critical edge to Johnson's descriptions of Levet and his life that shapes the figure into solidity, that makes this no indulgence in an 'urban–pastoral' ideal, as has been argued, but the totally convinced celebration of a genuine – the more genuine because its limitations are acknowledged – achievement.[46]

But it would not be true to say that the poem is quite free from the social snobberies and class feeling that surrounded the friendship of the two men. It is rather that Johnson knows he must negotiate inhibitions and barriers in himself as much as in his readers (hence perhaps the repeated recitations of the poem before publication), in order to secure a response to Levet that is as unsnobbish and direct as Levet's to his patients. There are blemishes in the poem: awkwardness in the appeal to 'letter'd arrogance' and an unnecessary concessive quality in stanza seven:

> His virtues walk'd their narrow round,
>   Nor made a pause, nor left a void;
> And sure the eternal Master found
>   The single talent well employed.

'Sure' might well convey doubt whilst appearing to express certainty. And pressures and tensions felt by the author may be detected in the very terms in which that praise is offered. There is a kind of disjunction or distance – despite the claim that Levet *fills* Affection's eye' – created by the poem's own evident, if subdued, sophistication. It manifestly belongs to a world of 'letters' to which its subject is alien. It begins with an allusion to the Roman punishment of *damnare in metallum*, thus setting the poem within a frame of learned melancholy grandeur. The phrasing – 'obscurely wise and coarsely kind' – is witty, refined, and balanced. The manners of the line are those of another world to Levet's. Into such a gap between the poem and its subject might rush all kinds of betrayals – patronage and sentimentality not being the least of them. What tone can the poem find, what bridge can it make, between its own informed and learned pessimism and Levet's narrow purposiveness? Johnson is in danger too of putting forward Levet as a type of simple integrity, but of dyeing the poem too deeply with his own complicated unhappiness.

The dangers of reflexive egoism can be detected, even whilst they are overcome, in

> The busy day, the peaceful night,
>   Unfelt, uncounted, glided by . . .

The chord of this praise might be heard leaving discords echoing behind it: the pangs of longing, of envy, ('How different from my life!'), of awareness how rare such fulfilment is, even, behind these, resentment and criticism. This may be particularly so for those who bring to the poem memories of Johnson's own private meditations on time misspent or wasted, those repeated records of turbulent and disturbed nights, of which the note made at 10.30 pm on Good Friday, 1775, is typical:

> When I look back upon resoluti[ons] of improvement and amendments, which have year after year been made and broken, either by negligence, forgetfulness, vicious idleness, casual interruption, or morbid infirmity, when I find that so much of my life has stolen unprofitably away, and that I can descry by retrospection scarcely a few days properly and vigorously employed, why do I yet try to resolve again? . . .

But one must be careful how far one reads into the poem one's knowledge of Johnson's state. Of course such knowledge – of restless nights, of days which do not 'glide by' but pass over, empty and fruitless – may enhance one's appreciation of these lines. But to allow it to determine one's reading would be in conflict with a most important feature of the poem, its strong and vigorous rhythm. At the same time there is an implicit relationship between Johnson and Levet in the poem – or between the poem and its subject. The meditation I have quoted goes on, ' . . . why do I yet try to resolve again? I try, because Reformation is necessary and despair is criminal. I try in humble hope of the help of God.' The effort is movingly, almost palpably, present: the effort of summoning resources drained by memories of past failures, once more to move forward. It is the 'toil' of the poem's opening lines: 'As on we toil from day to day'. This is a mind and spirit acutely conscious of time, of that effort and need in some way to defeat time, escape from its treadmill which, calling upon hope, all the more firmly condemns one to time's servitude. And time is conceived of as something that resists, that abrades human purpose. In contrast:

> The modest wants of ev'ry day
> The toil of ev'ry day supplied.

Levet's life and work 'glide' on the stream of time, so he is not conscious of it. He is not condemned to hope because he is satisfied with the present; more importantly, he knows nothing beyond the present.

Yet in describing the order and harmony of Levet's life we are, I think, describing the poem's own order. The easy complementary cadence of the two lines, whilst it defines the satisfactory, absorbed pattern of Levet's life, at the same time expresses the speaker's own wholehearted harmony and pleasure. Johnson's letters for these years, the letters of a sickly man surrounded by an ailing household, offer a documentary contrast:

Mrs. Williams is in a feeble and languishing state, with little hope of growing better. She went for some part of the autumn into the country, but is little benefited; and Dr. Lawrence confesses that his art is at an end. Death is, however, at a distance; and what more than that can we say of ourselves? I am sorry for her pain, and more sorry for her decay. Mr Levett is sound, wind and limb ...[47]

Poor Mrs Williams, whose tedious history one can piece together from the references in Johnson's letters, may be the unnamed antithesis of Levet in the poem. Her 'slow decline' and 'cold gradations of decay' suffuse the letters themselves with a generalised, unenergetic sadness. In contrast, the poem's firmly placed stresses:

> Well tried through many a varying year,
> See Levet to the grave descend ...

maintain a purposive momentum. 'See' is the poem's cue to read the firmness of these stresses as imitative of Levet's stoutness, his sound-ness of wind and limb and purpose. The common classical-humanist metaphor of life as a journey is newly realised in this poem by its rhythm, its evocation of the figure's specific activity, Levet's actual walking across London, to wherever his aid is summoned, his reserves of energy made tangible and concrete in the renewed and diverse commitments made as each stanza begins. When the reader comes to:

> His virtues walk'd their narrow round,
> Nor made a pause, nor left a void ...

he or she will already have felt this as much more than an abstract idea or metaphor: the concreteness is in the poem's strong rhythm. Its steady, decisive momentum, freer, moving closer to an easy pattern with an extra syllable as the poem reaches the climax of its fellow-feeling with Levet – 'His frame was firm, his powers were bright' – makes it apparent that more is involved than simply moral 'virtue', and that Levet's capacity to help others is the result of his own essential spiritual and psychological soundness.

The poem's close, in its great linguistic intensity, implies that Levet does now 'fill' the attention of the author:

> Then with no throbbing fiery pain,
>   No cold gradations of decay,
> Death broke at once the vital chain
> And free'd his soul the nearest way.

These lines return to the thought of death by 'sudden blast or slow decline' with which the poem began, only to introduce, in Levet's case, the idea of a seemingly miraculous intervention in, and exemption from, the common fate. The phrase 'the vital chain' is another with multiple meaning. It picks up the poem's opening metaphor in a reminder that all human beings are 'condemned' as slaves are. In another sense the phrase alludes to the traditional idea that the soul is enchained in the body. In a third, and dominant sense, it is, appropriately enough, a quasi-medical term (compare 'the vital powers' of *Rambler* 85, for instance) implying the inter-related physiological processes that constitute life – what Bichat was to call 'that ensemble of functions which resists death.' Johnson is also perhaps remembering Shakespeare's phrase 'Bardolph's vital thread' quoted in the *Dictionary* under 'vital'. In yet a fourth sense it suggests the chains that link us, as human beings, together – the social ties alluded to earlier in the poem.

The original reading of these lines in the *Gentleman's Magazine* differs from that generally adopted and in some ways it intensifies their latent implications:

> Death broke at once the vital chain,
> And *forc'd* his soul the nearest way. (My italics)

'For, Death thou art a mower too.' Here, rather, we can imagine death as a surgeon, acting with speed and skill, submitting the patient to the necessary act with a movement whose very concentrated strength is the focus of experience and the wish to avoid unnecessary pain. Just as the surgeon cuts for the stone or forces a dislocated joint back into place, so Death, the image of the compassionate, no-nonsense doctor that Levet was does what must be done with the minimum of fuss. Johnson's imaginative and intellectual resources are, in their turn, completely concentrated in the service of his friend's memory, rendering him the same direct, unsnobbish service as Levet rendered to his patients.

The poem's deep sympathy of purpose with Levet is embodied in the medical language with which it constitutes its tribute. It is the poem of a writer who sees the doctor's activities as pastoral rather than as narrowly or specifically medical. As doctor to the poor, Levet is their 'friend', bringing 'useful care'. He reaches those neglected by society, possibly by official medicine, including them within the human community, the 'narrow round' of his medical parish. In using this phrase I do not mean to suggest that Levet engaged – as, for example, Methodist preachers still occasionally did – in any form of spiritual healing. He was no folk doctor, no representative of an 'alternative' medical tradition, which, strictly speaking, did not emerge until the next century. What we can learn of his education and practice, little as it is, has been enough to show that, on the contrary, he was thoroughly orthodox. Though unlicensed, he shared the premises and presumably the practices, that were so widely diffused. His training was among the best exponents of an emerging 'scientific' surgery. In a further meaning of the line, Levet carries the torch of Enlightenment rationality into the dark caverns of suffering: Johnson's commendation of his 'useful care' is another expression of that ameliorist optimism Johnson expounds and commemorates in his *Literary Magazine* reviews, as when he speaks of Stephen Hales' 'long life spent in the service of mankind'.

Johnson's celebration of Levet is the focus of a broad conception of the doctor's vocation, a vocation which he valued so strongly throughout his life because it exemplified, above all, the practice of charity. This emphasis is entirely of a piece with his praise of the College of Physicians (and by implication of Thomas Lawrence) in the life of Samuel Garth, author of *The Dispensary*:

Whether what Temple says be true, that physicians have had more learning than the other faculties, I will not stay to enquire; but, I believe, every man has found in physicians great liberality and dignity of sentiment, very prompt effusion of beneficence, and willingness to exert a lucrative art where there is no hope of lucre. Agreeably to this character, the College of Physicians, in July 1687, published an edict, requiring all the fellows, candidates, and licentiates, to give gratuitous advice to the neighbouring poor.

Johnson's emphasis is all the more striking in the likelihood that the motives of the College were in fact considerably more mixed: having failed to control the invasions of the apothecaries upon their practice the physicians, in setting up a dispensary, made a foray into the enemy's own country.[48] Johnson's explicit commendation of the College means that the critical reflections on more affluent doctors which were necessary if Levet's virtues were to be brought out should not be extended too far. It is safe to say that Johnson does not intend any general reflections on the organised profession. On the contrary, it is because the profession is well known for its charity that he applies for Levet's honorary membership. True, Levet is quite without 'liberality and dignity of sentiment'. The poem notices, instead, his narrowness, his lack of refinement, his coarseness. But as Johnson said to Mrs Thrale, 'Levet, madam, is a brutal fellow, but I have a good regard for him; for his brutality is in his manners, not in his mind'.[49] It is Levet's 'prompt effusion of beneficence' above all which entitles him to be honoured as a worthy member of the profession.

In his history of *The People's Health, 1830–1910*, F. B. Smith tells the story of Francis Bonney, parish medical officer of Brentford, dismissed in 1843 for acts which can only be thought of as humane and compassionate, however much they may have transgressed official guidelines. Smith remarks: 'There must have been many Bonneys in the towns and parishes of Britain, but as elsewhere in this history, evidence of the good that men do is sparse, whilst the evidence of their inhumanity is abundant.'[50] There would have been many Levets in the burgeoning London of the mid eighteenth century, but they have all retired from the eye of history. Johnson's poem enables us to recover something of such a life otherwise lost in the obscurity in which it was lived, and celebrates, for the first time, such a life, with the dignity and seriousness previously only accorded physicians in the official traditions.

7

THERAPEUTIC FRIENDSHIP

MANY OF Johnson's friends besides Levet were doctors, and many of his friendships took on a medical or therapeutic cast. As is the case with most people who suffer from chronic illness, friendship and therapy, of various kinds, became deeply intertwined. His doctors became friends, and his friends, like Mrs Thrale, became doctors. This chapter, by way of an epilogue, will examine some of the other relationships in Johnson's life which have this therapeutic aspect. Picking up threads from earlier chapters, it will glance at some of the medical figures who populated that long life, but it will also review some of the conflicts, the struggles for various forms of power, that were an inevitable part of Johnson's relationships to his medical attendants. Johnson had his own medical convictions, which he did not suppress. So I shall also discuss the way in which Johnson, by virtue of his learning and his experience of illness, became himself a counsellor, a doctor-figure for his friends, and consider especially the role he played in the sometimes complementary history of James Boswell.

Johnson's letter to Dr Lawrence announcing the death of 'our old friend Mr Levett' symbolises his position at the confluence of many streams of eighteenth-century medicine. Focusing on him, we can see our way through some of the labyrinthine recesses, the confusion of obsolete practices, genuine advances, preposterous claims and conflicting theories that characterised a medicine only loosely and unsatisfactorily organised as a profession, and still largely – though this took many different forms – governed by an entrepreneurial spirit. He had known the most eminent and the most skilled, the most humble and the most disreputable, and it was not always the eminent who were skilled or the humble who were disreputable. He had known Richard Bathurst, the failed city physician, and William

Hunter the fabulously wealthy and successful surgeon. At one end of his life in London (and of the medical scale) he prevailed upon Hunter to present his *Journey to the Western Islands* to the King; at the other he remembered, he told Boswell in 1779, the quack Joshua Ward, once famous for his pill and drop.[1] These preparations of antimony had been the subject of much controversy in the late 1730s and 40s. In the December 1742 issue of the *Gentleman's Magazine* sandwiched between Johnson's life of Sydenham 'from the new translation by John Swan M.D.' and Johnson's *Account of the Harleian Library* is a letter attacking Ward's recently advertised cure for the gout which cites Robert James' *Medicinal Dictionary* on antimony's properties, declaring that 'antimony has in all times, since its medicinal Virtues were first discover'd, afforded the Empirics their most boasted Secrets ...'[2]

If Ward's drop was nevertheless one of the most successful quack medicines of the first half of the century (enabling Ward to establish a hospital for poor patients near St James' Park), its place was undoubtedlly taken by Robert James' fever powders and pill in the second. These too, curiously enough, were founded on antimony.[3] He took out a patent for the powder in 1747, and in 1748 his *Dissertation on Fevers* responds vehemently, though not very convincingly, to the charge that this was tantamount to 'quackery'. The chemical formula of the powder remained the subject of much dispute throughout the rest of the century. James, who has made many appearances in this book, is another figure, like Levet, who suggests how difficult to classify may be some aspects of the eighteenth-century medical scene. Active and energetic (especially in his own vindication), admitted licentiate of the College of Physicians in 1745, but never attaining any higher rank, author or translator of numerous books, including the pioneering *Dictionary*, it is difficult to know whether he would have thought of himself as a success or a failure. He published nothing after his *Treatise on Canine Madness*, in 1760, though he left behind him a *Vindication of the Fever Powders* including a self-defence, in which, as Johnson told Boswell, he appealed to Garrick and Johnson, his old friends, as witnesses in his defence against a charge of habitual drunkenness.

He died in 1776, and Johnson honoured him in the life of Edmund Smith in recalling the early days at Gilbert Walmsley's in Lichfield. 'At this man's table I enjoyed many cheerful and instructive hours, with companions such as are not often found; with one who has lengthened, and one who has gladdened life; with Dr James, whose skill in physick will be long remembered, and with David Garrick ...' In less elegiac vein, Johnson told Boswell that James had, in fact, not been sober for twenty years.[4] Someone having observed that 'Dr James was little known by people of rank, fashion, or talents', though, as we have seen, he attended Mrs Thrale's mother, Johnson added 'His company, Sir, was like his conversation, coarse. – James and gentlemen were never seen together.'[5]

James and Johnson and another old schoolfellow, the surgeon Edmund Hector, had been in company, possibly in Lichfield, when Johnson composed the impromptu verses 'To Laura' printed in the *Gentleman's Magazine* of July 1743. Another school companion of the three was Charles Congreve, who made a career in the church, and who arrived in London in 1774, an elderly valetudinarian in search of medical advice. The series of letters in which Johnson reported on this renewed acquaintance to Hector and John Taylor make up a vivid portrait of the hypochondriacal type Johnson despised and feared in equal proportions. 'He sent to me one that attends him as an humble friend, and she left me a direction. He told me he knew not how to find me ... His room was disordered and oppressive, he has the appearance of a man wholly sunk into that sordid self-indulgence which disease, real or imaginary, is apt to dictate', he wrote. 'Now and then I call on Congreve', he told Taylor, a few months later, 'though I have little or no reason to think that he wants [i.e. is in want] or wishes to see me. I sometimes dispute with him, but I think he has not studied. He has really ill health, and seems to have given way to that indulgence which sickness is always in too much haste to claim. He confesses a bottle a day.'[6] A year later in March 1776 he wrote:

I called the other day upon poor Charles Congreve, whom I had not seen for many months. He took no notice of my absence, nor appeared either glad or sorry to see me, but answered everything with monosyllables, and seemed heavy and drowsy, like a man muddled with a full meal; at last I enquired the hour, which gave him hopes of being delivered from me, and enabled him to bounce up with great alacrity and inspect his watch. He sits in a room about ten feet square, and though he takes the air every day in his chaise, fancies that he should take cold in any other house, and therefore never pays a visit.[7]

What Johnson castigates as indulgence is really very little different from what has come to be known, after Talcott Parsons, after Freud, as the 'secondary gain' from illness. Congreve 'converses only with those who hope to prosper by indulging [him]' and shows no sign of interest in the world lest he should damage his claim to that secondary advantage – were he to study or to visit, to initiate any action, the reality – or severity – of his illness might be put in question and his privileged status jeopardised. Johnson declines to authenticate his illness, and is thus an unwelcome visitor. Congreve, Johnson tells Hector, is one of 'a species of Beings with which your profession must have made you much acquainted, and to which I hope acquaintance has made you no friend. Infirmity will come, but let us not invite it; Indulgence will allure us, but let us turn resolutely away. Time cannot be always defeated, but let us not yield till we are conquered.'[8]

This temperamental preference for vigorous action led to many conflicts with his own doctors. There is no doubt that Johnson formed deep and dependent attachments to both Thomas Lawrence and Richard Brocklesby, but his relationship to each of them was full of disagreements on both the theoretical and practical level. As we have seen in chapters 1 and 2, Johnson was constantly usurping his doctor's role and prescribing treatment for himself. Like many other middle-class people in the eighteenth century, he had been alerted to the possibility of taking care of one's own health.[9] In his later years especially, he watched his diet carefully, travelled for changes of air, and monitored his bodily functions – as his journals record – in pursuit of that proper relation to the Galenic 'non-naturals' which was the goal of health. Intensely grateful for his physicians' attendance and concern, and therefore wary of transgressing or violating their professional instructions, he was yet moved continually to take aggressive measures of his own. Frustrated by the failure of his doctor's treatment to work, he wanted to take matters into his own hands: but characteristically, he always sought his doctor's blessing, pestering Lawrence until permission for large bleedings, or to try a new drug, was reluctantly given. Lawrence (and Heberden) rested a good deal of trust in the power of nature to act and heal gradually. Johnson preferred, as the Levet poem has it, 'vigorous remedy': large doses and – as we have seen – drastic bleeding.

No more poignant illustration of the dependence mixed with temperamental and ideological disagreements which constituted the friendship with Lawrence can be found than Mrs Thrale's account of Johnson's last visit in 1782:

He was himself exceedingly ill, and I accompanied him thither for advice. The physician was, however, in some respects more to be pitied than the patient: Johnson was panting under an asthma and dropsy; but Lawrence had been brought home that very morning struck with the palsy, from which he had, two hours before we came, strove to awaken himself by blisters: they were both deaf, and scarce able to speak besides; one from difficulty of breathing, the other from paralytic debility.... 'You (said Johnson) are *timidè* and *gelidè*, finding that his friend had prescribed palliative not drastic remedies. It is not *me*, replies poor Lawrence in an interrupted voice: it is nature that is *gelidè* and *timidè*.[10]

Lawrence's stroke was the first of a series, which eventually totally deprived him of the power of speaking or writing. He retired to Canterbury, where he died in June 1783, only a fortnight before Johnson suffered his own stroke. Johnson missed him deeply. On 16 April 1783 he was still writing in the same dependent strain to the mortally ill Lawrence 'Since your departure I have often wanted your assistance as well as your conversation.' On the morning of the stroke he gave thanks that he could still write, a mercy not enjoyed 'by my Dear friend Laurence, who now perhaps overlooks me as I am writing and rejoices that I have what he wanted.'[11]

'Postquam tu discesseris quo me vertam?' Johnson had asked him in May 1782.[12] After Lawrence's departure Johnson more or less doctored himself, sometimes with help from Dr Pepys and Sir Richard Jebb, Mrs Thrale's doctors. But on the morning after his stroke on 17 June he called in Doctors Heberden and Brocklesby. He explained to Mrs Thrale what had happened after the crisis was past:

That Dr [Pepys] is offended I am very sorry, but if the same state of things should recur, I could not do better. Dr Brocklesby is, you know, my neighbour and could be ready at call, he has for some time very diligently solicited my Friendship; I depended much upon the skill of Dr Heberden, and him I had seen lately at Brocklesby's. Heberden I could not bear to miss, Brocklesby could not decently be missed, and to call three, had made me ridiculous by the appearance of self importance.[13]

On 30 March 1783 Boswell had called on Johnson and had met Dr Brocklesby there.[14] Johnson and Brocklesby had been acquainted at least as early as 1775. But this was the first time Brocklesby had been called upon as a doctor, and we would not be wrong to suspect that even then it was with a certain reluctance. Brocklesby was necessary in order to have Heberden, and when Johnson describes his doctors, the phrasing always suggests Heberden's precedence.

Thomas Percival, one of the first medical writers to give some attention to the ethics of consultation, insisted that visits to the patient must be together. 'No visits should be made, but in concert, or by mutual agreement; no statement or discussion of the case should take place before the patient or his friends, except in the presence of each of the attending gentlemen of the faculty, and by common consent', he advised, insisting that doctors must respect each other's professional opinion, 'cooperating by mutual concession and the benevolent discharge of professional duty.'[15] John Gregory's *Lectures on the Duties and Qualifications of a Physician* shows a similar anxiety about the 'unhappy jealousies and animosities among those of the profession'.[16] The attention these first writers on medical ethics give to the politics of medical consultation shows how difficult the situation could sometimes be when a patient called upon more than one doctor. Fairly complex questions of etiquette were involved when a patient called in two or more doctors or when these were required to consult with surgeons, for there was no hierarchy among physicians. In theory, both doctors had equal authority. Heberden could not be counted a consultant and Brocklesby a general practitioner: the terms did not yet exist. But that in practice is what they became. Heberden (who was living at Windsor) stayed to see the crisis pass and the patient mending, and after a week left the scene, leaving Brocklesby in charge of the day to day management of the case. Brocklesby then became what Johnson called his 'physician in ordinary', visiting almost every day, and thus in a sense replacing both Levet and Lawrence. Whilst he was away in Ashbourne and Lichfield in the summer and autumn of 1784, Johnson wrote a regular bulletin of his condition to Brocklesby, sometimes asking him to consult with Heberden. Twice he wrote directly to Heberden himself, once asking him to call.[17] But there is no evidence of conflict between the two doctors; they were friends, but most importantly treated Johnson without charge, so the dangers warned of by the ethicists probably never arose. Pepys had presumably given his advice freely too, and was naturally put out to find others consulted in the emergency. The absence of fees made Johnson the more personally indebted, at the same time as it may have encouraged his tendency to play the role of partner in the treatment. In his letters to Brocklesby we can see Johnson balancing the two attitudes – grateful dependence on his doctor on the one hand with the urge to think that he himself knows best on the other. Johnson was often pressing new treatments upon Brocklesby, sometimes asking him to consult with Heberden about them. It was he who suggested the cantharides as a diuretic. Brocklesby apparently was reluctant, but gave him permission.[18]

Johnson was to become as dependent on Brocklesby as he had been on Lawrence, but there were barriers to his choice of Brocklesby, impediments to the unimpeded confidence Johnson had probably enjoyed with his earlier physician. Yet Brocklesby was by no means an undistinguished doctor. Educated at Edinburgh and Leyden (another of 'Boerhaave's men') he was a Fellow of the Royal Society, and published in the *Philosophical Transactions*. In 1749 he had brought out a book called *Reflections on Antient and Modern Musick with the application to the cure of Diseases* and in 1763 *Observations on Diseases of the Army*. He was on the army hospital board during the Seven Years War.[19] In the late sixties he published in the *Medical Observations and Enquires*. Richard Brocklesby was also, from 1776 onwards, the physician of Edmund Burke.

One of his papers, as we have seen, concerned experiments on live animals, which Johnson would have read with horror, and may have remembered. But the barrier to Brocklesby's acceptance was undoubtedly the latitude of his religious convictions. In Boswell's 1775 journal report Johnson says 'he had heard Dr Brocklesby, a man once a Quaker and afterwards loose in his notions, say that he did not believe there were in England above two hundred infidels'.[20] Brocklesby was well known for the freedom of his religious beliefs. Johnson was thus in his last days forced by circumstances to depend upon the kindness and professional experience of a man whose religious opinions, he knew, were a possible threat to his own serenity. He received and repeatedly expressed his gratitude for an attention and charity which Brocklesby demonstrated without also having the firm Christian beliefs which had underpinned Lawrence's (and presumably Levet's) kindness and which were deeply associated in Johnson's mind with the special reverence due to the doctor. His final struggle with life became also a struggle towards a death-bed conversion in which Brocklesby's reclamation would be the endorsement or confirmation of his own. He repeatedly tried to balance or reciprocate Brocklesby's kindness with the gift of faith: to conquer Brocklesby's scepticism would be to cancel his indebtedness with an inestimable benefit, but it would also be to assuage his own anxieties. Johnson was dying, but he was also seeking psychological peace – a peace which Brocklesby's conversion would have brought appreciably nearer. The most telling (though perhaps exaggerated) account of the ensuing drama is by Hannah More:

Dr Brocklesby, his physician, was with him; he said to him a little before he died, Doctor, you are a worthy man, and my friend, but I am afraid you are not a Christian! what can I do better for you than offer up in your presence a prayer to the great God that you may become Christian in my sense of the word. Instantly he fell on his knees, and put up a fervent prayer; when he got up he caught hold of his hand with great earnestness, and cried, Doctor, you do not say Amen. The Doctor looked foolishly, but after a pause, cried, Amen! Johnson said, My dear doctor, believe a dying man, there is no salvation but in the sacrifice of the Lamb of God; go home, write down my prayer, and every word I have said, and bring it me tomorrow. Brocklesby did so...[21]

Brocklesby himself told Boswell that 'he made me on Nov 28 write down some serious Dicta on the Subject and Importance of Faith'.[22] But though repeatedly petitioned by Johnson, he remained quite unconvinced. Even in the letter to Boswell which relates Johnson's struggles with him, a letter full of grief and reverence for the dead man, he calls Johnson's religion, unequivocally, 'Superstition'. Nor was this conflict the only one. Johnson asked Brocklesby if he ever prayed: Brocklesby answered by quoting the stoic conclusion of Juvenal's tenth satire, whereupon Johnson, the classical scholar now in ascendent over the penitent Christian, angrily corrected his quotation. Less than a week before he died, according to Sir John Hawkins, he was ridiculing Brocklesby's method of judging of his condition by taking the pulse.[23]

Johnson's confidence in his medical knowledge, a confidence as I have shown largely warranted, is clear in the many dozens of letters of medical advice he himself wrote. They range from the letter of December 1755 to Hill Boothby – 'Give me leave, who have thought much on Medicine, to propose to you an easy and I think a very probable remedy' – through his letters to the Thrales about Henry's stroke, to a series advising John Taylor at Ashbourne, and his letters to James Boswell. Partly because of his informally acquired medical knowledge, partly because of his long experience of chronic and multiple illness, partly because of his stature as a scholar and moralist, Johnson became a doctor-figure to many, especially his later, friends and acquaintances. This is a role, too, which I think Johnson cultivated. His advice is offered dogmatically, he writes as a qualified authority. 'A striking feature of Johnson's prose', begins a mono-graph, 'is the relative infrequency of imperative sentences; the great moralist seldom commands.'[24] But when the moralist wears the mantle of the physician nothing is more common. Injunctions to 'do this' and 'do that' fill Johnson's letters of medical advice. One to John Perkins of July 1782 is almost a parody:

I am much pleased that You are going a very long Journey, which may by proper conduct restore your health and prolong your life.

Observe these rules

1. Turn all care out of your head as soon as you mount the chaise
2. Do not think about frugality, your health is worth more than it can cost.
3. Do not continue any day's journey to fatigue.
4. Take now and then a day's rest.
5. Get a smart sea sickness if you can.
6. Cast away all anxiety, and keep your mind easy.

This last direction is the principal; with an unquiet mind neither exercise, nor diet, nor physick can be of much use.[25]

One might think this dogmatism strange, given that one of the recurrent themes of the *Rambler* essays is the futility of giving advice. 'Admonition or reproof', says *Rambler* 155, for example, can hardly persuade, 'since it impresses no new conviction, nor confers any powers of action or resistance. He that is gravely informed how soon profusion will annihilate his fortune, hears with little advantage what he knew before … He that is told how certainly intemperance will hurry him to the grave, runs with his usual speed to a new course of luxury, because his reason is not invigorated, nor his appetite weakened.' This of course applies to moral advice, but as the letter just quoted makes abundantly plain, Johnson's medical directions usually contain large doses of instruction about psychological attitudes. Johnson does tell his correspondents how much they ought to exercise, what drugs to take, to guard against excessive heat or cold (etc.), but these dictates are almost always enveloped in what cannot be called other than psychological counselling. A principal tenet of Johnson's therapeutic rationale is expressed most succinctly to John Taylor. 'There is no distemper', he writes, 'not in the highest degree acute, upon which the mind has not some influence.'[26] Physiological disease does not exist in isolation from the patient's family or social circumstances: the whole situation must be understood, and attended to, if his or her condition is to be ameliorated. He insists that an agitated or disturbed or even just an excited mind will exert a malign influence on a body prone to illness. Not even Thrale's stroke ('above all, keep your mind quiet, do not think with earnestness even of your health') or the fever from which Goldsmith died ('made, I am afraid, more violent by uneasiness of mind') are exceptions to this rule.[27] 'The management of the mind' is always one of the main targets of Johnson's therapeutic regime.

It can be argued then that in his letters Johnson does offer a form of emotional and mental therapy to his friends. But, as I have suggested, the extent to which Johnson anticipates Freud has been much exaggerated. There is no psychoanalysis by post. Johnson's approach is 'not radical but palliative': he differs from traditional advice-givers only in the force with which he urges his recommendations and the intensity with which he communicates his participation in his friend's distress. He has much to say, as had George Cheyne, about such traditional resources as diversion, exercise and diet, implying as he did in the *Rambler*, that putting the faculties into motion or activity will dislodge or replace mental as well as physical noxae. He urges the importance of companionship, friendship and the sharing of confidences. 'Do not nurse vexation in solitude', he counsels Taylor, 'You will hardly be at rest till you have talked yourself out to some friend or other ...' 'I honestly recommend [Miss Hudson] to your pity', he told Mrs Thrale, 'for nothing but the opportunity of emptying her bosom with confidence can save her from madness.'[28] This companionship in suffering is what many of Johnson's letters themselves offer. 'I know' is a key phrase, as when he writes to Thomas Cumming, then in the last stages of illness:

> Mrs Williams, who likewise has good judgement, desires me to persuade you with all my power to return to Clerkenwel, where you may have her visits and Mr Levet's, and be more within reach of all that you can want. For this removal You and I know yet a better reason, the necessity of abstracting you from your own thoughts, and of driving by external objects out of your mind, these troublesome and intrusive images which with so little reason, have by taking advantage of a distempered body, harrassed you so long.
>
> I do not say put these painful imaginations out of your head, I know that they have got a dominion which you cannot control...[29]

'You and I know': we perhaps glimpse here, in Bacon's phrase, a previous 'civil shrift or confession' between the two. To John Taylor he writes:

Your uneasiness at the misfortunes of your Relations, I comprehend perhaps too well. It was an irresistible obtrusion of a disagreeable image, which you always wished away but could not dismiss, an incessant persecution of a troublesome thought neither to be pacified nor ejected ... Such has of late been the state of my own mind...'[30]

It is this recognition of another's suffering and stabilising reflection in his own that Johnson offers in his letters of condolence too. 'I know that such a loss is a laceration of the mind. I know that a whole system of hopes, and designs, and expectations is swept away at once, and nothing left but bottomless vacuity. What you feel, I have felt...'[31]

Johnson's letters of medical and psychological advice do more than reiterate familiar consolations. Much of what he says could probably be duplicated in the letters of any aging and ailing man to his old and equally ailing friends. Yet there is much more significance in the letters than this, I suggest, partly because their dogmatic manner is so predominant an ingredient in their prescriptions. It is likely that Johnson knew what he was doing and that he was consciously using the authority which – especially in the second half of his life – his writing had brought him. He enlists the prestige of the moralist behind the advice of the friend. The letters are themselves acts in which resistance against indulgence, courage, resolution and hope are instilled by what Johnson once called 'the contagion of example.'

This brings us, finally, to James Boswell, who was of course one of the principal recipients of Johnson's emotional therapy, besides being, as Mrs Thrale suggested, one of Johnson's 'best physicians' himself. One of the things that united the two men and one of their first topics of conversation in July 1763 was 'melancholy' and the means to alleviate it. 'It gave me great relief to talk of my disorder with Mr Johnson', Boswell wrote in his journal, 'and when I discovered that he himself was subject to it, I felt that strange satisfaction which human nature feels at the idea of participating distress with others; and the greater person our fellow sufferer is, so much the more good does it do us.'[32] Both sufferers believed in their condition as an inherited – and quasi-physiological – entity. Johnson's avowal in the Hebrides that 'I inherited a vile melancholy from my father ...'[33] is complemented by Boswell's 'It is certain that I am subject to melancholy. It is the distemper of our family. I am equally subject to excessive high spirits. Such is my constitution.'[34] (Boswell's brother John, incidentally, was often described as 'insane'.) Boswell's accounts of his own disorder run the gamut of eighteenth-century medical or pseudo-medical explanation, but they all tend to represent it as a physiological condition. Sometimes it is melancholy, sometimes 'want of spirits', sometimes the spleen, the vapours, sometimes nerves, sometimes 'hypochrondriak uneasiness'. 'The slight irregularity of supping out and sitting a little late last night had hurt my nerves', he wrote under 30 July 1782 for example, 'so that I was a good deal afflicted with hypochrondria today....'[35] What Johnson called 'morbid melancholy' and Boswell by preference, 'hypochondria' may have been in fact very different conditions, with different causal ontologies. It seems safe to say at least that Johnson's depressive miseries (they might in the nineteenth century have been diagnosed as neurasthenia) had very different constituents from Boswell's.

'Melancholy' though, conceived as a specific disease entity, fundamentally physiological, was something the two men felt they had in common, and many of their conversations are about it. Yet, because melancholy was thought of as 'constitutional', these conversations, however earnest as to the symptoms and treatment, do not enquire into its causes as a subject demanding equal – if not more – exploration. And, as Frank Brady remarks, Boswell's 'incessant self-commentary observes rather than analyses his emotions'.[36] So that when the topic of melancholy is discussed in Boswell's *Life of Johnson*, and in the Journals from which the *Life* was drawn, we always have the impression that it is artificially isolated from other aspects of their lives which seem to cry out for association with it, and the area of their intimacy is correspondingly circumscribed.

'Melancholy' really leads us then, into other, more secret aspects of the two men's friendship. The conversation at Oxford, recorded under Tuesday, 18 March 1776, in which, as Boswell reports, Johnson told him that it was 'madness' to 'think down' melancholy thoughts and declared that 'the management of the mind is a great art', is one of the most famous in the *Life*. If a man is subject to melancholy, Boswell asks, should he not provide amusements for himself? 'Let him take a course of chymistry, or a course of rope-dancing, or a course of any thing to which he is inclined at the time. Let him contrive to have as many retreats for his mind as he can, as many things to which it can fly from itself.'[37] In the Journal, this conversation and advice refer directly to Boswell, who adds slyly: 'I *thought* of a course of concubinage, but was afraid to mention it.'[38] In these early months of 1776 Boswell is thinking a good deal, in fact, about what he calls 'concubinage': and in conversations on ostensibly respectable topics

Johnson is surreptitiously being invited to join in his inner debate. Sexually 'too many' as he calls it, for his wife, Boswell wonders whether, for instance, since the patriarchs had more than one wife, and Luther did not condemn 'concubinage', his sexual adventures may not be permissible. 'My appetite that way was naturally strong', he wrote in his journal for the same day he had the conversation with Johnson just quoted. 'I *must* venture to consult Dr Johnson upon it. For he can, by his noble counsel, make my judgement clear and my resolution vigorous.'[39] On their journey to London Johnson once again 'bid me divert melancholy by every means but drinking. I thought then of women, but no doubt he no more thought of my indulging in licentious copulation than of my stealing.'[40] Thus whilst Johnson thinks they are speaking of melancholy they are in fact discussing sex, though this is concealed from readers of the *Life*, as it was concealed – or half-concealed – from him.

When they arrived at London, they split: Johnson went straight to the Thrales': Boswell, on the other hand, 'in a kind of brutal fever' headed for St James' Park and 'was relieved by dalliance'. 'Brutally feverish' later that night, having 'madly' drunk a whole bottle of claret, he went once again to the Park and then, coming home, was picked up by a strumpet 'and in my drunken venturousness, I lay with her'. Though anxious about the consequences, he had sex with various prostitutes in various locales, including 'Charing Cross Bagnio', on the next three nights.[41] By 4 April, he suspected symptoms of 'the venereal disorder', reinfection by gonorrhea.[42] He went to see Sir John Pringle, who confirmed his own diagnosis, on 10 April. Pringle referred him to Andrew Douglas, who instilled a urethral irrigant by syringe. As Dr William Ober, on whose account of Boswell's venereal diseases I am relying here, remarks, 'One can only imagine the discomfort caused by instilling acid into an already inflamed, pus-producing urethra'.[43] Boswell during this London visit incurred, according to Ober's chronology, his eleventh bout of gonorrhea.

All this time Boswell was seeking means to introduce the topic of 'concubinage' and his anxieties to Johnson. Disguised as discussion of sexual morality, or marriage, or as hypothetical legal questions, he repeatedly raises the topic of sexual licence. They discuss marriage in Birmingham on 22 March and again in Lichfield on the 25th, when Johnson makes his allusion to 'the mechanical reason' why women marry.[44] 'If I have a daughter who is debauched by a man, but nobody knows it, should I keep her in my house?' Boswell enquires on

5 April. On 7 April, 'I repeated to [Johnson] the argument of a lady of my acquaintance, who maintained that her husband's having been guilty of numberless infidelities released her from conjugal obligations . . .' But whether his intention was to draw Johnson into some formal concession about adultery or to introduce the confession of his own weaknesses, he got nowhere at all. 'I mentioned the licensed stews of Rome. That he strongly censured. "Then sir", said I, "you would allow no fornication at all." "To be sure, sir", he said, "I would punish it much more than is done, and so restrain it." '[45] If Angelo-Johnson guessed what was preoccupying Boswell's mind, I can find no evidence – despite what is sometimes asserted – that Johnson ever knew about Boswell's infidelities, and certainly Boswell concealed his medical condition from him. In 1779, attacked in the same way, Johnson repeated his position: 'to whore is wrong in a single man, and one cannot have more liberty by being married.'[46] 'I wrote to him as to a Confessor',[47] Boswell told Brocklesby after Johnson's death, but it seems unlikely that Boswell ever wholly 'emptied his bosom with confidence'. Johnson's own struggles and anxieties forced limits on their intimacy.

But despite – or because of – the circumscribed nature of their discussions, it seems clear that Boswell's melancholy, and to some extent his self-destructive sexual excursions, were alleviated by his association with Johnson. It was the 'awe' that Boswell felt in Johnson's company, he once confessed to him, that kept away his melancholy.[48] It is equally clear that Johnson and manliness are closely connected in his mind. One biographical reason for this is obvious. Boswell's father, the Laird of Auchinleck, eminent judge of the court in which his son was an advocate, powerful and respected member of Edinburgh society, cast a life-long shadow over his eldest child, a shadow which deliberately blighted that son's self-esteem. Brady speaks of the father's 'life-long undermining of his self-confidence'.[49] The Laird was not only a dominant and aggressive father: for reasons of his own he systematically attacked his son's pride in himself. Psychological 'castration' is the way two writers at least have described the Laird's extraordinary act of showing his resentment of his son's marriage by re-marrying himself on the very same day.[50]

References to his father's tyrannies in Boswell's letters and journals are routinely followed by compensatory recollections of Johnson, as for example, in this letter to Temple in September 1767: 'The time was when such a letter from my father as the one I enclose would have depressed me. But I am now firm, and, as my revered friend Mr Samuel Johnson used to say, I feel the privileges of an independent human being.'[51] Johnson is not just a substitute father figure, who, unlike the real father, loved and admired him (and could be brought to say so on occasion). Nor was it simply that when he was in London or with Johnson James Boswell was a social success, mingling with eminent and successful men, admired and liked for his own achievements. 'I thought myself of some real personal consequence while I made one of such company', he writes.[52] (His father presented him with a different picture of his life in London: in an interview recorded on 27 December 1775 in the Journal the Laird, in a 'diabolical-like passion', 'threw out some morose, contemptuous reflections: as if I thought myself a very wise man, and was the reverse, and how I went to London among the *geniuses*, who despised me. He abused Dr Johnson ...'[53]) Johnson was also a sage, someone who gave advice, advice which almost always convinced Boswell and settled his uncertainties. Nor was he an overbearing sage: his advice was almost always surrounded by reassurance and respect. But the curative effect Boswell felt through his friendship with Johnson was not simply attributable to this, nor that Johnson appeared a lofty and inspiring moral example. 'Mental qualities are communicated by contagion as certainly as material qualities', he remarks in his Journal, apropos the assimilation of 'high manly notions'.[54] Johnson brought him 'by contagion' what he felt himself to lack, 'firmness', independence and resolution. His company and his friendship and letters make Boswell feel not only that he himself is valuable, but that he is firm and resolute, everything that he cannot feel he is in the vicinity of his father.

It seems clear then, that Johnson was associated for Boswell with the instillation, or restoration, of quintessentially masculine qualities. The medical expression which Boswell uses in the *Life* to praise *The Rambler*, which he read before he met Johnson, is interesting. 'I will venture to say, that in no writings whatever can be found *more bark and steel for the mind*, if I may use the expression; more that can brace and invigorate every manly and noble sentiment.'[55] This notion that Johnson, and his works, act to instill bracing and 'manly' qualities runs through Boswell's whole relationship with the older man. Through his writings, then in his conversation and letters Johnson became bound up, in complex and interacting ways, with Boswell's aspirations towards full 'manliness' which he may have dimly grasped might have involved renunciation of his compulsive sexual defiance of his father. The refrain runs through the whole twenty years Boswell knew Johnson, from the *Inviolable Plan*, the memorandum that Boswell composed for himself whilst in Utrecht in October 1763:

You are now determined to form yourself into a man ... The Rambler showed you that vacancy, gloom, and fretfulness were the causes of your woe, and that you was only afflicted as others are. He furnished you with principles of piety and philosophy to support the soul at all times.... from this time you fairly set out upon solid principles to be a man....[56]

to, for example, these notes in December 1780:

Was still in very bad spirits, but just resolved to bear my distress. Thought I had no *spirit*, no manly firmness.... While quite sunk, and in a state of everything seeming 'stale, flat, and unprofitable', I tried to read some of Dr Johnson's *Preface* to Milton, and was at once animated and ennobled.[57]

Johnson, through what he was, and what he said, instilled a manliness associated in Boswell's mind with sexual resolution and abstinence. It seems essential to this conception of manliness, in fact, that sexuality is reduced to silence. (And indeed, for all his recording on paper of his sexual temptations and adventures Boswell did not like to talk about sex. Unlike Wilkes, who noticed the fact, he no more talked bawdy than Johnson did.) Johnson's work, like his conversation, is significant for the extent to which sexuality is repressed or excluded from it. Boswell clearly found Johnson a sustaining presence, as did others, because in an age of increasing doubt and 'infidelity', and in an age filled with signs of political unease, he expressed with confidence and resolution an orthodox religious and political position. But Johnson was important to Boswell not only because as a sage, a seer, he could quell the doubts and insecurities of the age. There was a more personal, more intimate element in his dependence, and it seems fair enough to say that this was bound up with Johnson's seeming to embody in his writings, and subsequently in his conversations and letters, an ideal of manliness, an ideal firmness, resolution and self-control, which Boswell felt he could acquire for himself by association or by contagion. The level of Boswell's emotional dependence on Johnson is illustrated vividly in his conduct on becoming, at last, Laird of Auchinleck himself. As he writes to Johnson:

I came to this place [Auchinleck], with my wife and children, on Wednesday the 18 September and took possession of the seat of my ancestors on Dr Johnson's birthday.... I hovered here in fluttering anxiety [the opposite of manly firmness] to be with you till Tuesday the 24: and on that day, though my dear wife had the night before a disagreeable return of her spitting of blood and was very uneasy to think of my going away, I set out. I felt myself drawn irresistibly. I imagined I could neither act nor think in my new situation till I had talked with you ... But ... I was stopped by an express that my wife had been seized with her alarming complaint of spitting of blood more violently than ever and that she entreated I might return. I hastened home again; and the agitation of her spirits being calmed, she has ever since been pretty easy. But that calm she owes to you. For while I was still intent on flying away to you, your excellent letter forcibly dissuading me from *deserting my station* arrived and at once settled me.[58]

Though rationalised as the need to obtain Johnson's advice, it is evident that more urgent and primitive needs are operative here. Margaret Boswell seems to have known what was going on. But the most interesting evidence of the role that Johnson played in Boswell's psychological life is the dream he records (but does not of course, examine) of Thursday, 13 December 1781:

Awaked this morning remarkably well. Had a good dream in the night of being in company with a steady English counsellor, with whom I had a good deal of conversation which animated me, as the English character so agreeably does; and I recollected distinctly a peculiar phrase which he used: that a man should acquire 'preciseness and peremptoriness of mind.' It was well dreamt. I was in strong spirits all day, and was sensible that a great deal of my unhappiness is mere cloud which any moment may dissipate. I thought that at any period of time, a man may disencumber himself of all the *accessories* of his identity, of all his books, all his connexions with a particular place, or a particular sphere of life; and retaining only his consciousness and reminiscence, start into a stage of existing quite new.[59]

This steady English counsellor – stripped even of his identity as Johnson – is, too, disencumbered: a mere voice, like the unmediated presence Boswell felt when his mind was 'elevated wonderfully' by reading *Taxation No Tyranny*: 'a being directly impressing us, as the soul of that writing.'[60] For the Johnson who played such an important role in Boswell's psychological life was inherently a disembodied Johnson. It is a Johnson who, though ungainly and uncouth in physical appearance, suffering from many and varied physical complaints, and living a private life of anguish and disturbance, is quickly assimilated, in the *Life*, to the vigorous and manly Johnson of the writings, the undisturbed and triumphantly balanced sage. Boswell's own needs dictate the presentation of a Johnson whose physical condition can be separated from his importance as hero and authority.

The impression one takes away from the *Life* that Johnson's chronic ill-health is fully documented is misleading. In fact, and apart from his introductory and general remarks, almost all the information about Johnson's illnesses is recorded in footnotes, supplied by later editors from such sources as the *Prayers and Meditations*, or in letters quoted by Boswell without comment. He takes no notice, for example, of the collapse at Oxford in 1768, although he had followed Johnson there.[61] Of 1769, in which Johnson, recovering from this illness, published nothing, he merely notes: 'His Meditations too strongly prove that he suffered much both in body and mind', an acknowledgement immediately followed by the reinstatement of Johnson as the idealised hero of mental fight: 'yet he was perpetually struggling against evil, and nobly endeavouring to advance his intellectual and devotional improvement'. (Mrs Thrale, by contrast, added the marginal note in her copy of the *Life*: 'Ay & against the King's Evil.')[62] Only in the last years, from 1782 onwards, is Boswell forced by his reliance on the letters to acknowledge that Johnson was chronically ill: 'however it will appear from his letters that the powers of his mind were in no degree impaired', he adds.[63]

Boswell did not know that Johnson was almost blind in one eye, but where Johnson's illnesses were concerned it was Boswell who was blind, prevented by his own anxieties and needs from seeing, and acknowledging, Johnson as he was. William C. Dowling has argued that the *Life* deconstructs itself:[64] that the Johnson whose voice speaks when the prayers and poems are quoted from is radically opposed to the idealised and disembodied sage Boswell's own commentary promotes. As Dowling suggests, Boswell plays down the despair and anxiety we glimpse in the prayers, and has of necessity to minimise his hero's physical and psychological maladies. He occasionally thinks of Johnson's future death, and occasionally of his infirmities, but only to dismiss his fears and remind himself of Johnson's, as it were trans-cendental, power. Reading the *Life* of Denham, for example, in London in 1778, he is overwhelmed with admiration once more. 'I thought of his having been ill. I thought of his death. I could not at this moment think gloomily even of that. I could not suppose a mind so extensive, so distinguishing, so luminous, but in a state of exalted felicity. Oh! let me cultivate with respectful and affectionate assiduity the friendship of this great and good man with whom I enjoy an intimacy to which I could not have hoped to attain. But I have attained.'[65] With the wonderful transparency that is his gift Boswell lets us see just how it is that it is his own needs that are met in the friendship. Boswell did not know and could not have known the Johnson known to Levet and Lawrence, to Hector and Mrs Thrale. In order for Johnson to function for Boswell he must appear as the image of mental and spiritual health. That is why the emphasis on Johnson in this book has been so different from the emphasis in the *Life* and one of the reasons why the *Life* pays so little attention to Johnson's medical condition (although this kind of amnesia is not uncommon in biography): Johnson for Boswell is doctor, not patient.

The relationship came to a tragic impasse in Johnson's last year, when we witness the exigent interplay of their psychological needs, now abrading one against the other. In 1784, when Johnson was plainly dying, Boswell was in Scotland. He wrote, by his own admission, 'a letter filled with dejection and fretfulness'. Johnson, at Ashbourne, lonely and ill, replied, reiterating his usual advice, and expressing it, perhaps, the more roughly because, as always, he was trying to strengthen himself. His answer, writes Boswell, 'was chiefly in terms of reproach, for a supposed charge of "affecting discontent, and indulging the vanity of complaint".'[66] 'Write to me often and write like a man', he said. Under the pressure of his own distress, the sage who imparted manliness was, perhaps, becoming dangerously like the nagging, castrating, father. Johnson must have felt that he had crossed this border for he wrote again, two days afterwards, a more conciliatory letter of advice, emphasising, 'I mean it well, for I love you with great ardour and sincerity.' Boswell's depression continued, though, and he wrote to Johnson only to conjure him 'not to do me the injustice of charging me with affectation'.[67] It was now impossible to separate the lofty unimpaired mind from the suffering man.

After this, 'I was with much regret long silent' but whether the regret was retrospective or concurrent is unclear. 'To pay a visit, or write a letter to a friend, does not surely require much activity, yet such small exertions have appeared so laborious to a Hypochondriak, that he has delayed from hour to hour, till friendship has grown cold for want of having its heat continued ...', wrote Boswell in his essay series *The Hypochondriack*.[68] Johnson wrote again on 3 November a letter which in the *Life* Boswell says 'it was not a little painful to me to find ... he still persevered in arraigning me as before, which was strange in him who had so much experience of what I suffered'. Whatever the 'arraignment' (Johnson now collapsed into his father?) was, it is censored. In his journal Boswell noted on 12 November, 'I had received a letter from Dr Johnson that the dropsy increased upon him. I was callous by iteration of misery. Tonight I wrote a short letter to him in a kind of despair.'[69] And that, in effect, was the end of their relationship.

In revering Johnson as a sage, as a hero who is miraculously exempt from ordinary failings of mortality, Boswell is only an extreme representative of a wide-spread, if not universal, human urge. 'It is the most natural thing in the world that this should happen, for not only does one expect it oneself', writes Jung, perhaps rather conceitedly, of the 'mana-personality', 'but everybody else expects it too. One can scarcely help admiring oneself a little for having seen more deeply into things than others, and the others have such an urge to find a tangible hero somewhere, or a superior wise man, a leader and father, some undisputed authority ...'[70] Johnson himself understood this, as he demonstrates in *Rasselas*, chapter 18. Rasselas, the idealistic young prince, finds a man who, as he tells Imlac, 'can teach all that is necessary to be known, who, from the unshaken throne of rational fortitude, looks down on the scenes of life changing beneath him'. When he at last gains access to this sage he finds him crushed by the very misfortunes he claimed to be above. Rasselas leaves, disillusioned, 'convinced of the emptiness of rhetorical sound, and the inefficacy of polished periods and studied sentences'. The polish and the study are Johnson's own in this very sentence, and he thus implicates himself in the tragic inevitability of this process.[71]

Many others since Boswell have continued to reverence – the last word of the *Life* – Johnson's tragic authority. It has been an authority bound up, as it was for Boswell, with a notion of masculinity, of 'manliness', a conception which seems to involve self-conquest, tenderness and sensitivity joined with vigour, illness withstood, chronic anxiety and division countered with 'robust' commonsense. It rests, in short, on the conversion of the vulnerabilities of the sufferer into the abilities of the Doctor. As I remarked in beginning, Samuel Johnson is Doctor Johnson, the scholar, the moralist, the literary dictator, but also the sage, and by implication, the healer. And as such he continues to be turned to as a salutary example in the midst of suffering, even by doctors themselves. Oliver Sacks, for instance, bewildered and dismayed by the devastating mental effect of neurological damage to his knee, thinks with relief of Johnson's clarifying sanity.[72] Arthur Kleinman, describing the day-to-day defeats and the coping ('what a trivialising word') that make up the life of the chronically ill, thinks of Johnson's life as an exemplary victory over just such conditions.[73]

But it is not just his biography, copiously preserved as it is, which makes Johnson an important figure for those who seek to think about illness beyond the bounds of contemporary biomedicine. To read the Levet poem, wrote Leslie Stephen, 'and realise the deep manly sentiment which it implies, without tears in one's eyes is to me at least impossible'.[74] The poem is Johnson's last published work, though not his last poem. To use the modern term, it is his last statement, bringing to culmination a life-time's thinking on moral matters, often in their association with or in their guise as medical ones, a life-time's work which had engaged sometimes centrally, sometimes tangentially with medical writings and the medical profession. He had known medicine in all its branches – official, unlicensed, and self-help. Through him men (and women, since Mrs Thrale was also a notable 'dabbler in physick') of diverse backgrounds, training and ambitions met and were involved in the practice of medicine. But more than this, he was an intensely honest, watchful and articulate patient. His suffering was at the very centre of his view of life. Illness was not for him an aberration, an intrusion into the normal course of life, an episode gone through, recovered from and then quickly forgotten, as it happily is for most of us, but a condition to be permanently reckoned with, the essential ground of human life. Suffering penetrated his work, sometimes erupting almost out of control as in the review of Soame Jenyns, sometimes moulded and directed as in the *Rambler* essays. Besides suffering he thought too about health, in the poem on Levet, and perhaps in one of the last poems he wrote in which he remembers himself as a boy learning to swim at Stowe pool in Lichfield, enjoying what Boswell said he never knew, the natural joy of a free and vigorous use of his limbs. To think about him, about his 'case', is to be reminded, too, what doctors (as well as medical historians) occasionally forget, that the *raison d'être* for medicine is, after all, the suffering of the patient.

NOTES

Introduction

1 Marc Bloch, *The Royal Touch*, translated by J. E. Anderson (1973), p. 220: '"Her Majesty" would seem to have performed the healing gesture for the last time on 27 April 1714, rather more than three months before her death.'

2 Matthew Baillie's *The Morbid Anatomy of some of the most important parts of the human body* (1793), is the first systematic textbook to treat morbid anatomy as a separate subject. A supplementary work, *A Series of Engravings, ... intended to illustrate the morbid anatomy of some of the most important parts of the human body*, was issued in book form in 1803. It has long been thought that the engraving (fasc. 2, plate 6, fig. 1) published in this atlas is of a section of Johnson's lung, and it has been republished as such in several twentieth-century textbooks (e.g. C. Singer's *A Short History of Medicine* (1928; reprinted 1944). In 'A dissertation upon the lung of the late Dr Samuel Johnson, the great lexicographer', Harold D. Attwood (*The Lancet* (21/28 December 1985), 1,411–13), has shown that Baillie's description of Johnson's case in his first edition does not marry with the engraving, which probably is of interstitial fibrosis. The claim that the specimen is Johnson's originates in Squibb, G. J., 'Last illness and post-mortem examination of Samuel Johnson, the lexicographer and moralist, with remarks,' *London Journal of Medicine* 1 (1849), 615–23. Squibb got his information from 'Dr Latham, Snr.', (John Latham, 1761–1843), an associate of Squibb at, and President of, the Royal College of Physicians. See P. James Bishop, 'Samuel Johnson's lung', *Tubercule* 40 (December 1959), 478–81. Lawrence C. McHenry Jr. reproduces both the engraving and the original drawing in 'Samuel Johnson's emphysema', *Archives of Internal Medicine* 119 (January 1967), 98–105, p. 99.

3 Oliver Sacks, *Migraine, Understanding a Common Disorder* (Berkeley and L.A., 1985), preface, p. xvii.

4 Lester King, *Medical Thinking, A Historical Preface* (Princeton, 1982), especially chapters 12, 13 and 14.

5 *Diaries*, p. 106 (March 29 1766).

6 *Literary Magazine* 1 (1756), p. 85.

7 *Miscellanies*, II, p. 280.

8 Sir Humphry Rolleston, 'Medical aspects of Samuel Johnson', *Glasgow Medical Journal*, 4 (April 1924), 173–91, p. 184.

1 Johnson's medical history: facts and mysteries

1 *Boswell's Life of Johnson*, edited by G. B. Hill, revised by L. F. Powell, 6 vols., 2nd edn, IV, Appendix I, p. 465. (Oxford, 1964), IV, Appendix I, p. 465 (hereafter *Life*).
2 Hugh Honour, *Neo-classicism* (Harmondsworth, 1968), p. 120.
3 *Life*, IV, p. 465.
4 *Johnsonian Miscellanies*, arranged and edited by G. B. Hill, 2 vols. (Oxford, 1897), I, p. 224 (hereafter *Miscellanies*); 'Dr Naked', The Marquis of Landsdowne, ed., *The Queeney Letters*, 1934, p. 258.
5 *Miscellanies*, I, p. 344.
6 *Life*, I,. p. 94, and V, p. 18.
7 *Miscellanies*, II, p. 396. Other races include one with Baretti in 1775 (*Life*, II, p. 386.)
8 Roger Lonsdale, *Dr Charles Burney, A Literary Biography* (Oxford, 1965), p. 286. This is, of course, a metaphor.
9 For Falstaffian references in letters to Mrs Thrale, see letters 552, 553, 645, 658, 817.3; Paul Fussell, 'Boswell and his Memorable Scenes' in *The Boy Scout's Handbook and other Observations* (New York and Oxford, 1982), p. 153.
10 *Life*, I, p. 250.
11 *Life*, IV, p. 425.
12 Samuel Johnson, *Diaries, Prayers and Annals*, ed. E. L. Macadam, Jr. with Donald and Mary Hyde (New Haven and London, 1958), p. 3 (hereafter *Diaries*).
13 P. P. Chase, 'The ailments and physicians of Dr Johnson', *Yale Journal of Biology and Medicine* 23 (1951), 370–79. L. C. McHenry Jr. and R. MacKeith, 'Samuel Johnson's childhood illnesses and the King's Evil', *Medical History* 10 (1966), 386–399.
14 Aleyn Lyell Reade, *Johnsonian Gleanings*, Part X, *Johnson's Early Life; The Final Narrative* (1946; reprinted New York, 1968), p. 22.
15 *Diaries*, p. 5.
16 T. C. Allbutt (ed.), *A System of Medicine* (1897), IV, p. 397.
17 McHenry and MacKeith, 'Samuel Johnson's childhood illnesses', pp. 388, 390.
18 *Ibid.*, p. 388.
19 *Diaries*, p. 4.
20 Reade, *Gleanings*, X, p. 25; Keith Thomas, *Religion and the Decline of Magic* (Harmondsworth, 1978), p. 231, notes that 'the healing power of the exiled dynasty became an indispensable element in Jacobite propaganda after 1688'.
21 Richard Wiseman, *Several Chirurgicall Treatises* (1686), The Fourth Book, Ch. 1, 'Of the Cure of the Evil by the King's Touch', p. 246.
22 T. Smollett, MD, *An Essay on the External Use of Water* (1752), p. 11.
23 C. MacLaurin, *Mere Mortals* (1925), p. 13.
24 This operation is not mentioned in the surviving pages of the *Annals*. It would have been performed in the years covered by the pages of the manuscript 'which were torn out by [Johnson] himself, and destroyed', according to the first editor, 'Richard Wright Surgeon', in 1805 (*Miscellanies*, I, p. 127). Mrs Piozzi says 'the scrophulous evil' terribly afflicted his childhood' (*Miscellanies*, I, p. 152). Photographs of the death mask are in McHenry and MacKeith, 'Samuel Johnson's childhood illnesses'.
25 Marshall Waingrow (ed.), *The Correspondence and other Papers of James Boswell Relating to the Making of the Life of Johnson* (1969), p. 85.

26 George Cheyne, *The English Malady, or a treatise of Nervous Disease of all kinds* (1733), p. 184. This passage is marked in Boswell's copy of the fifth edition of this work (1735), now in the Johnson Birthplace library.

27 Arthur Murphy, in *Miscellanies*, I, pp. 450–1; Sir John Hawkins, *The Life of Samuel Johnson L.L.D.* (2nd edn 1787), p. 287 (hereafter Hawkins).

28 McHenry and MacKeith, 'Samuel Johnson's childhood illnesses', p. 394.

29 Hawkins, p. 318, *Miscellanies*, I, p. 152; *Life*, I, p. 41. Boswell writes: 'There is amongst his prayers one inscribed "When my EYE was restored to its use", which ascertains a defect that many of his friends knew he had, though I never perceived it. I supposed him only to be nearsighted.' (It was only after his death that Johnson's *Prayers and Meditations* was published by William Strahan in 1785.)

30 McHenry and MacKeith, 'Samuel Johnson's childhood illnesses', pp. 394–5.

31 *Miscellanies*, I, p. 344; 'His eyes flashed with indignation' at one of Boswell's *faux pas. Life*, I, p. 464.

32 *Anecdotes by the Rev. Dr. Thomas Campbell*, in *Miscellanies*, II, p. 52.

33 *Life*, IV, p. 160 n.1.

34 *Diaries*, p. 348.

35 'Oct. 15 Monday. The Palais Royal very grand large and lofty. – A very great collection of pictures. – three of Raphael. – Two Holy Family. – One small piece of M. Angelo. – One room of Rubens. – I thought the pictures of Raphael fine' (*Life*, II, p. 392).

36 *Miscellanies*, II, pp. 298–9.

37 *Miscellanies*, II, p. 343 (Thomas Tyers).

38 *Life*, IV, Appendix F.

39 *Life*, I, p. 377 n.2.

40 *Miscellanies*, II, p. 325. Roger Bacon is probably the inventor meant.

41 McHenry and MacKeith suggest Johnson had 'a high degree of myopic astigmatism which could not be corrected by the optical knowledge of the time' ('Samuel Johnson's childhood illnesses', p. 395 n). Thomas Tyers says Johnson 'was assured [spectacles] would be of no service to him'. *Miscellanies*, II, p. 343).

42 *Miscellanies*, II, p. 254.

43 *Diaries*, pp. 245–6, 158.

44 *Life*, V, pp. 18, 141. Also III, p. 187 where Johnson describes Islam 'distinctly and vividly': 'It was wonderful how accurate his observation of visual objects was, notwithstanding his imperfect eyesight, owing to a habit of attention', IV, p. 311. *The Literary Magazine*, I (1756), p. 78.

45 *Miscellanies*, I, p. 152.

46 McHenry and MacKeith, 'Samuel Johnson's childhood illnesses', p. 397.

47 It may be that Johnson's hearing difficulties were of the type which made background noise pleasing to him. There are numerous reports of his composing whilst in a crowded room and he could read whilst travelling in a carriage. 'He had a table by one of the windows, which was frequently surrounded by five or six ladies engaged in work or conversation' (*Miscellanies*, II, p. 414). Both Frances Reynolds and Sir John Hawkins thought that music was actively painful for Johnson to hear. Sir F. D. MacKinnon thought he had *paracusis Willisii* – ability to hear in noisy conditions (*Life*, I, p. 500 n). (His hearing may also have deteriorated (as is implied in *Miscellanies*, II, p. 318 [Steevens].)

48 *Life*, III, p. 197.

There is undoubtedly sympathy with this figure, but hidden within the chapters on the astronomer is also a critique of the pursuit of useless knowledge. Johnson's commendation of Raphael's reproof of Adam's curiosity after the planetary motions in the *Life of Milton* is only one place in his work where he criticises the search after 'star-knowledge', in John Hardy's phrase, rather than the cultivation of self-knowledge. More importantly, and more perceptively, the chapters provide a parodic extrapolation and reversal of the Enlightenment fantasy (see, for example, *Robinson Crusoe*) that it might be possible to appropriate the natural world completely to the purposes of man.[66] To subjugate Nature to the rule of Reason is a common urge, of which the astronomer's dreams are one version, and Johnson's own enterprises are another. The hubristic desire for total control over the natural world is a madness, like Xerxes' in the lines of Juvenal long known by heart to Johnson before he translated them as:

> ... Madness fires his Mind
> The Waves he lashes and enchains the Wind.

Such mad ambition is not unknown to scholars, moralists and lexicographers. In *Adventurer* 137 attention is given to the claim that 'no age was ever made better by its authors, and that to call upon mankind to correct their manners, is like Xerxes, to scourge the wind and shackle the torrent'. More significantly, in the closing passages of the Preface to the *Dictionary*, Johnson speaks of his early hopes that his enterprise might fix the language, and that it was in his power 'to change sublunary nature'. 'I have indulged expectation which neither experience nor reason can justify', he confesses, and declares that 'to enchain syllables and lash the wind are equally the undertakings of pride'.[67] The day-dreams of benevolent power of the astronomer, 'the regulator of the year', are thus not so very different from the day-dreams of Samuel Johnson, the regulator of the language, and these chapters castigate them just as the chapter of *Rasselas* about the Arab who is bored to death with his harem, might well be thought to castigate Johnson's fantasies of life in a seraglio.[68] Johnson saw that his own dreams and ambitions had the seed of madness in them. The turret of the astronomer is a metaphoric transposition of the attic at Gough Square.

In chapter 46 the Princess and Pekuah, her maid, visit the astronomer who 'was pleased to see himself approached with respect by persons of so splendid an appearance' and Johnson's case history begins to approach the question of cure. Pekuah's 'conversation took possession of his heart': he wants to see more and more of them, and so they invite him to the house of Imlac, 'where they distinguished him by extraordinary respect'. 'From this time the astronomer was received into familiar friendship, and partook of all their projects and pleasures: his respect kept him attentive, and the activity of Rasselas did not leave much time unengaged.'

This may be linked with Johnson's later and more famous remark to Boswell in 1777 that 'a madman loves to be with people whom he fears; not as a dog fears the lash; but of whom he stands in awe'.[69] Superficially this resembles such commonplaces of mad-doctor's doctrine as Thomas Willis's statement that 'indeed for the curing of Mad people, there is nothing more effectual or necessary than their reverence or standing in awe of such as they think their Tormentors.'[70] But this is an argument for brutal treatment to subdue the animal wildness of the insane, as Willis continues, 'Furious Madmen are sooner, and more certainly cured by punishments and hard usage, in a strait room, than by *Physick* or Medicines'. Johnson's position is completely misunderstood if it is assumed that he is speaking in favour of hard usage of the mad. On the contrary, his ideas about therapy resemble those to be announced by the humanitarian guardians of the insane over half a century later. The Quaker, Samaul Tuke, at York, found the patients' 'desire for esteem' a powerful agent towards their management and cure: 'This principle in the human mind which doubtless influences in a great degree, though often secretly, our general manners; and which operates with peculiar force on our introduction into a new circle of acquaintance.'[71] The astronomer is now mingling with personages of whom he stands in awe and he naturally wishes to aquit himself well with them. Johnson's theory, like that of those who supposedly revolutionised the treatment of the insane in the first decades of the nineteenth century, is that as a result of this his mind will have less time and energy to spend on its own problems and delusions and they will therefore diminish. Rasselas, his sister and her maid surround the astronomer with just such a 'fictional family' as the managers of early asylums created to subdue the manifestations of insanity in their patients. Since this theory and the institutional treatment it promoted have come under attack for substituting inner compulsions, inner guilts, inner chains, for the external restraints previously employed by mad-house keepers,[72] it is worth pointing out that Johnson's stress is on the contrary fact, the consider the variety of medical practice it becomes very difficult to substantiate a hard-and-fast division between orthodox and unorthodox medicine, or to use this division as an index to the probable nature or standard of practice. A dissenting minister, James Clegg of Chapel-en-le-Frith in Derbyshire took up the practice of medicine, having learned the rudiments from a physician in near-by Macclesfield. When he was threatened with prosecution he bought an MD from Aberdeen and became, by this process, a 'legitimate' physician.[6] 'Sir' John Hill, one of the most notorious quacks of the mid eighteenth century (though he made important contributions to botanical knowledge and Johnson used him in the *Dictionary*), similarly got his degree from one of those universities, as Sir John Hawkins sourly remarked, which would scarce refuse one to an apothecary's horse. And John Mudge, called by Boswell 'the celebrated physician', whom Johnson consulted by letter about his sarcocele in 1783, was actually an irregular; he obtained his MD at King's College, Aberdeen, only in 1784, when he was over sixty.[7]

The diffusion of medical practice and knowledge throughout the kingdom was recognised, if in an ambiguous manner, in a work such as William Buchan's *Domestic Medicine* (the first of many editions appeared in 1769), which steers its way carefully between maintaining the necessity of professional medical assistance and at the same time plausibly offering help and advice to the middle classes who, it implicitly acknowledges, act as physicians for their families and servants.[8] Much earlier, the proposals for the *Medicinal Dictionary* make it clear that it is at least partly aimed at readers who practise medicine as a branch of charity. Not much is as yet known of the ordinary literate person's knowledge of medicine in the eighteenth century, since medical historians have tended to concentrate so much on official medicine and the lives and achievements of a few star names. But there were, then as now, lots of publications aimed at the medical self-help market.[9]

It is as hard to find out much about the lives and therapeutic practices of the unlicensed doctors. Unlike the official physicians, they kept no records of consultations. They were sometimes employed by the overseers of the poor and given the deferential title of 'Dr' in the accounts of payment, but they must frequently, even more often than qualified doctors, have received their fees in the form of payment in kind. They probably lived from hand to mouth. The itinerant quacks have at least left behind them the newspaper advertisements in which their healing powers and their royal patrons are touted. But the lives of these obscure men, never meeting the junctures of official power, must have almost entirely perished, leaving no memorial behind.[10]

Robert Levet is one who would have gone into the dark with the rest but for his friendship with Samuel Johnson. The two men first met at about the same time (1746) that James was thundering against empirics. Levet may have lived with Johnson before 1762, but certainly for about twenty years he was an inmate of Johnson's household, occupying the garret at Bolt Court. One night in January 1782, when Johnson was with Mrs Thrale, he was musing alone in his room about his future and he resolved (so he later told Boswell) that, if he were to set up house elsewhere, he would at all events try to retain Levet's companionship. In the morning the servant, probably Frank Barber, brought him word of Levet's death. Johnson wrote that day to Thomas Lawrence:

> Sir,
> Our old friend Mr Levett, who was last night eminently cheerful, died this morning. The man who lay in the same room hearing an uncommon noise got up: and tried to make him speak, but without effect, he then called Mr Holder the apothecary, who though, when he came, he thought him dead; opened a vein but could draw no blood. So has ended the long life of a very useful, and very blameless man.[11]

Lawrence was retired by this time, but still being consulted almost daily by Johnson, who was suffering a particularly severe bout of asthmatic trouble. In the following spring Johnson was reciting to his friends and giving out copies of his famous memorial verses on Levet. Eventually the poem found its way into print in the *Gentleman's Magazine* for August 1783:

On the Death of Dr ROBERT LEVET,
by Dr. JOHNSON

Condemn'd to hope's delusive mine,
  As on we toil from day to day,
By sudden blasts, or slow decline,
  Our social comforts drop away.

Well tried through many a varying year,
  See LEVET to the grave descend;
Officious, innocent, sincere,
  Of ev'ry friendless name the friend.

had bouts of frantic exhilaration, his drunkenness was as notorious as his praying; his illness was manifested in behaviour that was publicly sensational: he prayed in St James' Park and routed all the company. In this respect he conformed to his contemporaries' expectations. 'All agreed that it was the essence of lunacy to be visible, and known by its appearance', writes Porter, reviewing eighteenth-century cultures of madness. For 'Burton's or Boswell's contemporaries',

madness gave itself away. The mad looked quite peculiar. They went near-naked, tore their clothes or dressed fantastical, their hair festooned with straw. They acted oddly: now motionless, withdrawn: now preternaturally violent. They gobbled strange foods, such as vermin and dung, or refused to eat. They moved and gesticulated incessantly, apparently never sleeping, racked by tics and convulsions. Some bayed at the moon, or howled like dogs. Others tried to kill themselves. Altogether they were sub- or anti-human.'[54]

It is this traditional notion of the madman as beast or brute (a notion that was reflected in the often brutal treatment meted out to the insane) that the astronomer's story confronts, and against this background that its emphasis on the 'uncertain continuance of reason' has its shocking force. All Johnson's stress is upon the similarities between the state of madness and 'normal', socially accepted, behaviour. The dramatic structure of the chapters depends upon the contrast between the astronomer's public reputation – 'his integrity and benevolence are equal to his learning', says Imlac – and the sudden revelation of his inner life. The astronomer is guarded in demeanour, perfectly sober and reasonable in conversation. He is slow and reluctant to communicate his belief in his powers to Imlac, and when he does communicate his secret, the confession is accompanied by signs of guilt and anxiety. His obsession consumes and torments him, but he passes for a normal, in fact a supremely admirable, man.

One seeks for models among Johnson's acquaintances for this portrait, because there seem to be no precedents for this in fiction or medical texts. But there are brief instances in the literature on insanity which may have offered hints towards the construction of the astronomer's obsession, as well as towards its accompanying emotions. Richard Brocklesby's *Reflections on Antient and Modern Music, with the application to the cure of diseases* (1749), for instance, gives an account of the onset of insanity which has some resemblances to Johnson's (as well as to Locke's). The insane person, Brocklesby writes, at last come[s] to dwell upon the same subject so long, till the mind has imposed a sort of mechanical necessity on the organs that excite this idea, still to go on in the same manner; hence it sometimes happens, the person shall strive with his utmost efforts to get rid of that particular thought, yet it will in spite of his endeavours rush upon his mind, and dwell with him continually, sometimes the whole external face of things is changed . . .[55]

But rather than give examples from his own observation, Brocklesby, like Thomas Arnold, falls back upon a classical instance:

A woman, mentioned by TRALLIAN [de arte Medica, Lib. i, cap. xvii] continually held up her middle finger, on which she imagined she was supporting the whole world, and was in perpetual anxiety lest she should suffer her finger to give way, and destroy the world, with its inhabitants . . .[56]

Similarly the astronomer's responsibilities demand 'unremitted vigilance'. He declares 'If the task of a king be considered as difficult, who has the care only of a few millions, to whom he cannot do much good or harm, what must be the anxiety of him, on whom depend the action of the elements and the great gifts of light and heat!' Supreme power, that is also unending punishment: that is the paradox of the insane obsession.

But if there are passing mentions of guilt and anxiety in the literature as an accompaniment or constituent of insane delusions, there are no precedents for the central and extended attention Johnson gives to this aspect of the astronomer's experience. Nor are there formal precedents for another fundamental aspect of Johnson's presentation, his allowing a madman a voice. It is the astronomer in fact who initiates the whole discussion of madness, when he breaks his silence and makes his disclosure to Imlac in chapter 45: it is the astronomer who, in revealing his delusion, reveals that he has 'reasoned long against his conviction': it is the astronomer's voice which speaks of the 'fear, disquiet and scrupulosity' that accompanies this conviction (chapter 46) and later tells of his struggles against the inveterate persuasion that rushes upon his soul. This madman is endowed with self-reflection, self-consciousness, and a self-knowledge that tragically approaches completeness: Johnson even has him say, 'I sometimes suspected myself of madness'. This dramatic presentation of the astronomer's experience sets up some conflicts with the theory of insanity Imlac expounds. Some of the nuances of his speeches in fact suggest interpretations more consonant with later developments in the history of psychology.

tal beings intruding into the turmoil of mortal life.'[62] But though this sense of a foreign presence, a spectre, is a consistent part of the astronomer's experience, Johnson's account or analysis of insanity gives no explanation for it or its origins. It is simple enough for the modern reader to read the astronomer's descriptions of an apparently external force as reports, in effect, of the unconscious. The sage's anxiety is for him, and for Johnson, explained by the burdensomeness of his task, but a modern reading of such a case would suggest that it is on the contrary connected to an inner reality hidden from him. Its presence would be the sign that the real pressures behind his fantasy were not being directly expressed in it. Such an interpretation might go on to suggest that the astronomer's guilt attaches to his original, hidden, fantasy, or to his 'indulgence' in it, but has been transferred in his conscious mind to its symptoms. The process of repression has split it from its original cause and attached it to another idea which is then mistaken for it. The primordial fantasy has become distorted into a fantasy of power (or perhaps of power of a different sort) at the same time as the emotions have been transformed, in ways for which analogies would be found in the phobias, from pleasure to 'fear, disquiet and scrupulosity'. The super-ego, to adopt later Freudian terminology, though, has not been deceived: it can read that code which to the ego is baffling, and thus punishes the obsessive fantasy as much as it would punish the original idea of which the fantasy is a symptom. Such an explanation of the astronomer's misery is of course not remotely like anything that Johnson's account gives a hint of: I offer it only to underline the suggestion that the 'unremitting anxiety' which accompanies the delusion, as well as the process of 'going mad' itself, is not explicable in the terms that Johnson had available to him, and to suggest how far he is from the Freud to whom he has been so often compared.[63]

What account of the astronomer's guilt Johnson gives is in Imlac's remarks in chapter 46. 'When melancholick notions take the form of duty', he says, 'they lay hold on the faculties without opposition, because we are afraid to exclude or banish them.' The astronomer's duties are carried out under the eyes of a jealous, punishing god, but this assumption is too deeply engrained in Johnson's thought to be made explicit here. Imlac's discussion seems to escape from the point in another respect: the astronomer's are not merely melancholic notions, they are obsessive convictions. He really believes he has supernatural powers, his scruples and dutifulness are merely its accompaniment or consequence. Yet Imlac's earlier remarks about the origins of insanity do contain some insight that can be applied illuminatingly to the astronomer's particular case. Why does his delusion take this form? Not, as common sense would reply, that having so much to do with the skies, his dreams naturally concern them. Rather the question is, why are these dreams of power?

When we are alone we are not always busy; the labour of excogitation is too violent to last long; the ardour of enquiry will sometimes give way to idleness or satiety. He who has nothing external that can divert him, must find pleasure in his own thoughts, and must conceive himself what he is not; for who is pleased with what he is? He then expatiates in boundless futurity, and culls from all imaginable conditions that which for the present moment he should most desire, amuses his desires with impossible enjoyments, and confers upon his pride unattainable dominion. The mind dances from scene to scene, unites all pleasures in all combinations, and riots in delights which nature and fortune, with all their bounty, cannot bestow.

In time some particular train of ideas fixes the attention, all other intellectual gratifications are rejected, the mind, in weariness or leisure, recurs constantly to the favourite conception, and feasts on the luscious falsehood whenever she is offended with the bitterness of truth.[64]

The motive force, so Johnson's account suggests, is the desire of pleasure, and the mechanism, to use a Jungian term, is compensatory. There is an antithesis, a balance between the fantasy and the reality – between 'the lusciousness of falsehood' and 'the bitterness of truth'. The astronomer's delusion of power can then be thought of as a compensation for his actual powerlessness. When he has emerged from belief in his gifts, Imlac's concluding advice is 'keep this thought always prevalent, that you are only one atom of the mass of humanity, and have neither such virtue nor vice, as that you should be singled out for supernatural favours or afflictions'. For the astronomer, the surrender of his delusion is almost a confession of his life's failure. 'I have passed my time in study without experience', he says sadly:

'in the attainment of sciences which can, for the most part, be but remotely useful to mankind. I have purchased knowledge at the expence of all the common comforts of life; I have missed the endearing elegance of female friendship, and the happy commerce of domestick tenderness. If I have obtained any prerogatives above other students, they have been accompanied with fear, disquiet and scrupulosity; but even of these prerogatives, whatever they were, I have, since my thoughts have been diversified by more intercourse with the world, begun to question the reality.'[65]

'Mr', of course, is a courtesy title too. Sometimes we hear of Mr Frank Barber. These questions of social protocol are not merely extrinsic to the poem but germane to its whole nature. It everywhere acknowledges that it belongs to a context where social distinctions, professional arrangements, etiquette, loyalties and class feeling constitute invisible expectations and constraints. The poem may thus tell us a good deal about both Levet's practice and about medical conditions of the time, and so I think it does. But it does not yield this information easily, nor is it on the surface. Attempting to analyse the poem as an historical document involves first confronting or negotiating certain aspects of Johnson's conscious poetical method. His poems eschew detail and particularity in conformity with deeply held convictions. Writing of Samuel Butler's *Hudibras* Johnson declares that 'the manners, being founded on opinions, are temporary and local, and therefore become every day less intelligible and less striking'. 'All poems describing manners require notes after fifty years', he said with some disapproval. His conception of human nature, his theory of poetry and his practice of poetry are all consistent, and all what we may call a-historical. His premise is that human nature is uniform, not only 'from China to Peru' not only from high to low but throughout historical time. 'The interests and passions, the virtues and vices of mankind, have been diversified in different times, only by unessential and casual varieties', he wrote in *Adventurer* 95; 'such is the constitution of the world, that much of life must be spent in the same manner by the wise and the ignorant, the exalted and the low. Men, however distinguished by external accidents or intrinsick qualities, have all the same wants, the same pains and ... the same pleasures' (*Idler* 51). As the word 'constitution' implies, Johnson's thinking on this matter is often based on an analogy with the human anatomy; as all men and all women share the same anatomical characteristics, so their differences are 'casual' and 'inessential', external and – Johnson declares – much less important.

Poetry, Johnson argues, should address itself to, and elicit a response from, essential human nature – that part of present and future readers which might be thought independent of historical times and circumstances. If it is to succeed in this it obviously should not entangle itself with contemporary manners and social conditions, for 'poetry' as Johnson writes in *Rambler* 36, 'cannot dwell upon the minuter distinctions, by which one species differs from another, without departing from that simplicity of grandeur which fills the imagination; nor dissect the latent qualities of things, without losing its general power of gratifying every mind by recalling its conceptions.' It 'has to do rather with the passions of men, which are uniform, than their customs, which are changeable.' His view is consistent throughout his career. It appears again, for instance, in his famous judgement of Gray's *Elegy* ('The Churchyard abounds with images which find a mirrour in every mind, and with sentiments to which every bosom returns an echo' – a remark made, in completing the *Lives of the Poets*, not a year before composing his own elegy for Levet.)

As we might expect then, the poem is written in language which seems plain, general, even stereotypical. But its apparently generalised language is very different from the common run of eighteenth-century commemorative verses, including Gray's *Elegy*, however much Johnson's poem conforms to the conventional format of such poems. Compare it with one of its prototypes, the memorial verses 'On the Death of Dr Cheyne' published after George Cheyne's death in 1734:[36]

> Of Virtues, common to the Race
>   Of Mortals he possest;
> Yet heighten'd with uncommon Grace,
>   They stood his own confest.
>
> Discreetly wise, and temperate,
>   Where Folly keeps her Court;
> And Luxury in pompous State
>   Enjoys her feastful Sport.
>
> Learned, yet affable, and free,
>   His Treasures to dispense,
> With unaffected Modesty,
>   Sound Judgment, manly Sense.
>
> Learned yet humble and devout
>   He grateful spent his Days;
> And studiously his Gifts laid out
>   In the great Giver's Praise.
>
> Like him beneficently kind,
>   Nor Impotent to save;
> To Rich and Poor an equal Friend
>   Like Baiae's balmy Wave.

as much as his readers, when he calls on 'letter'd arrogance' to put aside its snobbish preconceptions and squeamishness and pay tribute to Levet. It is as if the poem acknowledges a slight inhibition in the poet, which is a reflection of anticipated resistance within the tradition and the audience of polite literature, or as if the poet must expose a division within himself, between his 'affection' and his social or intellectual loyalties. The lines recall Gray's

> Let not Ambition mock their useful toil,
>   Their homely joys, and destiny obscure;
> Nor Grandeur hear with a disdainful smile,
>   The short and simple annals of the poor.

But in Johnson's case the address to 'letter'd arrogance' is more militant. One does not need to suppose that 'letter'd' is particular rather than general – that Johnson might have had in mind the letters MD – to feel that in turning the self admonition outwards to a putative reader the poem effects a successful transition to a more politically edged mode. There are similarities with the concluding passages of Johnson's life of another friend, Richard Savage, and its impassioned scorn of those whose affluence and refinement lead them to look down on a man whose life was not so comfortable as their own. The next stanza of the poem continues the praise of Levet:

> When fainting nature called for aid
>   And hov'ring death prepar'd the blow,
> His vig'rous remedy display'd
>   The power of art without the show.

Levet's practice demonstrated the skill, the courage and quickness of an accomplished surgeon or physician. That is obviously the meaning of the first half of this last line. But what does 'without the show' imply? The term 'art' is closely associated with the professional guild, corporation or company, a group of men solely empowered by charter to practise a particular craft or skill. Each medical corporation had its own constitution, arms and privileges. The line is not simply neutral, descriptive of Levet's own demeanour, but may involve a reflection upon the 'show', in the first place the armorial bearings, the gold-topped cane and all the other trappings of the official medical corporations. It certainly defends Levet from the condescending attitudes that are epitomised in Hawkins' remark that 'his external appearance and behaviour were such, that he disgusted the rich, and terrified the poor'.

If this is so, then specific, locally charged references are latent in the seeming orotund grandeur of the lines. This is even more true of the next stanza, the fifth:

> In Misery's darkest caverns known
> His useful care was ever nigh,
> Where hopeless anguish pour'd his groan,
> And lonely want retir'd to die.

In one reading, like the Dungeon of Giant Despair, the caverns are metaphors for that misery we call 'deepest': 'Suffering is permanent, obscure and dark', Wordsworth was to write. The phrase 'dark caverns' is one of those expressions which attempts to communicate or search out through the use of a metaphor the pain of a pathological mental state whose essence is the absence of the power of articulation, of energy, will and hope. The cavern suggested may be that cavern which is the human skull. Yet here Levet's 'useful care' is 'nigh'. This certainly implies that the caverns have geographical reality, are places which one can approach. 'Caverns' must also then describe the actual dwelling places of the poor, must subliminally remind the reader that Levet's patients might literally live underground in darkness, in the basements and cellars of London's slums. The darkness that surrounds Levet and his patients is actual, then: but on a third level of meaning it is, once again, metaphysical. 'We have histories of diseases, but not of health, biographies of doctors but not of the sick', writes Roy Porter, lamenting as so many recent medical historians do, our lack of knowledge of the patient, especially the poor patient.[43] The images of mines and caverns in the poem co-operate with the 'obscurity' that surrounds Levet to suggest the invisibility of these poor patients and their doctor to the eye of history, or to the official records of society, compiled by its articulate self-conscious possessors of tradition and authority. These patients have, the poem goes on to suggest, erased themselves from notice and from history. As 'self-respecting' poor, they have chosen to withdraw from the public stage and die in isolation. Levet visits

> Where hopeless anguish pour'd his groan,
> And lonely want retir'd to die.

(Or, in the version which Johnson repeated to Boswell: 'And labour steals an hour to die'.) The phrase 'pourd his groan' implies not merely the inarticulacy of the acutely suffering, but – 'poured' in the 'cavern'

Yet still he fills affection's eye,
   Obscurely wise, and coarsely kind;
Nor, letter'd arrogance, deny
   Thy praise to merit unrefin'd.

When fainting nature call'd for aid,
   And hov'ring death prepar'd the blow,
His vig'rous remedy display'd
   The power of art without the show.

In misery's darkest caverns known,
   His useful care was ever nigh,
Where hopeless anguish pour'd his groan,
   And lonely want retired to die.

No summons mock'd by chill delay,
   No petty gain disdain'd by pride,
The modest wants of ev'ry day
   The toil of ev'ry day supplied.

His virtues walk'd their narrow round,
   Nor made a pause, nor left a void,
And sure th'Eternal Master found
   The single talent well employ'd.

The busy day, the peaceful night,
   Unfelt, uncounted, glided by,
His frame was firm, his powers were bright,
   Tho' now his eightieth year was nigh.

Then with no throbbing fiery pain,
   No cold gradations of decay,
Death broke at once the vital chain,
   And forc'd his soul the nearest way.

Johnson's friends and biographers were inclined to disapprove of Johnson's friendship with Levet. Hawkins described him as 'one of the lowest practitioners in the art of healing that ever sought a livelihood by it'. Mrs Thrale called him 'that odd old surgeon whom [Johnson] kept in his house to tend the out-pensioners'. Boswell wrote of 'his humble friend Mr Robert Levet, an obscure practiser in physick amongst the lower people'.[12] All three were amused, even slightly scandalised, at Johnson's respect for his friend's abilities. 'Johnson', wrote Hawkins, 'whose credulity in some instances was as great as his incredulity in others, conceived of him as of a skilful medical professor, and thought himself happy in having so near his person one who was to him, not solely a physician, a surgeon, or an apothecary, but all.'[13] Boswell was particularly amused on Good Friday 1773, breakfasting with Johnson on tea and cross buns, to hear Frank, the negro servant, refer to '*Doctor* Levet'. There is no doubt that Johnson did value Levet's abilities highly. Writing to Thomas Cumming, a Quaker acquaintance who was desperately ill, in May 1774, for instance, he says 'I have been talking of your case with my Friend Mr Levet, who has had great practice, and of whom I have a very high opinion'. He urges Cumming to move to Clerkenwell, where Levet might visit him, and adds encouragingly, 'Ther[e] is a man now living whom Mr Levet restored from ulcerated lungs after many Physitians had deserted him'.[14]

After Johnson's death an anonymous correspondent to the *St James Chronicle* supplied an account of Levet's life, which was reproduced, after some 'mistakes' had been corrected, in the *Gentleman's Magazine* of February 1785. Among other things this gives the following details of Levet's medical education:

Mr Levett, though an Englishman by birth, became early in life a waiter at a coffee-house in Paris. The surgeons who frequented it, finding him of an inquisitive turn, and attentive to their conversation, made a purse for him, and gave him some instructions in their art. They afterwards furnished him with the means of other knowledge, by procuring him free admission to such lectures in pharmacy and anatomy as were read by the ablest professors of that period. Hence his introduction to a business, which afforded him a continual, though slender maintenance. Where the middle part of his life was spent, is uncertain. He resided, however, above twenty years under the roof of Johnson, who never wished him to be regarded as an inferior, or treated him like a dependent. He breakfasted with the doctor every morning, and perhaps was seen no more by him till midnight. Much of the day was employed in attendance on his patients, who were chiefly of the lowest rank of tradesmen. The remainder of his hours he devoted to Hunter's lectures, and to as many different opportunities of improvement as he could meet with on the same gratuitous conditions. 'All his medical knowledge', said Johnson, 'and it is not inconsiderable, was obtained through the ear. Though he buys books, he seldom looks into them, or discovers any power by which he can be supposed to judge of an author's merit.'

This is a rather different history than we would guess from Johnson's poem, with its reference, for instance, to Levet's 'narrow round' and 'single talent'. (Neither Johnson nor Mrs Thrale had travelled abroad before their brief visit to Paris and Northern France in September 1775. Neither could speak French with any fluency.)

other favours from Hunter, procured Levet this one, too.[28] William Hunter has not gone down in history as a generous or charitable man, to say the least.

It will have been noticed that Levet's contemporaries do not agree in their descriptions of his occupation, his trade or profession – whichever it was. 'Physician in ordinary', was Arthur Murphy's term. 'A necessary man, a surgeon', Mrs Thrale once called him. 'Mr Levat, I suppose sir', she cheekily asked Johnson on another occasion, 'has the office of keeping the hospital [she seems to have meant Johnson's ailing household], in health? For he is an apothecary.'[29] Hawkins' description 'not solely a physician, a surgeon or an apothecary but all' has already been given. We can assume, I think, that Levet supplied drugs for his poor patients; those who could scarcely afford to pay their doctor would not have been able to afford apothecary's fees as well. The remark that his patients 'were chiefly of the lowest class of tradesman' is interesting too. Levet's patients might not have been then the totally destitute, for these might have been in the care of the Overseers of the poor. We may imagine Levet scraping a living between the very poor and the lower middle classes who could afford a surgeon or apothecary. It was a time when London seems to have been well supplied with official and licensed practitioners of medicine.[30] One characteristic of Levet that caused some amusement to Johnson is notable too. 'Johnson would observe, he was, perhaps, the only man who ever became intoxicated through motives of prudence. He reflected, that if he refused the gin or brandy offered him by some of his patients he could have been no gainer by their cure, as they might have had nothing else to bestow on him. This habit of taking a fee, in whatever form it was exhibited, could not be put off by advice or admonition of any kind. He would swallow what he did not like, nay what he knew would injure him, rather than go home with an idea, that his skill had been exerted without recompence.'[31] Levet's behaviour in other words was a way of laying hold of status: he took payment, of whatever kind, to remind his patients that he was, to use a modern term, a health care professional. It also, of course, ministered to his patients' self-respect.

One of the few weapons available to the College of Physicians in its fitful forays against unlicensed doctors throughout the century was to instruct its members to refuse to co-operate or consult with unqualified men. It is fascinating, therefore, to find the ex-President of the College, through Johnson's agency, doing just that (though Levet of course, as a surgeon-apothecary, or whatever, was not a rival physician.) Levet carried out minor surgery and prescribed drugs to Johnson's household on Thomas Lawrence's instructions. On one occasion at least, in January 1777, Levet came to the rescue when a bleeding which had been ordered by Lawrence failed to stop. Johnson's letter to Lawrence announcing Levet's death is sufficient evidence of the respect and friendship uniting the three men. It suggests that medical relations during the century were a good deal more complicated than the propaganda of the likes of Robert James would lead one to think.

Most upper and middle class patients of the time clearly recognised the distinctions between the different categories of practitioner, and indeed insisted on them.[32] Johnson's friends and biographers are no exception. Johnson himself, we happen to know, was perfectly well informed about them. In February 1775 he wrote to Thomas Lawrence for clarification, on Boswell's behalf, of whether it could be held invidious to call a man 'Doctor of Medicine' rather than 'Physician' in England. A Doctor Memis or Menis had brought a court case against the Royal Infirmary of Aberdeen which had given him this title in its charter (the grounds being presumably that the title implied that he was not officially qualified), and Boswell was appearing for the defence.[33] He wrote the same day to Boswell:

I consulted this morning the President of the London College of Physicians, who says, that with us, *Doctor of Physick* (we do not say *Doctor of Medicine*) is the highest title that a practicer of Physick can have; that *Doctor* implies not only *Physician*, but teacher of physick; that every *Doctor* is legally a *Physician*, but no man, not a *Doctor*, can practice Physick but by *licence* particularly granted. The Doctorate is a licence of itself.[34]

Moreover, Johnson, as Chapman noted, 'is, as a rule, punctilious in the use of titles.'[35] Yet Johnson's poem commemorating Levet, an unlicensed practitioner, an 'empiric', was entitled, on its first appearance, 'On the Death of *Dr* Robert Levet' – an open defiance, it might seem, of professional protocol. The poem's subsequent history confirms that this was how it was perceived. In all of the numerous magazine reprintings of the poem during Johnson's last year this title is reproduced exactly, but in the posthumous *Works* of 1787 it becomes 'On the Death of Mr Robert Levet', with (in later editions) the explanatory sub-heading, 'A Practiser in Physic'. Johnson's poem addresses itself in part to 'lettered arrogance', but lettered arrogance it seems was not so easily placated.

became completely unco-ordinated, and she had no contact with reality. Except for those periods, she remained all through her illness, even when most insane, terribly sane in three-quarters of her mind. The point is that her insanity was in her premises, in her beliefs'. See Leonard Woolf, *An Autobiography*, 2 vols (Oxford, 1980), II: 1911–69, p. 112.

18 Dewhurst, *John Locke*, p. 101.

19 Leslie Stephen, *English Literature and Society in the Eighteenth Century* (1904), p. 46.

20 Locke, *Essay*, p. 112.

21 *Ibid.*, p. 337.

22 *Ibid.*, p. 341. I quote this not only for the pleasant oddness of it, but because it reveals so clearly the insufficiency of Locke's theory to account for the phenomena he describes. As Freud was to point out, a theory based only on false connections in the mental apparatus cannot explain disorders afflicting motility.

23 *Ibid.*, p. 338.

24 David Hartley, *Observations on Man, his frame, his duty and his expectations*, 2 vols. (1749), 'Of Imperfections in the Rational Faculty', I, section 6, p. 402.

25 Thomas Arnold, *Observations on Insanity*, 2nd edn, 2 vols. (1802), II, p. 166.

26 Richard Mead, *Medical Precepts and Cautions*, in *The Medical Works of Richard Mead*, 3 vols. (Edinburgh, 1763), I, p. 41.

27 George Cheyne, *Essay of Health and Long Life* (1724), pp. 155–7.

28 'If the matter of indulgence be a single thing, it has *with* before it; if it be a habit it has *in*: as, he indulged himself *with* a draught of wine; and, he indulged himself *in* shameful drunkenness'. Johnson's *Dictionary*, 6th edn (1785), under 'Indulge'.

29 *Rasselas*, p. 105.

30 *Rasselas*, p. 104.

31 Dewhurst, *John Locke*, p. 310.

32 John Monro, *Remarks on Dr Battie's Treatise on Madness* (1758), p. 16.

33 Battie, *Treatise*, pp. 27, 16.

34 Dewhurst, *John Locke*, p. 310; Hartley, *Observations*, pp. 402–3.

35 J. K. Wing, *Reasoning About Madness* (1978), p. 65.

36 John Haslam, *Observations on Madness and Melancholy*, 2nd edn (1808), p. 220.

37 Haslam, *Observations*, pp. 47–8.

38 Thomas Arnold, *Observations on Insanity*, 2 vols. (1782), I, pp. 136–7n.

39 'There is no doubt that Johnson, though not a physician, was basing his portrait on a schizophrenic whom he had actually observed.' Kathleen M. Grange, 'Dr. Samuel Johnson's account of a schizophrenic illness in *Rasselas* (1750)', *Medical History* 6, (1962), 166–7.

40 Roy Porter, *Mind-Forg'd Manacles*, (1987), p. 58.

41 *Miscellanies*, I, p. 199.

42 *Miscellanies*, I, p. 148.

43 *Life*, I, p. 397.

44 Appendix G to *Life*, I, p. 548, citing Sir F. D. Mackinnon, *Cornhill Magazine* (October 1924), p. 470.

45 William Hayley, *The Life and Letters of William Cowper Esq.*, 4 vols. (1809), I, p. 107.

46 *Life*, I, p. 397.

47 Arthur Sherbo, *Christopher Smart: Scholar of the University* (East Lansing, 1967).

48 Quoted in Moira Dearnley, *The Poetry of Christopher Smart* (1968), p. 115.

49 *Collected Poems of Christopher Smart*, ed. N. Callan, 2 vols. (Harvard, 1949), I, p. 245.
50 Dearnley, *Smart*, p. 34.
51 Johnson and Newbery may have known each other as early as 1745, for Newbery was the publisher of the *Medicinal Dictionary*. Three letters exist in which Johnson, in 1751, asks Newbery for loans: in 1759, whilst he was living in the Temple, he wrote Newbery a promissory note for £42.19.10. Johnson wrote for him in *The Student* in 1751, and the Introduction and 'Advertisement' to a collection of voyages and travels called *The World Displayed* in 1759. When the *Idler* was collected in volume form, Newbery was its publisher. It was at this time that Johnson helped Smart by writing for the *Universal Visiter*, a monthly journal Smart was contracted to produce when he become ill: 'I wrote for some months ... for poor Smart, while he was mad, not then knowing the terms on which he was engaged to write, and thinking I was doing him good. I hoped his wits would soon return to him. Mine returned to me, and I wrote in "The Universal Visiter" no longer' (*Life*, II, p. 345). Johnson possibly wrote articles for the months in which Smart was also still contributing (see Roland B. Botting, 'Johnson, Smart and the *Universal Visiter*', *Modern Philology* 36 (1939), 293–300). His kindness towards the family is clear from a letter (1154, undated, but probably 1757) in reply to one from Smart's wife Anna Maria in Ireland. (She was temporarily there, acting, it seems, as an agent for the Fever Powders).
52 See Richard Weindorf, '"Poor Collins" reconsidered', *Huntingdon Library Quarterly* 42 (1978–9), 91–116.
53 *Letters* 57, 96.
54 Porter, *Mind-Forg'd Manacles*, p. 35.
55 Richard Brocklesby, *Reflections on Antient and Modern Music, with application to the cure of diseases* (1749), p. 46.
56 Thomas Arnold, *Observations on Insanity*, I, p. 116.
57 *Rasselas*, p. 100.
58 *Rasselas*, p. 115.
59 Bernard de Mandeville MD, *A Treatise of Hypochondriak and Hysterick Passions ... in three dialogues* (1711), p. 46.
60 Otto Finichel, *The Psychoanalytic Theory of Neurosis* (1947), p. 18.
61 C. E. Jung, *Modern Man in Search of a Soul* (1933; reprinted 1981), p. 90.
62 See, for instance, 'Neurosis and psychosis' (1924), in *On Psychopathology* (Penguin Freud Library, Vol. 10, 1979), p. 214.
63 Kathleen Grange suggests that not only is the history of the astronomer an extended and detailed study of a schizophrenic illness, but that Johnson gave 'a remarkably clear formulation and rational discussion of concepts resembling those of Freud' (*Journal of Nervous and Mental Disease* 135, 2 (August 1962), 93–8, p. 93). 'All power of fancy over reason', says Imlac, 'is a degree of insanity; but while this power is such as we can controul and repress, it is not visible to others, nor considered as any depravation of the mental faculties; it is not pronounced madness but when it becomes ungovernable, and apparently influences speech or action.' Speaking of this as a use of 'the concept of repression', Grange gives it as 'an example of Johnson's contribution to the science of psychiatry' ('Schizophrenic illness', pp. 163–4). Three observations could immediately be made. 'Repression' in this psychological sense is used by Robert Burton and others well before Johnson (*The Anatomy of Melancholy*, (1621–51) Part I, section 2, Mem. 3, Subs. 4:

Some few discreet men there are, that can govern themselves, and curb in these inordinate affections, by religion, philosophy and such divine precepts, of meekness, patience, and the like; but most part, for want of government, out of indiscretion, ignorance, they suffer themselves wholly to be led by sense, and are so far from repressing rebellious inclinations, that they give all encouragement unto them, leaving the reins, and using all provocations to further them...' (Everyman edition, I, p. 258)

Johnson's citations of 'repress' in the *Dictionary* are all in the political sense of 'to crush, to put down, to subdue' and suggest that when he uses the verb he is thinking of the mind on the model of the state. Secondly, 'repression' is not, of course, Freud's term: it is his translator's word for the German 'Verdrangung', which might more accurately have been rendered as 'ousting' or 'repulsion' (Bruno Bettelheim, *Freud and Man's Soul* (1983), pp. 93–4). James Strachey's choice of the word (he also tended to add italics, making it a technical term) is obviously influenced by its prior currency in English in psychological contexts. Most importantly, Johnson's usage refers to what cannot be called other than a conscious process.

W. J. Bate has been the most eloquent exponent of Johnson's anticipation of Freud. He remarks that 'The part of Johnson that really anticipates psychoanalysis is not to be found in simple thrusts that cut through a complacent sentimentalism about human nature':

It is to be found in Johnson's studied and sympathetic sense of both inner 'resistance' and what in psychoanalysis are called 'defense mechanisms' or, in Johnson's phrase, 'the strategems of self-defence'. In particular, he anticipates the concept of 'repression' as he turns on the way in which the human imagination, when it is frustrated in its search for satisfaction, doubles back into repression, creating a 'secret discontent', or begins to move ominously into various forms of imaginative projection. (W. J. Bate, *Samuel Johnson* (1978), p. 306)

But when Johnson writes (in *Rambler* 76), 'No man yet was ever wicked without secret discontent', the discontent he plainly refers to is the voice of conscience and reason. It is perfectly conscious, and explicitly results from crimes that are 'apparent and confessed'. When Johnson uses the verb 'repress' as he does in the last sentence of the essay, and in *Rasselas*, he employs it in its traditional sense of a conscious exertion of will: 'the faculties are engaged in resisting reason, and repressing the sense of the divine disapprobation'. Roy Porter has more recently remarked 'as an anatomist of the psyche Johnson certainly has affinities with Freud' (Porter, 'The hunger of imagination: approaching Samuel Johnson's melancholy', in *The Anatomy of Madness*, ed. Bynum Porter and Shepherd, 2 vols. (1985), I: *People and Ideas*, p. 71). These affinities, though, I suggest, if they exist, are not to be found in any anticipations of Freudian theory or concepts.

64 *Rasselas*, p. 105.
65 *Rasselas*, p. 113.
66 M. Horkheimer and T. W. Adorno, *Dialectic of Enlightenment*, trans. John Cumming (1973), passim.
67 'Preface' to *Dictionary*, paras. 84, 85.
68 *Life*, V, p. 216.
69 *Life*, II, p. 6.

70 Thomas Willis, *The Practice of Physick: two discourses concerning the soul of Brutes* (1684) quoted in A. Scull, 'The domestication of madness', *Medical History* 27 (1983), 233–48, p. 238.

71 Quoted in M. Foucault, *Madness and Civilization*, trans. R. Howard (1973), p. 248.

72 Scull, 'The domestication of madness; Scull, *Museums of Madness* (New York, 1979).

73 Porter, *Mind-Forg'd Manacles*, p. 146.

74 Francis Bacon, *The Advancement of Learning and New Atlantis*, ed. Arthur Johnston (Oxford, Clarendon Press, 1980), pp. 163–4.

6 Dr Robert Levet

1 Robert James, *A Dissertation on the Gout and Rheumatism* (1745), pp. 84, 86–7.

2 In 1765 there were forty-six Fellows and sixty-three licentiates, after the College had recruited many unlicensed doctors the previous year. Sir George Clark, *A History of The Royal College of Physicians of London*, 3 vols. (Oxford, 1966), II, p. 738 (Appendix II).

3 Irvine Loudon, 'The nature of provincial medical practice in eighteenth century England', *Medical History* 29 (1985), 1–32, p. 16.

4 Marner 'had inherited from his mother some acquaintance with medicinal herbs and their preparation'. His reputation as a healer is based on his relieving by 'a simple preparation of fox-glove' a woman suffering from 'the terrible symptoms of heart disease and dropsy' (*Silas Marner* [1861] Edinburgh, n.d.) pp. 6, 13). The period must be the later years of the eighteenth century.

5 An example, among many, is Thomas Dyer, the subject of Jonathan Barry's 'Cultural habits of illness: the enlightened and the pious in eighteenth century Bristol', in *Patients and Practitioners*, ed. R. Porter (Cambridge, 1985), pp. 145–76.

6 Loudon, 'Provincial medical practice', p. 8.

7 Hawkins, p. 211. Hill's degree was from St Andrews. Juanita G. L. Burnby, *A Study of the English Apothecary from 1660 to 1760* (1983), p. 77.

8 C. J. Lawrence, 'William Buchan: medicine laid open', *Medical History* 19 (1975), 20–35; Charles M. Rosenberg, 'Medical text and social context: explaining William Buchan's *Domestic Medicine*', *Bulletin of the History of Medicine* 57 (1983), 22–42.

9 In 'Prescribing the rules of health: self-help and advice in the late eighteenth century', *Patients and Practitioners*, ed. Porter, pp. 249–82, for instance, Ginnie Smith examines sixty-two titles published between 1770 and 1820.

10 Michel Foucault, 'The life of infamous men', in *Power, Truth, Strategy*, ed. M. Morris and P. Patton (Sydney, 1979), pp. 76–91.

11 Letter 757.

12 Hawkins, p. 396, Mrs Thrale, *Miscellanies*, I, p. 227; Boswell, *Life*, I, p. 243.

13 Hawkins, p. 401.

14 Letter 354.1.

15 Hawkins, pp. 397–8, 396–7.

16 John Hunter gave lectures, but it was William Hunter's that were fashionable and famous.

17 Antoine Louis, *Eloge* of Morand, quoted in Toby Gelfand, 'The "Paris Manner" of dissection: student anatomical dissection in early eighteenth century Paris', *Bulletin of the History of Medicine* 46 (1972), 99–130, p. 119.

18 *Ibid.*, pp. 104–5, 108.

19 *Ibid.*, p. 125, quoting Harrison's *A Short Comparative View on the Practice of Surgery in the French Hospitals* (1750).

20 *Gentleman's Magazine* 55 (1785), 101.

21 As Gelfand argues in 'Paris Manner'.

22 George C. Peachey, *A Memoir of William and John Hunter* (Plymouth, 1924), p. 45.

23 Hawkins, pp. 401–2.

24 C. H. Brock (ed.), *William Hunter 1718–1783, A Memoir by S. F. Simmons and John Hunter* (Glasgow, 1983), p. 5.

25 *Miscellanies*, I, pp. 198–9.

26 Treacher, *Catalogue of Preparations*, p. lxiii, quoted in W. F. Bynum and Roy Porter (eds.), *William Hunter in the Eighteenth Century Medical World* (Cambridge, 1985), p. 23.

27 William Wadd, *Mems, Maxims and Memoirs* (1827), p. 189.

28 Through Allan Ramsey, Johnson asked Hunter to go and see a young artist, possibly Mauritius Lowe (1746–93). I am grateful to Dr C. H. Brock for information about Hunter. William Cruikshank became Hunter's assistant in 1769–70. He was later Johnson's surgeon.

29 *Miscellanies*, I, p. 120; *The Diary and Letters of Madame D'Arblay*, with notes by W. C. Ward, 3 vols. (London, n.d.), I, p. 96.

30 Samuel Foart Simmons, *Medical Register* of 1783, gives over 960 medical personnel serving a population of about 800,000, a ratio of 1:850.

31 *Gentleman's Magazine* 55 (1785), 102.

32 Joan Lane, '"The doctor scolds me": The diaries and correspondence of patients in eighteenth century England', in *Patients and Practitioners*, ed. Porter, pp. 205–48.

33 Bertram H. Rodgers, 'The medical aspect of Boswell's "Life of Johnson" with some account of the medical men mentioned in that book', *Bristol Medical-Surgical Journal* 29 (1911), 135.

34 Letter 378.

35 *Letters*, II, p. 265 n.1.

36 Charles F. Mullett (ed.), *The Letters of Doctor George Cheyne to Samuel Richardson (1733–1743)* (Columbia, Missouri, 1943), pp. 128–9. The poem has eleven verses: I quote verses 2–7: it may be by Charles Wesley.

37 The phrase quoted is from *An Essay of Health and Long Life* (1724), preface, p. xvi; *Life*, III, p. 27. On Cheyne, see Lester S. King, 'George Cheyne, Mirror of Eighteenth Century Medicine', *Bulletin of the History of Medicine* 48 (1974), 517–39.

38 Katharine C. Balderston (ed.), *Thraliana, the Diary of Mrs Hester Lynch Thrale, 1776–1809*, 2nd edn, 2 vols. (Oxford, 1951), I, pp. 531–2.

39 *Miscellanies*, I, pp. 205, 226–7.

40 *Gentleman's Magazine* 52 (1782), p. 47.

41 Harold Perkin, *The Origins of Modern English Society, 1780–1880*, (1969, 1972), chapter 2, 'The Old Society.'

42 Hawkins, p. 404; *Life*, I, p. 243.

43 Porter, Introduction to *Patients and Practitioners*, ed. Porter, p. 1.

44 John Stowe, *Survey of London*, quoted in Clark, *History*, II, p. 1.

45 *The Letters of John Wesley*, II, p. 95, quoted in A. Wesley Hill, *John Wesley Among the Physicians* (1955), pp. 15–16.

46 T. F. Wharton, *Samuel Johnson and the Theme of Hope* (1984), p. 162.

47 Letter 502.
48 Burnby, *English Apothecary*, p. 108.
49 *The Diary and Letters of Madame D'Arblay*, I, p. 96.
50 F. B. Smith, *The People's Health 1830–1910* (1979), p. 52.

7 Therapeutic friendship

1 *Life*, III, p. 389.
2 Gentleman's Magazine 12 (December 1742), 636.
3 J. K. Crellin, 'Dr. James's fever powder', *British Society for the History of Pharmacy, Transactions* 1, 3 (1974), 136–43.
4 *Life*, III, p. 389.
5 J. L. Clifford, *Dictionary Johnson* (1979), p. 44.
6 Letters 369, 387.
7 Letter 461.
8 Letter 460.
9 William Coleman, 'Health and hygiene in the *Encyclopédie*: a medical doctrine for the bourgeoisie', *Journal of the History of Medicine* 29 (1974), 399–421.
10 *Miscellanies*, I, pp. 198–9.
11 Letter 833.3; Letter 850. Johnson revised his *Dictionary* in 1774. In the sixth edition the discussion of the problem of the etymology of bachelor (which Ménage derived from 'bas chevalier') is supplemented by the remark 'Dr Lawrence observed, that Menage's observation is much confirmed by the practice in our universities of calling a Bachelor, *Sir*'; which makes Lawrence one of the select band of Johnson's friends mentioned or commemorated in the *Dictionary*.
12 Letter 779.1.
13 Letter 863.
14 *Life*, IV, p. 176.
15 Thomas Percival, *Medical Ethics*, (Manchester, 1803), pp. 32, 53.
16 John Gregory, *Lectures on the Duties and Qualifications of a Physician* (1782), p. 36.
17 Letter 930 (February 1784), Letter 1022.
18 Letter 987.
19 Jessie Dobson, *John Hunter* (Edinburgh and London, 1969), p. 49.
20 Charles Ryskamp and Frederick A. Pottle (eds.). *Boswell: The Ominous Years, 1774–1776* (1963), p. 146.
21 *Miscellanies*, II, p. 205–6. Miss More's informant was Dr Pepys.
22 Marshall Wingrow, *The Correspondence and other Papers of James Boswell, Relating to the Making of "The Life of Johnson"* (1969), p. 32.
23 Hawkins, p. 588.
24 Paul Kent Alkon, *Samuel Johnson and Moral Discipline* (Evanston, 1967), p. ix.
25 Letter 796.
26 Letter 277.
27 Letters 622, 357.
28 Letters 165, 865.
29 Letter 354.1.
30 Letter 277.
31 Letter 466; compare letter 580 to Elphinston.

32 Frederick A. Pottle (ed.), *Boswell's London Journal 1762–1765* (1950; reprinted 1952), p. 308 (22 July 1763).

33 *Johnson's Journey to the Western Islands of Scotland and Boswell's Journal of a Tour to the Hebrides*, ed. R. W. Chapman (1924; Oxford, 1948), p. 302.

34 Frederick A. Pottle (ed.), *Boswell in Holland 1763–1764* (1952), p. 221 (17 April 1764).

35 Frederick A. Pottle and Joseph Reed (ed.), *Boswell, Laird of Auchinleck 1778–1782* (1977), p. 466.

36 Frank Brady, *James Boswell, The Later Years 1769–1795* (1984), p. 235.

37 *Life*, II, 440.

38 Ryskamp and Pottle (eds.), *Ominous Years*, p. 286.

39 *Ibid.*, pp. 286–7.

40 *Ibid.*, p. 303.

41 *Ibid.*, pp. 303–7.

42 *Ibid.*, p. 315.

43 William Ober, *Boswell's Clap and other Essays* (Evanston, Illinois, 1970), p. 19.

44 Ryskamp and Pottle (eds.), *Ominous Years*, p. 298.

45 *Ibid.*, p. 316.

46 Pottle and Reed (eds.), *Laird of Auchinleck*, p. 143.

47 Waingrow, (ed.), *Correspondence*, p. 30.

48 Frederick A. Pottle and Charles McC. Weis (eds.), *Boswell in Extremes 1776–1778* (1971), p. 169.

49 Brady, *Later Years*, p. 299.

50 Lawrence Stone, *The Family, Sex and Marriage, in England 1550–1800* (abridged edn, Penguin Books, 1979), p. 362: Ober, *Boswell's Clap*, p. 32: 'History records few more striking examples of the use of synchronous sexual competition by a father to perpetuate castration anxiety in his son'.

51 Frank Brady and Frederick A. Pottle (eds.) *Boswell in Search of a Wife 1766–1769*, (1957), p. 96.

52 Brady, *Later Years*, p. 35 (10 April 1772, at Oglethorpe's).

53 Ryskamp and Pottle (eds.), *Ominous Years*, pp. 205–6.

54 Pottle and Reed (eds.), *Laird of Auchinleck*, p. 150, (9 November–18 December 1779).

55 *Life*, I, p. 215.

56 Pottle (ed.), *Boswell in Holland*, p. 375.

57 Pottle and Reed (eds.), *Laird of Auchinleck*, pp. 272–3.

58 *Ibid.*, p. 481.

59 *Ibid.*, p. 415.

60 Ryskamp and Pottle (eds.), *Ominous Years*, p. 80.

61 *Life*, II, p. 47.

62 *Life*, II, 69. *Boswell's Life of Johnson*, ed. Fletcher, p. 406.

63 *Life*, III, 136.

64 William C. Dowling, *Language and Logos in Boswell's 'Life of Johnson'* (Princeton 1981) especially chapter 3, 'Structure and absence'.

65 Pottle and McC. Weis (eds.), *In Extremes*, p. 221.

66 *Life*, IV, p. 379.

67 *Life*, IV, p. 389.

68 Margaret Bailey, *Boswell's Column* (1951), p. 50.

69 *Life*, IV, 380 n.1.
70 C. G. Jung, 'The relations between the ego and the unconscious', in *Two Essays on Analytic Psychology, Collected Works*, 2nd edn (New York, 1966), VII, 233–4.
71 S. L. Goldberg, 'Augustanism and the tragic', *The Critical Review* (Melbourne) 17 (1974), 21–37, p. 25.
72 Oliver Sacks, *A Leg to Stand On* (1984), p. 59.
73 Arthur Kleinman MD, *The Illness Narratives: Suffering, Healing and the Human Condition* (New York, 1988), pp. 143–4, 170.
74 Leslie Stephen, *Samuel Johnson* (1878); reprinted 1909, p. 149.

BIBLIOGRAPHY

Place of publication is London, unless otherwise noted.

Medical and other works published before 1810

Mark Akenside, *Oratio anniversaria, quam ex Harvaii instituto in theatro collegii regalii medicorum Londonensis*, 1760.

Robert Anderson MD, *The Life of Samuel Johnson L.L.D. with Critical Observations on his Works*, 1795.

John Arbuthnot MD, *An Essay Concerning the Nature of Aliments, 3rd Edition, to which are added Practical Rules of Diet*, 1734.

Thomas Arnold, *Observations on Insanity*, 1782.

Matthew Baillie, *A Series of Engravings, Accompanied with Illustrations, which are intended to illustrate the Morbid Anatomy of Some of the most Important Parts of the Human Body*, 1803.

William Battie MD, *A Treatise on Madness*, 1758.

Richard Brocklesby, *Reflections on Antient and Modern Musick with the application to the cure of diseases*, 1749.

Economical and Medical Observations, in 2 parts, 1764.

William Buchan, *Domestic Medicine, or a Treatise on the Prevention and Cure of Diseases*, Edinburgh, 1769.

Elizabeth Carter, trans., *All the works of Epictetus, which are now extant, consisting of his Discourses etc.*, 1758.

A. Cornelius Celsus, *Of medicine*, in eight books, trans. James Grieve MD, 1756.

George Cheyne, *The English Malady, or, A Treatise of Nervous Diseases of all Kinds*, 1733, 5th edition, 1735.

The Natural Method of Cureing the Diseases of the Body, and the Disorders of the Mind Depending on the Body, in 3 parts, 1742.

An Essay of Health and Long Life, 1724.

F. Clifton, trans., *Hippocrates upon Air, Water and Situation; upon Epidemical Diseases and upon Prognosticks*, 1743.

Richard Cromwel, *The Happy Sinner*, 1691.

Erasmus Darwin, *Zoonomia, or the Laws of Organic Life*, 2 vols., 1796.

[Benito Geronimo Feijoo], *An Exposition of the Uncertainties in the Practice of Physic, Written Originally in Spanish and Translated from the Seventh Edition*, 1751.

Sir John Floyer, *ΦAPMAKO–BAΣANOΣ: or The Touch-stone of Medicines, Discovering the Vertues of Vegetables, Minerals and Animals by their Tastes and Smells*, 2 vols., 1687, 1691.

 The Preternatural State of the Animal Humours Described by their Sensible Qualities, 1696.

 An Enquiry into the Right Use and Abuses of the Hot, Cold, and Temperate Baths in England, 1697.

 The history of Cold Bathing, both Ancient and Modern, in Two Parts, (1702), 6th edition, 1732.

 A Treatise of the Asthma (1698), 2nd edition, 1717.

 The Physician's Pulse Watch, or an ESSAY *to Explain the Old Art of Feeling the Pulse, and to Improve it by the Help of a Pulse-Watch*, 1707.

 Medicina Gerocomica: or, the Galenic Art of Preserving Old Men's Healths, 2nd edition, 1724.

John Freind, *The History of Physick from the time of Galen, to the Beginning of the Sixteenth Century, Chiefly with Regard to Practice, in a Discourse to Dr. Mead*, 2 vols., 4th edition, 1744–50, reprinted New York, 1973.

John Gregory, *Elements of the Practice of Physic*, 2nd edition, 1774.

Stephen Hales, *Statical Essays: Containing Haemastaticks or, An Account of some Hydraulick and Hydrostatical Experiments made on the Blood and Blood-Vessels of Animals*, 2 vols., 1733.

David Hartley, *Observations on Man, his Frame, his Duty and his Expectations*, 2 vols., 1749.

John Haslam, *Observations on Madness and Melancholy*, 1809.

William Hawes MD, *An Account of the late Dr. Goldsmith's Illness so far as it relates to the Exhibition of Dr. James's Powders*, 1774, 4th edition, 1780.

John Hawkins, *The Life of Samuel Johnson, L.L.D.*, 1787.

William Hayley, *The Life and Letters of William Cowper Esq.*, 4 vols., 1809.

William Heberden, 'Remarks on the Pulse', *Medical Transactions of the Royal College of Physicians* 2 (1772).

 Commentaries on the History and Cure of Diseases, 1802, reprinted New York, 1962.

J.-B. van Helmont, *Oriatrike, or Physick Refined, the Common Errors therein Refuted and the Whole Art Reformed and Rectified*, 1662.

William Hunter, *Medical Commentaries*, part I, 1762.

Robert James, *A New Method of Preventing and Curing the Madness caused by the Bite of a Mad Dog*, 1743.

 A Medicinal Dictionary, including Physic, Surgery, Anatomy, Chymistry and Botany, together with a History of Drugs, 3 vols., 1743–5.

The Modern Practice of Physic as Improv'd by the celebrated Professors H. Boerhaave and F. Hoffman ... with a Translation of Boerhaave's Aphorisms with the Commentaries of Dr Van Sweiten, so far as was necessary to explain the doctrine laid down, 1746.

A Dissertation on the Gout and Rheumatism, 1746.

A Dissertation on Endemical Diseases (F. Hoffman] *together with a Treatise on the Diseases of Tradesmen* [B. Ramazzini], 1746.

A Dissertation on Fevers and Inflammatory Distempers, 1748.

A Dissertation of Fevers and Inflammatory Distempers, 8th edn, *To which are now first added ... a Vindication of the Fever Powder and a short treatise on the diseases of Children*, 1778.

A Treatise on Canine Madness, 1760.

[Samuel Johnson (and Robert James)], *A General Account of the Work*, [Proposal for the *Medical Dictionary*], 1743.

Bernard Mandeville, *Discourse on Hypochondriac Affections*, 1711.

Richard Mead, *The Medical Works of Richard Mead*, 3 vols., Edinburgh, 1763.

John Monro, *Remarks on Dr Battie's Treatise on Madness*, 1758.

Thomas Percival, *Medical Ethics*, 1803, 3rd edition, 1849.

Sir John Pringle, *Observations on the Nature and Cure of Hospital and Gaol-Fevers*, 1750.

Observations on the Diseases of the Army, 1765.

John Quincy MD, *Lexicon Physico-Medicum, or a New Medicinal Dictionary*, 1719.

Medicinas Statica; being the Aphorisms of Sanctorius, translated in English, with large Explanations. To which is added Dr. Keil's Medicina Statica Britannica, 1723.

Pharmacopoeia Officinalis & Extemporanea: or, a Compleat English Dispensatory (1718), 12th edition, 1742.

Peter Shaw, *A New Practice of Physic*, 2 vols., 1726.

Tobias Smollett, *Essay on the External Use of Water*, 1752.

Richard Wiseman, *Several Chirugicall Treatises*, 1676.

George Young MD, *A Treatise on Opium, founded upon Practical Observations*, 1753.

Contemporary periodicals

The Critical Review or Annals of Literature
Gentleman's Magazine
Literary Magazine, or the Universal Review
London Magazine
Monthly Review
Philosophical Transactions

Works published after 1810

J. L. Abbott, 'Dr. Johnson, Fontenelle, le Clerc, and the six "French" Lives', *Modern Philology* 63 (November 1965).

Erwin H. Ackerknecht, *Therapeutics from the Primitives to the 20th Century*, New York, 1973.

Medicine at the Paris Hospital, 1794–1848, Baltimore, 1967.

Paul Kent Alkon, *Samuel Johnson and Moral Discipline*, Northwestern, 1967.

D. G. Allan and R. E. Schofield, *Stephen Hales: Scientist and Philanthropist*, 1980.

T. C. Allbutt, ed., *A System of Medicine*, 4 vols., 1897.

Aristotle, *The Works*, translated into English under the editorship of W. D. Ross, Oxford, 1925.

J. K. Aronson, *An Account of the Foxglove and its Medical Uses, 1785–1985*, 1985.

Margery Bailey, *Boswell's Column, being his Seventy Contributions to the London Magazine under the Pseudonym 'The Hypochondriack' from 1778 to 1783*, 1951.

John Barlow, *Man's Power over Himself to Prevent or Control Insanity*, 1843, 2nd edition, 1849.

Jonathan Barry, 'Piety and the patient: medicine and religion in eighteenth-century Bristol', in R. Porter, ed., *Patients and Practitioners*, Cambridge, 1985, pp. 145–75.

W. J. Bate, *Samuel Johnson*, 1978.

F. V. Bernard, 'The Hermit of Paris and the Astronomer in *Rasselas*', *Journal of English and Germanic Philology* 67 (1968), 272–8.

Bruno Bettelheim, *Freud and Man's Soul*, 1983.

Joseph Bliss *et al.*, 'Sensory experiences of Gilles de la Tourette Syndrome', *Archives of General Psychiatry* 37 (December 1980), 1,343–7.

Marc Bloc, *The royal Touch*, trans. J. E. Anderson, 1973.

E. A. Bloom, *Samuel Johnson in Grub Street*, Providence, Rhode Island, 1957.

Roland B. Botting, 'Johnson, Smart, and the *Universal Visiter*' *Modern Philology*, 36 (1938–9), 293–300.

O. M. Brack Jr. and Thomas Kaminski, 'Johnson, James and the *Medicinal Dictionary*', *Modern Philology* 81 (May 1984), 378–400.

Frank Brady, *James Boswell: The Later Years 1769–1795*, 1984.

Frank Brady and Frederick A. Pottle, eds., *Boswell in Search of a Wife 1766–1769*, 1957.

W. Russell Brain, 'Thomas Lawrence, M.D., F.R.C.P. (1711–83)' *Medical History* 1 (October 1957), 293–396.

Some Reflections on Genius and Other Essays, 1960.

C. H. Brock, ed. *William Hunter 1718–1763, A Memoir by S. F. Simmons and John Hunter*, Glasgow, 1983.

Juanita G. L. Burnby, *A Study of the English Apothecary from 1660 to 1760*, 1983.

Frances Burney, *Memoirs of Doctor Burney, by his daughter Madam D'Arblay*, 3 vols., 1832, reprinted 1972.

Robert Burton, *The Anatomy of Melancholy* (1621–51), 2 vols., 1932, reprinted 1948.

W. Bynum, R. Porter and M. Shepherd, eds., *The Anatomy of Madness*, 2 vols., 1985.

W. F. Bynum and Roy Porter, eds., *William Hunter and the Eighteenth Century Medical World*, Cambridge, 1985.

Max Byrd, *Visits to Bedlam, Madmen and Literature in the Eighteenth Century*, South Carolina, 1974.

N. Callan, ed., *Collected Poems of Christopher Smart*, 1968.

H. S. Carter, 'Samuel Johnson and some eighteenth century doctors', *Glasgow Medical Journal* 32 (July 1951), 218–27.

J. Chadwick and W. N. Mann, eds., *The Medical Works of Hippocrates*, Oxford, 1950.

Arnold Chaplin MD, *Medicine in England during the Reign of George III*, 1919.

Sir George Clark, *A History of the Royal College of Physicians of London*, 3 vols., Oxford, 1966.

Edwin Clarke, ed., *Modern Methods in the History of Medicine*, 1971.

J. L. Clifford, *Young Samuel Johnson*, 1955.

  Dictionary Johnson, 1979.

William Coleman, 'Health and hygiene in the *Encyclopédie*: a medical doctrine for the bourgeoisie', *Journal of the History of Medicine* 29 (1974), 399–421.

Sir Zachary Cope, *William Cheselden, 1668–1752*, Edinburgh and London, 1953.

  The Royal College of Surgeons of England, A History, 1959.

C. D. N. Costa, ed. *Seneca*, 1974.

J. K. Crellin, 'Dr. James's fever powder', *Transactions of the British Society for the History of Pharmacy* 1, 3 (1974), 136–43.

Leopold Damrosch, *Samuel Johnson and the Tragic Sense*, Princeton, New Jersey, 1972.

L. A. Dayton *et al.*, 'Symptomatic and pulmonary response to acute phlebotomy in secondary polycythemia', *Chest* 68 (1975), 785–90.

Moira Dearnley, *The Poetry of Christopher Smart*, 1968.

Robert de Maria, *Johnson's Dictionary and the Language of Learning*, Oxford, 1986.

Kenneth Dewhurst, *Dr Thomas Sydenham (1624–1689): His Life and Original Writings*, Berkeley, 1966.

  John Locke (1632–1704), Physician and Philosopher, A Medical Biography, with an Edition of the Medical Notes in his Journals, 1963.

Anne Digby, *Madness, Morality and Medicine: A Study of the York Retreat 1796–1914*, Cambridge, 1985.

Klaus Doerner, *Madmen and Bourgeoisie, A Social History of Insanity and Psychiatry*, trans. Neugroscel and Steinberg, Oxford, 1981.

Jane B. Donegan, *Women and Men Midwives, Medicine Morality and Misogyny in Early America*, Westport, Connecticut and London, 1976.

Jean Donnison, *Midwives and Medical Men*, 1977.

F. N. Doubleday, 'Some medical associations of Samuel Johnson', *Guy's Hospital Reports* 101 (1952), 45–51.

William C. Dowling, *Language and Logos in Boswell's Life of Johnson*, Princeton, 1981.

Donald D. Eddy, *Samuel Johnson, Book Reviewer in the* Literary Magazine or Universal Review; *1756–1758*, New York and London, 1979.

Knud Faber, *Nosography, The Evolution of Clinical Medicine in Modern Times*, 2nd edition 1930, reprinted New York 1976.

J. D. Fleeman, ed., *Early Biographical Writings of Dr. Johnson*, Farnborough, 1973.

Michel Foucault, *The Birth of the Clinic, an Archeology of Medical Perception*, trans. A. M. Sheridan, 1973.

Madness and Civilization, trans. R. Howard, 1973.

Power, Truth, Strategy, ed. M. Morris and P. Patton, Sydney, 1979.

R. K. French, *Robert Whytt, The Soul and Medicine*, 1969.

Sigmund Freud, *Gesammelte Werke, Vol. XI, Vorlesungen Zur Einfürung in die Psychoanalyse*, 1940.

An Outline of Psycho-Analysis, trans. James Strachey, 1940, reprinted 1973.

Civilization and its Discontents, trans. Joan Riviere revised by James Strachey 1930, reprinted 1973.

On Psychopathology: Inhibitions, Symptoms and Anxiety and Other Works, The Penguin Freud Library, vol. 10, 1981.

On Metapsychology: The Theory of Psychoanalysis, The Penguin Freud Library, vol. 11, 1984.

Arnold J. Friedhoff and Thomas N. Chase, *Gilles de la Tourette Syndrome*, New York, 1982.

Paul Fussell, *The Rhetorical World of Augustan Humanism*, Oxford, 1965.

The Boy Scout's Handbook and other Observations, New York and Oxford, 1982.

Toby Gelfand, 'The "Paris Manner" of dissection: student anatomical dissection in early eighteenth century Paris', *Bulletin of the History of Medicine*, 46, 2 (1972), 99–130.

D. D. Gibbs, 'Sir John Floyer, M.D., (1649–1734)', *British Medical Journal* 25 (January 1969), 242–5.

'The physician's pulse watch', *Medical History* 15 (1971), 187–90.

S. L. Goldberg, 'Augustanism and the tragic', *The Critical Review* (Melbourne) 17 (1974), 21–37.

Kathleen M. Grange, 'Dr. Samuel Johnson's account of a schizophrenic illness in *Rasselas*', *Medical History* 6 (1962), 162–88.

'Samuel Johnson's Account of Certain Psychoanalytic Concepts', *Journal of Nervous and Mental Disease* 135, 2 (1962), 93–8.

Ernest Gray, *Portrait of a Surgeon, a Biography of John Hunter*, 1952.

Donald Greene, 'Johnson's contributions to the *Literary Magazine*', *Review of English Studies* 7 (October 1956), 367–92.

'Johnson as stoic hero', *Johnsonian Newsletter* 24 (June 1964), 7–9.

'"Pictures to the mind"; Johnson and imagery', in *Johnson, Boswell and their Circle*, ed. Mary Lascelles *et al.*, Oxford, 1965.

Samuel Johnson's Library, An Annotated Guide, University of Victoria, 1975.

R. M. Gummere, *Seneca the Philosopher and his Modern Message*, 1922.

Allen T. Hazen, 'Samuel Johnson and Dr. Robert James', *Bulletin of the History of Medicine* 4 (1936), 455–65.

Ernest Heberden, 'William Heberden the Elder (1710–1801): aspects of his London practice', *Medical History* 30 (1986), 303–21.

George Birkbeck Hill, ed., *Boswell's Life of Johnson*, 6 vols., Oxford, 1887.

G. B. Hill, *Johnsonian Miscellanies*, 2 vols., Oxford, 1897.

Geoffrey Holmes, *Augustan England, Professions, State and Society 1680–1730*, 1982.

M. Horkheimer and T. W. Adorno, *Dialectic of Enlightenment*, trans. John Cumming, 1973.

Michael Hunter, *Science and Society in Restoration England*, Cambridge, 1981.

Richard Hunter and Ida MacAlpine (eds.), *Three Hundred Years of Psychiatry 1535–1860, A History Presented in Selected English Texts*, 1963, reprinted New York, 1982.

Stanley W. Jackson, *Melancholia and Depression, From Hippocratic Times to Modern Times*, New Haven and London, 1986.

W. Jaeger, 'Aristotle's use of medicine as model of method in his Ethics', *Journal of Hellenic Studies* 77 (1957), 54–61.

N. D. Jewson, 'Medical knowledge and the patronage system in 18th century England', *Sociology* 8 (1974), 369–85.

Johnson, Boswell and Their Circle: Essays Presented to L. F. Powell, ed. Mary Lascelles *et al.*, Oxford, 1965.

Arthur Johnston, ed., *Francis Bacon, The Advancement of Learning and the New Atlantis*, Oxford, 1974.

Carl Gustav Jung, *Modern Man in Search of a Soul*, trans. W. S. Dell and C. P. Baynes, 1933, reprinted 1969.

Thomas Kaminski, *The Early Career of Samuel Johnson*, Oxford, 1987.

Lester S. King, *The Medical World of the Eighteenth Century*, Chicago, 1958.

The Growth of Medical Thought, Chicago, 1963.

"George Cheyne, mirror of eighteenth century medicine", *Bulletin of the History of Medicine* 48 (1974), 517–39.

The Philosophy of Medicine, the Early Eighteenth Century, Cambridge, Mass., 1978.

Medical Thinking, A Historical Preference, Princeton, 1982.

Desmond King-Hele, *Doctor of Revolution, The Life and Genius of Erasmus Darwin*, 1977.

Desmond King-Hele, ed., *The Letters of Erasmus Darwin*, Cambridge, 1981.

Arthur Kleinman, *The Illness Narratives, Suffering, Healing and the Human Condition*, New York, 1988.

Louis Mansfield Knapp, *Tobias Smollett, Doctor of Men and Manners*, Princeton 1949, reprinted New York, 1963.

Paul J. Korshin, *Johnson after Two Hundred Years*, Philadelphia, 1986.

Joseph Wood Krutch, *Samuel Johnson*, 1948.

Donald Lane and Antony Storr, *Asthma, the Facts*, Oxford, 1983.

Joan Lane, '"The doctor scolds me": The diaries and correspondence of patients in eighteenth century England', in R. Porter, ed., *Patients and Practitioners*, Cambridge, 1985.

Margaret Lane, *Samuel Johnson and his World*, 1975.

J. Laplanche and J.-B. Pontalis, *The Language of Psycho-Analysis*, trans. D. Nicholson-Smith, 1973.

Mary Lascelles, *Facts and Notions, Collected Criticism and Research*, Oxford 1972.

C. J. Lawrence, 'William Buchan: medicine laid open', *Medical History* 19 (1975), 20–35.

W. E. H. Lecky, *A History of England in the Eighteenth Century*, 7 vols., 1892.

Daniel le Clerc, *Histoire de la médecine*, The Hague, 1729, reprinted Amsterdam, 1967.

John Locke, *An Essay Concerning Human Understanding* (1690), 25th edition, 1824.

Roger Lonsdale, *Dr. Charles Burney, A Literary Biography*, Oxford, 1965.

Reginald S. A. Lord, 'The white veins: conceptual difficulties in the history of the Lymphatics'. *Medical History* 12 (1968), 174–82.

Irvine Loudon, 'The nature of provincial medical practice in eighteenth-century England', *Medical History* 29 (1985), 1–32.

Medical Care and the General Practitioner, 1750–1850, Oxford, 1986.

E. L. McAdam Jr. and A. T. Hazen, 'Dr. Johnson and the Hereford Infirmary', *Huntingdon Library Quarterly* (April 1940), 359–67.

Ruth K. McClure, 'Johnson's criticism of the Foundling Hospital and its consequences', *Review of English Studies* n.s. 28 (1976), 17–26.

Michael MacDonald, *Mystical Bedlam: Madness, Anxiety and Healing in Seventeenth Century England*, Cambridge, 1981.

Lawrence C. McHenry Jr., 'Samuel Johnson's "The Life of Dr Sydenham"', *Medical History* 8 (1964), 181–6.

'Dr. Samuel Johnson's medical biographies', *Journal of the History of Medicine and Allied Sciences* 14 (1967), 298–310.

C. Maclaurin, *Mere Mortals*, 1925.

Henry Meige and E. Feindel, *Tics and their Treatment*, with a Preface by Professor Brissaud, trans. S. A. K. Wilson, 1907.

John H. Middendorf, ed., *English Writers of the Eighteenth Century*, New York and London, 1971.

Charles F. Mullett, ed., *The Letters of George Cheyne to Samuel Richardson (1733–43)*, Columbia, Missouri, 1943.

William B. Ober, *Boswell's Clap and other Essays*, Southern Illinois, 1979.

David Owen, *English Philanthropy 1660–1960*, Cambridge, Mass., 1965.

James F. Palmer, ed., *The Medical Works of John Hunter F.R.S.*, 4 vols., 1835.

George C. Peachey, *A Memoir of William and John Hunter*, Plymouth, 1924.

T. Whitmore Peck and K. Douglas Wilkinson, *William Withering of Birmingham, M.D. F.R.S.*, Bristol and London, 1950.

Harold Perkin, *The Origins of Modern English Society, 1780–1880*, 1969.

George Pickering, *Creative Malady*, 1974.

Charles W. Pierce, *The Religious Life of Samuel Johnson*, 1983.

Roy Porter, 'The rage of party: a glorious revolution in English psychiatry?', *Medical History*, 27 (1983), 35–50

'William Hunter; a surgeon and a gentleman', in *William Hunter and the Eighteenth Century Medical World*, Cambridge, 1985.

'Lay medical knowledge in the eighteenth century: the evidence of the *Gentleman's Magazine*', *Medical History* 29 (1985), 138–68.

Mind Forg'd Manacles, 1987.

Roy Porter, ed., *Patients and Practitioners, Lay Perceptions of Medicine in Pre-Industrial Society*, Cambridge, 1985.

Frederick A. Pottle ed., *Boswell's London Journal 1762–1763*, 1952, reprint of 1950 ed.

Boswell in Holland, 1763–1764, 1952.

Frederick A. Pottle and Joseph W. Reed, eds., *Boswell, Laird of Auchinleck 1778–1783*, London and New York, 1977 (Yale editions).

Pottle, Frederick A., and Charles Ryskamp, eds., *Boswell: the Ominous Years 1774–1776*, 1963.

Pottle, Frederick A. and Charles McC. Weis, eds., *Boswell in Extremes 1776–1778*, 1971.

Pottle, Frederick A. and William K. Wimsett, eds., *Boswell for the Defence, 1769–1774*, 1960.

Maurice Quinian, *William Cowper, A Critical Life*, Minneapolis, 1953.

George Qvist, *John Hunter 1728–93*, 1981.

D. H. Rawlinson, 'Presenting its evil to our minds: Imagination in Johnson's pamphlets', *English Studies*, 70 (1989), 315–27.

A. L. Reade, *Johnsonian Gleanings*, 10 vols., reprinted New York, 1968.

Stanley Joel Reiser, *Medicine and the Reign of Technology*, Cambridge, 1978.

Guenter B. Risse, 'The renaissance of bloodletting: a chapter in modern therapeutics', *Journal of the History of Medicine* 34 (1979), 3–22.

Louis H. Roddis, *James Lind, Founder of Nautical Medicine*, 1971.

Betsy Rodgers, *Cloak of Charity, Studies in Eighteenth Century Philanthropy*, 1949.

Bertram M. H. Rogers, 'The medical aspect of Boswell's Life of Johnson with some account of the medical men mentioned in that book', *Bristol Medical-Chirurgical Journal* (1910), 289–310; (1911), 124–145.

Charles E. Rosenberg, 'Medical text and social context: explaining William Buchan's *Domestic Medicine*', *Bulletin of the History of Medicine* 57 (1983), 22–42.

Jacob Rosenbloom, 'The history of pulse timing with some remarks on Sir John Floyer and his physician's pulse watch', *Annals of Medical History* 4 (1972), 97–9.

G. S. Rousseau, 'John Wesley's *Primitive Physic* (1747)', *Harvard Library Bulletin* 16 (1968), 242–56.

G. S. Rousseau and Roy Porter, eds., *The Ferment of Knowledge, Studies in the Historiography of Eighteenth Century Science*, Cambridge, 1980.

Nicholaas A. Rupke, ed., *Vivisection in Historical Perspective*, Wellcome Institute series in the History of Medicine, 1987.

Oliver Sacks, *A Leg to Stand On*, 1984.
Migraine, Understanding a Common Disorder, Berkeley and Los Angeles, 2nd edn, 1985.

Hilary St George Saunders, *The Middlesex Hospital, 1745–1948*, 1949.

Robert E. Schofield, *The Lunar Society of Birmingham*, Oxford, 1963.
Mechanism and Materialism, British National Philosophy in an Age of Reason, Princeton, 1970.

Richard B. Schwartz, *Samuel Johnson and the New Science*, Madison, Milwaukee, 1971.
Samuel Johnson and the Problem of Evil, Madison, Milwaukee, 1975.

Andrew Scull, *Museums of Madness*, New York, 1979.
'The domestication of madness', *Medical History* 27 (1983), 233–48.

Seneca, *Ad Lucilium epistulae morales*, with an English translation by R. M. Gummere, 3 vols., Loeb Library, 1897.

A. K. Shapiro et al., *Gilles de la Tourette Syndrome*, New York, 1978.

Arthur Sherbo, *Christopher Smart, Scholar of the University*, Michigan, 1967.

Wallace Shugg, 'Humanitarian attitudes in the early animal experiments of the Royal Society', *Annals of Science* 24 (1968), 227–38.

Henry E. Sigerist, 'A literary controversy over tea in 18th century England', *Bulletin of the History of Medicine* 22 (1943), 184–99.

Vieda Skultans, *English Madness: Ideas on Insanity, 1580–1890*, 1979.

F. B. Smith, *The People's Health 1830–1910*, 1979.

Wesley D. Smith, *The Hippocratic Tradition*, Ithaca and London, 1979.

R. D. Spector, *English Literary Periodicals and the Climate of Opinion in the Seven Years' War*, The Hague, 1966.

Leslie Stephen, *Samuel Johnson*, 1878.
English Literature and Society in the Eighteenth Century, 1904.

Stone, Lawrence, *The Family, Sex and Marriage in England 1500–1800*, abridged edn, Penguin, 1979.

James Stephen Taylor, *Jonas Hanway, Founder of the Marine Society: Charity and Policy in Eighteenth Century Britain*, London and Berkeley, 1985.

Owsei Temkin, *Galenism, the Rise and Decline of a Medical Philosophy*, Ithaca and London, 1973.

The Double Face of Janus and other Essays in the History of Medicine, Baltimore and London, 197.

Keith Thomas, *Religion and the Decline of Magic*, Harmondsworth, 1978.

Man and the Natural World, 1983.

Gary L. Townsend, 'Sir John Floyer (1649–1743) and his study of pulse and respiration', *Journal of the History of Medicine*, 22, 3 (1967), 286–316.

Hester Lynch Thrale, *Thraliana: The Diary of Mrs. Hester Lynch Thrale (later Mrs. Piozzi) 1776–1809*, ed. Katherine C. Balderston, 2nd edn, 2 vols., Oxford, 1951.

U. Tröhler, 'Brève histoire de l'expérimentation animale et des controverses qu'elle a suscitées', *Revue médicale de la Suisse Romande* 105 (1985), 817–29.

E. Ashworth Underwood, ed. *Science, Medicine and History*, 2 vols, Oxford, 1953.

'Boerhaave after three hundred years', *British Medical Journal*, 218 December 1968, 820–5.

Boerhaave's Men at Leyden and After, Edinburgh, 1977.

B. Vickers, *Francis Bacon and Renaissance Prose*, Cambridge, 1968.

Arthur J. Viseltear, 'Joanna Stephens and the eighteenth century lithontriptics: a misplaced chapter in the history of therapeutics', *Bulletin of the History of Medicine* 42 (1968), 199–220.

William Wadd, *Mems, Maxims and memoirs*, 1827.

John Wain, *Samuel Johnson*, 2nd edn, 1980.

Marshall Waingrow, ed., *The Correspondence and Other Papers of James Boswell Relating to the Making of the Life of Johnson*, 1969.

Howard Weinbrot, 'Samuel Johnson's unpublished manuscript notes to Dr. Thomas Lawrence's "De natura animali dissertatio"', *Huntingdon Library Quarterly* 38 (1974), 237–46.

Richard Weindorf, '"Poor Collins" reconsidered', *Huntingdon Library Quarterly* 42 (1978–9), 91–116.

A. Wesley Hill, *John Wesley among the Physicians*, 1958.

T. F. Wharton, *Samuel Johnson and the Theme of Hope*, 1984.

W. K. Wimsatt, Jr., *Philosophic Words, A Study of Style and Meaning in the Rambler and Dictionary of Samuel Johnson*, Yale, 1948.

J. K. Wing, *Reasoning about Madness*, Oxford, 1978.

Leonard Woolf, *An Autobiography*, 2 vols., Oxford, 1980.

Peter Wright and Andrew Treacher, eds., *The Problem of Medical Knowledge: Examining the Social Construction of Medicine*, Edinburgh, 1982.

Selected works concerned with the health and medical experiences of Samuel Johnson

Harold D. Attwood, 'A dissertation upon the lung of the late Samuel Johnson, the great lexicographer', *The Lancet*, (21/28 December 1985), 1,411–13.

Katharine C. Balderston, 'Johnson's vile melancholy', in *The Age of Johnson*, ed. F. W. Hilles and W. S. Lewis, New Haven, 1949, pp. 3–14.

P. J. Bishop, 'Samuel Johnson's lung', *Tubercule* 40 (1959), 478–81.

W. Russell Brain, 'A post-mortem on Dr. Johnson', *London Hospital Gazette* 37, (1934), 225–89.

'The great convulsionary', in *Some Reflections on Genius and Other Essays*, 1960.

Peter Pineo Chase, 'The ailments and physicians of Dr. Johnson', *Yale Journal of Biography and Medicine* 23 (1951), 370–9.

Macdonald Critchley, 'Dr. Samuel Johnson's aphasia', *Medical History* 6, (1962), 27–454.

William W. Fee, 'Samuel Johnson's "wonderful" remission of dropsy', *Harvard Library Buletin*, 232 (1975), 271–88.

Edward Hitschmann, 'Samuel Johnson's character, a psychoanalytic interpretation', *Psychoanalytic Review* 32 (1945), 208–18.

George Irwin, *Samuel Johnson: A Personality in Conflict*, Auckland and Oxford, 1971.

William Kenney, 'Dr. Johnson and the psychiatrists', *American Imago* 17 (Spring 1960), 76–82.

R. Macdonald Ladell, 'The neurosis of Samuel Johnson', *British Journal of Medical Psychology* 9 (1929), 314–23.

Lawrence, C. McHenry Jr., 'Medical case notes on Samuel Johnson in the Heberden Manuscripts', *Journal of the American Association* 195 (January 1966), 89–90.

'Dr Samuel Johnson's emphysema', *Archives of Internal Medicine*, 199 (January 1967), 98–105.

'Samuel Johnson's tics and gesticulations', *Journal of the History of Medicine* 22 (April 1967), 152–68.

'Art and medicine: Dr Johnson's dropsy', *Journal of the American Medical Association* 206, 11 (9 December 1968), 2,507–9.

Lawrence C. McHenry and Ronald MacKeith, 'Samuel Johnson's childhood illnesses and the King's Evil', *Medical History* 10 (1960), 386–99.

J. S. Madden, 'Samuel Johnson's alcohol problem', *Medical History* 11 (1967), 141–9.

T. J. Murray, 'Samuel Johnson's movement disorders, *British Medical Journal* 1 (1979), 1,610–14.

'Doctor Samuel Johnson's abnormal movements', in *Gilles de la Tourette Syndrome*, ed. Arnold J. Friedhoff and Thomas N. Chase, New York, 1982, pp. 25–30.

Peter M. Newton, 'Samuel Johnson's breakdown and recovery in middle-age: a life span development approach to mental illness and its cure', *International Review of Psycho-Analysis*, 11 (1984), 93–117.

Roy Porter, '"The hunger of imagination": approaching Samuel Johnson's melancholy', in *The Anatomy of Madness*, ed. Bynum, Porter and Shepherd, 2 vols., Cambridge 1986, I, pp. 63–88.

J. P. W. Rogers, 'Samuel Johnson's gout', *Medical History* 30 (1986), 133–44.

Sir Humphry Rolleston, 'Medical aspects of Samuel Johnson', *Glasgow Medical Journal* 41 (April 1924), 173–91.

'Samuel Johnson's medical experiences', *Annals of Medical History* new series I, (1929), 540–52.

J. G. Squibb, 'Last illness and post-mortem examination of Samuel Johnson, the lexicographer and moralist, with remarks', *London Journal of Medicine* I (1849), 615–23.

E. Verbeek MD, *The Measure and the Choice, A Pathographic Essay on Samuel Johnson*, Ghent, 1971.

Unpublished material

C. H. Brock, '"The greatest discovery both in physiology and pathology . . . since the discovery of the circulation": eighteenth century work on the Lymphatics', MS.

Richard Brocklesby, unpublished letters in the Wentworth Woodhouse Muniments, Sheffield City Libraries.

Sir John Floyer, unpublished materials including 'The Country Physician', in the Library of the Queen's College, Oxford.

Thomas Lawrence, *A Course of Lectures, Pathological and Therapeutic [Dictated to Mr. Clarke]*, 7 vols., 1751, in the Library of the Royal College of Physicians, London.

Bergen Evans, 'Dr. Johnson as a biographer', PhD thesis, Harvard University 1932, 2 vols.

INDEX

Descartes, René, 98
Desmoulins, Mr, 62
Desmoulins, Mrs, 210
Dickens, Charles, *Little Dorrit*,
 211–12
Digby, Anne, 48
digitalis, 55, 56, 61
Dionis, Pierre, 202
Dover, Thomas, 96
Dowling, William C., 240
Dryden, John, 107
Duverney, Joseph-Guichard, 202
Dyer, Thomas, 266 n5

Eddy, Donald D., 110, 257 n53
Eliot George (Mary Ann Evans), *Silas
 Marner*, 266
Epictetus, 143
experiments, quantitative medical, 71–2,
 142

Fee, William, W., 57, 58
Feijoo, Benito Geronim, *Exposition of
 the Uncertainties in the Practice of
 Physic*, 82
Fleury, Cardinal, 201
Floyer, Sir John (1649–1743) 2, 5, 16,
 38, 61, 71, 70–3, 74
 J recommends publication of 'loose
  piece' by, 74
 medical statics, 142
 Medicina Gerocomica, 72
 The Physician's Pulse Watch, 671, 71
 on new remedies, 78, 82
 Touchstone of Medicines, 73
 Treatise of the Asthma, 72
 used in *Dictionary*, 107, 108
Fontenelle, Bernard Le Bouvier de, 103
Foote, Samuel, 12
Foucault, Michel, 3, 35
Foundling Hospital, 115, 118–122,
 passim
Freind, Dr John, *History of Physick*,
 104–5
Freud, Sigmund, 42, 188, 225, 232, 263
 n22
 Freudian or psychoanalytic theories
  about J, 34, 41–2, 44, 100, 248–9
  n100
 Freudian interpretation of
  astronomer in *Rasselas*, 189
 J and Freud compared, 194, 232,
  264–5 n63

Fussell, Paul, 148

Galen, 61, 102, 135, 162
Galenic medicine, 16, 23, 38, 61, 65, 67,
 69, 71, 72, 75, 90, 150, 162, 174,
 177, 195, 226 see also Floyer
Galileo, 142
Garrick, David, 73, 182, 204, 224
Garth, Samuel, *The Dispensary*, 221
Gay, John, 109
Gazeteer, 121
Gelfand, Toby, 202
Gentleman's Magazine, 74, 75, 82, 92,
 93, 96, 97, 98, 99, 111, 116, 129,
 133, 158, 200, 204, 210, 211, 225 see
 also Cave, Edward
George III, King, 24
Gibbon, Edward, 204
Gilles de la Tourette syndrome *see*
 Tourette syndrome
Glisson, Francis, 135
Goldsmith, Oliver, 96–7
 Goody Two Shoes, 96, 181
Grange, Kathleen, 263 n39, 264 n63
Gray, Ernest, 143
Gray, James, 47
Gray, Thomas, *Elegy Written in a
 Country Churchyard*, 208, 213
Greene, D. J., 109, 110, 124, 159, 261
 n28
Gregory, Dr John, 227
Greswold, Henry, 25

Hales, Dr Stephen, 4, 93, 127, 138
Hall, Marie Boas, 87
Haller, Albrecht von, on sensibility,
 135–8
Hanway, Thomas, 109
 Foundling Hospital, 120–2
 Journal of an Eight Day's Journey,
  115–20
 on tea, 118–19
Harrison, John, 202
Hartley, David, 93, 167, 172
 Observations on Man, 174–5, 177, 179,
  180
Harvey, Gideon, *Morbus Anglicus, or the
 Anatomy of Consumptions* 107, 108
Harvey, William, 65, 76, 138, 141
Haslam, John, *Observations on Madness
 and Melancholy*, 179–80
Hawes, William, 96
Hawkins, Miss, 28